Chronobiology and Psychiatric Disorders

Chronobiology and Psychiatric Disorders

Edited by

Angelos Halaris, MD
Professor of Psychiatry and Pharmacology
Case Western Reserve University
Cleveland, Ohio

Elsevier
New York • Amsterdam • London

Elsevier Science Publishing Co., Inc.
52 Vanderbilt Avenue, New York, New York 10017

Sole distributors outside the United States and Canada:

Elsevier Science Publishers B.V.
P.O. Box 211, 1000 AE Amsterdam, The Netherlands

Library of Congress Cataloging-in-Publication Data

Chronobiology and psychiatric disorders.

  Includes bibliographies and index.
  1. Mental illness—Physiological aspects.
2. Chronobiology. I. Halaris, Angelos. [DNLM:
1. Chronobiology. 2. Mental Disorders—physiopathology.
QT 167 C5572]
RC455.4.B5C48 1987   616.89′071   87–17945
ISBN 0–444–01216–8

Current printing (last digit):
10 9 8 7 6 5 4 3 2 1

Manufactured in the United States of America

Contents

6. Induction of Depressive-Like Sleep Patterns in Normal Subjects 117
Scott S. Campbell and Juergen Zulley

7. A Chronobiologic Study of Depression: Discussion from a Methodologic Perspective 133
G. Dirlich, H. Barthelmes, L. von Lindern, R. Lund, and D. von Zerssen

8. What Is Wrong with Circadian Clocks in Depression? 159
Detlev von Zerssen

9. Phase Typing and Bright Light Therapy of Chronobiologic Sleep and Mood Disorders 181
Alfred J. Lewy and Robert L. Sack

14. Circadian Rhythm of Brain Serotonin: Physiologic Control and Pharmacologic Manipulation *291*
P. H. Redfern and K. F. Martin

15. Circadian Rhythms in Discrete Brain Regions *313*
Marian S. Kafka

Introduction

The existence of biologic rhythms was recognized by the ancient Greeks more than two-and-a-half millennia ago. The Greek poet Archilochus made reference to the rhythm that "governs man" and encouraged the understanding of such rhythm as a worthwhile endeavor. Written records dating back to the fifth and fourth centuries B.C. allude to rhythmical movements of flowers and leaves in response to sunlight. These early observations of diurnal rhythms, however, were interpreted as passive responses to cyclical changes in the environment. The inherent tendencies of living organisms to display rhythmic phenomena were not suspected to exist until much later. For example, Darwin, in his book, *On the Power of Movement in Plants* (1880), postulated that the circadian periodicity in leaf movements persisted in the absence of environmental cues and that this phenomenon reflected an inherent property of plants. The endogenous nature of circadian rhythms in mammalian organisms was not recognized until the late nineteenth and early twentieth centuries. Daily rhythms in body temperature were shown to persist independently of environmental factors and the sleep–wake cycle (Ogle, 1866). Simpson and Galbraith (1906) undertook the first scientific approach to the explanation of internally governed periodicities that was reminiscent of modern methodology. Using monkeys as experimental subjects, they conducted elaborate measurements of body temperature and concluded that the temperature rhythm is not only endogenous but it is synchronized by the light–dark cycle. Convincing confirmation of the endogenous nature of human circadian systems was presented by Aschoff (1960) and Aschoff and Wever (1962) following their groundbreaking experiments with subjects in temporal isolation. At about the same time, Erwin Bünning was engaging in the analysis of biologic rhythms. His findings were presented in a pioneering monograph in 1958 that laid the foundations for much of the research that followed. In the mid and late 1950s, Colin Pittendrigh provided strong evidence that circadian phenomena are not learned, and that they display endogenous properties, the periods of which are largely independent of environmental factors (Pittendrigh, 1954, 1958, 1960).

The association between circadian rhythms and medicine was established in the late 1960s and early 1970s. Conroy and Mills (1970), in their volume *Human Circadian Rhythms*, and Halberg and coworkers (1977) provided solid documentation of a host of biologic rhythms. A series of anatomic studies followed, and this led to the discovery of the seat of the circadian pacemaker in the suprachiasmatic nucleus of the hypothalamus. The concept of circadian oscillators was coined and the search was launched for the precise neuroanatomic location of these oscillators. The search continues.

During the last two decades a variety of physiologic functions, including sleep–wakefulness, feeding and drinking, endocrine and reproductive function, thermoregulation, and renal function were shown to be regulated by a system of clocks controlling basal levels of activity and responsivity to changes in the environment. The link between the biologic clock (or clocks) and behavior—normal and abnormal—was soon to be suspected. In the first ever published volume to review circadian phenomena in association with psychiatric conditions, Wehr and Goodwin (1983) state: "The existence of such temporal order in the organism raises the possibility that there are diseases that could be characterized as temporal disorders, in which the timing of biological rhythms is pathologically altered." Although disorders of sleep and arousal (delayed sleep-phase syndrome, narcolepsy) have been prime candidates for the study of disturbances in the timing of circadian rhythms, affective illnesses have been the focus of the most intense study in chronobiologic research during the last decade. There are strong reasons that mitigate in favor of a chronobiologic approach to the study of the pathophysiology of affective disturbances. Phenomenologically, manic-depressive illness is predominantly characterized by cyclicity and diurnal and seasonal variation. Depressive and manic episodes occur in cycles extending over days, months, and years, and they alternate with periods of normalcy or near-normalcy of varying length. These periods can last for days, months, or years. Seasonality in mood alterations of greater or lesser severity have been known to mankind for centuries. Diurnal mood swings are a cardinal feature of mania and depression and are generally accompanied by a disturbed diurnal rhythmicity in physiologic functions such as sleep architecture, thermoregulation, and endocrine function.

During the past 20 years clinical observations have led to the formulation of a host of chronobiologic theories to explain the affective disorders. A prominent position has been occupied by the phase-advance hypothesis, which postulates that the phase position of specific diurnal rhythms is advanced in depressed individuals, relative to controls. The hypothesis has received experimental support from sleep studies showing shortened REM latencies in depression and from numerous studies of body temperature, urinary electrolyte excretion, and levels of neurotransmitters and hormones, such as cortisol, prolactin, and melatonin. Most, but not all, studies have underscored the presence of phase aberrations among groups of patients with affective disorders. Although most of these studies present compelling evidence that phase advances in circadian rhythms are indeed observed in a variety of body functions, methodologic pitfalls require a critical evaluation of the results. Some of the most common pitfalls have been reviewed by Wehr and Goodwin (1983) and are also alluded to in this volume. Thus, the phase-advance hypothesis, although of heuristic value, cannot be considered as proven. Indeed, the theory has been challenged recently and arguments for and against it are presented by several authors in this volume.

Related hypotheses include the free-running and internal desynchronization theories of cyclic mood disorders. The free-running hypothesis was conceptualized by Halberg (1968), who postulated that a fast intrinsic rhythm of a pacemaker could escape from entrainment to the day-night cycle and begin to "free-run." Expanding on this theory, Kripke and coworkers (1978) described several subjects with free-running rhythms. A causal relationship, however, between this hypothesis and the pathogenesis of manic-depressive illness is far from established. The same holds true for the internal desynchronization hypothesis, which postulates that the strong and weak oscillators are out of phase. Although severe mental disturbances, including psychotic decompensation, depression, and suicide, have been noted in experimental subjects in whom a state of internal desynchronization was experimentally induced, most patients experiencing the condition in a laboratory setting have failed to report major affective disturbances. Finally, elaborations of the above hypotheses include photoperiodism, abnormal phase-angle

relationships between internal oscillators and rhythms, seasonal photoperiodism, genetic predisposition toward a fast-running intrinsic period of the strong oscillator, and age-related effects on oscillator coupling. It is not an understatement to claim that no single hypothesis has,
as of yet, convincingly explained the complexities associated with the
phenomenology and biology of affective disorders.

This volume is aimed at providing an update in the field of chronobiology research as it relates to psychiatric disorders, most notably the
affective illnesses. There was no intention to compile a comprehensive
review of basic and clinical findings in this rapidly expanding and fas-
cinating new development in biologic psychiatry. Rather, the volume
is intended to address both clinicians and basic scientists engaged in the
study of mood disturbances. To the actively engaged researcher, certain
chapters will serve as a concise update within their area of interest. To
the clinician who continues to marvel at the perplexities of affectively
ill patients, the volume provides incremental knowledge of the current
state of our understanding of this group of psychiatric disorders. It is
genuinely hoped that practical applications for treatment will eventually
evolve from the concepts and research endeavors presented in this
volume.

Angelos Halaris
May 1987

REFERENCES

Aschoff J (1960): Exogenous and endogenous components in circadian
rhythms. Cold Spring Harbor Symp Quant Biol 25:11–26.

Aschoff J, Wever R (1962): Biologische Rhythmen und Regelung. In Prob-
leme der zentralnervösen Regulation. Bad Oeyenhausener Gespräche V. Berlin-
Göttingen-Heidelberg, Springer, pp 1–15.

Bünning E (1958): Die Physiologische Uhr. Berlin, Springer.

Conroy RTWL, Mills JN (1970): Human Circadian Rhythms. London,
Churchill.

Darwin C (1880): On the Power of Movement in Plants. London, John
Murray.

Halberg F (1968): Physiologic considerations underlying rhythmometry,
with special reference to emotional illness. Symposium Bel-Air III. Geneva,
Masson et Cie, p 73.

Halberg F, Nelson WL, Cadotte L (1977): Living routine shifts simulated
on mice by weekly manipulation of light-dark cycle. In Halberg F (ed): XII
International Conference Proceedings, International Society for Chronobiology.
Milan, Il Ponte, pp 133–138.

Kripke DF, Mullaney DJ, Atkinson M, Wolf S (1978): Circadian rhythm disorders in manic-depressives. Biol Psychiatry 13:335–351.

Ogle JW (1866): On the diurnal variations in the temperature of the human body in health. St. George's Hosp Rep 1:220–245.

Pittendrigh CS (1954): On temperature independence in the clock-system controlling emergence in Drosophila. Proc Natl Acad Sci USA 40:1018–1029.

Pittendrigh CS (1958): Perspectives in the study of biological clocks. In Buzzati-Traverso AA (ed): Perspectives in Marine Biology. California, Scripps Institution of Oceanography, pp 239–268.

Pittendrigh CS (1960): Circadian rhythms and the circadian organization of living systems. Cold Spring Harbor Symp Quant Biol 25:159–182.

Simpson S, Galbraith JJ (1906): Observations on the normal temperature of the monkey and its diurnal variation, and on the effect of changes in the daily routine on this variation. Trans R Soc Edinb 45:65–106.

Wehr TA and Goodwin FK (1983): Circadian Rhythms in Psychiatry. Pacific Grove, CA, Boxwood.

Contributors

J. Arendt, PhD
Reader in Clinical Biochemistry, Department of Biochemistry, University of Surrey, Guildford, Surrey, England

David H. Avery, MD
Associate Professor, Department of Psychiatry, University of Washington School of Medicine, Harborview Medical Center, Seattle, Washington

H. Barthelmes, PhD
Information Specialist, Psychiatric Evaluation Research Unit, Max-Planck-Institut für Psychiatrie, Munich

Scott S. Campbell, PhD
Assistant Research Psychobiologist, Department of Psychiatry, University of California, San Diego; Research Psychobiologist, Veterans Administration Medical Center, San Diego, California

S. A. Checkley, MD
Consultant Psychiatrist, The Bethlem Royal Hospital and Maudsley Hospital, Beckenham, England

Emil F. Coccaro, MD
Instructor in Psychiatry, Mount Sinai School of Medicine, New York; Chief, Outpatient Psychiatry Specialty Clinics, New York

Kenneth L. Davis, MD
Professor of Psychiatry and Pharmacology, Mount Sinai School of Medicine, New York; Chief Psychiatry Service, Veterans Administration Medical Center, Bronx, New York

G. Dirlich, PhD
Staff Mathematician, Department of Biostatistics, Max-Planck-Institut für Psychiatrie, Munich

M. R. Eastwood, MD
Professor of Psychiatry and Preventive Medicine, Director of Geriatric Psychiatry Service, Clarke Institute of Psychiatry, University of Toronto, Toronto, Canada

Wolfgang Engelmann, PhD
Professor of Biology, Department of Biology I, University of Tübingen, Tübingen, West Germany

J. Christian Gillin, MD
Professor of Psychiatry, Director, Mental Health Clinical Research Center, Department of Psychiatry, University of California, San Diego; Staff Psychiatrist, Veterans Administration Medical Center, San Diego, California

Angelos Halaris, MD
Professor of Psychiatry and Pharmacology, Case Western Reserve University, Cleveland, Ohio; Vice Chairman, Department of Psychiatry, University Hospitals of Cleveland; Director, Department of Psychiatry, Cleveland Metropolitan General Hospital

Uriel Halbreich, MD
Professor of Psychiatry, Director, Biobehavioral Research, Department of Psychiatry, School of Medicine, State University of New York at Buffalo

David S. Janowsky, MD
Professor and Chairman, Department of Psychiatry, University of North Carolina, School of Medicine, Chapel Hill, North Carolina

Marian S. Kafka, PhD
Executive Secretary, Cellular Neurobiology and Psychopharmacology Subcommittee, National Institute of Mental Health, Rockville, Maryland

Daniel F. Kripke, MD
Professor of Psychiatry in Residence, Department of Psychiatry, University of California, San Diego; Staff Psychiatrist, Director, Sleep Disorders Clinic, Veterans Administration Medical Center, San Diego, California

Alfred J. Lewy, MD, PhD
Director, Sleep and Mood Disorders Laboratory, Professor of Psychiatry and Opthalmology, Associate Professor of Pharmacology, School of Medicine, Oregon Health Sciences University, Portland, Oregon

L. von Lindern, PhD
Head, Data Processing Unit, Max-Planck-Institut für Psychiatrie, Munich

R. Lund, PhD
Research Assistant, Nervenklinik der Universität München, Munich

K. F. Martin, PhD
Post-doctoral Research Fellow, Department of Physiology and Pharmacology, Medical School, Queens Medical Centre, Nottingham, England

Timothy H. Monk, PhD
Associate Professor of Psychiatry, Director of Human Chronobiology Research Program, Sleep Evaluation Center, Western Psychiatric Institute and Clinic, University of Pittsburgh School of Medicine, Pittsburgh, Pennsylvania

Daniel J. Mullaney, MS
Staff Research Associate, Department of Psychiatry, University of California, San Diego

P. H. Redfern, PhD
Reader in Pharmacology, Pharmacology Group, School of Pharmacy and Pharmacology, University of Bath, Bath, England

S. Craig Risch, MD
Associate Professor of Psychiatry, Department of Psychiatry, University of California, San Diego; Staff Psychiatrist, Veterans Administration Medical Center, San Diego, California

Robert L. Sack, MD
Associate Professor of Psychiatry, School of Medicine, Oregon Health Sciences University, Portland, Oregon

Larry J. Siever, MD
Professor of Psychiatry, Mount Sinai School of Medicine; Director, Outpatient Psychiatry Clinic, Veterans Administration Medical Center, Bronx, New York

C. Thompson, MD
Senior Lecturer, Charing Cross Hospital, London, England

J. L. Whitton, MD, PhD
Assistant Professor of Psychiatry, Clarke Institute of Psychiatry, University of Toronto, Toronto, Canada

Detlev von Zerssen, MD
Professor of Psychiatry, Head of Psychiatric Evaluation Research, Max-Planck-Institut für Psychiatrie, Munich

Juergen Zulley, PhD
Research Assistant, Sleep Laboratory in Department of Psychology, Max-Planck-Institut für Psychiatrie, Munich

1

Chronobiologic Instability of the Noradrenergic System in Depression

Larry J. Siever, Emil F. Coccaro, and
Kenneth L. Davis

Although abnormalities have been found in several amine neurotransmitter systems in depression and mania (Maas et al., 1973; Schildkraut et al., 1978a,b; Asberg et al., 1978; Goodwin and Potter, 1979; Potter et al., 1985), most studies have relied on measurements of neurotransmitter metabolites in biologic fluids from single samples [e.g., plasma or cerebrospinal fluid (CSF)] or cumulative samples collected over longer periods of time (e.g., 24-hour urinary collections). Neither method permits the evaluation of the natural time-dependent regulation of these systems, including circadian and ultradian periodicities. More recently, studies using multiple samples over extended time periods have suggested that there may be disturbances in the rhythmicity of these systems in depression.

The noradrenergic system has probably been one of the most extensively investigated of the neurotransmitter systems implicated in the pathogenesis of depression. Several studies have implicated altered concentrations of norepinephrine (NE) and/or its metabolites in biologic fluids in depression (Schildkraut et al., 1978a; Potter et al., 1985). More recent investigations have begun to focus on the time-dependent regulation or rhythmicity of the noradrenergic system. It has been proposed that the circadian rhythm of this system may be phase advanced in depression (Wehr et al., 1980; Wehr, 1984). Although this hypothesis has received experimental support (Wehr et al., 1980; DeMet et al.,

1

1982), more recent preliminary studies suggest that ultradian and circadian noradrenergic abnormalities in depression may be more consistent with an unstable or dysregulated noradrenergic system in depression (Siever and Davis, 1985). Evidence for the latter model, including preliminary data from our laboratory, is presented, after a discussion of the various conceptual approaches to the study of the noradrenergic system in depression and a review of recent research in this area.

NORADRENERGIC ACTIVITY: EXCESS OR DEFICIENCY?

In the earliest studies of the noradrenergic system, investigators measured concentrations of norepinephrine and/or its metabolites in biologic fluids to test hypotheses that predicted that in mania there would be an excess of metabolites, reflecting increased noradrenergic activity, whereas in depression there would be a deficiency of these metabolites, reflecting reduced noradrenergic activity (Schildkraut, 1965; Bunney and Davis, 1965).

Early evidence was reasonably consistent in demonstrating lower excretion of the NE metabolite 3-methoxy-4-hydroxyphenylglycol (MHPG) in depression than in mania or hypomania in the same patients followed longitudinally (Bond et al., 1972; Jones et al., 1973; Post et al., 1977; Wehr, 1977). The finding of decreased urinary MHPG in bipolar depressed patients has received reasonably consistent support (Potter et al., 1985), although a recent NIMH collaborative study found no significant differences between bipolar depressed patients and matched controls (Koslow et al., 1983). Urinary MHPG excretion in unipolar patients, on the other hand, may be increased (Schildkraut et al., 1978a,b). More recently, urinary norepinephrine itself as well as its metabolite normetanephrine has also been reported to be increased in unipolar patients (Koslow et al., 1983).

Cerebrospinal fluid concentrations of MHPG have been reported to be decreased in some (Post et al., 1973; Subrahmanyan, 1975) but not all studies (Wilk et al., 1972; Shaw et al., 1973; Ashcroft et al., 1976; Vestergaard et al., 1978) of depressed patients. Initial reports suggested that CSF NE was not different in depressed patients than in neurologic controls (Post et al., 1978; Christensen et al., 1980), but one study suggested that it may actually be higher in depressed patients than in normal controls (Post et al., 1980) and another study suggested that it was lower in bipolar depressed patients than in controls (Rudorfer et al., 1982).

More recently, investigators have explored measurements of plasma concentrations of NE and MHPG as conveniently obtained potential indices of noradrenergic activity. Plasma NE has fairly consistently been found to be increased in depressed patients compared to controls, although these increases have not always reached significance (Wyatt et al., 1971; Louis et al., 1975; Lake et al., 1982; Siever et al., 1983). Plasma MHPG has been found to be increased in bipolar patients in the manic state compared to the depressed state (Jimerson et al., 1981; Halaris, 1978), whereas increases in plasma MHPG concentrations in unmedicated depressed patients have not reached significance (Siever and Uhde, 1984; Charney et al., 1982; Jimerson et al., 1984).

The interpretability of these findings with regard to noradrenergic activity has been criticized from a number of vantage points. For example, it is usually assumed that concentrations of norepinephrine or its metabolites reflect release of norepinephrine from noradrenergic neurons, although differences in volume of distribution or clearance may also influence the concentrations measured (Potter et al., 1985). The central versus peripheral contribution to these measures remains uncertain. Although measures of plasma and urinary NE are derived from the periphery, estimates of the central contribution to the total body production of MHPG (reflected in urine and plasma concentrations) range from 20% (Blombery et al., 1980) to 60% (Maas et al., 1979). Peripheral and spinal cord noradrenergic activity may contribute to central CSF MHPG production, and CSF NE concentrations conceivably reflect spinal cord and central vascular sympathetic neuronal activity as well as that of brain (Kopin et al., 1983; Post et al., 1984). Thus, it is more accurate to regard some of these measures as peripheral (e.g., plasma NE) and others as whole body measures (e.g., plasma or urinary MHPG) of noradrenergic activity. Numerous other potential sources of difficulty in interpretation and methodologic artifact have been discussed elsewhere (Potter et al., 1983; Muscettola et al., 1981).

However, these methodologic concerns, which limit the interpretation of these findings, do not appear to account entirely for the considerable variations in results from study to study. It would appear that a simple model of excess or deficiency of noradrenergic metabolites in depression cannot easily accommodate the findings to date. Thus, interest has shifted towards examining the regulation of noradrenergic systems in depression, namely, variations in its activity over time, its response to stress, and its various control mechanisms (Maas et al., 1979; Siever and Davis, 1984, 1985; Wehr, 1984).

One logical investigative strategy that emerges from these considerations is the measurement of metabolites at multiple sampling times to evaluate the rhythmicities of the noradrenergic system. As discussed below, these studies have suggested abnormalities in the circadian regulation of noradrenergic activity.

NORADRENERGIC ACTIVITIES: PHASE ADVANCE?

Numerous studies have demonstrated that most biologic and behavioral systems do not operate at a constant level, but vary in their activity in organized, reproducible rhythms over a 24-hour period. The characteristic 24-hour pattern of activity for a particular system represents its circadian rhythm. These rhythms are generally believed to be regulated by the activity of the hypothalamic suprachiasmatic nucleus (SCN), which serves as a master pacemaker for a variety of physiologic functions.

Circadian rhythms have been documented for NE and its metabolites in various biologic fluids in humans including plasma NE (Lightman et al., 1981; Aronow et al., 1973; Levin et al., 1979), plasma MHPG (Markianos and Beckmann, 1976; DeMet et al., 1982), urinary NE (von Euler et al., 1955; Karki, 1956; Becker and Krenzer, 1970; Townsend and Smith, 1973), urinary vanillylmandelic acid (VMA) (Cymerman and Francesconi, 1975; Riederer et al., 1974; Reinberg et al., 1969), urinary MHPG (Wehr et al., 1980; Riederer et al., 1974; Cymerman and Francesconi, 1975), and CSF NE (Ziegler et al., 1976). In most studies, NE and its metabolites show higher concentrations in the daytime hours, with peak concentrations in mid-to-late afternoon and lowest concentrations in the early morning hours. Because of considerations of metabolism and diffusion from brain, particular indices may differ somewhat in their peak concentration times (DeMet et al., 1985).

As a number of investigators have interpreted the abnormal sleep patterns of depressed patients as indicative of a phase advance in its circadian rhythm in depression (Kripke et al., 1978; Wehr et al., 1980, 1984), it was hypothesized that the noradrenergic system might be phase advanced in its activity as well (Wehr et al., 1980). Initial studies focused on urinary excretion of noradrenergic metabolites as an index of noradrenergic activity. Riederer and associates (1974) evaluated the daily rhythm of VMA in 21 depressed patients and 13 controls in four 6-hour urinary collections. They found that, although normal control subjects showed increased VMA excretion in the morning and early afternoon hours, the depressed patients did not demonstrate this increase and had relatively low, nonvarying concentrations across the four collection periods.

Wehr and colleagues (1980) measured urinary MHPG concentrations from 3-hour collections throughout the 24-hour period in 10 bipolar patients and 14 normal controls. They found significant circadian rhythms in MHPG excretion in both groups, with a peak at 6:38 ± 46 minutes in the controls and 4:08 ± 31 minutes in the depressed patients. The difference between the two groups was significant, as were earlier maxima of temperature and motor activity in the depressed patients, consistent with the phase-advance hypothesis. Although it was noted that the depressed patients were older than the controls, the timing of the MHPG rhythm was not related to age in the patient group.

Giedke and colleagues (1982) also measured urinary excretion of MHPG at 3-hour intervals over 24 hours. Although maximal excretion tended to occur earlier in the day in depressed patients than in controls, minima did not differ. Unfortunately, the controls were somewhat younger (31 ± 11 years) than the patients (bipolars, 48 ± 10 years; unipolars, 48 ± 7 years) and some patients were taking medication. This study provides only limited support for the phase-advance hypothesis.

Because urine collections are cumulative measures, their usefulness is limited in defining the exact character of rhythmic disturbances of MHPG. Measurements of plasma metabolites, although constrained by half-life considerations, permit a more precise characterization of the timing of altered noradrenergic rhythms in depression.

Halaris and coworkers (DeMet and Halaris, 1984) have reported preliminary results of measurement of total MHPG concentrations from plasma samples drawn at 3-hour intervals over 24 hours in depressed patients and controls. Subjects were permitted to engage in their usual activities and were kept on a low monoamine diet. Both the normal subjects and the depressed patients appeared to demonstrate a circadian rhythm with a 24-hour periodicity. However, the peak MHPG concentration occurred 3 hours earlier in depressed patients than in controls, an interval similar to that noted in the Wehr study. In a small sample of patients, treatment with desipramine seemed to reverse this abnormality (DeMet et al., 1982).

Thus, there is empirical support for a phase-advance hypothesis, although studies to date have been limited in number. This hypothesis has heuristic value in explaining the sleep and activity disturbances of depression. According to this hypothesis, the depressed patients' natural circadian cycle may not conform to their environmental circumstances and might contribute to feelings of depression and lethargy, particularly in early morning hours, as well as to difficulty in maintaining expected sleep schedules. Also consistent with this hypothesis is preliminary work utilizing sleep deprivation and light manipulations that suggests that these interventions may ameliorate depression (Wehr, 1984; Lewy et al., 1985).

However, some evidence suggests that noradrenergic and other biologic system abnormalities may not be direct functions of a circadian phase advance, but may be better accommodated by models of instability or variability in these systems' control mechanisms, potentially resulting in a phase advance but equally likely to cause other disturbances in the time-dependent and stimulus-dependent regulation of these systems in depression.

NORADRENERGIC ACTIVITY: TOO UNSTABLE?

Although a phase-advance model might account for the apparent earlier peaks of noradrenergic metabolites in depressed patients, preliminary evidence suggests that the picture is more complex and may be better understood in terms of the chronobiologic instability or erratic output of this system (Siever and Davis, 1985). For example, in one case report, a bipolar patient in the depressed state showed multiple peaks of urinary MHPG concentrations (determined from a periodogram) throughout the day, whereas in remission the same patient evidenced the single expected afternoon peak (Pflug et al., 1982). In addition, in the depressed state, the peaks of urinary MHPG concentration were dissociated from those of urinary VMA and body temperature.

In the study of Giedke and colleagues (1982), the diurnal rhythms of urinary MHPG excretion that could be documented in the control group could not be demonstrated in the depressed patient groups, apparently due to the larger interindividual variability of diurnal MHPG excretion patterns in the depressed patients. The investigators interpreted these results in terms of desynchronization of the diurnal rhythm of MHPG. Despite the methodologic limitations of this study, it does tend to support a hypothesis of increased variability in the temporal organization of the noradrenergic system in depression. In the study of Halaris (Chapter 2, this volume), a phase-advanced peak of plasma MHPG concentrations in depressed patients appeared to be associated in many of these patients with the appearance of "unexplained" secondary peaks throughout the day. A subsequent analysis of these data suggested a secondary doubling of the 24-hour circadian rhythm, with an ultradian cycle of 12 rather than 24 hours (DeMet and Halaris, 1984).

These preliminary results regarding the noradrenergic system are at least consistent with models of chronobiologic instability in other indices such as rapid-eye-movement (REM) sleep and body temperature, for which more data are available. One group has suggested that the sleep abnormalities observed in depression are not consistent with an abnormal phase position of the REM sleep cycle, a low non-REM (NREM) sleep propensity, or circadian flattening but are consistent with increased amplitude of random fluctuations in the wake threshold (Beersma et al., 1984; Daan et al., 1984). They utilized the McCarley–Hobson model of NREM–REM regulation and demonstrated that observed results using such a model may be accounted for by an abnormal initial value of a variable representing the firing of the locus coeruleus (Beersma, Daan, and van den Hoofdakker, 1984). Avery and colleagues (1982) found a temperature minimum earlier in the night in depressed patients when ill, as compared to depressed patients in remission, but no phase advance in relation to normal controls. Nikitopoulou and Crammer (1976) found that daytime temperature appears more disorganized, with suggestions of a 12-hour rhythm in depressed patients compared to controls. They interpreted these data as resulting from a desynchronization and instability of circadian rhythms in depression. Pflug and colleagues (1982) also found instability of the circadian rhythm of temperature associated with depressive episodes, with more stable patterns during recovery.

As the noradrenergic system is implicated in thermoregulation (Tangri et al., 1974) and NREM–REM cycles (Hobson et al., 1976), and REM sleep is associated with heat retention, instability in these three functional systems might be expected to be associated. In fact, Avery and colleagues (1982) did find a relationship between increased REM latency and a greater decrease in nocturnal temperature. In the study by Wehr et al. (1980), temperature and urinary MHPG excretion were both phase advanced, but the phase advance was greater for urinary MHPG excretion. However, these associations are limited and do not permit inferences of causality.

The results of the studies of MHPG, in conjunction with the REM–NREM and temperature findings, thus raise the possibility that these rhythms may not only be phase advanced but also more unstable and desynchronized in the depressed state. These rhythms are ultimately controlled by the activity of the SCN. The SCN has an endogenous rhythmicity (Moore-Ede et al., 1983) that can be entrained by changes in the environment (day–night cycle) or modulated by other neural hormonal systems (Rusak and Zucker, 1979). The exact neurochemical mechanisms by which the SCN generates circadian rhythms are incompletely understood, but a number of neural models have been developed to account for its oscillatory activity (Kronauer et al., 1982; Daan and Berde, 1978; Carpenter and Grossberg, 1983). A "gated pacemaker" model is formulated in terms of mutually inhibitory on-cell/off-cell populations, with positive feedback signals gated by slowly accumulating neurotransmitters (Carpenter and Grossberg, 1983), conceptually similar to the REM–NREM sleep of McCarley and Hobson (1975). According to such a model, "noisy" or erratic activity of a relevant neurotransmitter system could alter the gating mechanism and contribute to an erratic and phase-advanced output of the master oscillator. This instability or erratic timing would be manifested in a variety of physiologic and behavioral systems.

Selected SCN neurons have been demonstrated to increase their activity in response to acetylcholine and glutamate and decrease their activity in response to norepinephrine, serotonin, and dopamine (Nishino and Koizomi, 1977). The catecholamines may be localized in afferent terminals in the capsule of the SCN (Moore, 1983). Thus SCN regulation of catecholamine neurotransmitter rhythms could conceivably depend on accumulation of these substances at catecholaminergic-sensitive neurons in the SCN. By this mechanism, an erratic increase in the output of an unstable noradrenergic system, for example, prior to the expected afternoon peak, might generate a false signal to the SCN, thus phase advancing and desynchronizing this system. "Noisy" periodicities in oscillatory systems also may result in frequency doubling (Farmer et al., 1980; Carpenter and Grossberg, 1983), as suggested in the previously mentioned studies.

Studies using the strategy of multiple sampling of noradrenergic metabolites over extended periods are, at this point, relatively few and preliminary. Thus, it is not possible at this time to characterize the apparent disturbances in rhythmicity of the noradrenergic system in depression with any precision or confidence, much less to determine their underlying biologic mechanisms. However, it appears worthwhile at this juncture to pursue these strategies further and consider the possibility that the putative chronobiologic abnormalities may be characterized as an instability in their rhythmicities. This possibility may be conceptualized in terms of a dysregulation of the noradrenergic system, consistent with a variety of studies that raise the possibility of faulty feedback control and responsiveness to environmental stimuli in this system (Siever and Davis, 1985). Whether these apparent abnormalities originate in the noradrenergic system, in other associated neurotransmitter systems, or represent more generalized properties of central neuronal systems, e.g., membrane regulatory processes, remains to be ascertained. However, they do suggest that strategies evaluating the regulation of this system over time may provide important information regarding the pathophysiology of depression.

IMPLICATIONS OF A MODEL OF CHRONOBIOLOGIC INSTABILITY

The abnormalities in the rhythmicity of norepinephrine parallel dysregulation in the circadian rhythms of the sleep–wakefulness cycle, temperature, and hypothalamo–pituitary–adrenal (HPA) axis in depression. At this point, it seems difficult to point to any single psychobiologic system as the "source" of the multiplicity of disturbances across these systems in depression. Rather, it is the configuration of these abnormalities and their relationships that require further exploration. In many instances, these abnormalities seem to be better accommodated by paradigms of altered stability or regulation than by models of increases or decreases in these systems' activity. Apparent phase advances in the diurnal rhythms of these variables may be a part of a broader and more generalized defect in the time-dependent and stimulus-dependent properties of these systems. Thus, these disturbances presumably imply disturbances in SCN pacing mechanisms, but not necessarily a localized primary SCN abnormality.

Disturbances in the adrenergic system are not confined to abnormalities in noradrenergic metabolite measures, which are presumably, in part, reflective of noradrenergic availability for intrasynaptic transmission. Both direct measures of receptor binding on blood elements (Garcia-Sevilla et al., 1981; Siever et al., 1984) and neuroendocrine indices of central adrenergic receptor responsiveness to psychopharmacologic challenge (Siever et al., 1981; Matussek et al., 1980; Checkley et al., 1981; Siever and Uhde, 1984) suggest that abnormalities in adrenergic receptors may be implicated in affective illness as well. Of particular interest is the α_2-adrenergic receptor, which is not only located postsynaptically but presynaptically as well and is inhibitory to noradrenergic firing and release in response to norepinephrine itself. Reduced MHPG and heart rate responses to clonidine, which presumably reflect inhibition of noradrenergic output, raise the possibility that these feedback inhibitory α_2-adrenergic receptors may be reduced in responsiveness in depressive illness (Siever and Uhde, 1984). Reduced feedback inhibition could contribute to unstable and poorly buffered activity in the noradrenergic system in depression (Siever and Davis, 1985).

There is some evidence for abnormalities in noradrenergic response to specific stressors in depressed patients that suggests inadequate buffering of the noradrenergic system in depression. As noted previously, concentrations of noradrenergic metabolites may be more variable in depressed patients under basal conditions. Changes in diet or activity also appear to cause alterations in excretion of urinary MHPG in depressed patients that do not occur in normal individuals (Muscettola et al., 1984; Goode et al., 1973; Beckmann et al., 1979). In contrast, discrete time-limited stimuli that lead to significant changes in urinary MHPG or plasma norepinephrine in normals may result in diminished responses in depressed patients (Buchsbaum et al., 1981; Ackenheil et al., 1980). Thus, the selectivity of response in the noradrenergic system may be different in depressed patients than it is in normal individuals. One might consider depressed patients to have exaggerated variability in response to less specific and appropriate stimuli and reduced responsiveness to discrete, appropriate stimuli.

There is some evidence that antidepressants may contribute to a reequilibration of the noradrenergic system in depression. DeMet and associates (1982) reported that desipramine alters the erratic, phase-shifted chronobiologic pattern of total plasma MHPG concentrations to conform more closely to the single late-afternoon peak observed in normal subjects. Antidepressants such as desipramine will decrease plasma and urinary concentrations of MHPG (Charney et al., 1982; Linnoila et al., 1982a,b). These changes have been interpreted as reflecting increased efficiency of the noradrenergic system (Linnoila et al., 1982a,b). Antidepressants such as clorgyline also may increase the efficiency of responsiveness of the noradrenergic system to the stimulus of standing (Ross et al., 1985).

These effects might be understood in the context of preclinical studies of the action of antidepressants on the noradrenergic system. Those antidepressants that affect the noradrenergic system, such as desipramine (DMI) and clorgyline, decrease the firing of the noradrenergic system (Svensson and Usdin, 1978; McMillen et al., 1980; Campbell et al., 1979). This decrease is apparently mediated by α_2-adrenergic receptors (McMillen et al., 1980) responding to local increases in noradrenergic availability secondary to reuptake blockade or monoamine oxidase (MAO) inhibition. Although decreases in the basal firing rate of the locus coeruleus are observed during antidepressant administration, responses to specific stimulation of the noradrenergic system may be normal or enhanced. β-Adrenergic receptors mediate inhibition of hippocampal neurons by noradrenergic neurons. Animals chronically treated with DMI show decreased hippocampal firing under basal conditions, which suggests decreased noradrenergic activity at β-adrenergic receptors (Huang, 1979; Huang, Maas, and Hu, 1980). This decrease is consistent with the documented decreases in β-adrenergic receptor responsiveness (Sulser, 1983) and decreased locus coeruleus firing rate (McMillen et al., 1980) following administration of DMI. In contrast, no difference in hippocampal firing was observed between the DMI-treated and untreated groups following electrical stimulation of the locus coeruleus (Huang, 1979; Huang et al., 1980). Similarly, although DMI lowers both firing of the locus coeruleus and MHPG accumulation acutely, the increment induced by locus coeruelus stimulation was not changed by DMI (Bareggi et al., 1978). These preclinical studies suggest that the basal activity of the locus coeruleus is reduced under basal conditions, but not under stimulated conditions, thus increasing the "signal-to-noise" ratio of the system. Such effects might not be expected to induce significant functional changes in a normally equilibrated system, but might suppress the "noisy" erratic basal activity of a dysregulated system while preserving its response to stimulation, thus increasing the efficiency of the system. These effects might account for the apparent "normalization" of circadian rhythms and improved efficiency of the noradrenergic system in depressed patients following long-term antidepressant treatment.

A model of dysregulated or unstable activity is not without precedent in medicine. For example, type II diabetes mellitus is a medical illness characterized by altered physiologic function of insulin. Both genetic factors and environmental factors such as body weight and diet may play a role in the onset and severity of diabetes (Albin and Rifkin, 1982), just as both genetic factors (Nurnberger and Gershon, 1984) and environmental factors such as stress or loss (Anisman and Zacharko, 1982) play a role in the pathogenesis of depression. The physiologic dysregulation of insulin could not, however, be simply detected as alterations of circulating insulin, as the concentrations may be increased, decreased, or normal (Albin and Rifkin, 1982). However, alterations in both the number of insulin receptors and effectance of receptors have been observed in type II diabetes (Kolterman et al., 1982). Some insulin receptors may play a feedback inhibitory role in insulin output in the pancreas, and this mechanism may be defective in obese individuals, who are at risk for type II diabetes (Elati et al., 1982). Thus, there may be broad similarities between insulin regulation in type II diabetes and noradrenergic regulation in affective illness, in which concentrations of norepinephrine or its metabolites may be normal, increased, or decreased and adrenergic receptors may be reduced in responsiveness.

There are also animal models that afford the possibility of delineation of biologic mechanisms not possible in clinical studies. The animal model of "learned helplessness" or uncontrollable shock is one in which the role of possible noradrenergic function has been investigated (Maier et al., 1969). Shocks administered to yoked rats will produce decreased food and/or water consumption, weight loss, poor motor performance as well as decreased aggressiveness, grooming, and sleep analogous to the vegetative symptoms observed in major depressive disorder. This syndrome may be reversed by antidepressant administration (Weiss et al., 1982).

Norepinephrine stores are reduced in the uncontrollable shock paradigm, apparently secondary to increased norepinephrine (Weiss et al., 1982, Anisman et al., 1980). Decreased noradrenergic availability would be predicted to result in feedback disinhibition of the firing of the locus coeruleus. The net result might be characterized by a pattern of an increased locus coeruleus firing rate, decreased norepinephrine released per nerve impulse, relative depletion of noradrenergic stores, and a functional understimulation of α_2-adrenergic receptors.

Although the exact character of noradrenergic alterations in this model require further clarification, pharmacologic studies using this paradigm are at least consistent with such a model. The noradrenergic depleting agents α-methyl-p-tyrosine and reserpine result in a behavioral deficit comparable to that induced by uncontrollable shock (Anisman et al., 1980). Piperoxane, which increases the locus coeruleus firing rate by blocking α_2-adrenergic receptors, also produces a behavioral syndrome similar to the uncontrollable shock syndrome (Weiss et al., 1982). Conversely, clonidine, an α_2-adrenergic agonist that reduces locus coeruleus firing, can reverse the uncontrollable shock syndrome (Weiss et al., 1982).

Thus, although the pattern of noradrenergic dysregulation implicated by this animal model remains inferential, it has limited empirical support and converges in several respects with the emerging clinical picture of noradrenergic dysregulation, namely, unstable and erratic basal activity reflected in disrupted circadian rhythms, inappropriate responses to stimulation, and ineffective feedback inhibition (Figure 1.1). Antidepressants may thus serve to increase the efficiency of this system by reducing basal firing, enhancing noradrenergic availability for responses to specific stimulation, and "normalizing" altered circadian rhythms (Figure 1.1).

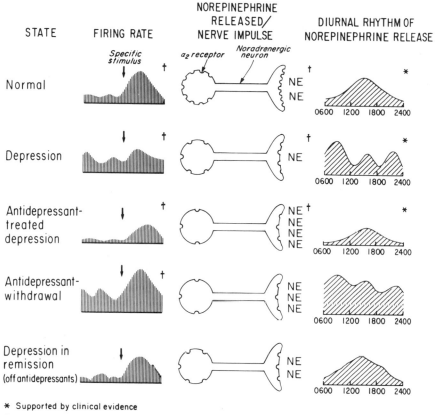

Figure 1.1. Model of Noradrenergic System in Depression. Source: Siever, LJ, Davis KL (1985), American Journal of Psychiatry 142:1017–1031. Reproduced with permission.

These considerations are raised to illustrate the possibility that observed alterations in circadian rhythmicities may represent one manifestation of an unstable or dysregulated noradrenergic system. This might then be expected to be associated with other indices of alterations in noradrenergic activity such as altered adrenergic receptor responsiveness or noradrenergic output. At this point, it is unclear what specific abnormality underlies the apparent dysregulation of this system. The multiple interactions among the noradrenergic system and other neurotransmitter systems and the evidence implicating serotonergic, cholinergic, and gabaergic neurotransmitter abnormalities in depression make it unlikely that the abnormalities in the noradrenergic system associated with depression should be considered in isolation or as somehow "primary" in the affective disorders. Rather, the configuration of neurotransmitter and neuromodulator abnormalities in depression requires further clarification. In this context, formulation of abnormalities in terms of instability or dysregulation rather than exclusively as increases or decreases in activity may be a useful vantage point from which to investigate these disordered systems.

In the neural model of the noradrenergic system in depression (Figure 1.1), the noradrenergic system is characterized by increased erratic firing rate at the locus coeruleus, which is less selectively responsive to specific stimuli compared to this system in normal individuals. The increased noradrenergic instability is associated with a subsensitivity of feedback inhibitory α_2-adrenergic receptors. As noradrenergic supplies become depleted, norepinephrine released per nerve impulse may decrease. The net accumulation of noradrenergic metabolites may be increased, decreased, or unchanged depending on the synthetic capacity of the noradrenergic system and degree of depletion as a function of phase of the illness. In any case, the normal time-dependent periodicities of these metabolite concentrations will be disrupted with a phase advance and altered conformation, e.g., unexpected erratic peaks in their circadian rhythm. Following long-term antidepressant administration, locus coereleus firing is pervasively decreased, but there is an increase in the "signal-to-noise" ratio both in the response to specific stimuli and in the coherence of the circadian rhythm, with a return to a normal afternoon peak of noradrenergic activity. The antidepressant-induced increased "signal-to-noise" ratio is a function of both a depressed basal noradrenergic firing rate and an increase in norepinephrine released per nerve impulse. The mechanisms for the increased norepinephrine released per nerve impulse may vary, but include the interaction of increased noradrenergic availability and α_2-adrenergic receptor downregulation. α_2-Adrenergic subsensitivity in the absence of depressed locus coeruleus firing is, however, maladaptive, as illustrated by the effects of abrupt antidepressant withdrawal. In this situation, firing rate increases and the α_2-adrenergic subsensitivity may contribute to a further dysregulation of noradrenergic output, which may be accompanied by agitation and depressive relapse. The noradrenergic system in remitted depressives off medication is relatively normal in its temporal organization and responsiveness, but the vulnerability remains for a dysregulated neurotransmitter–receptor interaction, as reflected in persistent α_2-adrenergic receptor subsensitivity. This vulnerability may translate into dysregulated noradrenergic output in response to stressful shifts in the internal or external environment. This model, although speculative, illustrates how associated alterations in a number of variables determining noradrenergic activity may interact to produce a dysregulated system.

REFERENCES

Ackenheil M, Albus M, Muller F, et al (1980): Catecholamine response to short-time stress in schizophrenic and depressive patients. In Usdin E, Kvetnansky R, Kopin IJ (eds.): Catecholamine and Stress: Recent Advances. Amsterdam, Elsevier.

Albin J, Rifkin H (1982). Etiologies of diabetes mellitus. Med Clin Am 66:1209–1226.

Anisman H, Zacharko RM (1982): Depression: The predisposing influence of stress. Behavioral and brain sciences 5:89–137.

Anisman H, Irwin J, Sklar LS (1979): Deficits of escape performance following catecholaminergic depletion: implications for behavioral deficits induced by uncontrollable stress. Psychopharmacol 64:163–170.

Anisman H, Pizzino A, Sklar LS (1980): Coping with stress, norepinephrine depletion and escape performance. Brain Res 191:583–588.

Aronow WS, Herding PR, DeQuatro V, et al (1973): Diurnal variation of plasma catecholamines and systolic time interval. Chest 63:722–726.

Asberg M, Bertilsson L, Thoren P, et al (1978): CSF monoamine metabolites in depressive illness. In Garattini S (ed): Depressive Disorders. FK Schattaner Verlag, Stuttgart, pp 293–335.

Ashcroft GG, Dow RC, Yates CM, et al (1976): Significance of lumbar CSF metabolite measurements in affective illness. In Tuomisto J, Paasonen MK (eds): CNS and Behavioral Pharmacology. Helsinki, Finland, University of Helsinki, pp 277–284.

Avery DH, Wildschiodtz G, Rafaelsen OJ (1982): Nocturnal temperature in affective disorder. J Affective Disord 4:61–71.

Bareggi SR, Markey K, Genovese E (1978): Effects of single and multiple doses of desipramine (DMI) on endogenous levels of 3-methoxy-4-hydroxy-phenylglycol-sulfate (MOPEG-SO$_4$) in rat brain. Eur J Pharmacol 50:301–304.

Becker EJ, Krenzer F (1970): Catecholamine excretion by healthy adults. Pfluger Arch 316:95–113.

Beckmann H, Ebert MH, Post RM, et al: (1979): Effect of moderate exercise on urinary MHPG in depressed patients. Pharmacopsychiatria 12:351–356.

Beersma DGM, Daan S, van den Hoofdakker RH (1984): Distribution of REM latencies and other sleep phenomena in depression as explained by a single ultradian rhythm disturbance. Sleep 7:126–136.

Beersma DGM, Daan S, van den Hoofdakker RH: The timing of sleep in depression—Theoretical considerations. Psychiatry Res (in press).

Blombery P, Kopin IJ, Gordon EK, et al. (1980): Conversion of MHPG to vanillylmandelic acid: Implications for the importance of urinary MHPG. Arch Gen Psychiatry 37:1095–1098.

Bond PA, Jenner JA, Sampson DA (1972): Daily variation of the urine content of 3-methoxy-4-hydroxyphehylglycol in two manic-depressive patients. Psychol Med 2:81–85.

Buchsbaum MS, Muscettola G, Goodwin FK (1978): Urinary MHPG, stress response, personality factors and somatosensory evoked potentials in normal subjects and patients with major affective disorders. Neuropsychobiology 7:212–224.

Bunney WE, Jr. and Davis JM (1965): Norepinephrine in depressive reactions: A review. Arch Gen Psychiatry 13:483–494.

Campbell IC, Murphy DI, Gallagher DW, et al (1979): Neurotransmitter-related adaptation in the central nervous system following chronic monoamine oxidase inhibition. In Singer TP, Van Korff RW, Murphy DL (eds): Monoamine Oxidase: Structure, Function, and Altered Functions. New York, Academic.

Carpenter GA, Grossberg S (1983): A neural theory of circadian rhythms: The gated pacemaker. Biol Cybern 48:35–59.

Charney DS, Heninger GR, Sternberg DE, et al (1982): Adrenergic receptor sensitivity in depression. Effects of clonidine in depressed patients and healthy patients. Arch Gen Psychiatry 39:290–294.

Checkley SA, Slade AP, Shur E (1981): Growth hormone and other responses to clonidine in patients with endogenous depression. Br J Psychiatry 138:51–55.

Christensen NJ, Vestergaard P, Sirensen T, et al (1980): Cerebrospinal fluid adrenaline and noradrenaline in depressed patients. Acta Psychiatr Scand 61:178–182.

Cymerman A, Francesconi RF (1975): Alterations of circadian rhythmicities of urinary 3-methoxy-4-hydroxyphenylglycol (MHPG) and vanillylmandelic acid (VMA) in man during cold exposure. Life Sci 16:225–236.

Daan S, Berde C (1978): Two coupled oscillators: Simulations of the circadian pacemaker in mammalian activity rhythms. J Theor Biol 70:297–313.

Daan S, Beersma DGM, Borbély AA (1984): Timing of human sleep: Recovery process gated by a circadian pacemaker. Am J Physiol 246:R161–R178, 1984.

DeMet EM, Halaris AE (1984): Tricyclic antidepressants reduce ultradian MHPG rhythm in depression. Neurosci Abstr 1:295.

DeMet EM, Halaris AE, Gwirtsman HE, et al (1982): Effects of desipramine on diurnal rhythms of plasma 3-methoxy-4-hydroxyphenylglycol (MHPG) in depressed patients. Psychopharm Bull 18:221–223.

DeMet EM, Halaris AE, Gwirtsman HE, Reno RM (1985): Diurnal rhythm of 3-methoxy-4-hydrophenylglycol (MHPG): Relationship between plasma and urinary levels. Life Sci 37:1731–1741.

Elati D, Nagulesparan M, Hershkopf RT, et al (1982): Feedback inhibition of insulin secretion by insulin. N Engl J Med 306:1196–1202.

Farmer D, Crutchfield J, Froehling H, et al (1980): Power spectra and mixing properties of strange attracters. Ann NY Acad Sci 357:453–472.

Garcia-Sevilla JA, Zis AP, Zelnic TC, et al (1981): Tricyclic antidepressant drug treatment decreases α_2-adrenoreceptors on human platelet membranes. Eur J Pharmacol 69:121–123.

Giedke H, Gaertner HJ, Mahal A, et al (1982): Diurnal variation of urinary MHPG in unipolar and bipolar depressives. Acta Psychiatr Scand 66:243–253.

Goode DJ, Dekirmenjian H, Meltzer HY, et al (1973): Relation of exercise to MHPG excretion in normal subjects. Arch Gen Psychiatry 29:391–396.

Goodwin FK, Post RM (1975): Studies of amine metabolites in affective illness and in schizophrenia: A comparative analysis. In Freedman DX (ed): Biology of the Major Psychoses. New York, Raven, pp 299–332. vol 54, 1975.

Goodwin FK, Potter WZ (1979): Noradrenergic function in affective illness. In Saletu B (ed): Proceedings of the 11th Collegium Internationale Neuro-Psychopharmacologium (CINP) Congress. New York, Pergamon, pp 127–137.

Halaris AE (1978): Plasma 3-methoxy-4-hydrophenylglycol in manic psychosis. Am J Psychiatry 135:493–494.

Halaris A (1987): Normal and abnormal circadian patterns of noradrenergic transmission. Chapter 2 in this volume.

Hobson JA, McCarley RW, McKenna TM (1976): Cellular evidence bearing on the pontine brain stem hypothesis of desynchronized sleep control. Prog Neurobiol 6:280–376.

Huang HY (1979): Chronic desipramine treatment increases activity of noradrenergic postsynaptic cells. Life Sci 25:709–716.

Huang HY, Maas JW, Hu G (1980): The time course of noradrenergic pre-and post-synaptic activity during chronic desipramine treatment. Eur J Pharmacol 68:41–47.

Jimerson DC, Nurnberger JI, Post RM, et al (1981): Plasma MHPG in rapid-cyclers and healthy twins. Arch Gen Psychiatry 38:1287–1290.

Jimerson DC, Rubinow DR, Ballenger JC, et al (1984): CSF norepinephrine metabolism in depressed patients: New methodologies. In Usdin E, Carlsson A, Dahlstrom A, Engel J (eds): Catecholamines Part C: Neuropharmacology and Central Nervous System Therapeutics Aspects. New York, Alan R. Liss, pp 123–129.

Jones FD, Maas FJ, Dekirmenjian M, et al (1973): Urinary catecholamine metabolites during behavioral changes in a patient with manic-depressive cycles. Science 179:300–302.

Karki NT (1956): The urinary excretion of noradrenaline and adrenaline in different age groups, its diurnal variations and the effect of muscular work on it. Acta Physiol Scand 39:1–96.

Kolterman OG, Scarlett JA, Olefsky JM (1982): Insulin resistance in non-insulin-dependent type 2 diabetes mellitus: Clinical endocrinology and metabolism 11:363–388.

Kopin IJ, Gordon EK, Jimerson DC, et al (1983): Relationship of plasma and cerebrospinal fluid levels of 3-methoxy-4-hydroxphenylglycol (MHPG): Their value as indices of noradrenergic activity. Science 219:73–75.

Koslow JH, Maas JW, Bowden CL, et al (1983): CSF and urinary biogenic amines and metabolites in depression and mania. Arch Gen Psychiatry 40:999–1010.

Kripke DF, Mullaney DJ, Atkinson M, et al (1978): Circadian rhythm disorders in manic-depressives. Biol Psychiatry 13:335–351.

Kronauer RE, Czeisler CA, Pilato SF, et al (1982): Mathematical model of the human circadian system with two interacting oscillators. Am J Physiol 242:R3–R17.

Lake CR, Pickar D, Ziegler MG, et al (1982): High plasma norepinephrine levels in patients with major affective disorders. Am J Psychiatry 139:1315–1318.

Lake CR, Ziegler MG, Kopin IJ (1976): Use of plasma norepinephrine for evaluation of sympathetic neuronal function in man. Life Sci 18:1315–1326.

Levin BE, Rappaport M, Natelson BH (1979): Ultradian variations of plasma noradrenaline in humans. Life Sci 25:621–628.

Lewy AJ, Sack RL, Singer C (1985): Bright light therapy of chronobiologic disorders. New Research Abstracts of the APA, NR 149.

Lightman SL, James VHT, Linsell C (1981): Studies of diurnal changes on plasma renin activity, and plasma noradrenaline, aldosterone and cortisol concentration in man. Clin Endocrinol 14:213–223.

Linnoila M, Karoum F, Calil HM, et al (1982a): Alteration of norepinephrine metabolism with desipramine and zimelidine in depressed patients. Arch Gen Psychiatry 39:1025–1028.

Linnoila M, Karoum F, Potter WZ (1982b): Effect of low-dose clorgyline on 24-hour urinary monoamine excretion in patients with rapidly cycling bipolar affective disorder. Arch Gen Psychiatry 39:513–516.

Louis WJ, Doyle AE, Anavekar SN (1975): Plasma noradrenergic concentration and blood pressure in essential hypertension, phaeochromocytoma and depression. Clin Sci Molec Med 48:2395–2425.

Maas JW, Dekirmenjian H, Fawcett J (1971): Catecholamine metabolism, depression and stress. Nature 230:330–331.

Maas JW, Dekirmenjian H, Jones F (1973): The identification of depressed patients who have a disorder of NE metabolism and/or disposition. In Usdin E, Snyder S (eds): Frontiers in Catecholamine Research. New York, Pergamon, pp 1091–1096.

Maas JW, Hattox SE, Greene NM (1979): 3-Methoxy-4-hydrophenyl-glycol production by human brain in vivo. Science 205:1025–1029.

Maier SF, Seligman MEP, Solomon RL (1969): Pavlovian fear conditioning and learned helplessness. In Campbell BA, Church RM (eds): Punishment and Aversive Behavior. New York, Appleton-Century-Crofts, pp 299–342.

Markianos E, Beckmann H (1976): Diurnal changes in dopamine-beta-hydroxylase, homovanillic acid and 3-methoxy-4-hydrophenylglycol in serum of man. J. Neural Transm 39:79–93.

Matussek N, Ackenheil M, Hippus H, et al (1980): Effect of clonidine on growth hormone release in psychiatric patients and controls. Psychiatry Res 2:25–36.

McCarley RW, Hobson JA (1975): Neuronal excitability modulation over the sleep cycle: A structural and mathematical model. Science 189:55–58.

McMillen BA, Warnack W, German DC, et al (1980): Effects of chronic desipramine treatment on rat brain noradrenergic responses to α-adrenergic drugs. Eur J Pharmacol 671:239–243.

Moore RY (1983): Organization and function of a central nervous system circadian oscillator; the suprachiasmatic nucleus. Fed Proc 42:2783–2789.

Moore-Ede MC, Czeisler CA, Richardson GS (1983): Circadian time-keeping in health and disease. Part 1: Basic properties of circadian rhythms. Physiol Rev 309:469–476.

Muscettola G, Potter WZ, Gordon EK, et al (1981): Methodological issues in the measurement of urinary MHPG. Psychiatry Res 4:267–276.

Muscettola G, Potter WZ, Pickar D, et al (1984): Urinary 3-methoxy-4-hydroxyphenylglycol and major affective disorders. Arch Gen Psychiatry 41:337–342.

Nikitopoulou G, Crammer JL (1976): Change in diurnal temperature rhythms in manic-depressive illness. Br Med J 1:1311–1314.

Nishino H, Koizomi K (1977): Responses of neurons in the suprachiasmatic nuclei of the hypothalamus to putative transmitters. Brain Res 120:167–172.

Nurnberger JI Jr, Gershon ES (1984): Genetics of affective disorder. In Post RM, Ballenger JC (eds): Neurobiology of Mood Disorders. Baltimore, Williams and Wilkins, pp 76–101.

Paykel ES, Myers JK, Dieneit MN, et al (1969): Life events and depression. A controlled study. Arch Gen Psychiatry 21:753–760.

Pflug B, Engelmann W, Gaertner JH (1982): Circadian course of body temperature and the excretion of MHPG and VMA in a patient with bipolar depression. J Neural Transm 53:213–215.

Post RM, Ballenger JC, Goodwin FK (1980): Cerebrospinal fluid studies of neurotransmitter function in manic and depressive illness. In Wood JH (ed): Neurobiology of Cerebrospinal Fluid. New York, Plenum, pp 685–717.

Post RM, Gordon EK, Goodwin FK (1973): Central norepinephrine metabolism in affective illness: MHPG in the ccrebrospinal fluid. Science 9:1002–1003.

Post RM, Jimerson DC, Ballenger JC, et al (1984): Cerebrospinal fluid norepinephrine and its metabolites in manic-depressive illness. In Post RM, Ballenger JD (eds): Neurobiology of Mood Disorders. Baltimore, Williams and Wilkins.

Post RM, Lake CR, Jimerson DC, et al (1978): Cerebrospinal fluid norepinephrine in affective illness. Am J Psychiatry 135:907–912.

Post RM, Stoddard FJ, Gillin JC, et al (1977): Alterations in motor activity, sleep, and biochemistry in a cycling manic-depressive patient. Arch Gen Psychiatry 34:470–477.

Potter WZ, Muscettola G, Goodwin FK (1983): Sources of variance in clinical studies of MHPG. In Maas JW (ed): Basic Mechanisms and Psychopathology. New York, Academic, pp 145–165.

Potter WZ, Ross RJ, Zavadil HP (1985) Norepinephrine in the affective disorders: Classic biochemical approaches. In Lake CR, Ziegler MG (eds), Catecholamines in Psychiatric Disorders. Butterworth, Boston, pp 213–233.

Reinberg A, Halberg F, Ghata J, et al (1969): Rhythm ciradian de diverses fonctions physiologiques de l'homme adulte sain actif et au repos pouls, pression arterielle, excretions urinares des 17-OCHS, des catecholamines et du potassium. J Physiol 61:383–400.

Riederer T, Birkmayer W, Neumayer E, et al (1974): The daily rhythm of HVA, VMA, and 5-HIAA in depression syndrome. J Neural Transm 35:23–45.

Ross RJ, Scheinin M, Lesieur P, et al (1985): The effect of clorgyline on noradrenergic function. Psychopharmacol 95:227–230.

Rudorfer MV, Lesieur P, Ross RJ, et al (1982): Norepinephrine in depression up or down. New Research Abstracts of the APA, NR 46.

Rusak B, Zucker F (1979): Neural regulation of circadian rhythms. Physiol Rev 59:334–526.

Schildkraut JJ (1965): The catecholamine hypothesis of affective disorders: Review of supporting evidence. Am J Psychiatry 122:509–522.

Schildkraut JJ, Orsulak PJ, LaBrie RA, et al (1978a). Toward a biochemical classification of depressive disorders. II. Application of multivariate discriminant function to analysis of data on urinary catecholamines and metabolites. Arch Gen Psychiatry 35:1436–1439.

Schildkraut JJ, Orsulak PJ, Schatzberg AF, et al (1978b). Toward a biochemical subclassification of depressive disorders. Arch Gen Psychiatry 35:1427–1433.

Shaw DM, O'Keefe R, MacSweeney DA, et al (1973): 3-Methoxy-4-hydroxyphenylglycol in depression. Psychol Med 3:333–336.

Siever LJ, Davis KL (1985): Overview: Toward a dysregulation hypothesis of depression. Am J Psychiatry 142:1017–1031.

Siever LJ, Insel TR, Uhde TW (1981): Noradrenergic challenges in the affective disorders. J Clin Psychopharmacol 1:193–206.

Siever LJ, Kafka MS, Targum S, et al (1984a): Platelet alpha-adrenergic binding and biochemical responsiveness in depressed patients and controls. Psychiatry Res 11:287–302.

Siever LJ, Murphy DL, Slater S, et al (1984b): Plasma prolactin changes following fenfluramine in depressed patients compared to controls: An evaluation of central serotonergic responsivity in depression. Life Sci 34:1029–1039.

Siever LJ, Pickar D, Lake CR, et al (1983): Extreme elevations in plasma norepinephrine associated with decreased α-adrenergic responsivity in major depressive disorder: Two case reports. J Clin Psychopharmacol 3:39–41.

Siever LJ, Uhde TW (1984): New studies and perspectives on the noradrenergic receptor system in depression: Effects of the alpha-adrenergic agonist clonidine. Biol Psychiatry 19:131–156.

Subrahmanyan S (1975): Role of biogenic amines in certain pathological conditions. Brain Res 87:355–362.

Sulser F (1983): Deamplification of noradrenergic signal transfer by antidepressants: A unified catecholamine–serotonin hypothesis of affective disorders. Psychopharmacol Bull 19:300–304.

Svensson TH, Usdin T (1978): Feedback inhibition of brain noradrenaline neurons by tricyclic antidepressants. Alpha-receptor mediation. Science 202:1089–1091.

Tangri KK, Bhargava AK, Bhargava KP (1974): Interrelation between monoaminergic and cholinergic mechanisms in the hypothalamic thermoregulatory centre of rabbits. Neuropharmacology 13:333–346.

Townsend MD, Smith AJ (1973): Factors influencing the urinary excretion of free catecholamines in man. Clin Sci 44:253–265.

Vestergaard P, Sorensen T, Hoppe E, et al (1978): Biogenic amine metabolites in cerebrospinal fluid of patients with affective disorders. Acta Psychiatr Scand 58:88–96.

von Euler US, Hellner-Bjorkman S, Owman I (1955): Diurnal variations in the excretion of free and conjugated noradrenaline and adrenaline in urine from healthy subjects. Acta Physiol Scand 33:10–16.

Wehr TA (1977): Phase and biorhythm studies in affective illness. In Bunney WE (moderator): The switch process in manic-depressive psychosis. Ann Intern Med 87:319–335.

Wehr TA (1984): Biological rhythms and manic-depressive illness. In Post RM, Ballenger JC (eds): Neurobiology of Mood Disorders. Baltimore, Williams and Wilkins, pp 190–206.

Wehr TA, Gillin JC, Goodwin FK (1983): Sleep and circadian rhythms in depression. In Chase MH, Weitzman ED (eds): Sleep Disorders: Basic and Clinical Research. New York, Spectrum, pp 195–225.

Wehr TA, Muscettola G, Goodwin FK (1980): Urinary 3-methoxy-4-hydrophenylglycol circadian rhythm. Arch Gen Psychiatry 37:257–263.

Weiss JM, Bailey WH, Goodman PA, et al (1982): In Levy A, Speigelstein MV (eds): Behavioral Models and the Analysis of Drug Action. Amsterdam, Elsevier.

Weiss JM, Glazer HI, Pohorecky LA (1976): Coping behavioral and neurochemical changes: An alternative explanation for the original "learned helplessness" experiments. In Serban G, Kling A (eds): Animal Models in Human Psychobiology. New York, Plenum, pp 141–173.

Wilk S, Shopsin B, Gershon S and Suhl M (1972): Cerebrospinal fluid levels of MHPG in affective disorders. Nature 235:440–441.

Wyatt RJ, Portnoy B, Kupfer DJ, et al (1971): Resting plasma catecholamine concentrations in patients with depression and anxiety. Arch Gen Psychiatry 24:65–70.

Ziegler MG, Lake CR, Wood JH, et al (1976): Circadian rhythm in cerebrospinal fluid noradrenaline of man and monkey. Nature 266:656–658.

2

Normal and Abnormal Circadian Patterns of Noradrenergic Transmission

Angelos Halaris

The catecholamine hypothesis of affective disorders, as originally postulated by Bunney and Davis (1965) and Schildkraut (1965), has focused on norepinephrine (NE) as the neurotransmitter intricately linked to mania and certain types of depressive illness. A definitive causal relationship between aberrant noradrenergic transmission and affective illness has not been unequivocally established. This conceptual framework has provided the impetus for a host of innovative modifications and expansions of the original hypothesis. Among the more recent hypotheses, some of the more intriguing include the adrenergic receptor downregulation hypothesis (Banerjee et al., 1977; Sulser et al., 1978; Charney et al., 1981a,b), the phase-advance hypothesis of circadian rhythms (Papoušek, 1975; Kripke et al., 1978; Wehr and Goodwin, 1981), and the dysregulation hypothesis introduced by Siever and Davis (1985). It is beyond the scope of this chapter to address all of the creative approaches researchers have utilized in attempting to understand the precise mechanism(s) by which noradrenergic transmission and its pathophysiology may relate to mood states in normal and diseased states. This chapter focuses, rather, on circadian phenomena as they pertain to the metabolism of NE in normal and depressed individuals.

A multitude of studies have explored the possibility that altered noradrenergic function is tantamount to the pathophysiology of affective illness (Schildkraut, 1978). Noninvasive indicators of noradrenergic ac-

23

tivity in the central nervous system (CNS) include the measurement of 3-methoxy-4-hydroxyphenylglycol (MHPG), the principal CNS meta-bolite of NE (Axelrod et al., 1959; Maas and Landis, 1968, 1971), in various body fluids. The origin and distribution of MHPG in each of the principal body fluids has been reviewed elsewhere (DeMet and Halaris, 1979). Several studies have confirmed that MHPG levels in cerebrospinal fluid (CSF), urine, and plasma are altered with changes in mood states (Schildkraut and Kety, 1967; Gordon and Oliver, 1971; Halaris and DeMet, 1979; Ostrow et al., 1984). Significant elevations of MHPG lev-els have been associated with stressed normal subjects or manic patients (Cymerman and Francesconi, 1975; Halaris and DeMet, 1979). Urinary excretion of MHPG is significantly decreased in certain types of de-pressed patients, especially bipolar manic-depressives (Muscettola et al, 1984), and altered excretion rates of MHPG may be predictive of re-sponse to treatment with certain types of antidepressants (Fawcett et al., 1972; Beckmann and Goodwin, 1980; Rosenbaum et al., 1980). Despite these results, however, attempts to demonstrate consistent and unequivocal decreases in MHPG in depressed patients have failed. In-deed, both decreases and increases in baseline MHPG levels have been reported, and some studies have found no significant differences be-tween depressed patients and normal controls or other patient popu-lations. Furthermore, successful treatment of depressed patients with tricyclic antidepressants does not produce a sustained increase in MHPG levels, as might be expected if NE activity were directly related to the depressed mood state (Beckmann and Goodwin, 1975; Halaris and DeMet, 1980).

Methodologic improvements in the late 1970s (e.g., electron-cap-ture gas chromatography and high-performance liquid chromatogra-phy) have permitted more frequent sampling, which led to the discovery that plasma and urinary MHPG levels follow a distinct diurnal variation (Cymerman and Francesconi, 1975; Markianos and Beckmann, 1976; Hollister et al., 1978; DeMet et al., 1982). Since plasma MHPG is usually determined at a single time point (typically 9 AM), whereas urine samples are collected over 24 hours, the presence of a diurnal rhythm complicates the interpretation of data obtained with either approach. Furthermore, recent studies have suggested that the phase and/or period of diurnal MHPG rhythms may be altered in affective disorders (Wehr et al., 1980; DeMet et al., 1982). Wehr and coworkers (1980) were the first to dem-onstrate that urinary MHPG in manic-depressives showed a circadian rhythm that was phase advanced (i.e., had an earlier peak) of approx-imately 1–3 hours when compared with normal subjects. This finding of a phase advance was confirmed by Giedke et al. (1982), but these authors failed to find a clear diurnal rhythm of MHPG in their depressed patients. Pflug and colleagues (1982) also demonstrated this phase advance but related it to a shorter period length of MHPG in urine. It is possible that these divergent results may relate to the general methodologic difficulties of urinary measurements, although it is clear that both central and peripheral compartments of MHPG are highly correlated (Lingjaerde, 1983; Maas et al., 1982), and, further, that the urinary and plasma compartments of MHPG also have clear and consistent interrelationships (DeMet et al., 1985).

As noted above, phase advances in the rhythms of manic and depressed patients have been reported for both plasma and urine. Since blood sampling is conventionally performed at the same time of the day in both control and depressed subjects, a phase advance (or delay) in the diurnal rhythm could be mistakenly interpreted as indicating an increase (or decrease) in baseline MHPG levels of depressed subjects. Following our pilot studies, in which we measured baseline plasma MHPG levels in various groups of manic-depressives (Halaris and DeMet, 1979), and having been impressed with a greater than expected variability in values obtained from unipolar depressives, we chose to conduct diurnal measurements rather than single time point evaluations in carefully diagnosed groups of patients. It was felt that the capability to obtain instantaneous measurements of plasma MHPG levels would better define the diurnal rhythm and would more consistently delineate a pathologic pattern in depressives. Initial findings using this method demonstrated that MHPG levels peaked earlier in a patient with rapidly cycling bipolar illness (Ostrow et al., 1984) and that successful treatment with desipramine (DMI) caused a phase delay of the phase-advanced diurnal rhythm in three endogenously depressed patients (DeMet et al., 1982).

The first goal was to determine the pattern and parameters of the MHPG diurnal rhythm in healthy male volunteers. Data obtained from the first six normal volunteers have been presented elsewhere (DeMet et al., 1985). Subsequently, the study was expanded to include a total of 12 male volunteers. The experimental design and approach to the data analysis is outlined below. The next project involved a population of primary major depressives who were studied before and after 4 weeks of treatment with DMI. These data are also summarized in this chapter. A third project consisted of a comprehensive baseline evaluation, an acute treatment phase, and a long-term (1 year) followup phase, with diurnal MHPG being included as a possible marker/predictor of treatment response and/or relapse. The data from the latter project will be the subject of future publications.

NORMAL SUBJECTS

Twelve normal male volunteers were recruited by word of mouth from within the university community. They ranged in age from 23 to 42 years, with a mean ± SEM of 31.4 ± 1.5 years. All subjects received a thorough medical examination to ensure that they were in good physical health and that they were not consuming any pharmacologic agent. No subject had a prior history of emotional illness or any first- or second-degree relatives who had been treated for such illness. A history of drinking of more than five drinks in 1 week was an exclusion criterion. Each subject completed a Minnesota Multiphasic Personality Inventory (MMPI) and was interviewed by a clinical psychologist. No attempt was made to restrict diet, since preliminary studies had failed to establish a clear-cut effect of catecholamine-containing dietary items on total plasma MHPG levels in healthy individuals. Subjects were asked to refrain from any type of exercise, strenuous physical activity, and alcoholic beverages for at least 3 days prior to the study. A log was kept of the general level of activity and the types and amounts of dietary items consumed.

Blood samples were collected via an indwelling antecubital vein catheter that was kept patent by flushing it with sterile citrate–phosphate–dextrose buffer (CPD-A). The samples were collected at 3-hour intervals around the clock, and every effort was made to avoid disturbing the subjects' sleeping patterns. Subjects slept in an environment that was already familiar to them. Total (free plus conjugated) plasma MHPG samples were measured by electron-capture gas chromatography as described by Halaris et al. (1977).

Plasma MHPG values were best fit to a cosine function by nonlinear least squares regression (procedure NLIN; SAS Institute, Cary, North Carolina). The NLIN Program was set to evaluate the residual sum of squares and arrive at a best set of starting variables for baseline, amplitude, phase, and period. The residuals of each of these parameters were then iteratively regressed on the partial derivatives of the cosine model by the Gauss–Newton method. Convergence criteria were met for the data sets of each of the 12 subjects within 15 iterations. The nonlinear regression method permitted us to estimate the period of the diurnal rhythm of plasma MHPG. However, this method cannot distinguish between harmonics of the principal rhythm. Therefore, for comparison, the results were also fit to a cosine function with a fixed period of 24 hours using a general linear regression model (procedure GLM; SAS Institute). The resulting estimates of baseline, amplitude, and phase were subjected to paired *t* tests. No significant difference was found

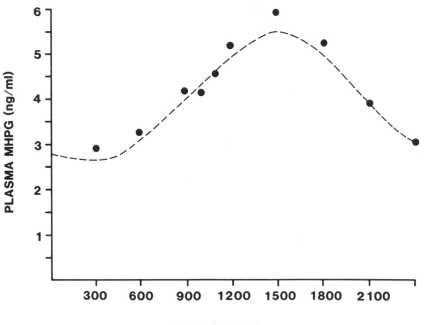

Figure 2.1. Computer-generated fit of the diurnal MHPG values from a typical (nearest to the mean) normal subject using the NLIN procedure.

between the two fitting methods with regard to any of the estimated parameters.

Figure 2.1 shows the computer-generated fit of the diurnal data from a typical normal subject. Figure 2.2 presents the mean ± SEM values at each time point for the 12 normal subjects studied. Both figures illustrate the sinusoidal shape of the diurnal curve. Using the above described procedures, the following values (mean ± SEM) were obtained for the component functions of the diurnal curve: baseline, 4.05 ± 0.33 ng/ml; amplitude, 1.46 ± 0.12 ng/ml; acrophase, 15.25 ± 0.52 hours; and period, 21.81 ± 0.83 hours. The correlation of the goodness of fit of the observed values to the cosine model was 0.92 ± 0.02 ($p <$ 0.001) (vide infra). The baseline values generated by the model were correlated with the observed 9:00 AM MHPG values. The correlation was high ($p <$ 0.0005), indicating that the diurnal acrophase was relatively consistent among normal subjects and that the 9:00 AM time point corresponds to a baseline crossing for a rhythm with a period fixed at 24

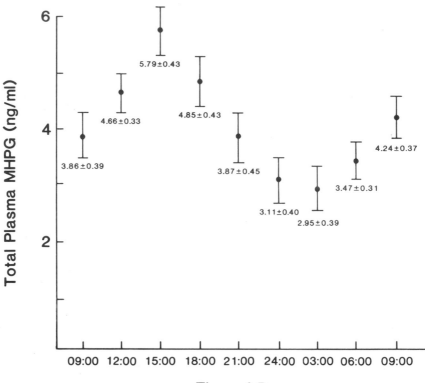

Figure 2.2. Normal circadian pattern of total plasma MHPG from 12 healthy male subjects. Values are the mean ± SEM for each time point during a 24-hour period.

hours. However, although the 9:00 AM value may be identical to the computed baseline value in normal male volunteers, 9:00 AM values may not accurately describe baseline levels in depressed patients with disturbed diurnal rhythms (DeMet et al., 1982; Wehr and Wirz-Justice, 1982).

A goal of this study was to establish criteria for a comparison of the various types of MHPG measurements that have appeared in the literature. Most investigators have employed either 9:00 AM plasma samplings or measurements obtained from 24-hour urine collections. However, both plasma and urinary levels undergo a diurnal variation, so that the two measures yield fundamentally different information. Plasma MHPG samples collected at fixed time points would be expected to reflect changes in amplitude, acrophase, or baseline of a diurnal rhythm but do not permit an estimation of these parameters unless they are collected at regular intervals throughout the 24-hour period. On the other hand, 24-hour urinary levels are a good index of the average (baseline) MHPG production but fail to provide any temporal information. Therefore, to permit a direct comparison between plasma and urinary values, it is necessary to measure a number of plasma samples over time and establish a diurnal baseline.

TEMPERATURE RHYTHM

In an effort to detect a functional relationship between body temperature and MHPG rhythms, oral temperature measurements were performed at the same time intervals as blood drawings. Subjects kept a careful log of food consumption and activity in order to record any variables that might introduce a masking effect into the measurement, for example, eating ice cream or taking a hot bath prior to the body temperature measurement. No such masking phenomena were recorded.

Individual temperature rhythms were fitted with the cosine models used for the MHPG data. Neither model produced a significant fit. The failure of these models to provide an adequate description of the results was due to a larger sampling variability than was evident in the MHPG determinations. A similar problem has been encountered in previous studies (Horne and Ostberg, 1977), where individual acrophases were estimated using a least squares fit to a polynomial function. Figure 2.3 shows the fit obtained using a cubic polynomial (SAS program). For comparison, both temperature and plasma MHPG measurements are shown for the same individual described in Figure 2.1. The mean acrophase, estimated by the polynomial fit, was 15.50 ± 2.45 hours for oral temperature and 14.53 ± 0.81 hours for plasma MHPG. No significant differences were found between the plasma MHPG and temperature acrophases determined in this way, or between the acrophases estimated for plasma MHPG using the polynomial as opposed to the cosine fits. Although no significant difference could be demonstrated between the plasma MHPG and temperature acrophases, the results do not necessarily imply a functional relationship between these two rhythms. Individual MHPG and temperature peak times failed to show any significant correlation ($r = 0.06$). Nevertheless, the results do indicate that the oral temperature and plasma MHPG rhythms are synchronized under normal conditions. The failure to find a direct corre-

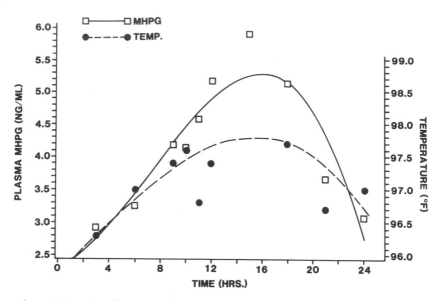

Figure 2.3. Diurnal temperature and MHPG rhythm from a typical normal male subject. The fit was obtained using a cubic polynomial.

lation between these rhythms in individual subjects suggests some degree of autonomy in their temporal control.

The temperature acrophase found in the present study occurred somewhat earlier than previously reported (Horne and Ostberg, 1977). The latter study attempted to relate oral temperature rhythms to activity cycles and distinguished between morning, evening, and intermediate subtypes. The intermediate subtype showed a bimodal temperature curve, with maxima occurring at ca. 2:30 and 8:25 PM. The present results appear to reflect the earlier of these peaks.

DEPRESSED SUBJECTS

A total of 18 patients completed at least the baseline portion of the study. Patients were diagnosed using DSM-III and Research Diagnostic Criteria (RDC) (Spitzer et al., 1975) for primary major depressive disorder, either unipolar or bipolar. On the basis of a structured interview, patients were further classified as either retarded or agitated, endogenous or nonendogenous, and unipolar patients as either recurrent or single ep-

Table 2.1.

Subjects	Healthy Controls	Depressed Patients	
		Pretreatment	Posttreatment
N	12	18	10
Age (± SEM)	31.4 ± 1.5	47.9 ± 2.9	45.6 ± 3.6
HAM-D	<5	25.8 ± 2.1	9.5 ± 2.1
Subtypes (N)			
Endogenous		11	6
Retarded		11	6
Unipolar		14	7
Recurrent		6	6
Responders			5
Nonresponders			5

isode (Table 2.1). Patients were free of any psychoactive medication for at least 3 weeks prior to the study. No attempt was made to impose dietary or normal activity restrictions (no physical exercise was permitted) because no consistent effect of either on plasma MHPG levels had been found in preliminary studies. The presence of schizophrenia, alcohol, or substance use served as exclusion criterion. All subjects were required to refrain from the use of alcoholic beverages for at least 3 days prior to the experiment (Latenkov, 1984). Patients underwent a thorough physical examination and routine laboratory tests, including thyroid function tests. The patients ranged in age from 29 to 80 years, with a mean ± SEM of 47.9 ± 12.3 years.

Blood samples were collected via an indwelling antecubital catheter as described above for normal subjects. The samples were collected at 3-hour intervals around the clock and efforts were made to avoid disturbing the sleeping patterns of the subjects as much as possible. All subjects slept in an environment that was familiar to them. Following the completion of the first diurnal MHPG collection, patients were treated with a daily dose of 150 mg of DMI for a total of 4 weeks. Changes in clinical status were determined weekly by means of the Hamilton Rating Scale for Depression (HAM-D). The diurnal rhythm of MHPG levels in plasma was reexamined following the 4 weeks of treatment. Total (free plus conjugated) MHPG samples were measured by electron-capture gas chromatography (Halaris et al., 1977). The plasma MHPG values for each subject were best fit to a cosine function using a nonlinear least squares regression procedure (SAS Institute; procedure

NLIN). The NLIN procedure was set to evaluate the residual sum of squares and to arrive at the best set of values for baseline (mean of all the raw MHPG values), amplitude, acrophase, and period length. The residuals of each of these parameters were then iteratively regressed on the partial derivatives of the cosine model by the Gauss–Newton method. Pearson product moment correlation coefficients between the observed MHPG values and those values from the predicted model were used as an indication of how well the observed MHPG values fit the model. A lower correlation indicated larger residuals and, therefore, failure to fit into a distinct diurnal rhythm. This correlation will be referred to as the *goodness-of-fit* measure. The resulting estimates of baseline, amplitude, peaktime, and period were subjected to analysis of variance (ANOVA). Patients who had at least a 50% decrease in HAM-D scores or whose score dropped below 10 following treatment were classified as treatment responders. Pre- and post-HAM-D scores and MHPG values were compared using a repeated measures ANOVA.

Figure 2.4 demonstrates the composite diurnal curves for observed and predicted MHPG values in normal volunteers and in depressed patients before and after DMI treatment. The goodness of fit for the whole group of depressed patients prior to treatment (0.82 ± 0.03) was significantly lower than for volunteers (0.92 ± 0.02) [$t(28) = 2.54, p = 0.02$] (Figure 2.5). An examination of subtypes of depression further indicated that the retarded depressives demonstrated a significantly lower goodness of fit to the cosine model (0.78 ± 0.04) than either the nonretarded depressives (0.88 ± 0.03) or the volunteers [$F(2,27) = 5.15, p = 0.01$] (Figure 2.6). Depressed patients demonstrated a significantly earlier acrophase (13.04 ± 0.64 hours) compared to normals (15.25 ± 0.52 hours) [$t(28) = 2.46, p = 0.02$]. This was especially true for the endogenous depressives, whose acrophase occurred approximately 3 hours earlier (12.53 ± 1.02 hours) than it did in healthy volunteers. The depressed subjects did not differ from normals with respect to baseline MHPG, amplitude, or period length. However, of the 14 patients with unipolar depression, the 6 who had recurrent depressions had a significantly longer period (25.21 ± 1.31) than did the patients experiencing their first depressive episode (20.36 ± 1.55), whereas normal subjects did not differ significantly from either group (21.81 ± 0.83) [$F(2,23) = 3.46, p = 0.05$].

Complete diurnal MHPG data were available on only 10 of the 14 patients who completed the treatment phase of the protocol. Following treatment, the HAM-D scores of this group of 10 patients decreased significantly, from 21.0 ± 1.73 to 9.5 ± 2.12 [paired-$t(9) = 3.69, p = 0.005$]. The depressed group did not differ from the normals on any

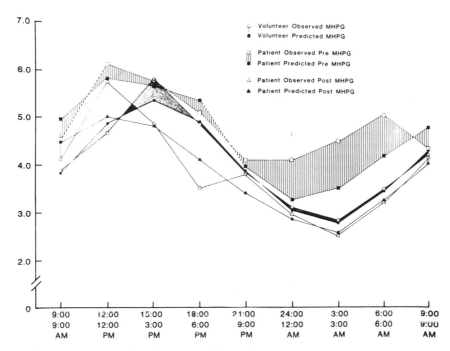

Figure 2.4. Observed and predicted diurnal MHPG curves in normal male subjects ($N = 12$) and depressed patients before treatment ($N = 18$) and following treatment with desipramine ($N = 10$).

MHPG parameter when the diurnal measurements were repeated at the end of the acute treatment phase. Differences were noted, however, among subtypes of depressed patients following treatment. The mean pretreatment goodness of fit value for the six retarded depressives with complete MHPG data was 0.74 ± 0.04 and increased significantly to 0.91 ± 0.03 following DMI treatment [paired-$t(5) = 4.53, p = 0.006$], becoming comparable to the volunteers. The nonretarded depressives showed a nonsignificant decrease, from 0.88 to 0.81 (Figure 2.7). Following treatment with DMI, the six endogenous depressives with post-treatment data showed a suggestive shift in peaktime, 11.73 ± 1.38 hours to 14.70 ± 1.29 hours [paired-$t(5) = 2.44, p = 0.059$] that was also comparable to that of the normal subjects. No such shift was observed among the nonendogenous depressives.

To determine patterns of association among the estimated parameters in depressed and control subjects, correlations were calculated between the 9:00 AM value of MHPG and the other parameters. The results

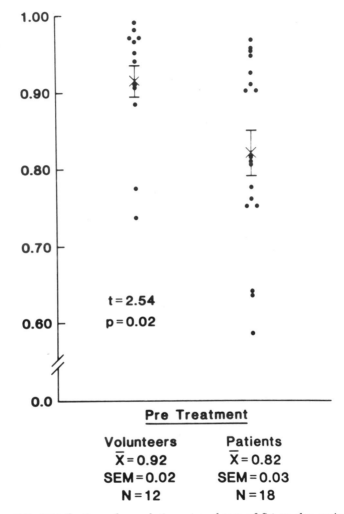

Figure 2.5. Distribution of correlations (goodness of fit) to the cosine model in the group of healthy subjects as compared to the whole group of depressed patients before treatment with desipramine. The difference is statistically significant ($p = 0.02$).

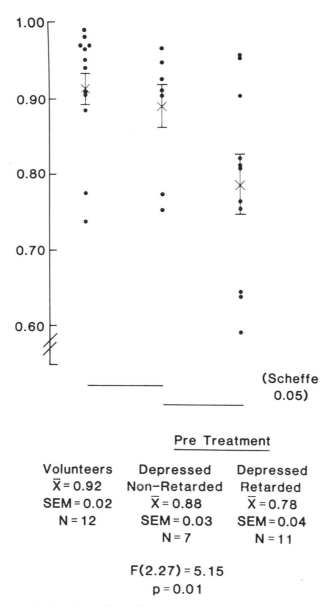

Figure 2.6. Distributions of correlations (goodness of fit) to the cosine model in the group of healthy subjects as compared to the subgroups of retarded and nonretarded depressed patients. The goodness of fit is significantly reduced in the retarded depressives compared to the nonretarded group $(p = 0.01)$.

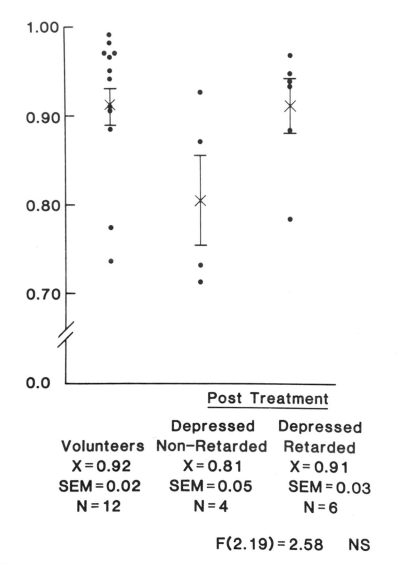

Figure 2.7. Distributions of correlations (goodness of fit) to the cosine model in the group of healthy subjects as compared to the subgroups of retarded and nonretarded depressed patients posttreatment. There was no significant difference among these three groups.

Table 2.2. Intercorrelations Among MHPG Parameters and 9:00 AM MHPG

Subjects	N	r	p
Normal			
MHPG 9:00 AM vs. baseline MHPG	12	0.91	0.001
Depressed			
MHPG 9:00 AM vs. baseline MHPG	18	0.82	0.004
Acrophase vs. period	18	0.78	0.0001
Amplitude vs. baseline MHPG	18	0.70	0.001

are reported in Table 2.2. MHPG drawn at 9:00 AM correlated highly with baseline MHPG in both the depressed and control groups. In the depressed patients, period correlated significantly with peak time, and amplitude appeared to correlate with baseline. In contrast, age of the subjects did not correlate with any MHPG variable in either patients or volunteers.

ULTRADIAN MHPG RHYTHM IN DEPRESSION

As described above, previous studies from our laboratory and others have shown that a variety of circadian rhythms, including that of MHPG, are phase advanced in certain depressed patients. We have described a 2–3 hour MHPG phase advance in depression compared to a normal male control group ($p < 0.05$) and noted that the MHPG rhythm tends to normalize after successful treatment with the tricyclic antidepressant, DMI (DeMet et al., 1982). We noted, however, that although the normal circadian MHPG rhythm was well fitted by a simple COSINOR model, rhythms obtained from depressed patients pretreatment were not. In an effort to understand this observation, we constructed a two-cosine model and attempted to fit the patient rhythms as follows: MHPG = baseline + ampl #1 × COS (Phase #1 + time/24 hours) + ampl #2 × COS (Phase #2 + time/12 hours) (DeMet and Halaris, unpublished data). Using this two-cosine model with a 12- and 24-hour component, patient rhythms were successfully fitted. A comparison of ten unipolar depressed patients before and after 4 weeks of treatment with DMI showed that the amplitude of the 24-hour component was not altered by treatment and that it was indistinguishable from a normal MHPG rhythm. In contrast, the 12-hour component was significantly reduced

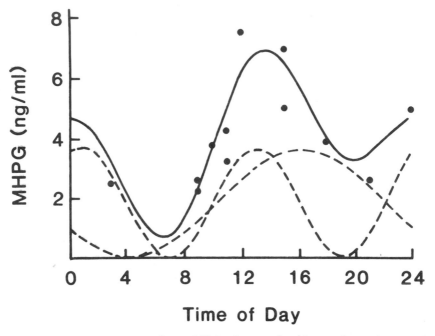

Figure 2.8. Apparent acrophase shift in depressed subjects prior to treatment (●———●). This apparent phase advance is probably due to the presence of an ultradian rhythm with an approximate 12-hour period.

($p < 0.025$) after treatment. This effect was evident in seven of the ten patients. Addition of the two components produced an apparent phase advance (Figure 2.8). Figure 2.9 illustrates the significant reduction in the amplitude of the 12-hour MHPG rhythm posttreatment with DMI in seven of the ten unipolar depressives. It appears therefore that an ultradian MHPG rhythm may be present during the acute stage of primary major depression, and its amplitude diminishes significantly when the patient is treated with a tricyclic antidepressant. The presence of such an ultradian rhythm during the acute phase of unipolar depression is currently being investigated. Its potential utility as a trait marker is being evaluated in ongoing studies. It is unclear at present whether such an ultradian rhythm is detectable in all subtypes of depressive illness.

DISCUSSION

The above results clearly demonstrate that the metabolism of NE, as reflected by levels of total plasma MHPG, undergoes diurnal variation

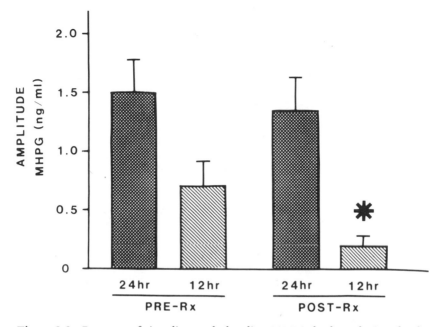

Figure 2.9. Presence of circadian and ultradian MHPG rhythms during the depressed mood state (prior to treatment). Posttreatment there is a statistically significant reduction in the amplitude of the ultradian rhythm only.

in normal male subjects and in depressed patients. This finding corroborates findings from previous investigations on the circadian rhythm of NE (Ziegler et al., 1976; Linsell et al., 1985; Fibiger et al., 1984; Latenkov, 1985; Mullen et al., 1981; Nishihara et al., 1985), and of catecholamine metabolites in healthy volunteers (Wehr et al., 1980; Giedke et al., 1982; Vorbrodt et al., 1985) and in depressed patients (Wehr et al., 1980; Pflug et al., 1982). Furthermore, the present results complement the findings in studies by Kafka (1985) demonstrating circadian rhythms in the densities of α_1- and β-adrenergic receptors and NE-stimulated cyclic adenosine monophosphate (cAMP) in rats, although these studies had remained unconfirmed for the α_2-adrenergic receptors (Jones et al., 1983) until recently. Kafka and coworkers have now confirmed the presence of diurnal rhythmicity in α_2-receptors in discrete regions of the rat brain (Kafka et al., 1986a; chapter 15 of this volume). A circadian MHPG rhythm in rat hippocampus and possibly in occipital cortex has also been described by Kafka and coworkers (1986b). Our finding of a phase advance in the MHPG rhythm in our depressed patient population is consistent with results from previous investigations (Wehr et al., 1980; Pflug et al., 1982; Giedke et al., 1982). In the present study, this abnormality was detected convincingly in the group of endogenous patients, and treatment with DMI largely corrected the phase shift. In contrast, the nonendogenous subgroup did not demonstrate such a phase abnormality.

The mean age of the healthy volunteers in this study was younger than that of the patients. However, age did not correlate consistently with any of the circadian MHPG variables examined. Other investigators have demonstrated that NE rhythms could be accounted for by sleep (Linsell et al., 1985; Nishihara et al., 1985), level of perceived stress (Fibiger et al., 1983; Brodan et al., 1982; Mullen et al., 1981), or alcohol intake (Latenkov 1985). Food does not appear to influence the rhythm of epinephrine or NE (Linsell et al., 1985; Mullen et al., 1981; Brodan et al., 1982). Effects of posture upon rhythms of NE are still controversial, with some investigators finding an effect of posture (Linsell et al., 1985; Fibiger et al., 1984), whereas others still detect the rhythm in volunteers who are confined to bed (Nishihara, 1985). Previous unpublished observations from our laboratory did not point to the need to control for food intake or feeding schedules. Many subjects were awakened at the time of nocturnal blood drawing, and this may have been stressful. Additionally, the effects of posture were not controlled for in this study. It is possible that these factors may have influenced the results, but this is rather unlikely, since volunteers and patients were studied and restudied under comparable and highly consistent conditions. Nevertheless, future investigations should more carefully control for temperature rhythms, posture, level of stress, and sleep parameters in order to further elucidate the concomitants of aberrant circadian MHPG rhythms.

The precise origin of peripherally measured MHPG remains controversial. In man, Maas et al. (1979) estimated that approximately 60% of the total body production of MHPG originates in the brain. However, a portion of free MHPG is converted to vanillylmandelic acid (VMA) in the periphery. Since the exact percentage of MHPG conversion into VMA is controversial (Blombery et al., 1980; Mårdh et al., 1981), it is uncertain exactly how much of the peripherally measured MHPG in blood and urine is of brain origin. This study does not make any claims that the observed circadian MHPG rhythm is central in origin. Certainly, the MHPG flux in the body has a circadian variation in both urine and plasma (DeMet et al., 1985). It is likely that such flux changes would also be seen in the CNS, at least for free MHPG. However, whether the central compartment drives or only participates in the circadian variations demonstrated is a question that requires more extensive investigation.

Depressed patients as a group exhibited a lesser degree of synchronization to the circadian cosine model than did volunteers. This was especially true in retarded depressives. Following treatment there was a partial correction of this desynchrony, which occurred significantly in retarded depressives. Nonretarded depressives did not demonstrate a correction in this parameter. Giedke and coworkers (1982) obtained similar results in a group of bipolar and unipolar depressives measuring urinary MHPG. Additionally, Giedke and coworkers (1982) conducted their measurements on a mixed sample of medicated and drug-free patients. This may have distorted their results, because the effects of the drugs were shown to lengthen the MHPG period. Pflug and colleagues (1982) demonstrated that the MHPG rhythm was dissociated from the temperature rhythm during the depression stage of a bipolar patient. During her well state the rhythms were resynchronized. It is possible that the level of desynchrony demonstrated in the present patient population may represent a shifting of one internal zeitgeber from another, or alternatively, an inability of the internal zeitgeber to adjust to external cues such as dawn or dusk (Lewy et al., 1984). Demonstration of ultradian periodicity in these MHPG rhythms would be supporting evidence for either of the above hypotheses (Wehr and Wirz-Justice, 1982).

The detection of an ultradian MHPG rhythm in at least a subpopulation of the depressed patients is an intriguing finding. The ultradian rhythm appears to be partially or fully responsible for the apparent phase advance and the poor fit of the MHPG circadian rhythm by the COSINOR model in the group of depressed patients. Neither the cause nor the mechanism by which such a rhythm emerges is understood. Even less well understood is the possible relevance to the pathophysiology of depressive illness. The fact that the amplitude of the ultradian MHPG rhythm diminishes with successful antidepressant drug treatment may be unrelated to the reversal of depressive symptomatology. However, an important clue may be found in the finding of an ultradian cortisol rhythm in some endogenous depressed patients described by Halbreich (see Chapter 3 of this volume). There are some striking similarities between the abnormalities noted in both plasma MHPG and plasma cortisol circadian rhythms in endogenous depressed patients. In both of these studies, the mean fitness of the cosinor curve was low, and a significant number of patients failed to show a circadian fluctuation in either rhythm compared to normal subjects. Halbreich hypothesized that the ultradian abnormality in the cortisol rhythm could be either in the frequency domain or in the magnitude of the secretory episode of cortisol. His spectral analysis revealed that the depressed patients displaying an ultradian cortisol rhythm had a somewhat lower frequency of secretory episodes but a higher variance density, which reflects the magnitude of the cortisol secretory episode. Similar considerations may apply to the ultradian MHPG rhythm observed in the untreated depressed patients of our study. It is tempting to speculate that the ultradian MHPG and cortisol rhythms may be somehow interconnected. The involvement of noradrenergic transmission in the regulation of the hypothalamic-pituitary-adrenal axis is well established. It appears therefore that a concomitant study of the diurnal MHPG and cortisol rhythms in the plasma of subtypes of depressed patients before and after recovery may elucidate the possible significance and underlying mechanism of ultradian rhythmicity in depression.

Like other investigators (Wehr and Wirz-Justice, 1982; Kripke et al., 1978; Pflug et al., 1982) we did find that subsequent to antidepressant drug treatment, patients demonstrated a longer period length than that of volunteers. This was especially true in patients who responded to treatment and in the endogenous subgroup. It is possible that the ameliorative effect of the tricyclic antidepressant may be related to the increasing circadian period length caused by these drugs. As period length increases, phase is delayed. Although we could not demonstrate on repeated-measures ANOVA a significant change in our patients with respect to period length, we were able to show that in the depressives, period and acrophase were highly correlated, whereas in the normal volunteers they were not. It is hypothesized that period and phase are distinctly related, and that this relationship does not appear in volunteers because of the degree of synchronization of their zeitgebers.

SUMMARY

The metabolism of NE, as reflected by plasma levels of its major metabolite, MHPG, undergoes diurnal changes in populations of normal and depressed subjects. The normal circadian pattern of MHPG was characterized in 12 healthy male volunteers. The values were fit into a cosine model by the Gauss–Newton method. This nonlinear regression method permits the estimation of diurnal rhythm components: baseline, phase, amplitude, and period. For comparison, the diurnal temperature rhythm was estimated in the normal subjects. No direct correlation was found between the temperature and MHPG rhythms in normal male subjects, suggesting some degree of autonomy in the temporal control of these two rhythms. However, under normal conditions it appears that oral temperature and plasma MHPG rhythms may be synchronized.

The study further compared the diurnal plasma MHPG rhythm in primary major depressives ($n = 18$) and in the healthy volunteers ($n = 12$). Biochemical and psychologic measures were taken both at baseline and following treatment. Patients received DMI 150 mg daily for 4 weeks. Normal subjects had a significantly higher goodness of fit to the cosine model than patients, and patients demonstrated an earlier occurring acrophase. Endogenous depressives demonstrated the highest degree of phase advance. Retarded depressives demonstrated the poorest goodness of fit to the model. Patients did not differ from normals on either baseline MHPG, amplitude, or period length. Following treatment, the HAM-D scores of the patient group decreased significantly. Endogenous depressives demonstrated a significant phase normalization of approximately 3 hours of posttreatment, whereas retarded depressives showed a marked improvement in goodness of fit. Following treatment, the depressed group as a whole did not differ from the normals on any MHPG parameter. This study confirms and extends previous reports of an apparent phase advance in circadian noradrenergic rhythms in depressed patients. However, this phase advance could be accounted for by the appearance of an ultradian MHPG rhythm which disappears posttreatment.

The research summarized in this chapter is based on collaborative efforts with Edward M. DeMet, Ph.D., Harry E. Gwirtsman, M.D., John E. Piletz, Ph.D. and Abraham Wolf, Ph.D. Some of the results have been previously presented in the form of papers or abstracts.

REFERENCES

Axelrod J, Kopin IJ, Mann JD (1959): 3-Methoxy-4-hydroxyphenylglycol sulfate, a new metabolite of epinephrine and norepinephrine. Biochim Biophys Acta 36:576–577.

Banerjee SP, Kung LS, Riggi SJ, et al (1977): Development of β-adrenergic receptor subsensitivity by antidepressants. Nature 268:455–456.

Beckmann H, Goodwin FK (1975): Antidepressant response to tricyclics and urinary MHPG in unipolar patients. Arch Gen Psychiatry 32:17–21.

Beckmann H, Goodwin FK (1980): Urinary MHPG in subgroups of depressed patients and normal controls. Neuropsychobiology 6:91–100.

Blombery PA, Kopin IJ, Gordon EK, et al (1980): Conversion of MHPG to vanillylmandelic acid. Implications for the importance of urinary MHPG. Arch Gen Psychiatry 37:1095–1098.

Brodan V, Kuhn E, Veselkova A, Kaucka J (1982): The effect of stress on circadian rhythms. Czech Med 5(1):1–8.

Bunney WE Jr, Davis JM (1965): Norepinephrine in depressive reactions: A review. Arch Gen Psychiatry 13:483–494.

Charney DS, Menkes DB, Heninger GR (1981a): Receptor sensitivity and the mechanism of action of antidepressant treatment. Arch Gen Psychiatry 38:1160–1180.

Charney DS, Heninger GR, Sternberg DE, et al (1981b): Presynaptic adrenergic receptor sensitivity in depression. Arch Gen Psychiatry 38:1334–1340.

Cymerman A, Francesconi RF (1975): Alteration of circadian rhythmicities of urinary 3-methoxy-4-hydroxyphenylglycol (MHGP) and vanillylmandelic acid (VMA) in man during cold exposure. Life Sci 16:225–236.

DeLeon-Jones F, Maas JW, Dekirmenjian H, Sanchez J (1975): Diagnostic subgroups of affective disorders and their urinary excretion of catecholamine metabolites. Am J Psychiatry 132:1141–1148.

DeMet EM, Halaris AE (1979): Origin and distribution of 3-methoxy-4-hydroxyphenylglycol in body fluids. Biochem Pharmacol 28:3043–3050.

DeMet EM, Halaris AE, Gwirtsman HE, et al (1982): Effects of desipramine on diurnal rhythms of plasma 3-methoxy-4-hydroxyphenylglycol (MHPG) in depressed patients. Psychopharmacology Bull 18:221–223.

DeMet EM, Halaris AE, Gwirtsman HE, Reno RM (1985): Diurnal rhythm of 3-methoxy-4-hydroxyphenylglycol (MHPG): Relationship between plasma and urinary levels. Life Sciences 37:1731–1741.

Fawcett JA, Maas JW, Dekirmenjian H (1972): Depression and MHPG excretion: Response to dextroamphetamine and tricyclic antidepressants. Arch Gen Psychiatry 26:246–251.

Fibiger W, Singer G, Miller AJ, et al (1984): Cortisol and catecholamine changes as functions of time-of-day and self-reported mood. Neurosci Biobehav Rev 8:523–530.

Giedke H, Gaertner HJ, Mahal A (1982): Diurnal variation of urinary MHPG in unipolar and bipolar depressives. Acta Psychiatr Scand 66:243–253.

Gordon EK, Oliver J (1971): 3-Methoxy-4-hydroxyphenylethylene glycol in human cerebrospinal fluid. Clin Chim Acta 35:145–150.

Halaris AE, DeMet EM (1979): Studies of norepinephrine metabolism in manic and depressive states. In Usdin E, Kopin IJ, Barchas J (eds): Catecholamines: Basic and Clinical Frontiers. New York, Pergamon, pp 1866–1868.

Halaris AE, DeMet EM (1980): Open trial evaluation of a pyrrolidine derivative (AHR-1118) on norepinephrine metabolism. Prog Neuropsychopharmacol 4:43–49.

Halaris AE, DeMet EM, Halari ME (1977): Determination of plasma 3-

methoxy-4-hydroxyphenylglycol by pulsed electron capture gas chromatography. Clin Chim Acta 78:285–294.

Hollister LE, Davis KL, Overall JE, et al (1978): Excretion of MHPG in normal subjects. Arch Gen Psychiatry 35:1410–1415.

Horne JA, Ostberg O (1977): Individual differences in human circadian rhythms. Biol Psychiatry 5:179–190.

Jones SB, Bylund DB, Reiser CA, et al (1983): Alpha$_2$ adrenergic receptor binding in human platelets: Alterations during the menstrual cycle. Clin Pharmacol Ther 34:90–96.

Kafka MS (1985): The effect of antidepressants on circadian rhythms in brain neurotransmitter receptors. Acta Pharmacol Toxicol (Copenh) 56(Suppl 1):162–164.

Kafka MS, Benedito MA, Blendy JA, Tokola NS (1986a): Circadian rhythms in neurotransmitter receptors in discrete rat brain regions. Chronobiol Int 3:91–100.

Kafka MS, Benedito MA, Roth RH, et al (1986b): Circadian rhythms in catecholamine metabolites and cyclic nucleotide production. Chronobiol Int 3:101–115.

Kripke DF, Mullaney DJ, Atkinson M, Wolf S (1978): Circadian rhythm disorder in manic-depressives. Biol Psychiatry 13:335–351.

Kripke DF, Mullaney DJ, Atkinson ML, et al (1979): Circadian rhythm phases in affective illnesses. Chronobiology 6:365–375.

Latenkov VP (1985): Circadian rhythms of adrenaline and noradrenaline excretion in man in normal conditions and after alcohol intake. Biull Eksp Biol Med 99:344–346.

Lewy AJ, Sack RL, Singer CM (1984): Assessment and treatment of chronobiologic disorders using plasma melatonin levels and bright light exposure: The clock-gate model and the phase-response curve. Psychopharm Bull 20:561–565.

Lingjaerde O (1983): The biochemistry of depression. Acta Psychiatr Scand 302:36–51.

Linsell CR, Lightman SL, Mullen PE, et al (1985): Circadian rhythms of epinephrine and norepinephrine in man. Clin Endocrinol Metab 60:1210–1215.

Maas JW, Landis DH (1968): In vivo studies of metabolism of norepinephrine in central nervous system. J Pharmacol Exp Ther 163:147–162.

Maas JW, Landis DH (1971): The metabolism of circulating norepinephrine by human subjects. J Pharmacol Exp Ther 177:600–612.

Maas JW, Fawcett JA, Dekirmenjian H (1972): Catecholamine metabolism, depressive illness and drug response. Arch Gen Psychiatry 26:252–262.

Maas JW, Hattox SE, Greene NM, Landis DH (1979): 3-Methoxy-4-hydroxyphenethyleneglycol production by human brain in vivo. Science 205:1025–1027.

Maas JW, Kocsis JH, Bowden CL, et al (1982): Pretreatment neurotransmitter metabolites and response to imipramine or amitriptyline treatment. Psychol Med 12:37–43.

Mårdh G, Sjöqvist B, Änggård E (1981): Norepinephrine metabolism in man using deuterium labelling: The conversion of 4-hydroxy-3-methoxyphenylglycol to 4-hydroxy-3-methoxymandelic acid. J Neurochem 36:1181–1185.

Markianos E, Beckmann H (1976): Diurnal changes in dopamine-β-hydroxylase, homovanillic acid and 3-methoxy-4-hydroxyphenylglycol in serum in man. J Neural Transm 39:79–93.

Mullen PE, Lightman S, Linsell C, et al (1981): Rhythms of plasma noradrenaline in man. Psychoneuroendocrinology 6:213–222.

Muscettola G, Potter WZ, Pickar D, Goodwin FK (1984): Urinary 3-methoxy-4-hydroxyphenylglycol and major affective disorders. Arch Gen Psychiatry 41:337–342.

Nishihara K, Mori K, Endo S, et al (1985): Relationship between sleep efficiency and urinary excretion of catecholamines in bed-rested humans. Sleep 8:110–117.

Ostrow D, Halaris A, Dysken M, et al (1984): State dependence of noradrenergic activity in a rapidly cycling bipolar patient. J Clin Psychiatry 45:306–309.

Papoušek M (1975): Chronobiological aspects of cyclothymia. Fortsch Neurol Psychiatr 43:381–440.

Pflug B, Johnsson A, Ekse AT (1981): Manic-depressive states and daily temperature: Some circadian studies. Acta Psychiatr Scand 63:277–289.

Pflug B, Engelmann W, Gaertner JH (1982): Circadian course of body temperature and the excretion of MHPG and VMA in a patient with bipolar depression. J Neural Transm 53:213–215.

Rosenbaum AH, Maruta T, Schatzberg AF, et al (1980): Urine free cortisol and 3-methoxy-4-hydroxyphenylglycol in depressive disorders. In New Research Abstracts of the APA, Annual Meeting, NR13, May 1980.

Rosenbaum AH, Schatzberg AF, Maruta J, et al (1980): MHPG as a predictor of antidepressant response to imipramine and maprotiline. Arch Gen Psychiatry 137:1090–1092.

Schildkraut JJ (1965): The catecholamine hypothesis of affective disorders: A review of supporting evidence. Am J Psychiatry 122:509–522.

Schildkraut JJ (1978): Current status of the catecholamine hypothesis of affective disorders. In Lipton MA, DiMascio A, Killam KF (eds): Psychopharmacology: A Generation of Progress. New York, Raven, pp 1223–1234.

Schildkraut JJ, Kety SS (1967): Biogenic amines and emotion. Science 156:21–30.

Siever LJ, Davis KL (1985): Overview: Toward a dysregulation hypothesis of depression. Am J Psychiatry 142:1017–1031.

Spitzer RL, Endicott J, Robins E (1975): Research Diagnostic Criteria. New York, New York State Department of Mental Hygiene, New York State Psychiatric Institute, Biometrics Research.

Sulser F, Vetulani J, Mobley PL (1978): Mode of action of antidepressant drugs. Biochem Pharmacol 27:257–261.

Vorbrodt B, Krause E, Weinart O (1985): Circadian rhythm of 3-methoxy-

4-hydroxymandelic acid and 3-methoxy-4-hydroxyphenylacetic acid in urine. Pharmazie 40:264–266.

Wehr TA (1984): Biological rhythms and manic-depressive illness. In Post RM, Ballenger JC: Neurobiology of Mood Disorders, Baltimore, Williams and Wilkins, pp 190–206.

Wehr TA, Goodwin FK (1981): Biological rhythms and psychiatry. In Arieti S, Brodie HKH (eds): American Handbook of Psychiatry, 2nd ed. New York, Basic Books, vol 7, pp 46–74.

Wehr TA, Wirz-Justice A (1982): Circadian rhythm mechanisms in affective illness and in antidepressant drug action. Pharmakopsychiatry 15:31–39.

Wehr TA, Wirz-Justice A, Goodwin FK, et al (1979): Phase-advance of the sleep–wake cycle as an antidepressant. Science 206:710–713.

Wehr TA, Muscettola G, Goodwin FK (1980): Urinary 3-methoxy-4-hydroxyphenylglycol circadian rhythm. Arch Gen Psychiatry 37:257–263.

Ziegler MG, Lake CR, Wood JH, Ebert MH (1976): Circadian rhythm in cerebrospinal fluid noradrenaline of man and monkey. Nature 264:656–657.

3

The Circadian Rhythm of Cortisol and MHPG in Depressives and Normals

Uriel Halbreich

Patients with Major Depressive Disorder (MDD) and especially those with endogenous subtype (ED) very often report a circadian fluctuation in their mood. Many times they are more depressed in the morning, and in the evening they feel somewhat better. This clinical phenomenon raises the possibility that a circadian rhythm of biological mechanisms that might be involved in the pathophysiology of MDD-ED may also be disturbed. This notion is further strengthened by the frequency of sleep disturbances in depression—especially the early awakening—which can also be a manifestation of an abnormal rhythm. Hence it is understood that a search for a rhythm abnormality closely followed the discovery of many compounds that were putatively associated with depression. Abnormality of norepinephrine (NE) was suggested to be involved in the pathophysiology of depressions since the mid-1960s. Since this neurotransmitter is involved in the regulation of cortisol secretion and since adequate methods for direct assessment of NE activity in the central nervous system were unavailable, there has been a substantial interest in the involvement of cortisol in depression, especially

This chapter is based on several papers that were written in collaboration with Gregory M. Asnis, M.D., Susanna Goldstein, M.D., Richard Shindledecker, M.A., Nansie Sharpless, Ph.D., Jean Endicott, Ph.D., R. Swami Nathan, M.D., Barnett Zumoff, M.D., Byung-Jo Kang, M.D., Jacques Vital-Herne, M.D., Karl Zander, M.D., Jacques Eisenberg, M.D., and Ching-Ming Yeh, Ph.D.

when it has been found that cortisol secretion normally follows a circadian pattern (Hellman et al., 1970; Krieger et al., 1971; Weitzman et al., 1971). Therefore, in this chapter we will concentrate on studies of the normal and abnormal circadian rhythm of plasma cortisol and then on the circadian rhythm of MHPG—a main metabolite of NE.

THE NORMAL 24-HOUR RHYTHM OF CORTISOL AND ITS DISTRACTION

It is well documented that, normally, plasma levels of cortisol fluctuate widely with a cycle that is approximately 24 hours (Hellman et al., 1970; Krieger et al., 1971; Weitzman et al., 1971). The first secretory episode of cortisol occurs shortly after sleep onset, and then in a series of consecutive episodes plasma levels increase, reaching a peak in the late morning hours. Hormonal levels decrease in the afternoon and reach a nadir around sleep onset. This cycle is quite stable, and even with a change in the activity–rest cycle or an abrupt jet lag it takes 2–10 days for that cycle to adapt itself to the new situation.

The rhythm of cortisol can be disrupted in several ways. As is demonstrated later, disruption in one function does not necessarily imply that also other functions are abnormal, nor is it true that increase in basal levels of the mean 24-hour levels of cortisol is necessarily associated with an abnormal rhythm. Figure 3.1 (Halbreich et al., 1982), which shows the normal 24-hour rhythm of cortisol in 88 normal subjects (the shaded area), also shows that in patients with anorexia nervosa ($n = 29$) or carcinoma of the prostate ($n = 61$) the circadian rhythm of cortisol is almost intact. By contrast, in patients with Cushing's syndrome ($n = 13$) not only are the basal levels of cortisol markedly increased, but the 24-hour curve is flat, the fluctuations between high and low levels are significantly diminished, and there is almost no quiescent period during the late evening—when the normal value can reach almost a zero.

Abnormalities in the cortisol rhythm (or in any 24-hour rhythm) can be detected in various ways. The most accepted way is by fitting an optimal cosinor curve that "smooths" the peaks and troughs (Halberg, 1968; Nelson et al., 1981) and single possibly fortuitous extreme values. The fitness of the curve, which is basically the association between the actual observed values and the optimal values on the cosinor curve, can be disturbed if the fluctuations are not "ideal" and include a large number of intense secretory episodes. The amplitude, which is the dis-

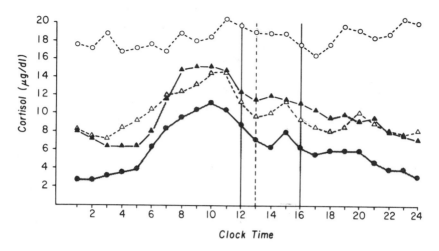

Figure 3.1. Mean hourly plasma cortisol concentrations in normal subjects and patients with increased levels of cortisol. The shaded area represents 1 SD from the mean plasma cortisol concentrations of the normal controls. ●———●, normal controls ($n = 88$); O———O, Cushing's syndrome ($n = 13$); ▲———▲, anorexia nervosa ($n = 29$); △———△, cancer of the prostate ($n = 61$). Reproduced, with permission, from Halbreich et al (1982): J Clin Endocrinol Metab 54:1262–1264.

tance between the "ideal" mean of the curve (the mesor) and the highest or lowest values of the cosinor curve, can be smaller—indicating a curve that is "flat" or larger than normal. The timing of the peak (the acrophase) can be advanced or delayed, as can be the timing of the nadir. In addition, one can measure the significance of the circadian rhythmicity (tA), which is a measure of the difference of the amplitude of the cosinor curve from a flat or a random curve during the 24-hour period.

Almost all of the above parameters were claimed to be abnormal in patients with endogenous depression.

THE 24-HOUR RHYTHM OF CORTISOL IN ENDOGENOUS DEPRESSION

The hypothalamic–pituitary–adrenal (HPA) axis has probably been the most extensively studied hormonal system in depression. Abnormalities of various components of that system, especially those that are related

to cortisol or its suppression by dexamethasone, have been widely studied (Carroll et al., 1976a, 1976b, 1981; Gibbons and McHugh, 1962;
Halbreich et al., 1985; Sachar et al., 1973; Schlesser et al., 1980; Stokes
et al., 1984). Within this context, it has been suggested that patients
with Major Depressive Disorder (MDD) Endogenous subtype (ED) not
only have increased basal levels of cortisol but also have a disturbed
circadian rhythm, primarily a "flattened curve" of cortisol secretion
(Fullerton et al., 1968; Green, 1967; Halberg et al., 1968; Lohrenz et
al., 1969; McClure, 1966; Sachar et al., 1973; Yamashita et al., 1969).
Some analyses of the pattern of the 24-hour fluctuations brought into
focus the timing of peak secretion (the acrophase), suggesting a shift of
its timing to an earlier hour—phase advance in ED patients (Wehr et
al., 1983). This suggestion, however, was based on studies that, meth-
odologically, were far from perfect. In some of them blood was drawn
only every 4 hours or even only twice a day. Most, including the most
widely cited study (Sachar et al., 1973), had a small sample size or were
a report on a single case. None of the earlier studies controlled for the
age variable, and in those studies that included normal controls, the ED
patients were usually older than the normals to whom they were compared (Carroll et al., 1976a, 1976b, 1981; Doerr et al., 1979; Fullerton,
1968; Gelenberg et al., 1978; Green, 1967; Halberg, 1968; Halberg et
al., 1968; Halbreich et al., 1985; Lohrenz et al., 1969; McClure, 1966;
Sachar et al., 1973; Schesser et al., 1980; Stokes et al., 1984; Wehr et
al., 1983; Yamaguchi et al., 1978; Yamashita et al., 1969).

In addition to the "flattened curve" and the phase advance, it has
also been suggested (Sachar et al., 1973) that ED patients have a large
number of secretory episodes of cortisol and that each episode is of
higher magnitude compared to normals (Hellman et al., 1970; Weitzman et al., 1971).

In our first round of 24-hour studies of depression, we compared
32 ED patients to 72 normal controls (Halbreich et al., 1985). It was
apparent that the difference between ED patients and normals was more
subtle than had been claimed previously.

The pattern of the 24-hour curve (Figure 3.2) did not show a
"flattened curve," nor was the time of the highest levels of cortisol
different from that of normals.

The assumption that the circadian rhythm of cortisol would be
disturbed in patients with higher levels of mean 24-hour plasma levels
of cortisol ($\bar{X}$24h PC) did not seem confirmed either.

Phase-angle analysis, which is summarized in Table 3.1, further
revealed that ED patients did not differ from normals in their mean
timing of peak secretion of the cortisol acrophase, although a large in-

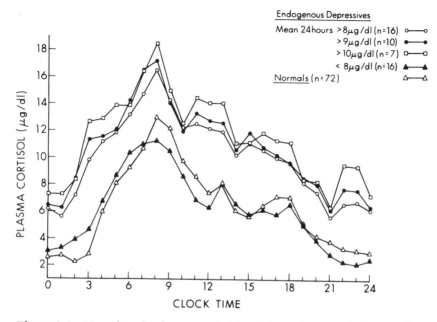

Figure 3.2. Mean hourly plasma cortisol levels in endogenously depressed patients with various levels of mean 24-hour plasma cortisol levels and normal subjects. ED patients: O——O, > 8 μg/dl (n = 16); ●——●, > 9 μg/dl (n = 10); □——□, > 10 μg/dl (n = 7); and ▲——▲ < 8 μg/dl (n = 16). Controls: △——△ (n = 72). [Reproduced, with permission, from Halbreich et al (1985): Arch Gen Psychiatry 42:909–914.]

dividual variability was shown. The acrophase of ED patients was at −161.9° ± 27.2°, which corresponds to ± 1 hour, 48 minutes (midnight is defined as 0°, and the 24-hour clock is divided into 360°, which means that every hour is 15°). The acrophase of the normals was at 10 hours, 48 minutes ± 2 hours, 32 minutes (−153.9° ± 38.1°). As is also shown in Table 3.1, there was no difference in acrophase between ED patients with high 24-hour levels of cortisol and those with low $\bar{X}$24h PC. As is described later, our more accurate results—compared to previous studies—are due to the wide age range of both ED *and* control subjects, because age is an important variable influencing the diurnal rhythm.

The 24-hour cosinor curve was not "flat" in ED patients. The amplitude of the ED patients did not differ from that of normals. Furthermore, if there were an association between flattening of the curve and cortisol hypersecretion in ED patients, we would expect a negative cor-

Table 3.1. Twenty-four-hour Rhythm of Cortisol Secretion: Time-Related Variables

	Normal Controls (n = 72)	Endogenously Depressed Patients		
		Total Sample (n = 32)	With Lower Levels of Cortisol (<8 µg/dl) (n = 16)	With Higher Levels of Cortisol (>10 µg/dl) (n = 7)
Actual $\bar{X}$24h levels of cortisol (µg/dl)	6.4 ± 1.9	8.1 ± 2.5[a]	6.1 ± 1.1	11.6 ± 1.7[b]
Mesor (µg/dl)	6.2 ± 2.0	7.5 ± 2.3	5.7 ± 1.0	10.6 ± 1.0[b]
Fitness of the cosinor curve (r^2)	0.42 ± 0.18	0.58 ± 0.19 (NS)[c]	0.61 ± 0.13	0.42 ± 0.30
Acrophase	10 hr 16 min ± 2 hr 32 min	10 hr 48 min ± 1 hr 48 min (NS)	10 hr 28 min ± 47 min	10 hr 44 min ± 1 hr 40 min (NS)
Amplitude (µg/dl)	3.7 ± 1.4	3.8 ± 1.1 (NS)	3.7 ± 1.2	4.3 ± 1.3 (NS)
Nadir (µg/dl)	1.2 ± 1.1	1.5 ± 1.6 (NS)	0.5 ± 0.7	3.3 ± 2.2[b]
Time of nadir	01 hr 19 min ± 1 hr 24 min	00 hr 38 min ± 1 hr 47 min[a]	0.1 hr 7 min ± 1 hr 31 min	00 hr 7 min ± 2 hr 12 min (NS)
Time of first secretory episode	02 hr 49 min ± 1 hr 30 min	01 hr 45 min ± 1 hr 54 min[a]	02 hr 24 min ± 1 hr 50 min	01 hr 7 min ± 2 hr 6 min (NS)
Age (yr)	33.5 ± 15.9	42.5 ± 15.1 (NS)	33.3 ± 11.5	55.1 ± 9.1[b]

Source: Halbreich U, et al (1985): Arch Gen Psychiatry 42:909–914. Reproduced with permission.
[a] $p < 0.01$ (ED patients *vs.* normal subjects).
[b] $p < 0.01$ (ED patients with high levels of cortisol *vs.* those with lower levels).
[c] Not significant.

relation between amplitude and $\overline{X}$24h PC, and this was not found ($r =$ 0.134). On an individual level, only three ED patients had an amplitude that was smaller than 1 SD of the normal mean, and none had an amplitude that was completely outside the normal range (2 SD). The same results were found by comparison of the ratio of amplitude to mesor (optimal mean of the cosinor curve). This method controlled for individual variability of $\overline{X}$24h PC. The mean ratio of the controls was 0.62 ± 0.20 and that of the ED patients was very similar (0.54 ± 0.20). Again, only eight ED patients had a ratio that was less than 1 SD of the normal mean and only one patient had a ratio lower than 2 SDs.

Although the morning, active secretion indices did not distinguish between depressives and normals, the two groups did differ in indices of rhythm that are pertinent to the quiescent early night period. The timing of the nadir was 40 minutes earlier in ED patients—0 hours, 38 minutes ± 1 hour, 47 minutes compared to the normals—1 hour, 19 minutes (AM) ± 1 hour, 24 minutes ($t = 2.091$, $p = 0.0391$). This difference, however, was mainly attributed to age ($F = 4.00$, $p = 0.0497$), and when age was controlled for, the difference between the ED patients and controls was still demonstrated but was insignificant ($p = 0.157$).

Depressives differed from normals in another parameter. The HPA system is probably activated earlier in ED patients. The first secretory episode of cortisol following the night nadir was at 1 hour, 45 minutes ± 1 hour, 54 minutes in the ED patients compared to 2 hours, 49 minutes ± 1 hour, 30 minutes in the normals ($t = 3.042, p = 0.0030$). Even though age had a significant effect on this variable ($F = 11.20, p = 0.0014$), and there was a significant negative correlation between age and time of the first secretory episode in ED patients and normals, still the group difference held even when age was controlled for ($F = 7.24, p = 0.0089$).

THE ULTRADIAN RHYTHM OF CORTISOL IN ENDOGENOUS DEPRESSION

Although the difference between the circadian rhythm of ED patients and that of normals was found to be rather subtle and was demonstrated mostly during the evening or early night hours, the mean fitness of the cosinor curve (r^2) was rather low, though statistically significant. Furthermore, 21 of the ED patients did not have a significant circadian fluctuation (tA). These two findings raise the possibility of an underlying rhythm that occurs in addition to the circadian rhythm and may increase the variance of the residuals around the optimal cosinor curve. This quantitative difference between ED and normal subjects was hypothesized to be due to differences in the number and magnitude of secretory episodes, or, in other words, an abnormality of ultradian (shorter than 24 hours) rhythm. Such an abnormality could be either in the frequency domain (number of episodes) or in terms of magnitude. These issues were studied by Fourier's analysis (spectral analysis). Indeed, as a group, ED patients had increased 4-hour variance density (magnitude of cortisol secretory episode), but they did not have a larger number of episodes per 24 hours (lower frequency). If anything, the opposite may exist (6.5 episodes per 24 hours in the ED patients as compared with 8.8 episodes per 24 hours in the normal group).

A further indication that the ultradian rhythm is the reason for the low fitness of the cosinor curve in ED patients is the finding that only 13 out of the 32 ED patients had an abnormal 4-hour magnitude of secretory episodes and all but one of them also had an insignificant 24-hour rhythm (tA).

The significance of the altered ultradian rhythm in the pathophysiology of ED is still unknown, as are its cause and underlying physiologic mechanisms.

AGE AND THE CIRCADIAN RHYTHM OF CORTISOL

Age has been shown to be a powerful variable in the determination of the levels and rhythms of various hormones. Hence, it was somewhat puzzling that some early studies reported that the circadian rhythm of cortisol does not change with age. These studies had some methodologic weaknesses because they included only small groups of patients and/or were performed with infrequent blood sampling. At present, one can unequivocally determine that age does influence the circadian rhythm of cortisol secretion. Our studies show a significant inverse correlation between age and acrophase (time of peak value—the amplitude—of the cosinor curve) ($r = -0.338, p = 0.0037$) among normal subjects. A tendency towards such a correlation could be demonstrated among depressed patients, but it did not reach significance ($r = -0.218, p = 0.228$). The importance of the variable of age in the timing of the peak secretion of cortisol is further demonstrated by analysis of covariance and regression analysis across groups (normals *and* depressives) ($F = 9.67$, df $= 1/101, p < 0.002$).

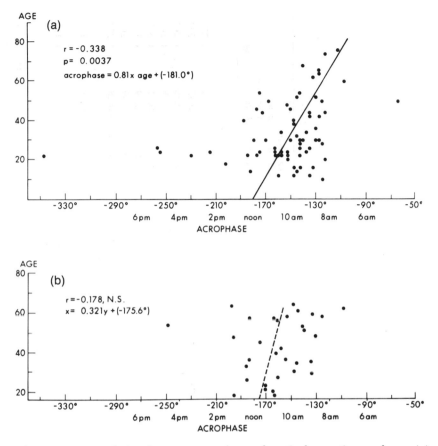

Figure 3.3. Correlation between acrophase of cortisol secretion and age. (a) Normal subjects ($n = 72$): $r = 0.338, p = 0.0037$, acrophase $= 0.81 \times$ age $+ (-181.0°)$. (b) Endogenously depressed patients ($n = 32$): $r = 0.178$, NS, $X = 0.321y + (-175.6°)$.

The relationship between age and the acrophase is shown in Figures 3.3(a) and 3.3(b).

Among normal subjects, age was positively correlated with the amplitude ($r = 0.26, p < 0.05$) and fitness of the cosinor curve ($r = 0.30, p < 0.01$) and was inversely correlated with the time of the first secretory episode of cortisol (at night) ($r = -0.27, p < 0.05$).

The depressed patients showed an even more significant inverse correlation between age and the fitness of the cosinor curve ($r =$

Table 3.2. Correlation Between Various Functions of Cortisol Secretion[a]

	Mean 1–4 PM Level	Amplitude	Acrophase	r^2	tA	Time of Nadir	Time of First Episode	Time From Nadir to First Episode	4-hr Variance Density	Age
Normal Subjects (n = 72)										
$\bar{X}$24h levels	0.80[b]	0.58[b]	0.01	−0.11	0.16	0.12	0.04	0.11	0.57[b]	0.37[b]
Mean 1–4 PM level		0.51[b]	−0.06	−0.10	−0.09	0.05	0.05	0.01	0.42[c]	0.23[d]
Amplitude			0.04	0.38[c]	0.10	−0.09	−0.06	0.02	0.56[b]	0.26[d]
Acrophase				−0.10	0.20	0.41[c]	0.40[c]	0.03	0.05	−0.34[e]
r^2					0.01	−0.03	−0.04	−0.02	−0.11	0.30[e]
tA						−0.23[d]	−0.28[d]	−0.10	0.29[e]	0.18
Time of nadir							0.77[b]	−0.23[d]	−0.09	−0.20
Time of first episode								0.43[c]	−0.08	−0.27[d]
Time from nadir to first episode									0.01	−0.13
4-hr variance density										0.11

table continues

Table 3.2. (continued)

Endogenously Depressed Patients (n = 32)

	Mean 1–4 PM Level	Amplitude	Acrophase	r²	tA	Time of Nadir	Time of First Episode	Time From Nadir to First Episode	4-hr Variance Density	Age
X̄24h levels	0.88[a]	0.13	0.29	−0.45[e]	−0.36[d]	−0.24	−0.26	−0.10	0.42[d]	0.55[c]
Mean 1–4 PM level		0.12	0.30	−0.43[e]	−0.39[d]	−0.20	−0.22	−0.11	0.45[e]	0.53[c]
Amplitude			0.22	−0.60[c]	−0.30	−0.03	0.04	0.20	−0.05	−0.06
Acrophase				0.04	0.59[c]	0.05	0.13	0.26	0.23	−0.22
r²					0.29	0.25	0.31	0.23	−0.28	−0.64[b]
tA						−0.04	−0.09	−0.17	−0.47[e]	0.04
Time of nadir							0.95[b]	0.02	0.05	−0.31
Time of first episode								0.33	0.04	−0.40[d]
Time from nadir to first episode									−0.01	−0.33
4-hr variance density										0.33

Source: Halbreich U, et al (1985): Arch Gen Psychiatry 42:909–914. Reproduced with permission.
[a] r² indicates the fitness of the curve; tA, significance of circadian rhythmicity.
[b] p < 0.0001.
[c] p < 0.001.
[d] p < 0.05.
[e] p < 0.01.

-0.64, $p < 0.0001$) as well as between age and the timing of the first secretory episode of cortisol ($r = -0.40$, $p < 0.05$).

The association between age and the various functions of cortisol secretion is summarized in Table 3.2.

The validity of these results is strengthened by two reports that were published in the same month: Sherman and colleagues (1985) reported an inverse correlation between age and acrophase ($r = -0.528$, $p < 0.001$) and age and nadir ($r = -0.543$, $p < 0.001$) in 34 normal subjects; and Linkowski and colleagues (1985) reported an inverse correlation of $r = -0.90$, $p < 0.02$ between age and time of the nocturnal nadir in seven normal subjects. This group of investigators did not find any age-related change in the timing of the morning acrophase. Although their suggestion that the maximal secretion of ACTH and cortisol and the minimal levels, or quiescent period, of ACTH and cortisol are controlled by different mechanisms—as previously suggested by Desir and coworkers (1981) and Krieger and Krieger (1967)—might be correct, they studied only seven normals.

The mechanisms underlying the age effects on the circadian rhythm of cortisol are still a matter of speculation. Age-related changes in the activity of several neurotransmitters that are involved in the regulation of cortisol have been demonstrated (McGeer and McGeer, 1978). However, the changes in basal levels of cortisol are not necessarily linked to changes in the rhythm. Age-related changes in oscillators' regulation are less well studied. The changes in the timing of the nadir and the first secretory episode can also be explained by changes in sleep onset that may occur with advancing age. This, however, does not provide an explanation for the advanced acrophase, and, as has already been mentioned, the regulation of the nadir and the acrophase may be mediated by different mechanisms. Additional investigations are needed in order to clarify this intriguing issue.

THE RHYTHM FUNCTIONS OF THE HPA SYSTEM ARE DISSOCIATED FROM EACH OTHER

The increased sophistication in the knowledge of the HPA system and its function brought with it the recognition that the system is not monolithic and abnormality of one of its functions does not necessarily imply that the others are disturbed as well. As is shown in Table 3.2., these various functions are only partially related to each other (Keller-Wood and Dallman, 1984). General statements on hyperactivity of the HPA system are not completely accurate. One should state which specific activity or function is disturbed.

The measured basal levels of cortisol are a manifestation of the overall set-point of activity of the HPA system, which may be elevated, as occurs in some depressives, alcoholics, and many other patients, or decreased, as is the case in patients with Edison's disease. One should realize that plasma cortisol is a different measure than urinary cortisol. Urinary cortisol, as well as salivary cortisol, is in the free form while plasma cortisol is mainly in the bound form.

The dexamethasone suppression test (DST), which is probably still the most extensively studied test in psychiatry, represents the delayed feedback mechanism in the HPA system that consists of a complicated set of stimulus–response and feedback mechanisms in that axis. The DST represents an active intervention by way of introducing an exogenous steroid into part of the system that is unable to distinguish between the endogenous product and the exogenous one. It has been shown (Asnis et al., 1981; Brown et al., 1985; Halbreich et al., 1985; Holsboer et al., 1984; Stokes et al., 1984) that there is only a partial overlap between cortisol hypersecretion and an abnormality of the feedback mechanism (abnormal DST). As is demonstrated in Table 3.2, the $\overline{X}$24h PC only partially correlates with most of the rhythm functions, and the correlation might be different in normals and depressives. For example, the amplitude correlates with the $\overline{X}$24h PC in normal subjects, but not in depressives.

The lack of correlation is not random and some systematic relationships do emerge. For example, the density of variance of the 4-hour ultradian rhythm—which can be viewed as a manifestation of the amount of cortisol secreted in each episode—is positively related to the $\overline{X}$24h PC. Such a relationship would be expected because more cortisol is needed in each episode to create a situation of increased mean 24-hour plasma levels. In addition, there is an inverse correlation between the density of variance of the same frequency and the tA, which is a mathematical representation of the significance of the circadian rhythm. Because the ultradian rhythm is actually a "noise" to the smoothness of the circadian cosinor curve, we would expect that the larger the "noise," the more reduced the significance and the clarity of the basic larger fluctuations would be. The cycle is closed by the finding that the "noise" (tA) is inversely correlated with the $\overline{X}$24h PC.

The selected associations between the various functions of the HPA system and their partial dissociation may also be examined by studying whether patients who show abnormality in one function will be abnormal in others. This approach is also important, as it will help to determine the clinical significance of treating the HPA system as a diversified cluster of distinguished mechanisms as opposed to a homogeneous one.

Table 3.3 shows a preliminary result of such an approach. When the overlap between the subgroups of ED patients who are abnormal in each of the HPA functions is analyzed with χ^2 tests, the relative lack of the association is further demonstrated. The squares were arranged in a way that significant χ^2 indicates association between the groups studied. It is worthwhile to note that almost all (12 of 13) ED patients who had abnormally high 4-hour density did not have a significant circadian rhythm (tA), which is in keeping with the other analyses. Six of the eight dexamethasone nonsuppressors also had abnormally low tA values. The cortisol hypersecretors tended to be normal in all other functions except DST and tA. The overlap between abnormal groups in all of the other functions were far from being significant.

It has been argued that the abnormal DST in depressives is "confounded" by the finding of an inverse correlation between the plasma level of dexamethasone and the postdexamethasone cortisol level. Mean plasma levels of dexamethasone, however, are not different in depressives compared to normals, and the inverse correlation exists within each group. Even when the plasma dexamethasone levels are controlled for (Carson and Halbreich, unpublished data), ED patients still have less suppressibility to the same plasma levels of dexamethasone than do normals.

The debate about "confounding factors" in hormonal tests is described and discussed in length elsewhere (Halbreich, in press). Suffice it to say that these factors further emphasize the need for a detailed and multidimensional approach to the study of psychiatric disorders and their biologic components. A narrow, rigid, and simple-minded attitude, in which additional factors that influence biologic parameters are perceived as "disturbing," is counterproductive. Instead, they should be incorporated into a well-rounded model, even if in the beginning such a model seems more complicated.

CLINICAL CORRELATES OF ABNORMALITIES OF THE HYPOTHALAMIC–PITUITARY–ADRENAL (HPA) SYSTEM

Even though the number of patients ($n = 32$) and hormonal determinations reported here is adequate for the analyses that were included in the previous sections, it is rather small once the group of ED patients

Table 3.3. Overlap (χ^2) Between Groups of Endogenous Depressives with Abnormal Cortisol Functions

	$\overline{X}$ 1–4-PM PC (n = 7)	DST (n = 8)	tA (n = 21)	r² (n = 8)	Acrophase (n = 4)	Amplitude (n = 3)	Amplitude Mean (n = 8)	4-h Density (n = 13)
$\overline{X}$24h PC (n = 7)	32.00[a]	4.93[b]	0.13	1.52	0.11	0.25	1.52	3.52
$\overline{X}$ 1–4-PM PC		4.93[b]	0.13	1.52	0.11	0.25	1.52	3.52
DST			0.41	0.89	0.71	3.87[b]	0.22	0.39
tA				0.42	4.88[b]	1.73	0.42	6.91[c]
r²					0.71	9.93[c]	8.00[c]	2.12
Acrophase						1.99[a]	0.71	0.42
Amplitude							9.93[c]	0.93
Amplitude Mean								2.12

[a] $p < 0.05$.
[b] $p < 0.001$.
[c] $p < 0.01$.

is divided according to clinical subtype or features. Hence the following data should be taken only as a demonstration of possible differential correlates of the various HPA functions.

Hypersecretion of cortisol was more prevalent among primary ED patients. All seven ED patients who had cortisol levels more than 2 SD above the normal mean had primary depression even though as a group the difference between primary and secondary ED patients did not reach significance (8.6 ± 2.7 vs. 7.1 ± 2.1 µg/dl, $t = 1.81, p = 0.07$). The positive correlation between $\overline{X}$24h PC and severity of depression, as measured by the Hamilton Depression Rating Scale (HDRS), also was significant only for the primary ($r = 0.728, p = 0.00023$), but not the secondary ED subjects ($r = -0.0094$, NS).

Levels of cortisol were also elevated in ED subjects with Psychomotor retardation ($n = 14$) compared to the nonretarded ED subjects ($\overline{X}$24h PC $= 9.4 \pm 2.1$ vs. 7.1 ± 2.0 µg/dl, $t = 2.826, p = 0.0083$; $\overline{X}$ 1–4-PM PC $= 9.2 \pm 2.2$ vs. 7.1 ± 2.1, $t = 2.706, p = 0.011$).

Dexamethasone nonsuppressors had higher HDRS scores (more severe depression) than did DST suppressors (30.0 ± 6.2 vs. 24.8 ± 5.2, $t = 2.17, p = 0.0373$).

Fitness of the 24-hour curve (r^2) was found to be inversely correlated with severity of depression ($r = -0.483, p = 0.005$). This is in accord with the finding that abnormally low r^2 was a distinguishing feature of the group of incapacitated ED patients ($r^2 = 0.24 \pm 0.14$ vs. 0.40 ± 0.13, $t = 3.385, p = 0.002$).

An abnormal ultradian rhythm distinguished unipolar ED patients ($n = 19$) from bipolar I patients ($n = 10$). The density of variance in the 4-hour block was 2.64 among the bipolar ED patients compared to 1.62 among the unipolar ED patients ($t = 2.697, p = 0.0032$). This is compatible with a tendency toward a less significant circadian rhythm (tA) among the bipolar ED patients ($\overline{X}$ tA BP $= 1.4, \overline{X}$ tA UP $= 2.08$, $t = 1.786, p = 0.085$). Powerful 4-hour ultradian rhythm (high density of variance) was also more prevalent among agitated ED patients ($n = 16$) than it was among the rest of the group (4-hour density of variance $= 2.23 \pm 1.12$ vs. 1.54 ± 0.84, $t = 1.944, p = 0.061$).

As was previously mentioned, a detailed study of the various functions of the HPA system as the dependent variable to which clinical parameters are related is premature at this point, and the above demonstrations are mere hints or promises for future studies. Another disclaimer to overemphasizing the significance of these data at present is the possibility that the same clinical phenomenology might result from different underlying pathophysiologic mechanisms. If this is the case, then the differences mentioned here might be secondary in importance and will be of significance only if patients differ in treatment response according to different pathologies.

THE NORMAL CIRCADIAN RHYTHM OF PLASMA MHPG AND ITS RELATIONSHIP WITH THE CIRCADIAN RHYTHM OF CORTISOL

3-Methoxy-4-hydroxyphenylglycol (MHPG) has been intensively studied because it is considered to be a main metabolite of norepinephrine (NE) in the brain (Maas, 1983). Changes in brain NE activity are reflected in changes in brain MHPG levels (Karoum et al., 1977; Maas et al., 1979), and levels of MHPG in peripheral body fluids are believed to be related to metabolite levels in the central nervous system (CNS) (DeMet and Halaris, 1979; Linnoila et al., 1982; Maas and Leckman, 1983; Maas et al., 1976). That relationship is quite complicated, and other peripheral NE metabolites might also be related to the CNS production of the neurotransmitter (Blomberg et al., 1980; Linnoila et al., 1986; Mårdh and Änggård, 1984; Mårdh et al., 1981). Nonetheless, although a substantial portion of plasma MHPG is probably of peripheral origin (Kopin et al., 1982), a high correlation between plasma and cerebrospinal fluid (CSF) MHPG has been obtained (Jimerson et al., 1981; Kopin et al., 1982). Hence, even if much of the MHPG in plasma is derived from peripheral sources, it is plausible that there is a close relationship between cerebral and peripheral NE mechanisms, and changes in plasma MHPG may reflect CNS changes in NE activity (Maas and Leckman, 1983).

In most of the early studies of MHPG, its levels were determined in urine. Urinary collections, however, are often complicated due to incomplete collections—a problem that is encountered even in inpatient clinical research centers and is more pronounced in outpatient studies. Furthermore, it was calculated (Kopin et al., 1984a) that brain MHPG must contribute less than 25% of urinary MHPG. Determinations of MHPG in the CSF are probably a better indication of brain MHPG, especially when values are adjusted for plasma MHPG contribution (Kopin et al., 1984a). Lumbar punctures, however, are inconvenient and cannot be repeated, as is required for determination of circadian rhythms. Determination of MHPG in plasma may be more controlled than in urine and it allows for serial frequent samplings. However, while urinary MHPG represents an integral measure over time, repeated single plasma samples might be subject to greater variability (Halbreich et al., 1986; Maas et al., 1980), which is apparent despite the 45–75-minute half-life time of the metabolite (Kopin et al., 1984b). Therefore, we measured integrated total plasma MHPG levels in samples collected continuously with a withdrawal pump over short periods of 2 hours for a total of 28 hours (Halbreich et al., in press, a).

Levels of plasma MHPG in normal subjects were reported to be higher during the afternoon than during the morning hours (DeMet et al., 1985; Leckman et al., 1980; Markianos and Beckmann, 1976; Swann et al., 1980; Sweeny et al., 1980). A circadian rhythm of urinary levels of the metabolite has also been demonstrated (Wehr et al., 1980).

Because NE is involved in the regulation of the HPA system and significant associations between urinary MHPG and some functions of the HPA system have been reported (Jimerson et al., 1983; Rosenbaum et al., 1983), it is of interest to examine the relationship between the diurnal rhythms of MHPG and cortisol. This is especially intriguing because the early interest in cortisol secretion as a "window into the brain" rose (Sachar et al., 1973) because of the assumption that changes in the level of cortisol are a mirror image of changes in NE activity in the brain.

Overnight studies of integrated plasma MHPG in 18 normal subjects (Halbreich, submitted) shows a clear diurnal rhythm (Figure 3.4).

Phase-angle analysis showed the acrophase to be at 14 hours, 55 minutes ± 2 hours, 33 minutes. The adjusted nadir was found to be at 4 hours, 38 minutes ± 2 hours, 49 minutes. The mean fitness of the cosinor curve (r^2) was 0.309 ± 0.232 and the mean amplitude was 2.39 ± 3.29 ng/ml. The amplitude was positively correlated with mean 24-hour plasma MHPG ($r = 0.57, p < 0.02$) as well as with age ($r = 0.547, p < 0.02$). Plasma MHPG tends to peak earlier with older age but the negative correlation between acrophase and age was not significant ($r = -0.402, p = 0.097$).

During most periods of the day, there was no significant correlation between plasma levels of cortisol and MHPG determined on the same sample. A consistent significant negative correlation was found, however, between plasma levels of the two compounds during subperiods of the afternoon and evening—when plasma levels of cortisol declined. The inverse relationship was more prominent when a time lag of one subperiod (2 hours) was introduced. The highest *negative* correlation was between plasma levels of MHPG between 6:00 and 8:00 PM and plasma levels of cortisol between 8:00 and 10:00 PM ($r = -0.623, p < 0.01$). Correlations were insignificantly *positive* during the night and became negative again after 8 AM.

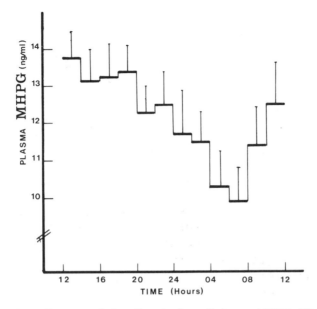

Figure 3.4. The normal circadian rhythm of plasma MHPG ($N = 18$).

These results suggest that the relationship between MHPG and cortisol is far more complicated than previously reported. The association between the metabolite and hormone depends on the time of day at which the level of each is determined. Only during the afternoon is there a significant association. These results also suggest that during different periods of the day various neurotransmitters have differing impacts on cortisol production: during the afternoon NE exerts a significant influence, which is associated with the decline in plasma cortisol levels, and during the night other mechanisms are more important for the regulation of cortisol.

THE CIRCADIAN RHYTHM OF MHPG IN DEPRESSIVES

The circadian rhythm of urinary MHPG has been reported to be different in depressed patients than in normals. Although the normal acrophase of urinary MHPG was found to be in the early evening (Hollister et al., 1978; Wehr et al., 1980), Wehr and coworkers (1980) noted that in depressed patients the acrophase occurred 2–3 hours earlier (phase advance). Indeed, for studies of circadian rhythms, urine sampling is not sufficiently frequent, and repeated blood drawing has a substantial advantage. DeMet and coworkers (1982), who drew blood every 3 hours, reported high variability of acrophase among ED patients. Some ED patients had an earlier acrophase whereas others had peak plasma MHPG levels later than did normals (DeMet et al., 1985). We have reported (Halbreich et al., 1987) that there might be at least two subgroups of ED patients according to their circadian rhythm. Furthermore, an ultradian rhythm of MHPG might exist in some but not all ED patients. Its existence is unclear at present, but if it does occur this might complicate the issue even further.

With 3-hour studies (Halbreich et al., in press, a) in the early afternoon—the afternoon continuous test (ACT)—we have reported that plasma MHPG is positively correlated with age in normal subjects. Although the mean afternoon MHPG level of the MDD-ED patients does not differ from that of normals, when the age variable is taken into account, there are ED patients whose afternoon MHPG level is higher or lower than age-matched normals. This is especially true for MDD-ED women, because the 1–4 PM period—during which the ACT was performed—includes the normal acrophase. These two subgroups might be another indication of the variability of the circadian rhythm of MHPG in ED patients. The ED patients with higher levels of afternoon "MHPG per age" might be those with the delayed phase whereas those with low afternoon "MHPG per age" might be those in whom the MHPG levels are already declining during the afternoon, so that they have an advanced phase.

At present, additional studies are being conducted in order to elucidate this issue. However, the finding that these two groups did not differ from each other in their clinical phenomenology raises a heuristic issue, namely, that similar affective symptomatology might be associated with different heterogeneous pathophysiologic processes—as is the case with some physical conditions such as hypertension or diabetes. If this is true, external validation of biologic subgroups and the distinction between disorders may rest not necessarily and solely on phenomenology but rather on pathophysiology (as well as genetics and course of illness) and its practical implications, for example, treatment responses. The finding that although various antidepressant drugs (with different initial mechanisms of action) have the same effect on patients (i.e., alleviation of symptoms) as well as the same biologic pattern (e.g., decreased plasma or CSF levels of MHPG and down regulation of β-adrenergic receptors), some MDD patients respond better to a specific one of these drugs than to others may also point to heterogeneity of initial pathophysiology with possible homogeneity of clinical consequences.

The reported studies were supported in part by NIMH grants #R0137111, #R0141423, and #R0129841, GCRC grants RR50 and RR53, and the Ritter's Foundation.

REFERENCES

Asnis GM, Sachar EJ, Halbreich U, et al (1981): Cortisol secretion and dexamethasone response in depression. Am J Psychiatry 138:1218.

Blomberg PA, Kopin JJ, Gordon EK, et al (1980): Conversion of MHPG to vanillylmandelic acid: Implications for the importance of urinary MHPG. Arch Gen Psychiatry 37:1095.

Brown WA, Keitner G, Qualls B, Haier R (1985): The dexamethasone suppression test and pituitary–adrenocortical function. Arch Gen Psychiatry 42:121.

Carroll BJ, Curtis GC, Mendels J (1976a): Neuroendocrine regulation in depression: I. Limbic system–adrenocortical dysfunction. Arch Gen Psychiatry 33:1039.

Carroll BJ, Curtis GC, Mendels J (1976b): Neuroendocrine regulation in depression: II. Discrimination of depressed from nondepressed patients. Arch Gen Psychiatry 33:1051.

Carroll BJ, Feinberg M, Greden JF, et al (1981): A specific laboratory test for the diagnosis of melancholia: Standardization, validation, and clinical utility. Arch Gen Psychiatry 38:15.

Dean S, Felton SP (1979): Circadian rhythm in the elderly: A study using a cortisol-specific radioimmunoassay. Age and Ageing 8:243.

DeMet EM, Halaris AE (1979): Origin and distribution of 3-methoxy-4-hydroxyphenylglycol in body fluids. Biochem Pharmacol 28:3043.

DeMet EM, Halaris AE, Gwirtsman HE, et al (1982): Effects of desipramine on diurnal rhythms of plasma 3-methoxy-4-hydroxyphenylglycol (MHPG) in depressed patients. Psychopharmacol Bull 18:221.

DeMet EM, Halaris AE, Gwirtsman HE, Reno RM (1985): Diurnal rhythm of MHPG: Relationship between plasma and urinary levels. Life Sci 37:1731.

Desir D, Van Cauter E, Fang V, et al (1981): Effects of "jet lag" on hormonal pattern. I. Procedures, variations in total plasma proteins and disruptions of adrenocorticotropin–cortisol periodicity. J Clin Endocrinol Metab 52:628.

Doerr P, von Zerssen D, Fischler M, Schulz H (1979): Relationship between mood changes and adrenal cortisol activity in a patient with 48 hour unipolar depressive cycles. J Affect Disord 1:93.

Fullerton DT, Wenzel FJ, Lohrenz FN (1968): Circadian rhythm of adrenal cortisol activity in depression: I. A comparison of depressed patients with normal subjects. Arch Gen Psychiatry 19:674.

Gelenberg AJ, Klerman GL, Hartman EL, Salt P (1978): Recurrent unipolar depressions with a 48 hour cycle: Report of a case. Br J Psychiatry 133:123.

Gibbons JL, McHugh PR (1962): Plasma cortisol in depressive illness. J Psychiatr Res 1:162.

Green R (1967): Morning and afternoon plasma 17-hydroxy-corticosteroid levels during affective psychosis. Int J Neurol Psychiatry 2:133.

Halberg F (1968): Physiologic considerations underlying rhythmometry with special reference to emotional illness. In de Ajuriaguerra F (ed): Cycles Biologiques et Psychiatrie. Paris, Mason et Cie, pp 73–126.

Halberg F, Vestergaard P, Sakai M (1968): Rhythmometry on urinary 17-ketosteroid excretion by healthy men and women and patients with chronic schizophenia: Possible chronopathology in depressive illness. Arch Anat Histol Embryol 51:301.

Halbreich U (in press): Hormones and depression—Conceptual transitions. In Halbreich U (ed): Hormones and Depression. New York, Raven.

Halbreich U, Zumoff B, Kream J, Fukushima DK (1982): The mean 1300–1600h plasma cortisol concentration as a diagnostic test for hypercortisolism. J Clin Endocrinol Metab 54:1262.

Halbreich U, Asnis GM, Shindledecker R, et al (1985): Cortisol secretion in endogenous depression: I. Basal plasma levels. Arch Gen Psychiatry 42:904.

Halbreich U, Sharpless NS, Goldstein S, Asnis GM (1986): Afternoon Continuous Test for MHPG in normals and depressives. Presented at annual meeting of the Society of Biological Psychiatry, Washington, D.C.

Halbreich U, Sharpless N, Asnis GM, et al (in press): Afternoon continuous plasma levels of "MHPG per age"—Distinctive biological subgroups of endogenous depression? Arch Gen Psychiatry.

Halbreich U, Goldstein S, Sharpless N, et al (1987): Two types of disturbed diurnal rhythm of plasma MHPG in endogenously depressed patients. Psychiat Res 20:79.

Halbreich U, Goldstein S, Sharpless N, Ryan J (submitted): Continuous plasma levels of MHPG-circadian pattern.

Hellman L, Nakada F, Curti J, et al (1970): Cortisol is secreted episodically by normal man. J Clin Endocrinol Metab 30:411.

Hollister LE, Davis KL, Overall JE, Anderson T (1978): Excretion of MHPG in normal subjects. Arch Gen Psychiatry 35:1410.

Holsboer F, Gerken A, Steiger A, Fass V (1984): Mean 14:00–17:00h plasma cortisol concentration and its relationship to the 1-mg dexamethasone suppression response in depressives and controls. Acta Psychiatr Scand 69:383.

Jimerson DC, Ballenger JC, Lake CR, et al (1981): Plasma and CSF MHPG in normals. Psychopharmacol Bull 17:86.

Jimerson DC, Insel TR, Reus VI, Kopin IJ (1983): Increased plasma MHPG in dexamethasone-resistant depressed patients. Arch Gen Psychiatry 40:173.

Karoum F, Moyer-Schwing J, Potkin SG, Wyatt RJ (1977): Presence of free, sulfate, and glucuronide conjugated MHPG in human brain, cerebrospinal fluid and plasma. Brain Res 125:333.

Keller-Wood ME, Dallman MF (1984): Corticosteroid inhibition of ACTH secretion. Endocrinol Rev 5:1.

Kopin IJ, Gordon EK, Jimerson DC, Polinsky RJ (1982): Relationship between plasma and cerebrospinal fluid levels of 3-methoxy-4-hydroxyphenylglycol. Science 219:73.

Kopin IJ, Jimerson DC, Markey SP, et al (1984a): Disposition and metabolism of MHPG in humans: Application to studies in depression. Pharmacopsychiatry 17:3.

Kopin IJ, Blomberg P, Ebert MH, et al (1984b): Disposition and metabolism of $MHPGCD_3$ in humans: Plasma MHPG as an important determinant of CSF levels of MHPG. Nobel Conference, Skokloster, Sweden.

Krieger D (1972): Characterization of normal temporal pattern of cortisol levels. J Clin Endocrinol Metab 34:380.

Krieger DT, Krieger HP (1967): Circadian pattern of plasma 17-hydroxycorticosteroids: Alteration by anticholinergic agents. Science 155:1421.

Krieger DT, Allen W, Rizzo F, Krieger HP (1971): Characterization of normal temporal pattern of plasma corticosteroid levels. J Clin Endocrinol Metab 32:261.

Leckman JF, Maas JW, Redmond DE Jr, Heninger FR (1980): Effects of oral clonidine on plasma MHPG in man. Life Sci 26:2179.

Linkowski P, Mendlewicz J, Leclercq R, et al (1985): The 24-hour profile of adrenocorticotropin and cortisol in major depressive illness. J Clin Endocrinol Metal 61:429.

Linnoila M, Karoum F, Potter WZ (1982): High correlation of norepinephrine and its major metabolite excretion rates. Arch Gen Psychiatry 521.

Linnoila M, Guthrie S, Lane EA, et al (1986): Clinical studies on norepinephrine metabolisms: How to interpret the numbers. Psychiatry Res 17:229.

Lohrenz FN, Fullerton DT, Wenzel FJ, et al (1969): Circadian rhythm of adrenal cortical activity in depression. Behav Neuropsychiatry 1:10.

Maas JW (ed) (1983): MHPG: Basic Mechanisms and Psychopathology. New York, Academic, 1983.

Maas JW, Leckman JF (1983): Relationship between central nervous system noradrenergic function and plasma and urinary MHPG and other norepinephrine metabolites. In Maas J (ed): MHPG: Basic Mechanisms and Psychopathology. New York, Academic, pp 33–43.

Maas JW, Hattox SE, Roth RH (1976): The determination of brain arteriovenous difference for MHPG. Brain Res 118:167.

Maas JW, Hattox SE, Green NM, Landis DH (1979): 3-Methoxy-4-hydroxyphenylglycol production by human brain in vivo. Science 205:1025.

Maas JW, Hattox SE, Landis DH (1980): Variance in the production of homovanillic acid and 3-methoxy-4-hydroxyphenethyleneglycol by the awake primate brain. Life Sci 26:252.

Mårdh G, Änggård E (1984): Norepinephrine metabolism in man using deuterium labelling: Origin of 4-hydroxy-3-methoxymandelic acid. J Neurochem 42:43.

Mårdh G, Sgöquist B, Änggård E (1981): Norepinephrine metabolism in man using deuterium labelling: The conversion of 4-hydroxy-3-methoxyphenylglycol to 4-hydroxy-3-methoxymandelic acid. J Neurochem 36:1181.

Markianos E, Beckmann H (1976): Diurnal changes in dopamine-beta-hydroxylase, homovanillic acid and 3-methoxy-4-hydroxyphenylglycol in serum of man. J Neural Transm 39:79.

McClure DJ (1966): The diurnal variation of plasma cortisol levels in depression. J Psychosom Res 10:189.

McGeer PL, McGeer EG (1978): Aging and neurotransmitter systems. In Finch CE, Potter AD, Kenny AD (eds): Aging and Neuroendocrine Relationships. New York, Plenum.

Nelson W, Liang Ton Y, Jung-Kuen L, Halberg F (1981): Methods for cosinor-rhythmometry. Chronobiologia 6:305.

Rosenbaum AH, Maruta T, Schatzberg AJ, et al (1983): Toward a biochemical classification of depressive disorders. VII: Urinary free cortisol and urinary MHPG in depression. Am J Psychiatry 140:314.

Sachar EJ, Hellman L, Roffwarg HP, et al (1973): Disrupted 24-hour patterns of cortisol secretion in psychotic depression. Arch Gen Psychiatry 28:19.

Schlesser MA, Winokur G, Sherman BM (1980): Hypothalamic–pituitary–adrenal axis activity in depressive illness: Its relationship to classification. Arch Gen Psychiatry 37:737.

Serio M, Piolanti P, Romano S, et al (1970): The circadian rhythm of plasma cortisol of subjects over 70 years of age. J Gerontol 25:95.

Sherman B, Wysham B, Phohl B (1985): Age-related changes in the circadian rhythm of plasma cortisol in man. J Clin Endocrinol Metab 61:439.

Stokes PE, Stoll PM, Koslow SH, et al (1984): Pretreatment DST and hypothalamic–pituitary adrenocortical function in depressed patients and comparison groups: A multicenter study. Arch Gen Psychiatry 41:257.

Swann A, Maas JW, Hattox SE, Landis DH (1980): Life Sci 27:1857.

Sweeney DR, Leckman JF, Maas JW, et al (1980): Plasma free and conjugated MHPG in psychiatric patients: A pilot study. Arch Gen Psychiatry 37:1100.

Wehr TA, Goodwin FK (eds) (1983): Circadian Rhythms in Psychiatry. Pacific Grove, CA, Boxwood.

Wehr TA, Muscettola G, Goodwin FK (1980): Urinary 3-methoxy-4-hydroxyphenylglycol circadian rhythm: Early timing (phase advance) in manic depressives compared with normal subjects. Arch Gen Psychiatry 37:257.

Weitzman FD, Fukushima DK, Nogeire C, et al (1971): Twenty-four hour pattern of the episodic secretion of cortisol in normal subjects. J Clin Endocrinol Metab 33:14.

Yamaguchi N, Maeda K, Kuromaru S (1978): The effects of sleep deprivation on the circadian rhythm of plasma cortisol levels in depressive patients. Folia Psychiatr Neurol Jpn 32:479.

Yamashita I, Morojoi T, Yamazaki K, et al (1969): Neuroendocrinological studies in mental disorders and psychotropic drugs: I. On the circadian rhythm plasma adrenocortical hormone in mental patients and metamphetamine and chlorpromazine-treated animals. Folia Psychiatr Neurol Jpn 23:143.

4

REM Sleep and Temperature Regulation in Affective Disorder

David H. Avery

The brain is a familiar and frequent cause (of melancholy), too hot or too cold . . . the brain itself being distempered . . . A hot and dry brain never sleeps well.

Robert Burton
The Anatomy of Melancholy, 1624

Rapid-eye-movement (REM) sleep and thermoregulation have a close, and complex interrelationship. Both processes have been found to be altered in some patients with affective disorder but have rarely been carefully studied in the same patients. This chapter (1) briefly reviews REM sleep findings in affective disorder, (2) focuses on the interrelationship between thermoregulation and sleep, especially REM sleep, (3) presents hypothesized temperature changes that follow from the REM sleep abnormalities, and (4) reviews temperature data from studies of depressed patients.

REM SLEEP AND AFFECTIVE DISORDER

Abnormal sleep architecture seems to characterize patients with primary affective disorder. Decreased slow wave sleep is a common but non-

This research was supported in part by NIMH fellowship 5 F32 MH 05799-01

specific finding in affective disorder (Gillin et al., 1979). In contrast, REM latency may be a good biologic marker with good sensitivity and specificity (Rush et al., 1982; Feinberg et al., 1982). Kupfer and associates, using well-diagnosed, drug-free patients, have found the REM latency (the period between sleep onset to the appearance of the first REM episode) in primary affective disorder to be significantly shorter than in both psychiatric and medical controls (Kupfer and Foster, 1972; Kupfer, 1976, 1978; Kupfer et al., 1978). Many other groups have confirmed this finding (Mendels and Chernik, 1975; Gillin et al., 1979; Vogel et al., 1980; Rush et al., 1982; Berger et al., 1982; Feinberg et al., 1982).

The REM latency is shorter in primary depressives than in nondepressed patients with insomnia (Gillin et al., 1979). The REM latency has been found to be shorter in primary depression compared to secondary depression (Kupfer, 1976a; Kupfer et al., 1978b) and shorter in endogenous than nonendogenous depression (Rush et al., 1982; Feinberg et al., 1982), but these findings are not universal (Berger et al., 1982). REM latency and other REM variables are also promising markers that may discriminate between primary depression and dementia (Reynolds et al., 1983a). Among depressives, the REM latency is shorter in the more severely depressed (Kupfer et al., 1976; Coble et al., 1981) and in those with psychotic depression (Coble et al., 1981).

REM latency increases during treatment with antidepressants (Kupfer et al., 1976, 1981a, 1982b; Gillin et al., 1978). Patients who respond well to antidepressant medication show a significantly greater lengthening of the REM latency and greater decreases in phasic and tonic REM than nonresponding patients after two nights of drug treatment (Kupfer et al., 1976, 1981b; Gillin et al., 1978).

There is evidence that the distribution of REM events is altered in affective disorder. Normally, the first REM period is the shortest and has the lowest density of phasic REM activity. There is a progressive increase in the duration and density over the first four or five successive REM periods (Verdone, 1968; Aserinsky, 1969; Benoit et al., 1974; Feinberg, 1974). In affective disorder, the first REM period is often longer than normal and often has a high REM density (Kupfer et al., 1978; Foster et al., 1976; Duncan et al., 1979; Kupfer, 1982; Kupfer et al., 1982a). REM sleep variables appear to change with age. REM latency decreases with age (Kupfer, 1976; Gillin et al., 1981). The percentage of REM sleep during the first half of the night increases with age (Hayashi and Endo, 1982). In spite of the influence of age on REM latency, REM latency is shorter in depressed patients than age-matched controls (Gillin et al., 1981). A study of REM distribution in affective disorder shows that the percent REM during the first third of the night is significantly greater than would be expected from adults of a similar age (Hayashi and Endo, 1982).

The REM sleep findings in affective disorder can be conceptualized as a phase advance of the circadian rhythm of REM sleep relative to sleep onset. REM sleep has a well-documented circadian rhythm with a tendency to occur between 4:00 AM and 12 noon (Webb and Agnew, 1977; Hume and Mills, 1977). In a time-cue-free environment, the REM latency shortens and the amount of REM during the first 3 hours of sleep increases, strongly suggesting a phase advance of REM sleep (Czeisler, 1978; Czeisler et al., 1980a,b; Zulley, 1979, 1980). In some subjects, the REM circadian rhythm period becomes different from the period of the sleep–wake cycle.

The REM sleep findings in affective disorder can also be conceptualized in noncircadian terms as a result of altered non-REM sleep. There is reciprocal inhibition occurring between REM and non-REM sleep. If non-REM sleep is deficient or inadequate, the REM findings could be explained. Zung (1969) postulated that "overarousal" might account for the findings. Kupfer and Foster (1978) have noted that the reduced slow-wave sleep in depression might cause the short REM latency. Vogel and colleagues (1980) have proposed an "extended sleep hypothesis" based on the similarity between sleep patterns in depressives and in normal controls after extended sleep. Borbély and Wirz-Justice (1982) have presented a more detailed noncircadian hypothesis based on Borbély's two-process model of sleep regulation (Borbély, 1982). They hypothesize that the sleep-dependent process (Process S) is deficient in depression. Support for these noncircadian hypotheses comes from a napping study of depressives (Kupfer et al., 1981b). Depressives napping at 10:00 AM and 4:00 PM had short REM latencies, which were not significantly different from their 11:00 PM values. In addition, the sleep latencies in these naps were long compared to naps in normal controls, suggesting that the sleep onset process is impaired. Reynolds et al. (1983b), in comparing REM latencies in depressed patients and controls, found a significant difference between groups in the amount of time between the shutting of lights and the onset of non-REM sleep, but found no difference in the amount of time between the shutting of lights and the onset of the first REM period.

Although many sleep abnormalities have been found in affective disorder, the most consistent and specific finding appears to be an abnormal distribution of REM events during sleep. The first REM period occurs relatively soon after sleep onset, has a long duration, and often has a high density of phasic REM activity.

CIRCADIAN TEMPERATURE RHYTHM

The circadian rhythm of body temperature is the result of oscillations of heat production and heat loss mechanisms. The normal circadian temperature pattern is determined primarily by the rhythm of heat loss mechanisms (Aschoff and Heise, 1972; Marotte and Timbal, 1981). Aschoff and Heise (1972) estimate that about 75% of the range of oscillation in core temperature is accounted for by circadian variations in heat loss and only 25% by variation in heat production. The body temperature begins to decrease in the evening, associated with increased vasodilatation and a lowered sweating threshold, to a temperature minimum between 2:00 and 6:00 AM. The temperature rise to a high temperature plateau during the day is associated with increased vasoconstriction and a higher sweating threshold (Smith, 1969; Wenger et al., 1976). The circadian rhythm of temperature has traditionally been viewed as being controlled by a single "shifting set point"; however, recent evidence indicates that the temperature rhythm is determined by multiple oscillating systems (Moore-Ede and Sulzman, 1977). These oscillating systems may become desynchronized from one another and create changes in the normal temperature rhythm.

CIRCADIAN INTERRELATIONSHIP BETWEEN THERMOREGULATION AND REM SLEEP

The onset of sleep is usually preceded by a fall in body temperature (Geschickter et al., 1966). During the first half of sleep the temperature continues to fall, associated with increased heat loss, a relatively high percentage of stage 3–4 sleep, and a low percentage of REM sleep. During the second half of sleep, the temperature rises, associated with decreased heat loss, a low percentage of 3–4 sleep, and a high percentage of REM sleep.

The general temporal association between REM and the rising body temperature is not merely a consequence of their common relationship to the sleep–wake cycle, but rather there is a close interrelationship between the two processes. In a study of the rhesus monkey, Crowley and colleagues (1971) found a significant correlation between the REM acrophase and the brain temperature nadir, the temperature nadir preceding the REM acrophase by only 1 hour. When the sleep–wake cycle is broken up by a series of 1-hour naps, occurring every 4 hours, the amount of REM has a significant negative correlation with the body temperature (Moses et al., 1975).

In a time-cue-free environment, core temperature and REM sleep both show a phase advance with respect to sleep onset (Czeisler, 1978; Czeisler et al., 1980a, 1980b; Zulley, 1979, 1980). Subjects studied in time-cue-free environments have shown a short REM latency, increased REM during the first 3 hours of sleep, and a temperature minimum occurring soon after sleep onset. In some subjects, the periodicity of the sleep–wake cycle became different from the REM periodicity. Even under these circumstances, increased REM in the first 3 hours of sleep was associated with the lowest temperatures (Czeisler, 1978a; Czeisler et al., 1980b; Zulley, 1979, 1980). Together, these studies indicate a strong coupling of the circadian rhythm of the REM events and the temperature rise that follows the temperature minimum.

INTERRELATIONSHIPS BETWEEN THERMOREGULATION AND INDIVIDUAL REM PERIODS

Other evidence for the close relationship between REM sleep and thermoregulation comes from studies focusing on physiologic changes during individual REM periods. Mammals become essentially poikilothermic during REM: the primary heat loss and heat production mechanisms are practically unresponsive to changes in environmental temperature or to heating or cooling of the preoptic nucleus (Parmeggiani, 1977; Henane et al., 1979). Studies of metabolic heat production rates in response to hypothalamic cooling show that thermosensitivity is greater during the waking state, less during non-REM sleep, and almost negligible during REM (Glotzbach and Heller, 1976). Minutes before and during REM, cold-induced shivering is suppressed in the cat (Parmeggiani et al., 1977). Even though *responsiveness* to thermal stress is almost absent during REM, under thermoneutral conditions, stage REM is usually associated with increasing body temperature (Parmeggiani, 1977; Henane et al., 1979).

In man, it is well-documented that sweating decreases during stage REM, whether the sweat rate is measured by electrodermal activity (Fujisawa, 1960; Hawkins et al., 1962; Broughton et al., 1965; Johnson and Lubin, 1966; McDonald et al., 1968; Koumans et al., 1968; Frexia et al., 1981; Gnirss and Schneider, 1975; Takagi, 1970) or by resistance hygrometer (Aschoff, 1972; Satoh et al., 1965; Ogawa et al., 1967). This suppression of sweating is even found at ambient temperatures of 35°

and 37° C (Shapiro et al., 1974). Stage 3–4 sleep is consistently associated with increased sweating (McDonald et al., 1968; Koumans et al., 1968).

At least three investigators have found correlations between phasic REM activity and peripheral vasoconstriction in man (Johnson and Karpan, 1968; Spreng et al., 1968; Khatri and Freis, 1967). During REM in the cat, there is a decrease in external iliac conductance and blood flow, and an associated increase in conductance and blood flow in the mesenteric, hypogastric, and renal arteries (Baccelli et al., 1974; Mancia et al., 1971). Thus, there appears to be a redistribution of blood flow away from the areas most capable of heat loss, the limbs, to an area with a low surface–mass ratio, the trunk.

Thus, heat retention through decreased sweating and peripheral vasoconstriction appears to be closely linked to stage REM. These thermoregulatory changes, together with the close temporal association of the REM acrophase to the temperature rise following the temperature minimum, point to the REM circadian rhythm as one of the major oscillating systems that determine body temperatures.

BRAIN TEMPERATURE CHANGES DURING REM SLEEP

Do the changes in thermoregulation occurring during REM have a significant influence on brain temperature? In most mammalian studies, paradoxical sleep is usually associated with increasing brain temperatures whereas temperature decreases are uncommon (Kawamura et al., 1966; Baker and Hayward, 1967; Satoh, 1968; Tachibana, 1969; Delgado and Hanai, 1966; Kovalzon, 1973).

How can the increase in brain temperature best be explained? The primary determinants of brain temperature are (1) the rate of cerebral blood flow, (2) the metabolic heat production of the brain itself, and (3) the temperature of the arterial blood.

It has consistently been found that the cerebral blood flow increases during REM (Townsend et al., 1973; Seylaz et al., 1971; Reivich et al., 1967; Meyer et al., 1979). Since the cerebral artery blood temperature is almost always cooler than the brain temperature, any brain temperature increase during REM occurs *despite* an increase in cerebral blood flow (Hayward and Baker, 1969). Furthermore, the increase in brain temperature during REM may precede the cerebral blood flow increase (Tachibana, 1969), so that it is unlikely that changes in cerebral blood flow cause the temperature increase during REM.

Heat production, as measured by total body oxygen consumption, has been found to be increased during REM in man (Brebbia and Altschuler, 1965) but not in the cat (Brebbia and Rechtschaffen, 1968). The possible role of increased neuronal activity in the brain temperature rise is not clear.

Some researchers have emphasized the importance of the cerebral artery temperature as the primary determinant of brain temperature changes (Baker and Hayward, 1967; Hayward and Baker, 1969; Horne, 1978). Increased aortic and cerebral artery temperatures and brain temperature precede the fast-wave activity and the hypotonia of REM sleep. Hayward and Baker (1969) conclude that the decreased heat loss through vasoconstriction leads to increased arterial and brain temperatures.

However, conflicting studies in the primate prevent an easy extrapolation of this model to man. Two investigations have found decreasing brain temperature during REM in primates (Hayward and Baker, 1969; Reite and Pegram, 1968), whereas other investigations have shown increases during REM (Hayward and Baker, 1968; Morishima and Gale, 1972).

The changes in the heat loss mechanisms and the cerebral artery temperature may precede stage REM itself, suggesting that the thermoregulatory changes may not simply be epiphenomena, but rather an integral part of the complex neurophysiologic events that precede the fast wave activity (Parmeggiani, 1977; Horne, 1978). In most mammals, the brain temperature increases associated with REM may be influenced by increased neuronal activity, but the major determinant is probably the cerebral temperature increase, which is closely related to the decreased peripheral heat loss mechanisms. If such a mechanism operates in man, the decreased sweating and increased vasoconstriction during REM should result in a cerebral artery temperature increase and a subsequent increase in brain temperature. A more conservative prediction is that during REM sleep a decrease in brain temperature is unlikely and that the brain temperature either rises or remains the same.

Ear canal temperature changes correlate well with tympanic membrane temperature (Cooper et al., 1964). Tympanic membrane temperature correlates well with esophageal and hypothalamic temperatures (Rawson and Hammel, 1963; Baker et al., 1972; Benzinger, 1969). The primary determinant of both tympanic membrane and hypothalamic temperatures is the temperature of the arterial blood (Baker et al., 1972). Carotid artery temperature change is a major determinant of the brain temperature changes associated with REM. Thus, ear canal temperature might be considered an index of brain temperature changes associated with REM.

EFFECTS OF TEMPERATURE ON REM SLEEP

The effects of REM-associated events on body temperature have been emphasized; however, temperature changes may have significant effects on stage REM.

Appropriate thermoregulation and normal sleep architecture, particularly the poikilothermic REM state, may at times become incompatible. Heller and Glotzbach (1977) and Parmeggiani (1977) have hypothesized that if the temperature conditions are not appropriate, better thermoregulatory states, non-REM sleep, or the waking state (the best) will occur rather than REM. In other words, the ratio of non-REM to REM and the ratio of waking to sleep will increase in situations in which precise thermoregulation is required.

Low or extremely high ambient temperatures will decrease the amount of REM in animals (Parmeggiani and Rabini, 1970; Schmidek et al., 1972) and in man (Beck et al., 1976; Buguet et al., 1979; Schmidt-Kessen and Kendel, 1973; Karacan et al., 1976, 1978). Increasing the body temperature by inducing fever will reduce REM sleep (Karacan et al., 1968).

The hypothalamic temperature may influence REM. The occurrence of REM is related to a narrow range of hypothalamic temperature—a temperature "gate" (Parmeggiani et al., 1975). Once an animal is in stage REM, warming the hypothalamus increases the duration of the REM period (Parmeggiani et al., 1974). The occurrence of REM may be increased by experimental manipulation of the hypothalamic and ambient temperatures. Heller and Glotzbach (1977) conclude that the stages of sleep and wakefulness are dependent not only on hypothalamic temperature but also on the interrelationship between the hypothalamic temperature and the peripheral temperature. If the relationship of these temperatures indicates a thermal error, a more appropriate thermoregulatory state, such as waking or non-REM sleep, is favored over a state such as REM, in which active thermoregulatory responsiveness is suspended.

Conversely, if the relationship between hypothalamic temperature and peripheral temperature indicates a trend towards thermoneutrality, the occurrence of REM sleep may be favored.

Brief skin temperature changes toward thermoneutrality may trigger REM sleep in rats (Szymusiak et al., 1980). Rats that were placed in a cool environment (23°C) were more likely to enter REM sleep when their skin was warmed during slow-wave sleep than were rats in a control group that did not have their skin warmed. Conversely, rats in a warm environment (34°C) were more likely to enter REM sleep if their skin temperature was cooled during slow-wave sleep than were rats in a control group. In addition, in both circumstances the REM latency was shortened by skin temperature changes toward thermoneutrality.

Thus, there is evidence for a strong interaction between thermoregulation and REM sleep. The REM-associated vasoconstriction and decreased sweating usually result in increasing body temperatures. On the other hand, thermal conditions in the body and in the environment may favor or prevent the occurrence of REM.

HYPOTHESES

The REM findings in affective disorder suggest at least four hypothesized types of altered thermoregulation in affective disorder.

Hypothesis I: "Phase Advance"

A phase advance (early timing) of REM events is suggested by the short REM latency and the long duration and high REM density of the first REM period in patients with depression. If there is a phase advance of REM events, one would hypothesize the temperature minimum would occur closer to sleep onset in patients with affective disorders (Figure 4.1, Hypothesis I).

Hypothesis II: "High Nocturnal Temperature"

Because heat retention processes are linked with REM events, and body temperature usually does not drop during stage REM, one would also predict that the normal temperature decrease during the first part of sleep would be blunted and that the body and brain temperature during sleep would be high (Figure 4.1, Hypothesis II).

This type of temperature pattern is also consistent with the de-

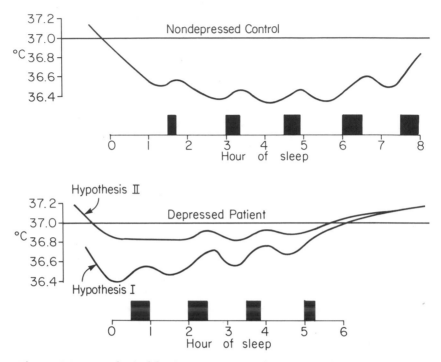

Figure 4.1. Hypothetical brain temperature changes in relationship to REM sleep.

creased stage 3–4 seen in affective disorder and Zung's "overarousal" hypothesis (Zung, 1969) referred to above. A low 24-hour temperature amplitude is another prediction that would be consistent with this hypothesis.

Hypothesis III: "REM and Temperature Rhythm Desynchrony"

A third hypothesis is that the REM circadian rhythm is uncoupled from the temperature circadian rhythm in affective disorder. As noted above, even in napping studies and in time-cue-free environments, these processes remain coupled. If the temperature acrophase were normal in depression while REM sleep were clearly phase advanced, the REM–temperature uncoupling hypothesis would be supported. More rigorous support for the hypothesis would come from demonstration of uncoupling of the two rhythms in depressed patients in a time-cue-free environment or in napping studies.

Hypothesis IV: "Drift Towards Thermoneutrality"

A fourth hypothesis, a "drift towards thermoneutrality" hypothesis, is also possible. As noted above, REM sleep is favored when the body appears to be moving towards a thermoneutral temperature, such as when the skin temperature is warmed in a cool environment or the skin temperature is cooled briefly in a warm environment (Szymusiak et al., 1980). Thus, a short REM latency may occur in affective disorder if the individual prior to sleep onset had a body temperature that was relatively distant from the temperature set point.

For example, depressed individuals may have a body temperature that is much higher than the temperature set point at sleep onset. Depressed individuals are known to have a high EMG activity (Lader, 1975), low forearm blood flow (Lader, 1975), and low sweat rate (Ward et al., 1983). EMG activity generates heat. Decreased forearm blood flow and decreased sweat rate both favor heat conservation. Together these findings suggest that individuals with depression should have a relatively high body temperature. Sleep onset itself, apart from the regulated circadian temperature rhythm, is associated with a decrease in body temperature (Zulley and Wever, 1982). With sleep onset, EMG activity decreases, sweating increases, peripheral vasodilatation occurs, and sweating increases. The decreased heat production and increased heat loss associated with sleep onset may allow the depressed person's temperature to "drift" towards the temperature set point without any active thermoregulation. This drift towards thermoneutrality may favor the onset of REM sleep.

In contrast, the nondepressed person just before sleep onset has a body temperature at the temperature set point. The temperature changes associated with sleep onset move the body temperature away from the temperature set point and create a state in which active thermoregulation is required, a state that does not favor the onset of REM sleep.

Hypothesis IV may be difficult to precisely test because of the difficulty in determining the "temperature set point." However, a high nocturnal temperature just prior to sleep onset would be consistent with this hypothesis.

TEMPERATURE RHYTHMS
IN DEPRESSION

Some *individuals* with depression demonstrate temperature findings consistent with the phase-advance hypothesis of depression (Wehr et al., 1983; Kripke et al., 1978; Pflug et al., 1976; 1981; Kramer and Katz, 1978). During the depression, the acrophase of the temperature rhythm is earlier than during recovery or earlier than the expected acrophase range for nondepressed controls. However, when a depressed *group* is compared with a nondepressed control *group*, the results are not consistent.

Kripke et al. (1979) compared 12 bipolar depressives and 5 unipolar depressives with 4 nondepressed controls and found no differences in oral temperature acrophase, amplitude of temperature rhythm, or mean temperature. Although the subjects were studied for at least 48 consecutive hours, only four to six oral temperature recordings per day were obtained. Temperature measurement during sleep was not systematically done. Many of the patients were taking psychotropic medications. Thus, these results are difficult to interpret.

Wehr et al. (1980) studied 10 bipolar depressives and 14 drug-free nondepressed controls, obtaining oral temperature every 3 hours during a 48-hour period (Figure 4.2). The study was especially well-controlled with regard to diet and environment. They found that the temperature maximum of the depressed group occurred 3–6 hours before that of the control group, but found no differences in the time of occurrence of the temperature minimum. The acrophase from the cosinor analysis of the depressed group was 1.4 hours earlier (NS) than in the control group. The temperature levels were higher in the depressed group at 7:00 AM, 4:00 PM, and 7:00 PM. When the data were reanalyzed, calculating the temperatures relative to the 24-hour mean, the depressed group had a significantly ($p < 0.001$) lower 1:00 PM temperature and significantly ($p < 0.05$) higher 7:00 AM temperature, a pattern consistent with a phase advance (Figure 4.2). However, the control group was significantly younger (21 years) than the depressed group (40 years), and age may be an important variable in studies of circadian rhythms. In one study (Avery et al., 1982a), a nonsignificant trend was found toward older control subjects having an earlier acrophase and an earlier temperature minimum. The acrophase in the control group (mean age 52) of the present study, 14:58, is earlier than reported values of younger control groups (Mellette et al., 1951; Winget et al., 1977). One study found an earlier minimum in older controls compared with young controls (Zepelin and McDonald, 1980); another study found no differ-

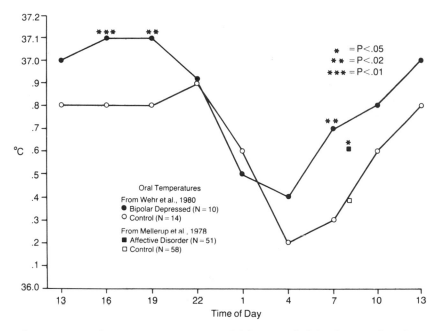

Figure 4.2. Oral temperatures across a 24-hour period in depressed patients and controls. (From Wehr et al, 1980.) Two data points from a similar study by Mellerup et al. (1978) have been added.

ence (Smallwood et al., 1985). Two studies found that older subjects had higher nocturnal temperatures than younger subjects (Smallwood et al., 1985; Weitzman et al., 1982); another study found the reverse (Zepelin and McDonald, 1980). When temperature rhythms of young and old subjects are studied in time-cue-free environments, the changes in the amplitude, level, and period of the temperature rhythm are found to be age related (Weitzman et al., 1982).

In a study by Avery and colleagues (1982a), high nocturnal rectal temperatures, high nocturnal ear canal temperatures (Avery, 1986), and low amplitude were found in depressed subjects compared with controls. No evidence was found for a phase advance for the depressed group.

The high nocturnal temperatures found in this study could not be explained by room temperature, the temperature of the beds' microclimate, age, sex, time of year, of psychoactive drugs (Avery et al., 1982a). Possible methodologic problems exist, however. In the study by Avery and colleagues (1982a), the rectal temperature was recorded continuously throughout the night, but daytime samples were taken only every 3 hours. In addition, some subjects were studied for only one 24-hour period. Of the 11 women in the study, 7 were postmenopausal—6 in the control group and only 1 in the depressed group. One unanswered question is whether postmenopausal women have different body temperatures compared to menstruating women (Avery et al., 1982a).

Some patients in the study by Avery and colleagues (1982a) demonstrated temperature minima and REM latencies that are consistent with the phase-advance hypothesis (Avery et al., 1982b); however, for the group as a whole there was no significant difference in acrophase. In addition, the temperature during the first 3 hours of sleep in the depressives was not low, as predicted by the phase-advance hypothesis, but high. There was only a nonsignificant trend ($p = 0.10$) for the temperature minimum to be later in the recovered state relative to the depressed state. When the temperature cycle is phase advanced relative to sleep onset in a time-cue-free environment, the amplitude of the temperature rhythm is reduced (Weitzman et al., 1982). It may be that the reduced amplitude seen in the depressives in the present study reflects such a shift.

Lund et al. (1983a) studied seven drug-free depressed patients intensively over a period of 8–21 days during the depression and for 14 days during remission. Nondepressed controls were studied over a 10–17-day period. Rectal temperatures were taken every 3 hours while the subjects were awake and then continuously during sleep. Although two of the seven depressed subjects appeared to have earlier temperature minima during depression than following recovery, there were no acrophase differences for the depressed group as a whole compared to their acrophases when recovered or compared to nondepressed controls.

Thus, in three of the four studies studying temperature rhythm in depression no strong evidence was found for a phase advance; the fourth found only suggestive evidence in bipolar depressives. Are there other explanations besides the above-mentioned methodologic problems to explain the lack of clear evidence for a phase advance of the temperature cycle?

1. Longer sampling periods may be necessary to demonstrate a phase advance. From the studies by Pflug et al. (1976, 1981), it is clear that during depression there is significant variability of the acrophase, with some days showing a phase advance and other days showing a normal acrophase.

2. A phase advance of the temperature oscillator may be "masked" by the sleep–wake cycle itself; sleep onset itself has a significant effect on body temperature (Zulley and Wever, 1982). It may be that the endogenous temperature oscillator is phase advanced relative to sleep onset in depression, but that the temperature drop associated with sleep onset makes the greater contribution to the cosinor analysis in the determination of the bathyphase. The hypothesis that the endogenous temperature rhythm in depression is phase advanced could be better tested in depressed patients and controls who are sleep deprived.

3. A phase advance of the temperature rhythm relative to sleep onset may be found only in some depressed patients and may simply not be characteristic for depressed patients as a group.

The high nocturnal temperature predicted by Hypothesis II was found by several investigators. Although Wehr and colleagues (1980) did not find an overall high nocturnal temperature, the 7:00 AM temperature in their depressed group was significantly higher than in the control group. In the study by Beersma et al. (1983), a control group was not used; however, in their 11 drug-free depressed patients, the nocturnal temperatures averaged well above 37.1°C for the entire group. Two studies by Avery et al. (1982a, unpublished data) and one study by Lund (1983b) show significantly increased nocturnal temperatures in drug-free depressed subjects compared with controls. In another study, Lund et al. (1983a) found that the nocturnal temperature was significantly higher during depression than following recovery in five of seven patients. In addition, Mellerup et al. (1978) found an elevated 7:00 AM temperature in depressed patients.

It could be argued that the high nocturnal temperatures in the Avery study were simply secondary to poor sleep in the depressed group. However, the rectal temperature was higher in the depressed group even at sleep onset. This finding is consistent with Hypothesis IV.

CORRELATIONS BETWEEN REM LATENCY AND TEMPERATURE RHYTHM

Only a few studies have simultaneously measured REM latency and the temperature rhythm. Schulz and colleagues published a case report of a patient with a short REM latency and early temperature minimum who experienced a lengthening of the REM latency and a phase delay of the temperature minimum associated with onset of treatment (Schulz et al., 1978).

Wehr studied five endogenous depressives who had short REM latencies and found that they also had early temperature minima. Three were restudied after recovery and found to have a phase delay of both temperature and REM sleep (Wehr et al., 1983).

Schultz and Lund (1983) studied REM latency and temperature rhythms in 15 endogenous depressive subjects and 10 control subjects over a 2–3-week period. Subjects who had at least one sleep-onset REM episode (a REM latency less than 20 minutes) during the study had a significantly smaller daytime–nighttime body temperature difference than did subjects without sleep-onset REM.

Data from a study by Avery et al. (1986) shed some light on the relationships between the REM latency and temperature rhythm variables. When all subjects were considered, the REM latency had a significant correlation with nocturnal temperature level and temperature amplitude but not with temperature rhythm. There were, in general, no significant correlations when 15 control patients were considered alone. It is possible that the range of the REM latencies and nocturnal temperature variables were not great enough to yield significant correlations. There did not appear to be any temperature variable, with the possible exception of nocturnal ear canal temperature, which was significantly ($p < 0.05$) correlated with REM latency within the control group.

However, within the depressed group alone there appeared to be significant correlations between mean nocturnal temperature and REM latency. Significant correlations become common only when the groups are considered as a whole. One might interpret these data as indicating that the association between REM latency and temperature variables is only secondary to their common relationship with depression. One might also interpret this finding to mean that by combining the two groups the range in the REM latency is great enough to yield a significant result. Nonetheless, it is notable that REM latency was significantly correlated with nocturnal temperature level and nocturnal temperature amplitude in the hypothesized directions.

No studies have as yet adequately tested Hypothesis III, which predicts uncoupling of the REM and temperature rhythms. Although the Avery study (1986) found no correlation between REM latency and the temperature acrophase, masking of the endogenous temperature rhythm by sleep might account for the lack of correlation.

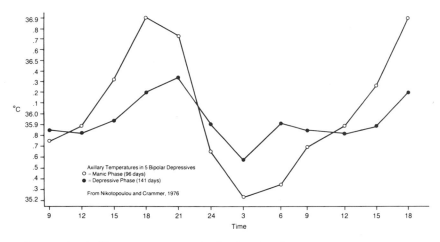

Figure 4.3. Axillary temperatures in five bipolar depressives during the manic phase and during the depressive phase. (From Nikitopoulou and Crammer, 1976.)

Other temperature rhythm abnormalities not necessarily predicted by the REM sleep findings have been observed in depression. For example, Kripke (1978) was able to document altered circadian periodicity in a rapidly cycling bipolar patient; the patient's temperature acrophase moved counterclockwise on subsequent days. When this patient was depressed, the acrophase was at about 5:00 PM. When this patient was manic, the acrophase was at about 11:00 PM.

Others have documented 8- and 12-hour components in addition to the 24-hour one. Nikitopoulou and Crammer (1976) found that bipolar depressives displayed a significant 12-hour component (Figure 4.3). Pflug et al. (1983) found a shift in the 8- and 12-hour components in outpatients associated with their depression.

None of the four hypotheses clearly explains all the temperature abnormalities found in depressed patients. Diagnostic heterogeneity, masking of the temperature rhythm, and day-to-day alterations in the temperature rhythm are variables that should be taken into account in future studies. It does appear, however, that temperature rhythm abnormalities in depression are common. Phenomenologic support for the frequency of thermoregulatory abnormalities in depression comes from a study of depressed outpatients and nondepressed patients with insomnia (Avery et al., 1984). Patients in each group who experienced early morning awakening were asked about temperature comfort at night and during the daytime and about the presence of night sweats. Depressed subjects experienced significantly more night sweats (51% vs. 10%, $p < 0.001$), nocturnal temperature warmth (59% vs. 31%, $p < 0.05$), and daytime temperature coolness (80% vs. 28%, $p < 0.001$). These were symptoms the depressed patients denied having prior to the depressive episode.

NEUROTRANSMITTERS IN REM SLEEP AND THERMOREGULATION

The close relationship between temperature and REM sleep raises the question of common abnormalities in neurotransmitter function. Just prior to the onset of REM there is a decrease in the firing rate of the noradrenergic locus coeruleus and a concomitant increase in the firing rate in the cholinergic FTG (pontine gigantocellular tegment field) neurons (McCarley, 1982).

Effects of adrenergic and cholinergic drugs on paradoxical sleep have also been studied. α-Adrenergic agents may suppress REM whereas α-adrenergic blocking agents may reverse this effect (Autret et al., 1977; Putkonen, 1978). Cholinergic agents shorten the REM latency, whereas anticholinergic agents lengthen it (Sitaram et al., 1975, 1979). Increased sensitivity to arecholine-induced REM induction has been found in drug-free recovered depressed patients and has been proposed as a possible trait marker (Sitaram et al., 1980).

Neurotransmitters in the hypothalamus play a major role in thermoregulation. Administration of norepinephrine to the anterior hypothalamus of the monkey results in a hypothermic response; acetylcholine elicits a hyperthermic response (Myers, 1976). Perfusion studies of the hypothalamus of the monkey show that norepinephrine is increased when the ambient temperature is raised; acetylcholine is increased when the ambient temperature is lowered (Myers and Chinn, 1973; Myers and Waller, 1973).

A short REM latency and high nocturnal temperatures might then be expected to result from increased cholinergic activity and/or decreased noradrenergic activity. On the basis of different evidence, an increased ratio of cholinergic activity to adrenergic activity has been hypothesized to be associated with affective disorder (Janowsky et al., 1972). This neurotransmitter hypothesis does not necessarily exclude the phase-advance hypothesis; the neurotransmitters and their receptors may have circadian rhythms (Wirz-Justice et al., 1980; Perry et al., 1977). Wehr et al. (1980) found a phase advance of the circadian rhythms of urinary

MHPG in bipolar depressives and Giedke et al. (1982) found a tendency for the maximum MHPG urinary excretion to occur earlier in the day in depressives.

Thus, both REM latency and high nocturnal temperature are not only associated with primary depression but also are physiologic findings consistent with an increased ratio of cholinergic activity to adrenergic activity.

SUMMARY

Thermoregulation and REM sleep are circadian processes that have a close but complex relationship. Increasing brain and body temperatures following the temperature minimum are associated with the occurrence of REM events. Each REM period is associated with suppression of heat loss mechanisms and rising brain and body temperatures. Abnormalities in REM sleep in affective disorder lead to several hypotheses concerning possible temperature rhythm abnormalities. A high nocturnal temperature and low 24-hour amplitude are common findings. Some individual patients have phase-advanced temperature rhythms. Although no single hypothesis explains all the data, it does appear that abnormal temperature rhythms are common in affective disorder.

REFERENCES

Aschoff J, Heise A (1972): Thermal conductance in man: Its dependence on time of day and on ambient temperature. In Itoh S, Ogata K, Yoshimura H (eds): Advances in Climatic Physiology. New York, Springer-Verlag.

Aserinsky E (1969): The maximal capacity for sleep: Rapid eye movement density as an index of sleep satiety. Biol Psychiatry 1:147–159.

Autret A, Minz M, Beillevaire T, et al (1977): Effect of clonidine on sleep patterns in man. Eur. J Clin Pharmacol 12:319–322.

Avery DH, Wildschiødtz G, Rafaelsen OJ (1982a): Nocturnal temperature in affective disorder. J Affective Disord 4:61–71.

Avery DH, Wildschiødtz G, Rafaelsen O (1982b): REM latency and temperature in affective disorder before and after treatment. Biol Psychiatry 17:451–457.

Avery DH, Dunner DL, Ishiki DM (1984): Nocturnal temperature discomfort and night sweats in primary depression and insomnia. Sleep Res 13:33.

Avery DH, Wildschiøodtz G, Smallwood RG, et al (1986): REM latency and core temperature relationships in primary depression. Acta Psychiatr Scand 74:269–280.

Baccelli G, Albertini R, Mancia G, Zanchetti A (1974): Central and reflex regulation of sympathetic vasoconstrictor activity to limb muscles during desynchronized sleep in the cat. Circ Res 35:625–635.

Baker MA, Hayward JN (1967): Autonomic basis for the rise in brain temperature during paradoxical sleep. Science 157:1586–1588.

Baker MA, Stocking RA, Meehan JP (1972): Thermal relationship between tympanic membrane and hypothalamus in conscious cat and monkey. J Appl Physiol 32:739–742.

Beersma DGM, van den Hoofdakker RH, van Berkestijn HWBM (1983): Circadian rhythms in affective disorders: Body temperature and sleep physiology in endogenous depressives. In Mendlewicz J, van Praag HM (eds): *Advances in Biological Psychiatry* Vol 11, pp 114–127, New York, Karger.

Beck U, Reinhard H, Kendel K, Schmidt-Kessen W (1976): Temperature and endocrine activity during sleep in man. Arch Psychiatr Nervenkr 232:245–256.

Benoit O, Parot S, Garma L (1974): Evolution during the night of REM sleep in man. EEG Clin Neurophysiol 36:245–251.

Benzinger TH (1969): Heat regulation: Homeostasis of central temperature in man. Physiol Rev 49:671–759.

Berger M, Doerr P, Lung R, Bronisch T, von Zerssen D (1982): Neuroendocrinological and neurophysiological studies in major depressive disorders: Are there biological markers for the endogenous subtypes? Biol Psychiatry 17:1217–1242.

Borbély AA (1982): A two process model of sleep regulation. Hum Neurobiol 1:195–204.

Borbély, AA, Wirz-Justice A (1982): Sleep, sleep deprivation, and depression. Hum Neurobiol 1:205–210.

Brebbia DR, Altschuler K (1965): Oxygen consumption rate and electroencephalographic stage of sleep. Science 150:1621–1623.

Brebbia DR, Rechtschaffen A (1968): Oxygen consumption rate during sleep in cats. Psychophysiology 5:245.

Broughton RJ, Poire R, Tassinari CA (1965): The electrodermogram (Tarchanoff effect) during sleep. Elektroencephal Clin Neurophysiol 18:691–708.

Buguet AGC, Roussel BHE, Watson WH, Radomski MW (1979): Cold-induced diminution of paradoxical sleep in man. EEG Clin Neurophysiol 46:29–32.

Coble PA, Kupfer DJ, Shaw DR (1981): Distribution of REM latency in depression. Biol Psychiatry 16:453–466.

Cooper KE, Cranston WI, Snell ES (1964): Temperature in the external auditory meatus as an index of central temperature changes. J Appl Physiol 32:739–742.

Crowley TJ, Halberg F, Kripke DF, Pegram GV (1971): Individual variation in circadian rhythms of sleep, EEG, temperature, and activity among monkeys: Implications for regulatory mechanisms. Biochronometry. Washington D.C., National Academy of Sciences.

Czeisler C (1978): Human circadian physiology: Internal organization of temperature sleep–wake, and neuroendocrine rhythms monitored in an environment free of time cues. Ph.D. dissertation, Stanford University.

Czeisler CA, Zimmerman JC, Ronda JM, et al (1980a): Timing of REM sleep is coupled to the circadian rhythm of body temperature in man. Sleep 2:329–346.

Czeisler CA, Weitzman ED, Moor-Ede MC, Zimmerman JC, Knauer RS (1980b): Human sleep: Its duration and organization depend on its circadian phase. Science 210:1264–1267.

Delgado JMR, Hanai T (1966): Intracerebral temperatures in free-moving cats. Am J Physiol 211:755–769.

Duncan WC, Pettigrew KD, Gillin JC (1979): REM architecture changes in bipolar and unipolar depression. Am J Psychiatry 136:1424–1427.

Feinberg I (1974): Changes in sleep cycle patterns with age. J Psychiatr Res 10:283–306.

Feinberg M, Gillin JC, Carroll BJ, Greden JF, Zis AP (1982): EEG studies in sleep in the diagnosis of depression. Biol Psychiatry 17:305–316.

Foster RG, Kupfer DJ, Coble P, McPartland RJ (1976): Rapid eye movement sleep density. Arch Gen Psychiatry 33:1119–1123.

Frexia i Baque E, Chevalier B, Grubar JC (1981): Spontaneous electrodermal activity during sleep in man: An intranight study. Sleep 6:77–81.

Fujisawa K (1960): The psychophysiological studies of sleep. Jpn Psychol Res 2:120–134.

Geschickter EH, Andrews PA, Bullard RW (1966): Nocturnal body temperature regulation in man: A rationale for sweating in sleep. J Appl Physiol 21:623–630.

Giedke H, Gaertner J, Mahal A (1982): Diurnal variation of urinary MHPG in unipolar depressives. Acta Psychiatr Scand 66:243–253.

Gillin JC, Wyatt PJ, Fram D, Snyder F (1978): The relationship between changes in REM sleep and clinical improvement in depressed patients treated with amitriptyline. Psychopharmacology 59:267–272.

Gillin JC, Duncan W, Pettigrew KD, et al (1979): Successful separation of depressed, normal, and insomniac subjects by EEG sleep data. Arch Gen Psychiatry 36:85–90.

Gillin JC, Duncan WC, Murphy DL, et al (1981): Age-related changes in sleep in depressed and normal subjects. Psychiatry Res 4:73–78.

Glotzbach SF, Heller HC (1976): Central nervous regulation of body temperature during sleep. Science 194:537–539.

Gnirss F, Schneider D (1975): Patterns of spontaneous autonomic activities during human NREM sleep. In Levin P, Koella WP (eds): Sleep 1974, Basel, Karger, pp. 352–355.

Hawkins DR, Puryear HB, Wallace CD, et al (1962): Basal skin resistance during sleep and "dreaming." Science 136:321–322.

Hayashi Y, Endo S (1982): All-night sleep polygraphic recordings of healthy aged persons: REM and slow-wave sleep. Sleep 5:277–283.

Hayward JN, Baker MA (1968): Role of cerebral arterial blood in the regulation of brain temperature in the monkey. Am J Physiol 215:389–403.

Hayward JN, Baker MA (1969): A comparative study of the role of the cerebral arterial blood in the regulation of brain temperature in five mammals. Brain Res 16:417–440.

Heller HC, Glotzbach SF (1977): Thermoregulation during sleep and hibernation. In Robertshaw D (ed): International Review of Physiology, Environmental Physiology II. Baltimore, University Park Press, Vol 15, pp 148–187.

Henane R, Buguet A, Bittel J, Roussel D (1979): Thermal rhythms and sleep in man: Approach to thermal comfort during sleep. Thermal Comfort Physiological and Psychological Bases. INSERM Symposia Series, Vol 75. Paris, Institut National de la Sante et de la Recherche Medicale.

Horne JA (1978): Dreaming sleep in man: A reappraisal. Perspect Biol Med 21(4):591–601.

Hume KI, Mills NJ (1977): Rhythms of REM and slow-wave sleep in subjects living on abnormal time schedules. Waking Sleeping 1:291–296.

Janowsky DS, El-Yousef MK, Davis JM, et al (1972): A cholinergic–adrenergic hypothesis of mania and depression. Lancet 2:632–635.

Johnson LC, Karpan WE (1968): Autonomic correlates of the spontaneous K-complex. Psychophysiology 4:444–452.

Johnson LC, Lubin A (1966): Spontaneous electrodermal activity during waking and sleeping. Psychophysiology 3:8–17.

Karacan I, Anch AM, Williams RL (1976): Recent advances in the psychophysiology of sleep and their psychiatric significance. In Grenell RG, Gabay S (eds): Biological Foundations of Psychiatry. New York, Raven, pp 440–497.

Karacan I, Thornby JI, Anch AM, Williams RL, Perkins HM (1978): Effects of high ambient temperature on sleep in young men. Aviat Space Environ Med 49:855–860.

Karacan I, Wolff SM, Webb WB, Williams RL (1968): The effects of fever on sleep patterns. Psychophysiology 5:255.

Kawamura H, Whitmoyer DI, Sawyer CH (1966): Temperature changes in the rabbit brain during paradoxical sleep. EEG Clin Neurophysiol 21:469–477.

Khatri IM, Freis ED (1967): Hemodynamic changes during sleep. J Appl Physiol 22:867–873.

Koumans AJr, Tursky B, Soloman P (1968): Electrodermal levels and fluctuations during normal sleep. Psychophysiology 5:300–306.

Kovalzon VM (1973): Brain temperature variations during natural sleep and arousal in white rat. Physiol Behav 10:667–670.

Kramer BA, Katz JL (1978): Circadian temperature variation and depressive illness. J Clin Psychiatry 39:439–444.

Kripke DF, Mullaney D, Atkinson M, et al (1979): Circadian rhythm phases in affective illnesses. Chronobiologia 6:365–375.

Kripke DF, Mullaney DJ, Atkinson M, Wolf S (1978): Circadian rhythm disorders in manic-depressives. Biol Psychiatry 13:335–351.

Kupfer DJ (1976): REM latency: A psychobiological marker for primary depressive disease. Biol Psychiatry 11:157–174.

Kupfer DJ (1978): Application of EEG sleep for the differential diagnosis and treatment of affective disorder. Pharmakopsychiatria 11:17–26.

Kupfer DJ (1982): EEG sleep as biological markers in depression. Biological Markers in Psychiatry and Neurology. London, Pergamon, pp 387–397.

Kupfer DJ, Foster FG (1972): Interval between onset of sleep and rapid-eye-movement as an indicator of depression. Lancet 2:684–686.

Kupfer DJ, Foster FG (1978): EEG and depression. In Williams RC, Karacan I (eds): Sleep Disorders. Diagnosis and Treatment. New York, Wiley, pp 163–164.

Kupfer DJ, Foster FG, Reich L, et al. (1976): EEG sleep changes as predictors in depression. Am J Psychiatry 133:622–626.

Kupfer DJ, Foster FG, Coble P, et al. (1978): The application of EEG sleep for the differential diagnosis of affective disorders. Am J Psychiatry 135:69–74.

Kupfer DJ, Gillin JC, Coble PA, et al (1981a): REM sleep, naps, and depression. Psychiatry Res 5:195–203.

Kupfer DJ, Spiker DG, Coble PA, et al. (1981b): Sleep and treatment prediction in endogenous depression. Am J Psychiatry 138:429–434.

Kupfer DJ, Shaw DH, Ulrich R, et al. (1982a): Application of automated REM analysis in depression. Arch Gen Psychiatry 39:569–573.

Kupfer DJ, Spiker DG, Rossi A, et al. (1982b): Nortriptyline and EEG sleep in depressed patients. Biol Psychiatry 17:535–546.

Lader M (1975): The Psychophysiology of Mental Illness. London, Routledge & Kegan.

Lund R, Kammerloher A, Dirlich G (1983a): Body temperature in endogenously depressed patients during depression and remission. In Wehr T, Goodwin FK (eds): Circadian Rhythms in Psychiatry, Pacific Groves, CA, Boxwood, pp 77–88.

Lund R, Schulz H, Berger M (1983b): REM sleep and body temperature in depressed patients during depression and remission and in control subjects. Presented at the 4th International Congress of Sleep Research, Bologna, Italy.

McCarley RW (1982): REM sleep and depression, common neurological mechanisms. Am J Psychiatry 139:565–570.

McDonald DG, Shallenberger HD, Carpenter FS (1968): Spontaneous autonomic responses during sleep and wakefulness. Psychophysiology 4:362–363.

Mancia G, Baccelli G, Adams DB, Zanchetti A (1971): Vasomotor regulation during sleep in the cat. Am J Physiol 220:1086–1093.

Marrotte H, Timbal J (1981): Circadian rhythms of temperature in man. Comparative study with two experiment protocols. Chronobiologia 8:87–99.

Mellerup ET, Widding A, Wildschiodtz G, Rafaelsen OJ (1978): Lithium effect on temperature rhythm in psychiatric patients. Acta Pharmacol Toxicol 42:125–129.

Mellette HC, Hutt BK, Askovitz SI, Horvath SM (1951): Diurnal variations in body temperatures. J Appl Physiol 3:665–675.

Mendels J, Chernik DA (1975): Sleep changes and affective disorder. In Flach FF, Draghi SC (eds): The Nature and Treatment of Depression. New York, Wiley.

Meyer JS, Sakai F, Karacan I, et al. (1979): Regional cerebral hemodynamics during normal and abnormal human sleep. Acta Neurol Scand Suppl 72(6).

Monroe LJ (1967): Psychological and physiological differences between good and poor sleepers. J Abnorm Psychol 72:255–264.

Moore-Ede MC, Sulzman FM (1977): The physiological basis of circadian timekeeping in primates. The Physiologist 20:17–25.

Morishima MS, Gale CC (1972): Relationship of blood pressure and heart rate to body temperature in baboons. Am J Physiol 223:387–395.

Moses JM, Hord DJ, Lubin A, et al (1975): Dynamics of nap sleep during a 40 hour period. EEG Clin Neurophysiol 39:627–633.

Myers RD (1976): Chemical control of body temperature by the hypothalamus: A model and some mysteries. Proc Aust Physiol Pharmacol Soc 15–32.

Myers RD, Chinn C (1973): Evoked release of hypothalamic norepinephrine during thermoregulation in the cat. Am J Physiol 224:230–236.

Myers RD, Waller MB (1973): Differential release of acetylcholine from the hypothalamus and mesencephalon of the monkey during thermoregulation. J Physiol 230:273–293.

Nikitopoulou G, Crammer JL (1976): Change in diurnal temperature rhythm in manic-depressive illness. Br Med J 1:1311–1314.

Ogawa T, Satoh T, Takagi K (1967): Sweating during night sleep. Jpn J Physiol 17:135.

Parmeggiani PL (1977): Interaction between sleep and thermoregulation. Waking Sleeping 1:123–132.

Parmeggiani PL, Rabini C (1970): Sleep and environmental temperature. Arch Ital Biologie 108:369–387.

Parmeggiani PL, Agnati LF, Zamboni G, Cianci T (1975): Hypothalamic temperature during the sleep cycle at different ambient temperatures. EEG Clin Neurophysiol 38:589–596.

Parmeggiani PL, Zamboni G, Cianci T, et al. (1974): Influence of anterior hypothalamic heating on the duration of fast wave sleep episode. EEG Clin Neurophysiol 36:465–470.

Parmeggiani PL, Zamboni G, Cianci T, Calasso M. (1977): Absence of thermoregulatory vasomotor responses during fast wave sleep in cats. EEG Clin Neurophysiol 42:372–380.

Perry EK, Perry RH, Tomlinson BE (1977): Circadian variations in cholinergic enzymes and muscarinic receptor binding in human cerebral cortex. Neurosci Lett 4:185–289.

Pflug B, Erikson R, Johnsson A (1976): Depression and daily temperature: a long term study. Acta Psychiatr Scand 54:254–266.

Pflug B, Johnsson A, Ekse AT (1981): Manic-depressive states and daily temperature. Some circadian studies. Acta Psychiatr Scand 63:277–289.

Pflug B, Johnsson A, Martin W (1983): Alterations in the circadian temperature rhythms in depressed patients. In Wehr TA, Goodwin FK (eds): Circadian Rhythms in Psychiatry. Pacific Grove, CA, Boxwood, pp 71–76.

Putkonen PTS (1978): Alpha- and beta-adrenergic mechanisms in the control of sleep stages. In Priest RG, Petscher A, Ward J (eds): Sleep Research. International Medical Publishers.

Rawson RO, Hammel HT (1963): Hypothalamic and tympanic membrane temperatures in rhesus monkey. Fed Proc Am Soc Exp Biol 22:283.

Reite ML, Pegram GV (1968): Cortical temperature during paradoxical sleep in the monkey. EEG Clin Neurophysiol 25:36–41.

Reivich M, Isaacs G, Evarts E, Kety SS (1967): Regional cerebral blood flow during REM and slow wave sleep. Trans Am Neurol Assoc 92:70–74.

Reynolds CF III, Spiker DG, Hanin I, Kupfer DJ (1983a): Electroencephalographic sleep, aging, and psychopathology: New data and the state of the art. Biol Psychiatry 18:139–155.

Reynolds CF III, Taska LS, Jarrett DB, et al. (1983b): REM latency in depression: Is there one best definition? Biol Psychiatry 18:849–863.

Rush A, Giles D, Roffwarg HP, Parker CR (1982): Sleep EEG and dexamethasone suppression test findings in outpatients with unipolar major depressive disorders. Biol Psychiatry 17:327–341.

Satoh T (1968): Brain temperature of the cat during sleep. Arch Ital Biol 106:73–82.

Satoh T, Ogawa T, Takagi K (1965): Sweating during daytime sleep. Jpn J Physiol 15:523–531.

Schmidek WR, Hoshino K, Schmidek M, Timo-iaria C (1972): Influence of environmental temperature on the sleep-wakefulness cycle in the rat. Physiol Behav 8:363–371.

Schmidt-Kessen W, Kendel K (1973): Einfluss der Raumtemperatur auf den Nachtschlaf. Res Exp Med 160:220–233.

Schultz H, Lund R (1983): Sleep onset REM episodes are associated with circadian parameters of body temperature. A study in depressed patients and normal controls. Biol Psychiatry 18:1411–1426.

Schultz H, Lund R, Doerr P (1978): The measurement of change in sleep during depression and remission. Arch Psychiatr Nervenkr 225:233–241.

Seylaz J, Mamo H, Goas JY, et al. (1971): Local cortical blood flow during paradoxical sleep in man. Arch Ital Biol 109:1–14.

Shapiro CM, Moore AT, Mitchel D, Yodaiken ML (1974): How well does man thermoregulate during sleep? Experientia 20:1279–1281.

Sitaram N, Moore A, Gillin JC (1975): Induction and resetting of REM sleep rhythm in normal man by arecoline: Blockade by scopolamine. Sleep 1:83–90.

Sitaram N, Moore AM, Gillin JC (1979): Scopolamine-induced super-sensitivity in normal man: Changes in sleep. Psychiatry Res 1:9–16.

Sitaram N, Nurnberger JI, Gershon ES, Gillin JC (1980): Faster cholinergic REM sleep induction in euthymic patients with primary affective illness. Science 208:200–202.

Smith RE (1969): Circadian variations in human thermoregulatory responses. J Appl Physiol 26:554–560.

Spreng LF, Johnson LC, Lubin A (1968): Autonomic correlates of eye movement bursts during REM sleep. Psychophysiology 4:311–323.

Szymusiak R, Satinoff E, Schallert T, Whishaw IQ (1980): Brief skin temperature changes towards thermoneutrality trigger REM sleep in rats. Physiol Behav 25:305–311.

Tachibana S (1969): Relation between hypothalamic heat production and intra- and extracranial circulatory factors. Brain Res 16:405–416.

Takagi K (1970): Sweating during sleep. In Hardy JD (ed): Physiological and Behavioral Temperature Regulation. pp 669–675. Springfield, Ill.: Thomas.

Townsend RE, Prinz PN, Obrist WD (1973): Human cerebral blood flow during sleep and waking. J Appl Physiol 35(5):620–625.

Verdone P (1968): Sleep satiation: Extended sleep in normal subjects. EEG Clin Neurophysiol 24:417–423.

Vitiello MV, Smallwood RG, Avery DH, et al. (1986): Circadian temperature rhythms in young adult males and elderly males. Neurobiol Aging 7:97–100.

Vogel GW, Vogel F, McAbee RS, Thurmond AJ (1980): Improvement of depression by REM sleep deprivation. Arch Gen Psychiatry 37:247–253.

Ward NG, Doerr HO, Storrie MC (1983): Skin conductance: A potentially sensitive test for depression. Psychiatry Res 10:295–302.

Webb WB, Agnew HW (1977): Analysis of the sleep stages in sleep–wakefulness regimens of varied length. Psychophysiology 14:445–450.

Wehr RA, Muscettola G, Goodwin FK (1980): Urinary MHPG circadian rhythm: Early timing (phase advance) in manic-depressives compared with normal subjects. Arch Gen Psychiatry 37:257–263.

Wehr TA, Gillin JC, Goodwin FK (1983): Sleep and circadian rhythms in depression. In Sleep Disorders: Basic and Clinical Research. Spectrum, pp 195–225.

Weitzman ED, Moline ML, Czeisler CA (1982): Chronobiology of aging: Temperature, sleep-wake rhythms and entrainment. Neurobiol Aging 3:299–309.

Wenger CB, Roberts MF, Stolwijk JAJ, Nadel ER (1976): Nocturnal lowering of thresholds for sweating and vasodilation. J Appl Physiol 41:15–19.

Wever R (1979): The Circadian System of Man: Results of Experiments Under Temporal Isolation. New York, Springer-Verlag.

Winget CM, DeRoshia CW, Vernikos-Danelis J, et al. (1977): Comparison of circadian rhythms in male and female humans. Waking Sleeping 1:359–163.

Wirz-Justice A, Kafka MS, Naber D, et al (1980): Circadian rhythms in rat brain alpha- and beta-adrenergic receptors are modified by chronic imipramine. Life Sci 27:341–347.

Zepelin H, McDonald CS (1980): Age and sex differences in physiological variables during sleep. Presented at the Association for the Psychophysiological Study of Sleep Meeting, Mexico City, June.

Zulley J (1979): Der Einfluss von Zeitgebern auf den Schlaf des Menschen. Frankfurt, A.M. Rita G. Fischer Verlag.

Zulley J (1980): Distribution of REM sleep in entrained 24 hour and free-funning sleep-wake cycles. Sleep 2:377–389.

Zulley J, Wever RA (1982): Interaction betwen the sleep–wake cycle and the rhythm of rectal temperature. In Aschoff J, Daan S, Groos G (eds): Vertebrate Circadian Systems, pp. 253–261. New York, Springer.

Zung W (1969): Effect of antidepressant drugs on sleeping and dreaming: III on the depressed patient. Biol Psychiatry 1:283–287.

5

Circadian Rhythms of Melatonin and Cortisol During Treatment with Desipramine in Depressed and Normal Subjects

C. Thompson, S.A. Checkley, and J. Arendt

Chronic antidepressant treatment leads to a number of physiologic and biochemical effects, including the downregulation of β-adrenergic and $5HT_2$ receptors. It has also been suggested that antidepressant drugs may alter the timing of circadian rhythms. Imipramine has been shown to modify the circadian rhythms of brain tryptophan and 5HT in rats (Martin and Redfern, 1982a,b). The circadian rhythms of a number of neuroreceptors have also been modified by imipramine. Wirz-Justice and colleagues (1980) showed a modification of the rhythms of α-and β-adrenergic receptors; Kafka and colleagues (1981) showed a modification of the rhythm of cholinergic receptors and Naber et al. (1980) showed a modification of the ultradian rhythm of dopamine receptors in the rat striatum. Clorgyline, a monoamine oxidase A inhibitor has also been reported to delay the phase position of neuroreceptor rhythms (Wirz-Justice et al., 1982) and locomotor activity rhythms in the hamster (Craig et al., 1981). Very little work has been carried out in humans, although tricyclic antidepressants can induce rapid cycling in manic-depressive patients, an effect that is assumed to be due to an alteration of circadian timekeeping (Wehr and Goodwin, 1979).

In addition to the studies of antidepressants, there is also a large body of literature on the circadian effects of lithium carbonate. Engelmann (1973) first showed a lengthening of the free-running period in a number of species on treatment with lithium, and this has been

followed with other evidence of slowing of behavioral rhythms (Hofmann et al., 1978; Kripke and Wyborney, 1980; McEachron et al.,
1981). Similar effects have also been found in acetylcholine, opiate, and
benzodiazepine receptor rhythms (Kafka et al., 1982) and in prolactin,
cortisol, parathyroid hormone, calcium, and magnesium rhythms
(McEachron et al., 1982; Strumwasser and Viele, 1980). In humans,
lithium delays the sleep rhythm under entrained conditions (Kripke et
al., 1979), and preliminary evidence suggests that it slows rhythms in
temporal isolation (Johnsson et al., 1980). However, the only study to
examine manic-depressive patients after chronic treatment failed to un-
cover any lithium effect on the rhythm of calcium, magnesium, or phosphate metabolism (Mellerup et al., 1976).

These findings have been integrated to suggest a single mechanism
of action of antidepressants. Based on this hypothesis, depression is
associated with abnormally early or phase-advanced circadian rhythms
(Wehr and Goodwin, 1981), which are normalized by the action of
antidepressants to lengthen the period and thus cause a phase delay
(Wehr and Wirz-Justice, 1982).

However, the clinical relevance of the studies described above is
uncertain, as they have largely been carried out in animals or normal
human volunteers. We have investigated the effects of desipramine in
depressed patients and in normal volunteers during 3 weeks of treatment
with desipramine at therapeutic doses. Two neuroendocrine markers—
melatonin and cortisol—were used to assess the effects of desipramine
upon the circadian system:

1. Melatonin has an endogenous circadian rhythm, with secretion
   occurring during the night hours (Lynch et al., 1975). There is
   strong evidence that this rhythm is driven by an oscillator in the
   suprachiasmatic nuclei of the hypothalamus (Klein and Moore,
   1979), which is in turn entrained to the light–dark cycle under
   normal conditions (Wurtman et al., 1963).

2. Cortisol also has a regular and reproducible circadian rhythm, with
   a peak at about 7:00 AM and a nadir at about 12:00 midnight. This
   rhythm also has an endogenous component and can be eliminated
   in the rat by ablation of the suprachiasmatic nucleus (Moore and
   Eichler, 1972). Thus, cortisol provides a marker of circadian
   activity.

The present study was designed to examine two other theories of
anti-depressant drug action as well. The norepinephrine uptake blockade theory predicts that nocturnal melatonin secretion will be increased

by desipramine because melatonin is released by norepinephrine acting upon a postsynaptic β-adrenergic receptor (Cowen et al., 1983).

An alternative theory of antidepressant action stems from the finding that chronic, but not acute treatment with antidepressants downregulates postsynaptic β receptors (Vetulani and Sulser, 1975). It has been postulated that this effect might represent the mechanism of action of antidepressants. If so, the secretion of melatonin should be reduced by desipramine after 3 weeks.

METHODS

Patients and Normal Volunteers

Depressed patients meeting Research Diagnostic Criteria (Spitzer et al., 1975) for major depressive disorder were selected. With the exception of night sedation with a benzodiazepine, they were drug free for 3 weeks. None suffered significant medical or other psychiatric illnesses, including alcoholism. Normal volunteers were selected from the hospital staff according to the same criteria: none had ever suffered from any psychiatric disorder.

Desipramine Treatment

Both the patients and the normal volunteers were treated for 3 weeks with desipramine (2 mg/kg body weight per day given in three divided doses). Plasma desipramine concentrations were measured using gas liquid chromatography (Braithwaite, 1979) after 1 and 3 weeks of desipramine treatment. No significant side effects were reported by either patients or subjects.

Sampling

Melatonin and cortisol were measured in plasma withdrawn hourly during 24-hour periods. At 9:00 AM on the first day of each test, a cannula was inserted into an antecubital vein. The cannula was connected via rigid, narrow bore tubing and a three-way tap to a minipump containing 2.5 ml of 1000 units per milliliter heparin solution, which was pumped into the vein over 24 hours. This technique allowed the cannula to remain undisturbed during sampling and for the subject to remain undisturbed during sleep. Sampling began 1 hour after insertion of the cannula. The initial 2 ml was discarded on each occasion and the remaining 8 ml was centrifuged immediately. The plasma was decanted into plastic storage bottles and frozen at −40°C.

All experiments were performed on a research ward. The subjects slept in single rooms and retired at their usual time. On very few occasions did the subjects awaken during nocturnal sampling. They were kept away from bright sunlight during the day; otherwise no special lighting arrangements were made. They were not allowed vigorous exercise or alcohol (Carr et al., 1981) but otherwise they took a normal diet and were occupied, within the confines of the ward, as usual. Twenty-four-hour blood sampling was performed both in the depressed patients and in the normal volunteers after 0, 1, and 3 weeks of treatment with desipramine. In the normal subjects a fourth 24-hour sampling was performed 1 week after desipramine was discontinued. This was not possible in the depressed group because the majority continued treatment for clinical reasons.

Pupil Tests

Each normal subject underwent pupil testing after 0, 1, and 3 weeks of treatment with desipramine. There were two tests each time:

1. Fifteen microliters of 2.5% tyramine was placed into the conjunctival sac of the right eye and the degree of dilation was recorded using a photographic technique every 15 minutes, up to 90 minutes, and measured as the ratio of the diameter of the right to the left pupil (Shur and Checkley, 1982). This provides a measure of inhibition of the norepinephrine uptake mechanism, as tyramine requires this uptake mechanism to exert its mydriatic effect.

2. The same procedure was carried out using 15 μl of 2.5% of the α_1-adrenoceptor agonist phenylephrine. The tyramine test was performed at the beginning of each 24-hour sampling procedure and the phenylephrine test was performed 24 hours later. The melatonin and cortisol assays were carried out in the biochemistry department of the University of Surrey using radioimmunoassay. Melatonin was measured by radioimmunoassay (Frazer et al., 1983) using tritiated tracer (NEN Ltd.) and antiserum 704/189 (Guildhay Antisera). The sensitivity ranged from 5 to 10 pg/ml of plasma, and the coefficients of the variation between assays were 13.5% and 16.3% at 339 and 75 pg/ml, respectively. Intraassay variability was 2.6% and 10% at 151 and 54 pg/ml, respectively. Cortisol was measured by routine radioimmunoassay using anti-

serum No. HP/A63k-IF (Guildhay Antisera). The interassay coefficient of variation was 5.4%–5.9% over the normal range and the sensitivity was 10 ng/ml. Total melatonin secretion was measured as the area under the curve between 11:00 PM and 9:00 AM; in most cases melatonin was undetectable in plasma at all other times of day.

RESULTS

Six depressed patients (three female, three male) agreed to take part in the study. The mean age was 45 (range 26–72). Four were assigned a diagnosis of endogenous depression according to both the Newcastle Scale (Carney et al., 1965) and the Research Diagnostic Criteria (Spitzer et al., 1975). Prior to treatment, the mean Hamilton Rating Scale score (Hamilton, 1967) was 21 (range 15–26). The mean height of the patients was 167 cm (range 156–185) and their mean weight was 60.9 kg (range 54–70). The six normal volunteers were all male. They had a mean age of 28 (range 24–30), a mean weight of 84.4 kg (range 62–110), and a mean height of 180 cm (range 170 188).

Melatonin

Figure 5.1 shows the mean hourly plasma melatonin concentrations for the depressed subjects at each stage of treatment with desipramine. The mean nocturnal melatonin secretion was calculated using the values between 9:00 PM and 9:00 AM inclusive, as mean melatonin levels were below the limit of detection for the assay at all other times. There was a significant increase in mean nocturnal melatonin secretion in the depressed group after 3 weeks of treatment with desipramine ($p < 0.02$ paired t test, two-tailed) but not after 1 week of treatment. Between 1 and 3 weeks of treatment there was a significant increase in melatonin secretion ($p < 0.05$ paired t test, two-tailed). The standard error bars appear to be large in Figure 5.1, but this is due to interindividual differences in the timing of secretion rather than in the total amount of secretion. No significant changes in the timing of the peak or of the time of onset of secretion were noted in this group.

Figure 5.2 shows the mean hourly melatonin level for normal subjects at each stage of the study. Mean daytime levels were higher in this group because one subject had high levels throughout the day. This subject's levels displayed a detectable rhythm, however, and he was included in the analysis because normative data for melatonin secretion

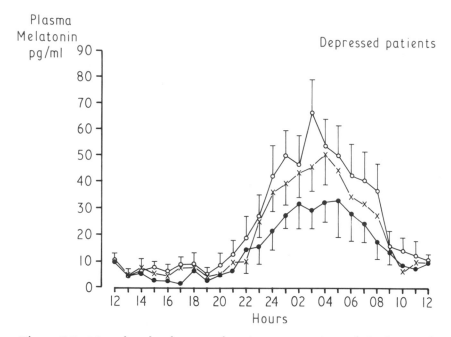

Figure 5.1. Mean hourly plasma melatonin concentrations of six depressed patients before desipramine treatment (●———●), after 1 week of desipramine 2 mgs/kg body weight (×———×), and after 3 weeks of desipramine (○———○):

is not available for large numbers of subjects and his pattern was not clearly abnormal. Using the same method as above, there were no significant differences between mean nocturnal melatonin plasma concentration at any stage of the study. However, an examination of Figure 5.2 suggests that the onset of secretion of melatonin and the entire rising phase of the curve occurred earlier during the administration of desipramine (week 1 and week 3) as compared with the two conditions before and 1 week after treatment. This was confirmed by calculating the mean values at each hour "on desipramine" and "off desipramine" for each subject and then plotting the mean curves for the group. Thus, N remains 6 in each condition. Paired t tests were performed every hour and melatonin levels were significantly greater "on desipramine" than "off desipramine" at 9:00 PM ($p < 0.01$) 10:00 PM ($p < 0.02$) 11:00 PM ($p < 0.01$), and 12:00 midnight ($p < 0.02$). An alternative analysis was performed using the mean time of onset of secretion for each subject under the two conditions. The mean time of onset while subjects were taking desipramine was 21.5 hours; after desipramine was discontinued,

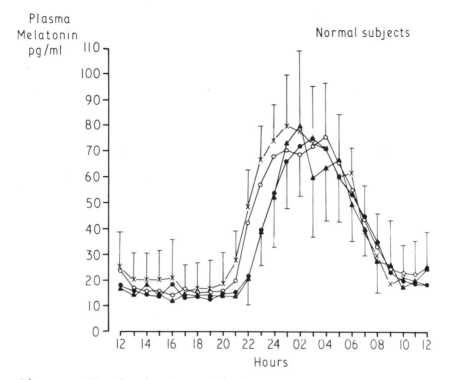

Figure 5.2. Mean hourly plasma melatonin concentrations of six normal subjects before desipramine (●———●), after 1 week of desipramine (○———○), after 3 weeks of desipramine (×———×), and 1 week after withdrawal of desipramine (▲———▲):

the mean time of onset was 22.9 hours. This was a significant advance of the onset of secretion by 1.4 hours ($p < 0.02$).

Cortisol

No significant differences were observed in the phase, amplitude, or mean 24-hour values of cortisol in either group. Neither was there a significant difference between groups at any stage of treatment (Figures 5.3 and 5.4).

Plasma Desipramine Concentrations

Mean desipramine levels after 1 week of treatment were 96 ng/ml (SEM ± 23.1) for the depressed group and 61.7 ng/ml (SEM ± 13.1) for the

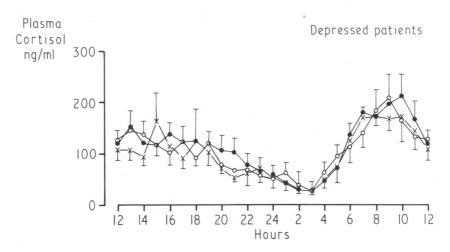

Figure 5.3. Mean hourly cortisol concentration of six depressed patients before despiramine treatment (O———O), after 1 week of desipramine (O———O), and after 3 weeks of desipramine (×———×):

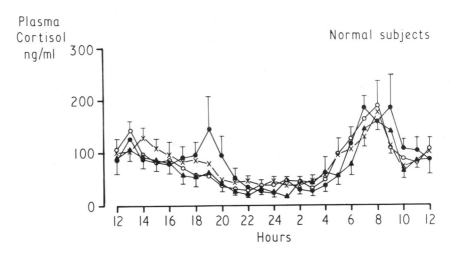

Figure 5.4. Mean hourly cortisol concentration of six normal subjects before desipramine treatment (O———O), after 1 week of desipramine (O———O), after 3 weeks of desipramine (×———×), and 1 week after withdrawal of desipramine (▲———▲):

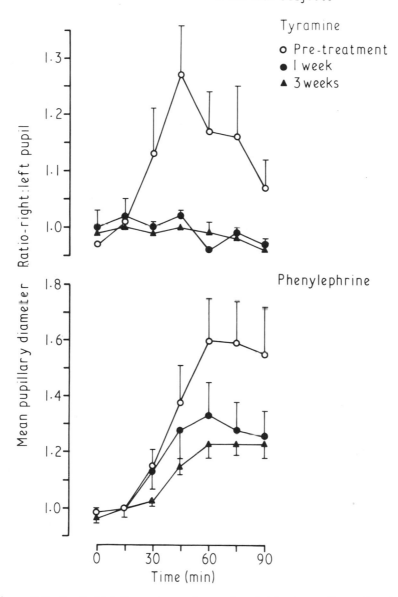

Figure 5.5. Pupil dilatation expressed as ratio of right (treated) pupil to left over 90 minutes following a drop of tyramine or phenylephrine. Results are shown for a group of six normal subjects before treatment with desipramine (O——O) and after 1 week (●——●) and 3 weeks of treatment (▲——▲) at 2 mg/kg body weight.

normal group. After 3 weeks of treatment mean levels were 108 mg/ml (SEM ± 35.4) for the depressed group and 76.2 ng/ml (SEM ± 14.1) for the normal group. These differences were not statistically significant, although in both cases there was a trend towards lower levels in the normal group.

Pupil Tests

Figure 5.5 shows the result of tyramine and phenylephrine tests for the normal subjects. A normal pupillary dilation was seen before treatment. The response to tyramine was inhibited during treatment ($p < 0.02$ at 1 week, $p < 0.05$ at 3 weeks, paired t test on area under curve) and the response to phenylephrine was attenuated although not significantly so. Thus desipramine, at this dose, blocked the reuptake of norepinephrine in normal subjects, as has been found previously for another group of depressed patients taking the same dose of desipramine (2 mg/ kg body weight) (Shur and Checkley, 1982).

In addition, the resting pupil diameter increased during desipramine treatment from 58.25 mm (projected diameter) before treatment to 64.4 mm at 1 week ($p < 0.02$) and 65.8 mm at 3 weeks ($p < 0.02$ compared with pretreatment value). This is further evidence that the net effect of desipramine is to increase noradrenergic neurotransmission.

Hamilton Rating Scales

In the depressed group, the mean score on the Hamilton Rating Scale was 21 prior to treatment (range 15–26). After 1 week it had fallen to 14 (range 6–20) and after 3 weeks to 13 (range 6–22). Following termination of the study, two patients improved further without a change of treatment.

DISCUSSION

This study was designed, in part, to test the hypothesis that antidepressant drugs slow the instrinsic period and delay the phase position of circadian rhythms, and that this constitutes their mechanism of action. Two separate groups of subjects were used, a clinically depressed group and a normal group. No attempt was made to match these groups and no comparison has been made between them.

In the depressed group, no changes in the timing of secretion of melatonin or cortisol were observed. However, the area under the curve of melatonin secretion increased significantly during desipramine treatment. These results lend no support to the circadian rhythm theory or to the β-receptor downregulation theory. They do support the reuptake blockade theory to a limited extent.

Because of the nature of this group, it was possible that the change in mental state itself, rather than the direct effects of the antidepressant, may have caused the alterations in melatonin secretion or, at least, constituted a confounding variable. For this reason, the normal group was also tested.

Unlike the depressed group, the normal group showed no increase in the area under the melatonin curve during desipramine treatment. This was true, despite the demonstrated effect of norepinephrine uptake blockade using the pupillary response to tyramine as a marker, and despite the increased noradrenergic tone using the resting pupil diameter as the measure.

However, the curves representing melatonin secretion in subjects taking desipramine at 1 week and 3 weeks were remarkably similar to each other, as were the curves representing melatonin secretion while subjects were not taking desipramine—before treatment and 1 week after withdrawal. Thus, these were combined to form the mean curve "on DMI" and the mean curve "off DMI," respectively. When these two curves are compared, it is seen that the secretion of melatonin began earlier during treatment than when off treatment, as shown by the greater melatonin values between 9:00 PM and 12:00 midnight in the former condition and also by the earlier timing of the onset of secretion. This is a post hoc analysis and will require replication in a further sample; however, two alternative interpretations might be considered.

1. The increase in melatonin during the rising phase of secretion was due to increased noradrenergic tone during treatment and was too small an effect to be detected using the analysis of the "area under the curve." The physiology of pineal activity would lead to the prediction that the rising phase of secretion would be more sensitive to the antidepressant drug effect because, at this time, melatonin secretion is actively driven by the sympathetic innervation of the pineal; this may explain why an increase was only detectable in the early part of the night. As night progresses, a rapid downregulation at pineal β adrenoceptors occurs, and this could obscure any initial drug effects.

2. The change in the onset of secretion may represent an underlying advance in the circadian system. This interpretation is contrary to most of the animal literature, in which it has been shown that antidepressants delay circadian rhythms (Wehr and Wirz-Justice, 1982). In addition, the timing shift was not seen in the peak of secretion or in the falling phase of the curve. Thus, an interpretation in terms of changes in circadian rhythms is difficult to sustain.

SUMMARY

Neither the depressed nor the normal group in the present study showed a delay in the phase position of either melatonin or cortisol secretion. Based on these findings, the circadian theory of the action of antidepressant drugs could not be supported. Similarly, no support was obtained for the receptor downregulation theory of antidepressant drug action. However, the theory of increased noradrenergic transmission due to reuptake blockade *was* supported by the melatonin results in the depressed group, and to some extent in the normal group of subjects.

REFERENCES

Braithwaite R (1979): Measurement of antidepressant drugs. Proc Anal Div Chem Soc 16:69–72.

Carney MWP, Roth M, Gartside RF (1965): The diagnosis of depressive syndromes and the prediction of ECT response. Br J Psychiatry 3:659–674.

Carr DR, Reppert SM, Bullen B, et al (1981): Plasma melatonin increase during exercise in women. J Clin Endocrinol Metab 53:224–225.

Cowen PJ, Fraser S, Sammon R, Green AR (1983): Atenolol reduces plasma melatonin concentration in man. Br J Clin Pharmacol 15:579–580.

Craig C, Tamarkin C, Garrick N, Wehr TA (1981): Long term and short term effects of clorgyline (a monoamine oxidase type A inhibitor) on locomotor activity and on pineal melatonin in the Hamster. In Abstracts Society for Neuroscience, 11th Annual Meeting.

Engelmann, W (1973): A slowing down of circadian rhythms by lithium ions. Z Naturforsch 28c:733.

Frazer S, Cowen P, Franklin U, Franey C, Arendt J. (1983): A direct radioimmunoassay for melatonin. Clin Chem 29:396–399.

Hamilton M (1967): Development of a rating scale for primary depressive illness. Br J Soc Clin Psychiatry 6:278–296.

Hofmann K, Gunderoth-Palmowski M, Weidenmann G, Engelmann W

(1978): Further evidence for period lengthening effect of lithium on circadian rhythms. Z Naturforsch 32c:231–234.

Johnsson A, Engelmann W, Pflug B, Klemke W (1980): Influences of lithium ions on the human circadian rhythms. Z Naturforsch 35c:503–507.

Kafka MS, Wirz-Justice A, Naber D, Wehr TA (1981): Circadian acetyl-choline receptor rhythm and its modification by chronic imipramine. Neuropharmacology 20:421–425.

Kafka MS, Wirz-Justice A, Naber D, et al (1982): Effect of lithium on circadian neurotransmitter receptor rhythms. Neuropsychobiology 8:41–50.

Klein DC, Moore RY (1979): Pineal N-acetyltransferase and hydroxy-in-dole-O-methyltransferase: Control by the retinohypothalamic tract and the suprachiasmatic nucleus. Brain Res 174:245–262.

Kripke DF, Wyborney VG (1980): Lithium slows rat circadian activity rhythms. Life Sci 26:1319–1321.

Kripke DF, Judd U, Hubbard B, et al (1979): The effect of lithium carbonate on the circadian rhythm of sleep in normal human subjects. Biol Psychiatry 14:545.

Lynch HJ, Wurtman RJ, Moscowitz MA, et al (1975): Daily rhythm in human urinary melatonin. Science 187:169.

McEachron DL, Kripke DF, Wyborney VG (1981): Lithium promotes entrainment of rats to long circadian light–dark cycles. Psychiatry Res 5:1.

McEachron DL, Kripke DF, Hawkins R, et al (1982): Lithium delays biochemical circadian rhythms in rats. Neuropsychobiology 8:12.

Martin KF, Redfern PH (1982a): The effects of clomipramine on the 24-hour variations of 5HT and tryptophan concentrations in the rat brain. Br J Pharmacol 76:288.

Martin KF, Redfern PH (1982b): Modification of 24-hour variations in brain tryptophan and 5HT concentrations by imipramine. Br J Pharmacol 77:51.

Mellerup ET, Lauritsen B, Dam H, Rafaelsen OJ (1976): Lithium effects on diurnal rhythm of Ca, Mg, and PO_4 metabolism in manic-melancholic disorder. Acta Psychiatr Scand 53:360.

Moore RY, Eichler VB (1972): Loss of circadian adrenal cortiscosterone rhythm following suprachiasmatic lesions in the rat. Brain Res 42:201–206.

Naber D, Wirz-Justice A, Kafka MS, Wehr TA (1980): Dopamine receptor binding in rat striatum: Ultradian rhythm and its modification by chronic imipramine. Psychopharmacology 68:45.

Shur E, Checkley SA (1982): Pupil studies in depressed patients: An investigation of the mechanism of action of desipramine. Br J Psychiatry 140:181–184.

Spitzer RL, Endicott J, Robins E (1975): Research Diagnostic Criteria. New York, New York State Department of Mental Hygiene, New York State Psychiatric Institute, Biometrics Research.

Strumwasser F, Viele DP (1980): Lithium increases the period of a neuronal circadian oscillator. Neurosci Abstr 241:5.

Vetulani J, Sulser F (1975): Action of various antidepressant treatments reduced reactivity of noradrenergic cyclic AMP generating system in limbic forebrain. Nature 257:495–496.

Wehr TA, Goodwin FK (1979): Rapid cycling in manic depressives induced by tricyclic antidepressants. Arch Gen Psychiatry 36:555.

Wehr TA, Goodwin FK (1981): Biological rhythms and psychiatry. In: American Handbook of Psychiatry VII, 2nd ed. New York, Basic Books.

Wehr TA, Wirz-Justice A (1982): Circadian rhythm mechanisms in affective illness and in antidepressant drug action. Pharmacopsychiatry 15:31–39.

Wirz-Justice A, Wehr TA, Goodwin FK, et al (1980a): Antidepressant drugs slow circadian rhythms in behavior and brain neurotransmitter receptors. Psychopharmacol Bull 16:45–47.

Wirz-Justice A, Kafka MS, Naber D, Wehr TA (1980b): Circadian rhythms in rat brain and adrenergic receptors are modified by chronic imipramine. Life Sci 27:341.

Wirz-Justice A, Kafka MS, Naber HD, et al (1982): Clorgyline delays the phase position of circadian neurotransmitter receptor rhythm. Brain Res 41:115–122.

Wurtman RJ, Axelrod J, Phillips LS (1963): Melatonin synthesis in the pineal gland: Control by light. Science 142:1071.

6

Induction of Depressive-Like Sleep Patterns in Normal Subjects

Scott S. Campbell and Juergen Zulley

During the past decade the study of sleep characteristics associated with depression has received considerable attention. The rationale behind such investigations has been primarily to describe biologic criteria that, when applied in conjunction with more traditional clinical methods, would aid in the differential diagnosis of affective disorders. An important extension of such investigations, however, has been the development of several hypotheses regarding psychobiologic foundations of affective disorders based on alterations in EEG sleep structure typically observed in depressed patients.

Generation of these theoretical models for the understanding of depressive disorders has been based, for the most part, on changes in two specific aspects of sleep structure—REM sleep and sleep continuity measures. Probably the most prominent feature of altered sleep structure associated with endogenous or primary depression is a significant shortening of REM sleep latency (i.e., the interval from sleep onset to the appearance of the first REM sleep epoch) (Hartmann, 1968; Hartmann et al., 1966; Kupfer, 1976; Kupfer and Foster, 1972; Snyder, 1968). The degree to which REM latency is shortened has been shown to be associated with the severity of the illness (Coble et al., 1981), and it has been proposed that, with the exception of drug withdrawal states and narcolepsy, shortened REM latency is a dependable marker for the diagnosis of primary depression (Kupfer, 1977).

Although in recent years the specificity of short REM latencies to endogenous depression has been questioned (cf. Gillin et al., 1984; Insel et al., 1982), this feature is, nevertheless, highly correlated with major depressive disorder and remains an important consideration in the description of putative biologic mechanisms mediating depressive states.

An additional qualification to the finding of shortened average REM latencies associated with depression was pointed out by Schulz and coworkers (1979). They showed that the average short latencies were the result of a bimodal distribution in REM latencies, with approximately one-third of latencies occurring within 20 minutes of sleep onset and a second peak occurring between 40 and 60 minutes following sleep onset.

In addition to shortened latency to REM sleep, other alterations in REM sleep measures observed in depressed patients indicate an advance of REM sleep toward the beginning of the sleep period. These include an increase in the "intensity" of early REM sleep, as measured by frequency of eye movements, as well as a lengthening of the first REM sleep period of the night, which often results in an increase in REM sleep amount during the first third of the sleep period.

With regard to sleep continuity measures, the sleep of depressed patients is generally characterized by increased awakenings throughout the sleep episode, resulting in reduced sleep efficiency indices. In addition, many patients exhibit early morning awakening, i.e., premature termination of sleep, leading to shortened total sleep times. Such shortened sleep times are descriptive of about 80%–85% of depressed patients (Gillin et al., 1984). In contrast, between 10% and 20% of depressed patients exhibit hypersomnia when compared with age-matched controls (Kupfer et al., 1975; Michaelis and Hofmann, 1973; Taub et al., 1978). Young patients and bipolar depressives are probably more likely to exhibit hypersomnia (Gillin et al., 1984). Finally, there is some evidence to indicate that depressed patients have "shallower" sleep, with increased amounts of stage 2 sleep and reductions in slow-wave sleep (stages 3 and 4).

Under certain conditions normal healthy subjects may exhibit some of the sleep-related characteristics associated with depressive disorders. Indeed, results of studies using normal subjects living in environments without time cues, or on altered sleep–wake schedules, have been instrumental in the development of hypotheses linking affective illness with biologic rhythm disturbance. In this chapter we discuss an experimental approach that appears to induce in normal, healthy young adults a majority of the changes in sleep structure typically associated with depression.

We begin by describing the experimental environment and present results of a study using nine subjects maintained in such an environment for 60 hours. This is followed by a discussion of the findings in relation to those of depressed patients, and in terms of their implications for theoretical models of depression.

METHOD

The Disentrained Environment

The experimental conditions employed in the present study have been described previously (Campbell, 1984). The term "disentrainment" was selected in order to distinguish the current conditions from those usually employed in human circadian research. Many aspects of the typical time-free environment remain essentially unchanged relative to daily life. That is, subjects are asked to continue their normal daily activities and are usually requested to structure their days by eating three designated meals per day and by avoiding naps during the major waking episode.

In contrast, a principal feature of the disentrained environment is the specific emphasis placed on removing from the environment all behavioral controls on the sleep process, and minimizing the occurrence of behaviors that may be incompatible with the sleep response. As such, the disentrained environment is characterized by highly static, basal conditions. In the current study, subjects were restricted to bed for 60 continuous hours, with the exception of in-room bathroom visits. Beds were situated singly in sound-dampened, windowless recording chambers, in which access to time-of-day cues was minimized.

During the period of disentrainment subjects were prohibited from reading, writing, exercise, listening to music, and so on. Subjects were instructed to lie as quietly as possible and at no time were instructions given relative to when or when not to sleep. Meals, consisting of sandwiches, vegetables, and noncaffeinated beverages, were served at irregular intervals, always during ongoing waking episodes. In addition, snacks were available ad libitum. Illumination was provided by a 60-W incandescent lamp placed on a bedside table, and control of light and darkness was at the discretion of each subject.

To summarize, the physical environment used in this study was essentially the same as environments employed in standard human circadian research. The primary difference was that during disentrainment no constraints were placed on the initiation of sleep, and behavioral options to sleep, including physical activity, were highly restricted.

Procedure

The subjects for this study were nine healthy young adults (four males and five females) between the ages of 18 and 25 years (mean 20.4 years). Each subject was confined to bed for 60 hours immediately following two nights of laboratory sleep. The EEG (central, frontal, and parietal leads) and EOG (recorded from the external canthus of each eye) of each subject were continuously monitored and each record was analyzed in 1-minute epochs following standard scoring procedures (Agnew and Webb, 1972a). Sleep onset was defined by the first epoch of stage 2 sleep (Agnew and Webb, 1972b; Johnson, 1973).

RESULTS

The results reported here are based on 84 sleep episodes recorded during the period of disentrainment. A sleep episode was defined as a period of at least 30 minutes of sleep, uninterrupted by more than 20 minutes of wakefulness. Such criteria for a sleep period accounted for all but eight sleep episodes (mean duration 7.3 minutes), which constituted less than 0.1% of all sleep recorded. Overall characteristics of these sleep episodes, relative to their durations and placement within the nychthemeron, have been reported in detail elsewhere (Campbell, 1984). The major emphasis here is placed on sleep measures that have been reported to be altered in the sleep of depressed patients.

REM Sleep Measures

Of the 84 sleep episodes, 11 (13.1%) recorded during disentrainment contained no REM sleep. Of the 11 sleep episodes containing no REM sleep, 8 occurred between 10:00 AM and 7:00 PM, corresponding to the descending slope of the circadian oscillation in REM sleep propensity. The absence of REM sleep during this interval resulted in the only significant difference ($p < 0.001$, two-tailed t test) in sleep stage percentages between day (7:00 AM to 11:00 PM) and night (11:00 PM to 7:00 AM) phases of the disentrainment period, as shown in Table 6.1. The following analyses are based on the 73 sleep periods containing REM sleep.

Latency. The median latency for REM episodes recorded during disentrainment was 47 minutes (mean = 44.1 minutes, SD = 29.7 minutes). This is compared with a median and mean latency on the baseline night

Table 6.1. Comparisons of Sleep Parameters in Disentrainment: Baseline Night versus Overall Disentrainment Period, Night Phase versus Day Phase, and First 24 Hours versus Second 24 Hours of Disentrainment. Mean Values Are Given, with Standard Deviations in Parentheses.

	Baseline Night (hr)	Overall Disentrainment (hr)	Night Phase (hr) (11:00 PM to 7:00 AM)	Day Phase (hr) (7:00 AM to 11:00 PM)	First 24 Hours	Second 24 Hours
Total sleep time	8.72 (1.58)	27.99 (5.39)	15.34 (3.30)	12.65 (4.91)	14.46[a] (2.28)	10.97 (2.36)
Sleep period length	8.72 (1.58)	2.99 (2.35)	5.52[b] (2.65)	1.93 (.98)	3.54 (1.92)	2.28 (1.44)
Total number sleep periods	9	84	24	60	39	33
Percent stage 0	2.99 (2.54)	3.59 (2.28)	3.50 (2.26)	3.64 (3.58)	2.94 (2.23)	4.48 (4.25)
Percent stage 1	1.78 (1.14)	3.28 (1.87)	3.88 (2.79)	2.81 (2.06)	3.03 (1.93)	3.74 (2.66)
Percent stage 2	53.06 (6.52)	58.41 (4.94)	56.37 (5.76)	60.80 (6.22)	59.69 (4.03)	56.68 (8.50)
Percent stage 3	5.47 (1.83)	4.33 (1.24)	4.13 (1.58)	4.94 (1.75)	4.15 (1.40)	4.66 (1.58)
Percent stage 4	13.42 (5.08)	9.86 (4.54)	8.89 (5.37)	11.01 (4.28)	8.39 (3.60)	11.39 (6.88)
Percent stage REM	23.55 (3.55)	20.47 (2.94)	23.13[b] (4.01)	17.54 (3.87)	21.77 (2.56)	19.02 (4.82)

[a] $p < 0.01$, two-tailed t test.
[b] $p < 0.001$, two-tailed t test.

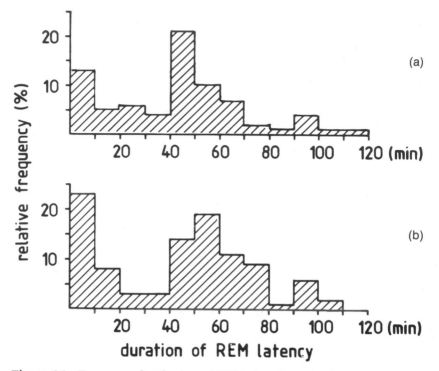

Figure 6.1. Frequency distribution of REM sleep latencies for sleep episodes recorded during disentrainment (a) compared to REM sleep latencies reported for a group of endogenously depressed patients (b) data from Figure 1 of Schulz et al., 1979.

of 82 and 91.2 minutes (SD = 28.9 min), respectively. The average REM latency for young adults (20–29 years) is reported to be 94 minutes (Williams et al., 1974).

Figure 6.1(a) shows that there was a tendency toward a bimodal distribution of REM sleep latencies recorded during disentrainment. Twenty-three percent of first REM episodes occurred within 20 minutes after sleep onset, 13% occurred between 20 and 40 minutes after sleep onset, and 48% occurred between 41 and 60 minutes after sleep onset.

Distribution. Under normal laboratory conditions, the first REM episode after sleep onset is usually substantially shorter in duration than succeeding REM episodes. This was also the case on the baseline night in the present study but was not the case during the period of disentrainment. Using REM sleep episodes that occurred during major (longest) nocturnal sleep periods of the first and second 24 hours of disentrainment, mean durations of successive REM episodes were calculated. The results of those calculations, along with those from the baseline night, are presented in Table 6.2.

On the baseline night, a sharp increase in the mean durations of successive REM episodes was evident from the first to the third REM episode, followed by a gradual decline in durations over the next three episodes. In contrast, during disentrainment mean REM period duration remained essentially constant across all REM periods recorded during nocturnal sleep episodes. On both nights, during disentrainment durations of the first REM episodes were significantly longer than on the baseline night (Wilcoxon matched pairs; $p < 0.05$ and p 0.01, respectively, two-tailed). Further, no significant difference was found between durations of all first REM episodes ($N = 73$) and all other REM episodes recorded during disentrainment (Mann–Whitney U test, $p < 0.05$, two-tailed).

Such increases in first REM episodes resulted in increases in REM percentages in the first third of the night, when compared to baseline values, for the first night of disentrainment (Wilcoxon test; $p < 0.02$, one-tailed), and for the two nights of disentrainment combined (Mann–Whitney U $= 36$; $p < 0.01$, one-tailed), but not for the second night of disentrainment considered alone. Mean REM percent in the first third of major sleep episodes increased from 11.6% on the baseline night to 21.1% during disentrainment.

The duration of the first, but not other, REM episodes recorded during disentrainment showed a clear circadian variation. As shown in Figure 6.2 there was a significant difference in the durations of first REM episodes occurring between 4:00 and 8:00 PM and those occurring during sleep episodes initiated between 12:00 midnight and 4:00 AM. No significant differences in durations of all other REM episodes were observed as a function of time of day.

Sleep Continuity Measures

Sleep–Waking Patterns. The 84 sleep episodes recorded during disentrainment comprised 47.6% of the disentrainment period. Average total sleep time was 27.99 hours (SD $= 5.4$ hours). Despite the large proportion of total time spent asleep, individual sleep episodes were of relatively brief duration. Only 6 of the 84 sleep episodes continued for as long as 7 hours. Eighty percent of sleep episodes were of less than 4 hours in length. The mean duration of all sleep periods was 2.99 hours (SD $= 2.4$ hours).

Table 6.2. Comparisons of REM Episode Durations on Baseline Night and During the Period of Disentrainment. (Nights 1 and 2 of Disentrainment were determined by taking the longest sleep episode of each subject with onset time after 11:00 PM.)

	REM Period (min)						
	1	2	3	4	5	6	7
Baseline (Night 2 in lab)	(N = 9)	(N = 9)	(N = 9)	(N = 8)	(N = 6)	(N = 3)	(N = 1)
Mean	11.0	27.7	31.6	30.1	23.3	24.0	33.0
(SD)	(7.1)	(16.8)	(17.7)	(12.9)	(11.2)	(11.5)	
Median	10.0	21.0	30.0	28.0	24.5	20.0	33.0
Disentrainment (Night 1)	(N = 9)	(N = 9)	(N = 8)	(N = 5)	(N = 4)	(N = 2)	(N = 2)
Mean	24.9[a]	22.0	26.5	19.8	31.3	24.5	26.0
(SD)	(11.0)	(9.6)	(12.4)	(5.8)	(21.7)		
Median	25.0	18.0	29.0	21.0	30.0	2.0	26.0
Disentrainment (Night 2)	(N = 9)	(N = 8)	(N = 7)	(N = 4)	(N = 1)		
Mean	27.0[b]	24.9	20.1	17.0	11.0		
(SD)	(10.6)	(10.8)	(9.6)	(8.1)			
Median	24.0	24.5	22.0	17.5	11.0		

[a] First REM episode significantly longer ($p < 0.05$, two-tailed, Wilcoxon test) than on baseline night.
[b] First REM episode significantly longer ($p < 0.01$, two-tailed, Wilcoxon test) than on baseline night.

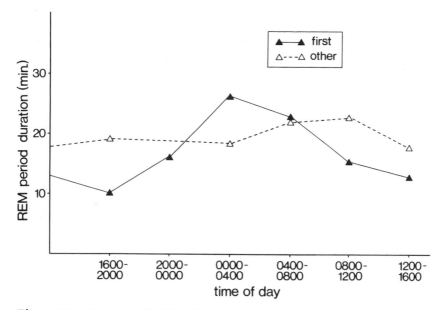

Figure 6.2. Duration of REM sleep episodes as a function of time-of-day. Course of mean durations of first REM sleep episodes is shown by the solid line. Course of all other REM episode durations is shown by the broken line. Only first REM sleep episodes showed significant circadian variation in mean duration.

Sleep episodes were initiated throughout the 24-hour day, with amounts of sleep occurring during the day phase (7:00 AM to 11:00 PM) and during the night phase (11:00 PM to 7:00 AM) being proportional to the amount of the disentrainment period comprised by each phase.

Structure of Sleep Episodes. Overall sleep stage percentages recorded during disentrainment were generally within normal limits for young adults (Williams et al., 1974), and did not differ significantly from percentages recorded on the baseline night. However, as can be seen in Table 6.1, there were nonsignificant increases in stages 0, 1, and 2 during disentrainment relative to baseline values of each stage. These increases were primarily at the expense of slow-wave sleep, which showed a nonsignificant decline as a percent of total sleep time in disentrainment.

Additionally, disruptions in the typical sequencing of sleep were evident when sleep episodes were analyzed individually. Less than half of all sleep episodes (47.6%, N = 40) were typical sleep periods, in the sense that both REM sleep and slow-wave sleep (SWS) were present and the usual sleep stage sequencing was observed (i.e., SWS occurred prior to the first epoch of REM sleep). In 26 sleep episodes the first REM sleep period was preceded only by stages 1 or 2, and 18 sleep periods recorded during disentrainment were incomplete, with 9 episodes showing no REM sleep, 7 episodes showing no SWS, and 2 episodes showing neither REM sleep nor SWS (Table 6.3).

DISCUSSION

Before discussing implications of the present findings in terms of theoretical models of depression, we begin this section by summarizing our results and comparing them to findings typically reported for depressed populations.

Comparisons with Depression. As with sleep in endogenous depression, the most impressive alterations in sleep measures recorded during disentrainment were observed relative to REM sleep. Average REM sleep latency recorded during disentrainment was about half that of baseline values and virtually identical to measures obtained from numerous depressed samples. Similarly, as shown in Figure 6.1, the group distribution of REM sleep latencies during disentrainment compared favorably with that obtained from a population of endogenously depressed patients (Schulz et al., 1979).

Advancement of REM sleep to an earlier position within the sleep period was also exhibited in the sleep of disentrained subjects in the form of increased durations of the first REM sleep episodes of major sleep periods. First REM sleep episodes did not differ in length from all other REM sleep episodes of the night. This is in marked contrast to sleep patterns recorded on the baseline night (Table 6.2) and is consistent with sleep patterns observed in endogenously depressed patients. Also consistent with such sleep patterns was the increase in REM percent during the first third of nocturnal sleep periods recorded during disentrainment.

Sleep continuity measures obtained from disentrained subjects were similarly consistent with the sleep patterns generally associated with major depressive disorder. Although the increases in percentages of stages 0, 1, and 2 observed during disentrainment were not statistically significant when compared to baseline values, such increases do suggest fragmentation of the sleep process. That such increases occurred primarily at the expense of slow-wave sleep also suggests a "shallowing"

Table 6.3. Classification of Sleep Episodes as a Function of Presence or Absence of REM Sleep and Slow-Wave Sleep (stages 3 and 4).

	Number of Episodes	Day Phase (7:00 AM to 11:00 PM)	Night Phase (11:00 PM to 7:00 AM)	Mean Duration (Standard Deviation) (min)
Slow-wave sleep and REM sleep present	66	44	22	211.14 (141.60)
No slow-wave sleep	7	6	1	68.40[a] (35.40)
No REM sleep	9	8	1	65.90[a] (37.80)
Neither slow-wave sleep nor REM sleep present	2	2	0	61.48[a]
Total	84	60	24	179.40 (141.00)

[a] Duration of sleep episode significantly shorter than complete sleep episodes, i.e., slow-wave sleep and REM present (Mann–Whitney U test, $p < 0.001$, two-tailed).

of sleep in disentrained subjects. Sleep fragmentation was further evident in the observation that subjects were unable to maintain sleep for prolonged periods (80% of all sleep episodes were of less than 4 hours duration), and in the finding that over half of all sleep episodes were characterized by the absence of REM sleep or SWS, or by atypical sleep stage sequencing.

The relatively large amounts of total sleep per 24 hours obtained by subjects in disentrainment make the present results comparable to those of depressed patients reported to exhibit hypersomnia rather than hyposomnia. The proportion of depressed patients exhibiting hypersomnia is reported to be only about 15%−20%. However, it is quite possible that the incidence of hypersomnia may be underestimated in depressed populations as a whole as a result of the typically controlled recording times employed in laboratory settings. As far as can be determined, only one study has reported sleep time per 24 hours in depressed samples (Shimizu et al., 1979). As such, the occurrence of sleep episodes throughout the nychthemeron has not been adequately assessed in this population.

Taken together, the sleep parameters described above indicate that the disentrained environment was effective in inducing, in normal young subjects, depressive-like sleep patterns.

Implications for Theoretical Models of Depression. Alterations in EEG sleep structure are perhaps the most well-established objective measures of biologic changes associated with endogenous depression. These highly characteristic structural alterations form, in large part, the foundation for theoretical models of depression. Implicit in such models is the assumption that these sleep disturbances reflect the malfunctioning of the same systems responsible for other symptoms of depressive disorders, such as flat affect, loss of appetite, and decreased motor behavior.

This assumption seems to be supported by the finding that the degree and speed with which sleep structure becomes normalized following administration of some tricyclic antidepressants is predictive of subsequent efficacy in treatment of the mood disturbance. Similarly, the finding that manipulations such as phase shifting sleep time, total sleep deprivation, and deprivation of REM sleep all have noticeable effects not only on sleep structure but also on affect suggests an intimate connection between depressed sleep patterns and depression proper.

It is also quite clear, however, that although these sleep disturbances are highly characteristic of endogenous depression, they are not specific to depressive disorders. Similar sleep patterns have been reported in other psychiatric disorders, in narcolepsy, and in normal subjects under certain conditions. That it was possible to induce depressed sleep patterns in healthy young adults in the present study indicates that the biologic correlates generally considered to be necessary (Gillin et al., 1984) and sometimes sufficient (Kupfer, 1977) for the diagnosis of endogenous depression may be observed in the absence of the other major behavioral manifestations of depression.

Thus, it is important that any theoretical model of depression that is based on alterations in the sleep patterns of depressed patients should also take into consideration the common characteristics of these other situations in which similar sleep patterns may be found.

One feature of the disentrained environment that appears to have contributed in large part to the atypical sleep patterns observed is the extremely basal, static level of behavior characterizing the environment. In short, there was nothing to do. As a result, subjects were unable to maintain prolonged episodes of wakefulness. It can be argued, then, that wakefulness during disentrainment was characterized by a reduced level of behavioral activity, relative to normal waking episodes. Consistent with this notion is the finding that subjects maintained in a disentrained environment, but *not* restricted to bed, exhibited fewer features of depressed sleep than did the subjects in the present sample (Campbell and Zulley, 1985). Moreover, the sleep patterns of subjects living in typical time-cue-free environments, in which usual daily activities are permitted to continue, are characterized by still fewer features of depressed sleep (Czeisler et al., 1980; Zulley, 1980).

In view of these findings, the existence of a gradient may be hypothesized in which the degree to which the sleep of normal subjects comes to resemble the sleep of depressed patients is inversely related to the level of behavioral arousal associated with the environment. Evidence presented by Schulz (1983) seems to support such a notion, since reduced somatic activity in normal subjects, immediately prior to sleep, resulted in significantly shorter REM latencies and higher amounts of REM sleep in the first half of the night. In further support of such a hypothesis is the finding that narcoleptics, who are known to exhibit sleep patterns quite similar to those seen in depression, have lowered habitual arousal levels relative to controls, as well as "a marked tendency to decreases in phasic arousal" (Levander and Sachs, 1985).

With regard to depression, Schulz and Lund (1983) have proposed that the REM sleep abnormalities typical of depression are a consequence of a flattening in the amplitude of a putative circadian arousal system. This proposal was based on the finding that subjects displaying REM sleep latencies of less than 20 minutes had significantly smaller variation around the daily mean of body core temperature than did subjects who never showed such short REM sleep latencies. Beersma et al. (1983) have also speculated that the disturbed sleep of endogenous depressives may be related to a circadian rhythm disturbance characterized by an extreme flattening of the endogenous temperature oscillation.

Based on these findings and the results of the present study, we offer the following hypothesis. Under any conditions in which waking episodes are characterized by sufficiently low levels of behavioral arousal, sleep episodes will be characterized by patterns similar to those observed in depression. In the case of normal, healthy adults, levels of behavior low enough to induce depressive-like sleep patterns occur primarily in contrived, extreme environments such as the one employed in the present study. Those experimental designs that have been most effective in inducing depressive-like sleep in normals have been those that produced extremely low levels of activity as a result of either sleep deprivation or absence of behavioral options (i.e., short sleep–wake schedules [Carskadon and Dement, 1975; Weitzman et al., 1974] and bed rest [the present study; Nakagawa, 1980], respectively).

However, for pathologic samples, such as narcoleptics and depressives, a much less dramatic reduction in levels of behavior may be adequate to trigger depressed sleep patterns. These individuals may be predisposed to exhibit such sleep alterations as a consequence of having lower set points of a putative arousal threshold. In terms of a current model of sleep regulation (Daan et al., 1984) this would correspond to an abnormally low level of the upper threshold, $\bar{H}$. Although the effects on sleep structure of varying levels of $\bar{H}$ have not been fully addressed, it has been shown that the fragmented sleep patterns observed in disentrainment, as well as in narcolepsy and depression, may be simulated by lowering the set point of this threshold.

The assumption of reduced levels of behavioral activity as a factor in depressive-like sleep patterns is not at odds with most theoretical models of depression, which are based on such atypical sleep patterns. Rather, the reduction in levels of behavior may best be viewed as an important intervening variable that contributes in large part to alterations in brain mechanisms that may, in turn, be manifested in the form of biological rhythm disturbance and/or cholinergic super-sensitivity. Indeed, these two leading hypotheses regarding the psychobiologic foundations of affective disorder may not be mutually exclusive but, rather, interactive. It is tempting to speculate that since behavioral levels show well-established circadian variation, the manifestation of alterations in brain mechanisms (e.g., cholinergic supersensitivity) would be influenced similarly by circadian effects. A direct test of this hypothesis would be a phase-response study of cholinomimetic agents such as physostigmine or RS86.

In conclusion, the present data serve to emphasize that changes observed in the sleep of endogenously depressed patients do not necessarily reflect alterations in the same physiologic systems governing other symptoms of depression. Instead, the results suggest that such sleep patterns may be regarded as epiphenomena of depression and "markers" of any condition in which reduced behavioral arousal is a principal feature.

REFERENCES

Agnew HW, Webb WB (1972a): Sleep stage scoring. Journals Supplement Abstract Service (American Psychological Association Ms. No. 293):

Agnew HW, Webb WB (1972b): Measurement of sleep onset by EEG criteria. Am J EEG Technol 12:127–134.

Beersma DGM, Hoofdakker RH, van den Berkestijn HWBW (1983): Circadian rhythms in affective disorders. Body temperature and sleep physiology in endogenous depression. In Mendlewicz J, van Praag HM (eds): Biological Rhythms and Behavior. Basel: Karger, pp 114–127.

Campbell SS (1984): Duration and placement of sleep in a "disentrained" environment. Psychophysiology 21:106–113.

Campbell SS, Zulley J (1985): Ultradian components of human sleep/wake patterns during disentrainment. In Schulz H, Lavie P (eds): Ultradian Rhythms in Physiology and Behavior. Berlin, Springer, pp 234–255.

Carskadon M, Dement W (1975): Sleep studies on a 90-minute day. EEG Clin Neurophysiol 39:145–155.

Coble PA, Kupfer DJ, Shaw DH (1981): Distribution of REM latency in depression. Biol Psychiatry 16:453–466.

Czeisler CA, Zimmerman JC, Ronda JM, et al (1980): Timing of REM sleep is coupled to the circadian rhythm of body temperature in man. Sleep 2:329–346.

Daan S, Beersma DGM, Börbely AA (1984): Timing of human sleep: Recovery process gated by a circadian pacemaker. Am J Physiology 246:R161–R178.

Gillin JC, Sitaram N, Wehr T, et al (1984): Sleep and affective illness. In Post RM, Ballenger JC (eds): Neurobiology of Mood Disorders. Baltimore, Williams and Wilkens, pp 157–189.

Hartmann E (1968): Longitudinal studies of sleep and dreams in manic-depressive patients. Arch Gen Psychiatry 19:312–329.

Hartmann E, Verdone P, Snyder F (1966): Longitudinal studies of sleep and dreaming patterns in psychiatric patients. J Nerv Ment Dis 142: 117–126.

Insel TR, Gillin JC, Moore A, et al (1982): The sleep of patients with obsessive-compulsive disorders. Arch Gen Psychiatry 39:1372–1377.

Johnson LC (1973): Are sleep stages related to waking behavior? Am Scientist 61:326–338.

Kupfer DJ (1976): REM latency: A psychobiological marker for primary depressive disease. Biol Psychiatry 11:159–174.

Kupfer DJ (1977): EEG sleep correlates of depression in man. In Hanin J, Usdin E (eds): Animal Models in Psychiatry and Neurology. Oxford, Pergamon, pp 181–188.

Kupfer DJ, Foster FG (1972): Intervals between onset of sleep and rapid-eye-movement sleep as an indicator of depression. Lancet 2:684–686.

Kupfer DJ, Foster FG, Detre TP, Himmelhoch J (1975): Sleep EEG and motor activity as indicators in affective states. Neuropsychobiology 1:296.

Levander S, Sachs C (1985): Vigilance performance and autonomic function in narcolepsy: Effects of central stimulants. Psychophysiology 22:24–31.

Michaelis R, Hofmann E (1973): Zur Phaenomenologie und Ätiopathogenese der Hypersomnia bei endogen phasischen Depressionen. In Jovanovic UJ (ed): The Nature of Sleep. Stuttgart, Fischer, pp 190–193.

Nakagawa Y (1980): Continuous observation of EEG patterns at night and in daytime of normal subjects under restricted conditions. I. Quiescent state when lying down. EEG Clin Neurophysiol 49:524–537.

Schulz H (1983): The influence of pre-sleep conditions on the temporal structure of sleep. Paper presented at the 4th International Congress of Sleep Research, Bologna, Italy.

Schulz H, Lund R (1983): Sleep onset REM episodes are associated with circadian parameters of body temperature. A study in depressed patients and normal controls. Biol Psychiatry 18:1411–1426.

Schulz H, Lund R, Cording C, Dirlich G. (1979): Bimodal distribution of REM sleep latencies in depression. Biol Psychiatry 14:595–600.

Shimizu A, Hiyama H, Yagasaki A, et al (1979): Sleep of depressed patients with hypersomnia: A 24-h polygraphic study. Waking Sleeping 3:335–339.

Snyder F (1968): Electrographic studies of sleep in depression. In Kline NS, Laska E (eds): Computers and Electronic Devices in Psychiatry. New York, Grune and Stratton, pp 272–301.

Taub JM, Hawkins DR, Van de Castle RL (1978): Electrographic analysis of the sleep cycle in young depressed patients. Biol Psychiatry 7:203–214.

Weitzman ED, Nogeire C, Perlow et al (1974): Effects of a prolonged 3-hour sleep–wake cycle on sleep stages, plasma cortisol, growth hormone, and body temperature in man. J Clin Endocrinol 38(6):1018–1029.

Wiliams RL, Karacan I, Hursch C (1974): Electroencephalography (EEG) of Human Sleep: Clinical Applications New York, Wiley.

Zulley J (1980): Distribution of REM sleep in entrained 24 hour and freerunning sleep–wake cycles. Sleep 2:377–389.

7

A Chronobiologic Study of Depression: Discussion from a Methodologic Perspective

G. Dirlich, H. Barthelmes, L. von Lindern, R. Lund, and D. von Zerssen

In this chapter a study of chronobiologic aspects of depression is reviewed from a methodologic point of view. The clinical study was based on long-term observations of a set of variables. The limited scope for experimentation in psychiatric research, the importance of environmental factors as confounding variables, and the complex structure of the observational data have contributed to the methodologic problems discussed here. As it is likely that similar problems will be encountered in similar studies in the future, we believe that an examination of these problems will prove useful to other researchers in the field.

The first efforts to introduce chronobiologic hypotheses into theoretical concepts of affective disorders were made in the late-1960s and mid-1970s (Halberg, 1968; Papoušek 1975). The rapidly progressing experimental and theoretical work on human chronobiology provided an appropriate frame of reference for the planned investigation (Wever, 1979). Unfortunately, the precise knowledge of how to perform empirical chronobiologic studies with mentally ill subjects was then largely lacking.

The study examined in this chapter was first conceptualized in 1975. It was performed by an interdisciplinary team of investigators at the Max Planck Institute for Psychiatry in Munich. The central goal of our project was the collection of a broad data base that would allow us to explore chronobiologic aspects of depression. An additional goal was to test, empirically, the "desynchronization hypothesis," which had received anecdotal support from studies performed by Pflug and coworkers (personal communication; Pflug et al., 1976) and Atkinson and coworkers (Atkinson et al., 1975). The results and conclusions from our study were published elsewhere (Schulz et al., 1979; Doerr et al., 1979; Emrich et al., 1979; von Zerssen et al., 1979; von Zerssen and Doerr, 1980; Dirlich et al., 1981; Schulz and Tetzlaff, 1982; Doerr and von Zerssen, 1983; Lund et al., 1983; von Zerssen et al., 1983; Lund et al., 1985; Schulz and Lund, 1985; von Zerssen et al., 1985; von Zerssen, chapter 8 in this volume). In this chapter, therefore, we focus our discussion on the design of the study and on the analysis of the data. Results are reported only to illustrate methodologic approaches and problems.

OVERVIEW

Ethical considerations limit the range of empirical studies that can be conducted with mentally ill subjects. Significant limitations and constraints must be taken into account and various tradeoffs must be made. We address some of these problems below. In the first part of this chapter, a description of the design of the study is presented. We also discuss some of the considerations that led to a scientifically promising and clinically tolerable compromise.

A central feature of the observational data collected in our study is their structure of multivariate time series. Data analysis and interpretation require a quantitative data reduction that, generally speaking, preserves "important information." In the second part of this chapter, we describe our general approach and some of the underlying considerations concerning the processing and analysis of the data. We have explored certain standard methods in chronobiology, leading to a stepwise reduction of the quantity and complexity of the data. Specifically, we describe the methods of educed waveforms and spectral analysis and we discuss how they relate to each other with respect to the information they represent.

DESIGN OF THE STUDY

Several constraints resulted from the main goal of our project, namely, the collection of a broad data base for an exploration of chronobiologic aspects of depression.

First, it was necessary to observe patients for extended periods of time in order to capture the ongoing psychobiologic processes. Second, we had to consider numerous variables because endogenous depression affects a wide spectrum of psychic, physiologic, and behavioral processes. Third, it was necessary to control intervening variables before and during the period of observation. These constraints resulted from the intention to perform a scientific experiment. They stood in stark contrast to the requirement to provide an appropriate clinical environment for the depressed patients. Finally, we were aware that extensive standardization of the environment and frequent long-term testing and observation would influence and modify the processes under investigation.

The design that emerged from extensive discussions in our research group is a compromise in which the foregoing constraints have been considered. It is described in detail in Table 7.1.

The design is determined by (1) the psychobiologic states under investigation, (2) the variables that we studied, (3) the environment in which the study was conducted, (4) the duration of the period of observation for each subject, and (5) the daily sampling schedule (Table 7.1).

The selection of the subjects was based upon the criteria summarized in Table 7.2. The design was tested in a pilot study with two subjects (one healthy subject and one patient). The same design was used in all experiments with 24 patients and 10 control subjects with minor modifications.

The process of conceiving and defining the design of our study can be regarded as a problem-solving procedure in which several tradeoffs played a central role. We discuss them in the following sections. In reality, these problems were closely interconnected, and their solutions had to be approached simultaneously. However, from a methodologic perspective it is helpful for the design of future studies of such nature to divide the planning stage into tasks such as those discussed here.

Tradeoff Problems in Planning the Study

A familiar problem encountered in the planning of empirical studies is the following: two factors, for example, Y and Z, that are relevant for the scientific value of the study must be weighed and balanced against each other. They are both functions of a variable X to which the investigator can assign different values. The task is to select the most appropriate value for X, one that yields a good tradeoff value for Y and Z. The following is a good example: an increase in the sample size (X) in general leads to greater reliability of the obtained results (Y). This is an

136

Table 7.1. Design of the Study.

Psychobiologic States	Subjects	Label
Endogenous depression	Ten patients	D
Symptom free remission	Same ten former patients	R
Mental health	Ten matched subjects	C

Observed Variables	Method	Label
Mood		
Adjective mood scale	Self-rating questionnaire	AMS
Visual analog scale	Self-rating	VAS (SR)
Visual analog scale	Observer's rating	VAS (OR)
Motor- and mental activity		
Motor activity of arm	Modified wrist watch	MAA
Motor activity of leg	Modified wrist watch	MAL
Calculation test	Add and subtract problems	CAL
Tapping speed	Finger tapping	TS
Excretion of saliva and urine		
Salivation rate	Dental role	SAL
Urine volume	Collected at sampling times	UV
Urinary sodium	Sodium in urine sample	NA
Urinary potassium	Potassium in urine sample	K
Neuroendocrine and vegetative processes		
Urinary free cortisol	In urine sample	CO
Body temperature	Rectal probe	TE

Environmental conditions
  Clinical ward routine (for all states, all subjects)
    Daily schedule of events
      Bed rest: 10:30 PM to 7:00 AM
      Breakfast: 8:00 AM
      Video session: 9:00 AM (only in D: Monday, Wednesday, Friday)
      Lunch: 11:30 AM
      Supper: 5:30 PM
Duration of observation period (for all states, all subjects):
  Minimum 14 consecutive days (preceded by three adaptation days in the state of depression)
Daily sampling schedule:
  7:00 AM, 10:00 AM, 1:00 PM, 4:00 PM, 7:00 PM, 10:00 PM, and 2:30 AM
    [no test of mental activity variables (TS, CAL) and salivation, and no monitoring of motor activity variables (MAA, MAL) at 2:30 AM]

Table 7.2. Criteria for the Selection of Subjects.

State of depression
  Unambiguous diagnosis: endogenous depression
  Very low likelihood of suicide
  Delay of drug treatment acceptable with respect to severity of symptoms and social
    circumstances
  No organic diseases (CNS, other)
  Age
    men: between 18 and 69
    women: after menopause and up to 69
  No drug treatment before start of observations
State of remission
  Former patient, subject in state D group
  Unambiguously in symptom-free state of remission
  No drug treatment, no lithium during last month
  No electroshock treatment during last 3 months
State of mental health
  No mental disease, no organic disease
  Matching criteria: age, sex

advantage with respect to the quality of the information, but it may also require that the study be of longer duration. This may create a disadvantage with respect to the utility of the study (Z). Such tradeoff situations are typically encountered in conceiving and designing clinical studies. They contribute significantly to many of the difficulties in conducting clinical research. We now discuss some of the tradeoff problems that had to be solved during the planning phase of our study.

Psychologic States and Sample Size. The state of depression (D) has two natural reference states: the state of mental health (C, for control), and the state of symptom-free remission (R). An investigation and comparison of the three states yields more information than a comparison of D with only one reference state. Moreover, a comparison of states D and R in the same subjects (alternative 1) is superior to a comparison of a group of patients in state D with a group of different subjects in state R (alternative 2) with respect to the quality of information. The obvious advantage of the first alternative is that intraindividual comparisons can be carried out whereas in the second case, only group comparisons are possible. We chose the first alternative (Table 7.1). A sample size of ten subjects in each state (D, R, C) was necessary for the compilation of an adequate data base and satisfied minimal sample size requirements for statistical analysis.

Our study included ten control subjects and ten patients observed in both D and R. As it was very likely that not all patients who had been observed during the state of depression would be available for observations during the state of remission, it was necessary to enlarge the sample size during the state D. Thus, we studied a total of 20 patients, 16 of whom met all of the selection criteria (Table 7.2) and yielded sufficiently complete data sets (von Zerssen et al., 1985). Moreover, in some cases we extended the period of observation in order to obtain more reliable data. Thus, at the end of the study, we had collected 760 days of observation and a sufficiently complete data base for ten subjects in the states D and R and for ten matched controls (Table 7.2). The intervals between the D and R periods of observation ranged from 4 to 36 months and delayed significantly the length of time needed to complete the study. The examples of data and results presented in this chapter are derived from the ten patients who were observed in both states D and R; we do not refer here to data of the control subjects or of a few additional endogenously depressed patients who took part in the study (see von Zerssen et al., 1985).

Variables. The composition of the set of variables can also be discussed in terms of the tradeoff problem. "Informational completeness" had to be weighed against the mental stress of the subjects and against the workload of the investigators. We used the following guidelines:

1. The variables had to capture the most important psychiatric aspects of depression: mood, which exhibits circadian and long-term fluctuations; motor and mental activity, which are usually reduced during the state of depression; salivation, which is reduced in depression; and cortisol, which is significantly increased in depression. An additional important aspect of depression is sleep, which was polygraphically recorded in our study (see Schulz et al., 1979; Schulz and Tetzlaff, 1982; Schulz and Lund, 1985; Lund et al., 1985). However, sleep is not discussed here because its analysis raises methodologic problems quite different from the ones discussed here.

2. The variables included in the study should be those that are the focus of human chronobiology research: body temperature, urine volume, urinary sodium and potassium, and urinary free cortisol, as well as mood, motor activity, and tests of psychomotor performance, namely, tapping and computation speed.

While the study was in progress, we excluded from the battery two variables of mental performance testing—"tapping at the most comfortable speed" and an "estimation of a time interval (10 seconds)." There was so much unsystematic variance in the data that it was impossible to obtain reliable information about circadian phenomena from them. However, we did add to the battery a mood rating scale and a retrospective rating of general activity, both of which were completed by observers. The latter variable is not discussed here.

The required frequency of the tests and the relatively short sampling interval (see below) imposed additional constraints on the final selection of variables. For example, it would have been impossible to measure plasma cortisol during the entire period of the study, nor was a continuous measurement of rectal temperature feasible. However, body temperature was continuously monitored during the time of bed rest (see Lund et al., 1983) for the majority of subjects.

Environmental Conditions. The choice of environmental conditions was also limited because patients during state D had to be admitted to the hospital due to the severity of their symptoms. We decided that the patients and subjects should be included in the daily routine schedule of the ward. The following facts had to be considered in making this decision: The structure of daily activities of subjects according to the strictly prescheduled ward routine undoubtedly acted as a strong zeitgeber (time cue) compared to an environment free of time cues. On the other hand, the normal working situation outside of the hospital also has a strict 24-hour schedule of numerous activities and is in this respect comparable to the ward routine. It cannot be ruled out that the ward routine, in combination with the daily schedule of observations, and especially with a forced awakening every night (see below), may have prevented the development or emergence of psychobiologic rhythms that were no longer coupled to the geophysical time. (If this were the case, our investigation should not be interpreted as an empirical test of the above-mentioned desynchronization hypothesis.) Finally, the alternative of reducing the influence of periodically active zeitgebers by organizing the activities of subjects according to their own intentions was technically too difficult to implement under the circumstances at the time of the study.

Duration of the Observation Period. It is well accepted that the reliability of data representing rhythmic processes increases with the duration of the observation period. In addition to this general rule, there was a special constraint for the period of observation in our case. As already mentioned, we were searching for desynchronized components in some variables with periods at the lower end of the circadian period range (ca. 22 hours) described by Pflug and colleagues (personal communication; Pflug et al. 1976) and Atkinson and colleagues (1975). According to a classical rule in chronobiologic experimentation, the hypothetical endogenous rhythm should advance for at least one complete cycle in relation to the geophysical 24-hour rhythm during the observation period. Therefore, at least 11 days of observation or 12 complete cycles of the hypothetical free-running rhythm had to be monitored. This argument must be viewed in connection with the frequency resolution of spectral analysis, which increases with the duration of the observation period, a relationship that is discussed in detail below.

The aforementioned factors support the choice of a relatively long period of observation. They must be weighed against reasons for the selection of a relatively shorter period of observation. The common denominator here is the increasing risk that during a longer period of observation systematic changes in the observed processes might occur. In particular, there is also the previously mentioned ethical problem of withholding treatment. Moreover, psychologic effects such as changes in the level of motivation due to stress from continued interruptions of sleep had to be considered. We therefore decided to abbreviate the observation period whenever it appeared to be necessary for ethical reasons. Indeed, we discontinued the observation earlier than planned in two cases during state D, and in two cases during state R.

Daily Sampling Schedule. In general, a higher sampling rate yields a better description of the processes under investigation. Continuous sampling—if possible—is optimal. However, since our study explored various circadian rhythms, a high sampling rate was theoretically not required: even two or three measurements per day should have been sufficient to estimate certain circadian components. The sampling theorem requires at least two measurements per cycle of the highest frequency of interest (Koopmans, 1974). Because our study was conceived as a comprehensive exploration of the chronobiology of depression, and not simply as an empirical test of the desynchronization hypothesis, we decided to perform seven measurements per day (Table 7.1). A similar schedule had been used in studies on human circadian rhythms before (Giedke et al., 1974). A sampling interval of 3 hours appeared to be short enough to provide informative descriptions of the assessed processes. The workload (15–20 minutes to carry out the measurements and tests for all variables) and the psychologic burden appeared to be tolerable for patients and control subjects. The daily schedule of observations was also compatible with the schedule of ward activities. A longer sampling interval of 4.5 hours was chosen for the bed rest period because a second interruption of sleep appeared to be an unbearable situation for the patients.

Summary

We have discussed the design of our study as a compromise guided by the concept of tradeoffs between the scientific quality of the data and the ethical and medical constraints imposed by the fact that we had to study patients suffering from depression. Obviously, a critical feature of the study is the set of intervening factors, in particular, effects on psychobiologic rhythms caused by environmental factors related to the clinical and experimental conditions.

EXPLORING THE INFORMATION CONTENT OF THE DATA

The starting point for the data analysis in our study is governed by three facts: (1) a set of questions or hypotheses rooted in the psychobiology of depression and/or in human chronobiology, (2) a data base compiled according to the above design, and (3) a conceptual framework and "toolkit" of chronobiologic and statistical standard methods. For a successful exploratory data analysis it was necessary that the questions, the structure of the data, and the tools matched each other. The situation encountered in our study can be briefly characterized as follows:

(1) The questions of our study were centered around the following aspects of the investigated processes:

> Regularities (in particular in the circadian period domain) in individual time series, namely, intraindividual regularities in single variables
>
> Intraindividual differences in the regularities between the states D and R, namely, disturbances of the biologic rhythms in single variables
>
> Systematic group differences between the states D, R, and C in single variables
>
> Commonalities and differences in comparing the different observed variables in the states D, R, and C

We have not attempted to define the fundamental concept of "regularity" rigorously, because a rigorous definition bears the danger of

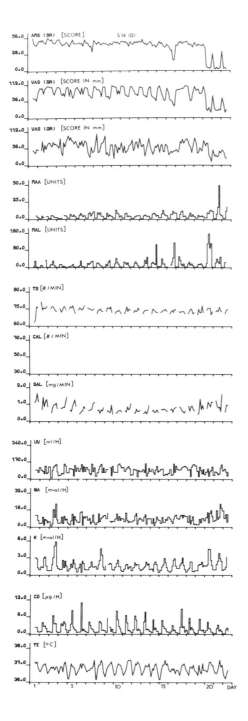
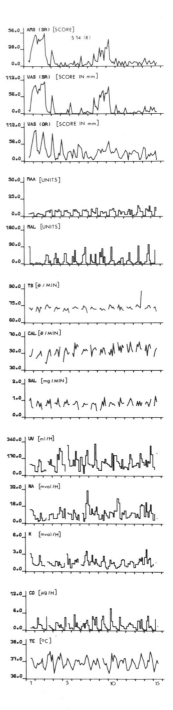

narrowing the scope of interest. Certainly, 24-hour rhythms and rhythms with deviating periods are interesting regularities. In particular, the waveform of such rhythms, their amplitude, and their position with respect to a temporal reference system are interesting features of the temporal structure of the observed processes.

(2) The counterpart to questions and hypotheses is the data base. The data from our study provide rough descriptions of psychobiologic processes. We measured 13 variables to capture different aspects of depression and performed 98 test sessions during the course of 14 days of observation. Thus, the description of one subject in one observation period involves 1274 data points. Such a "body of data" has a complex structure: it is a multivariate time series. A certain degree of redundancy in these data sets must be assumed, in the time dimension as well as between the different variables. An exploration of the actual information content of the data is the global goal of data analysis.

(3) The tools, namely, the methods and procedures used in the analysis of the data, are standard procedures in chronobiologic research. The guideline for our approach to data analysis was determined by the exploratory nature of the study: exhaustive search for temporal structures, maximal transparency of results, attention to unproven implicit models underlying the computational procedures, and caution in generalizing the findings.

Figure 7.1. Time courses of 13 variables (sequence from top to bottom according to Table 7.1) of one patient (S 14, male, 47 years) in the state of depression (*left*—observation period in July and August 1978) and in the state of remission (*right*—observation period in October 1979).
   Method. *x* axis—time (days), tickmarks at midnight; *y* axis—scale units identical for depression and remission. Raw data were sampled according to the sampling schedule (table 7.1). Graphical interpolation: spot-checking variables linearly, integrating variables by step functions assigned the same value, namely, raw value divided by sampling interval, to the interval preceding the measurement; missing values—blank (interruption).
   Remarks. *Depression*: trend in AMS; great local variation in VAS (OR), low reliability; increase in MAA and MAL towards the end of the observation period; learning effect in TS during the first days; no observation of CAL; missing values for TS and SAL at 2:30 AM; highly regular 24-hour time course in TE during days 8–12. *Remission*: dramatic variations in mood variables [AMS (SR) and VAS (SR)] during first days and again during days 8–10 with relatively better values during days 4–8 (with respect to depression) and days 11 to the end of the observation; relatively more MAA and MAL; absence of obvious differences between depression and remission in mental activity variables, salivation, urinary, neuroendocrine, and vegetative variables.

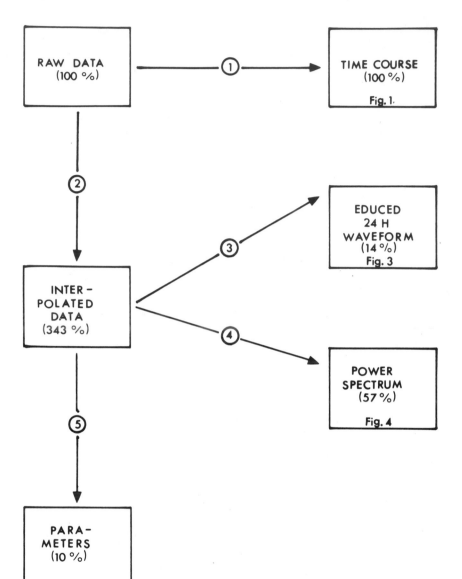

Figure 7.2. Steps in data analysis. Boxes represent data structures (left column) and results (right column). They contain the names of the data structures with respect to results, information about the reduction rate in percent of the raw data, and, for the results, references to the figures. Arrows represent computational procedures. They are labeled by numbers: (1) Graphical interpolation, linear for spot checking variables, respectively, step functions for integrating variables. (2) Interpolation of hourly values with the same interpolation tech-

Time Course Representation

The first step in analyzing the data was their presentation in the form of time courses, by means of which some information becomes evident. For example, Figure 7.1 shows two sets of data describing one subject during a state of depression and the same subject during a state of remission. Such data presentation enables us to answer certain questions by mere visual inspection, e.g., missing data points, outliers, trends or changes of level, differences in global mean values, and obvious differences in the degree of regularity.

However, some questions cannot be answered solely by visual inspection. Are there significant periodic components? Are there temporally stable relations between the variables? Are there phase differences between state D and state R? Are there differences in the relative magnitude of the 24-hour components? The information required to answer these questions is not evident. It has to be extracted, decoded, and presented by means of special computational procedures. The most useful of these procedures are described below.

Strategy of Data Analysis

The general strategy for data analysis is depicted in Figure 7.2. Two standard methods in circadian rhythm research, namely, spectral analysis and educed waveforms play a central role in our approach (Dirlich et al., 1981). Spectral analysis is particularly useful in the search for periodic components. A computation of educed waveforms for dominant periods, which either may be expected due to experimental conditions or have been detected by means of spectral analysis, is a powerful approach to extract and represent periodically recurring components in the data (Enright, 1981). Educed waveforms unveil the shape and magnitude of such periodically recurring components, which we will call rhythms.

Because our study was carried out in an environment with a pattern of events and activities recurring periodically every 24 hours, a frequency synchronization of the psychobiologic processes to the geophysical time was to be expected. Therefore, we assumed that the mea-

---

niques as in (1) combined with three-point moving average smoothing procedure. (3) Computation of educed 24-hour waveforms (details in the legend of Figure 7.3). (4) Computation of power spectra (details in the legends of Figures 7.4 and 7.5). (5) Computation of a condensed set of parameters of the 24-hour educed waveforms and of the spectra. The results described in Zerssen et al. (1985) stem from these data.

146

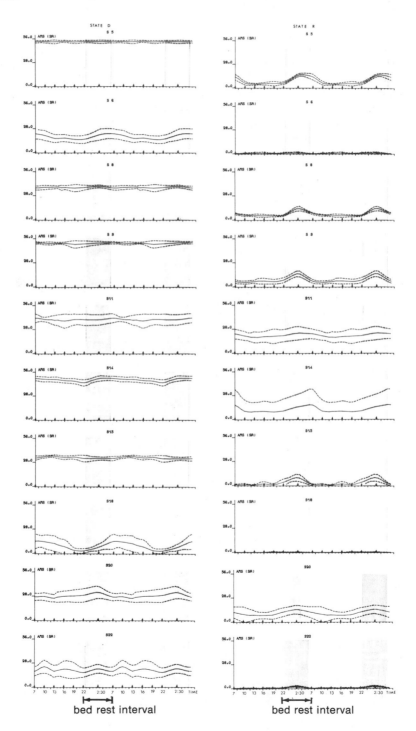

sured variables should display significant 24-hour components in the spectral representation and that educed 24-hour waveforms should yield distinctly typical curves for each variable, with interindividual variations. In addition, we wished to examine the hypothesis that free-running rhythms might contribute to the observed time courses in certain variables. Spectral analysis appeared to be the appropriate method for this exploration.

An important result of our study is the absence of any significant rhythms in the circadian period range, with periods deviating from 24 hours and amplitudes significantly greater than the noise component in all variables either in the state of depression or in the state of remission (von Zerssen et al., 1985). In the majority of cases, the 24-hour rhythms were marked and the 24-hour spectral components were prominent.

Educed 24-hour Waveform

Educed 24-hour waveforms were computed for all observations in the data base. An illustration of this approach is given in Figure 7.3, which shows the educed 24-hour waveforms of one variable, AMS, for the ten subjects in the states of depression and remission.

Educed waveforms allow a visual comparison of different observations. The quantity of data on which educed waveforms are based is 14% of the quantity of the raw data in the present case (Figure 7.2). By analyzing the data, certain questions can be answered: What is the amplitude of the educed waveform? At what time of day does the maximum occur? Other questions, however, cannot be answered by this approach: What is the origin of the relatively big error component in the educed waveform of subject 14 in state R (compare Figures 7.1 and 7.3)? What is the temporal relation between different educed waveforms?

Figure 7.3. Educed 24-hour waveforms of Adjective Mood Scale [AMS (SR)] from ten subjects in the state of depression (*left*) and in the state of remission (*right*).

Method. The computation is based on interpolated hourly values: for all values assigned to the geophysical time t ($t = 0-24$ hours) the mean value $m(t)$ and the standard deviation $s(t)$ were computed; these mean values $m(t)$ (*solid line*) and standard deviations $s(t)$ (*dashed lines*) were graphically represented as a standard double plot (Dirlich et al., 1981).

Remarks. Compare the educed waveforms for subject S 14 with the respective data in figure 7.1—distinct 24-hour rhythms are lacking in several cases, which is not only due to ceiling effects (e.g., S 8 in depression). The educed waveform represents the shape of the 24-hour rhythm, but it does not allow one to infer details about the sources of the residual variation.

Power Spectra

The last two questions are typical of problems for which spectral representations of the data are suitable. The spectral representation of a function is fundamentally different from a time domain representation because the parameter in the spectral representation is frequency and length of the period, not time. Both forms of representation are informationally equivalent in principle, which means that time-course representations contain the same information as spectral representations. Indeed, transformations of a function from the time domain into the frequency domain, and back into the time domain by means of an inverse spectral transformation, yield the original function (Figure 7.4). The difference between the two forms of representation lies in the accessibility of the information. For instance, information about the presence of sinusoidal components "pops out" from a spectral representation but it is more or less "hidden" in a time-course representation. In contrast, information about the amplitude at a certain time point is evident from a time-course representation but is hidden in a spectral representation. We discuss certain rules that will facilitate the interpretation of spectral representations.

Time Course and Power Spectrum. In order to demonstrate some properties of spectral analysis, we use an observed time course of the body temperature (Figure 7.5A left). A widely used spectral representation is the power spectrum (Figure 7.5 right).

Relationship Between Educed Waveform and Power Spectrum. Like the educed waveform, the power spectrum yields a drastic reduction of the data: in the present case with 98 tests during the observation period of 14 days the reduction is about 50% in relation to the raw data (Figure 7.2). What is the relationship between the educed waveform and the power spectrum with respect to the information represented by the two methods?

The educed 24-hour waveform of the temperature data and the respective power spectrum are shown in Figure 7.5B. The power spectrum has a typical form: power is assigned only to the spectral components at 24.0, 12.0, 8.0, and 6.0 hours. Together, these components constitute the 24-hour rhythm. This kind of power spectrum is typical for 24-hour rhythms, that is, strictly periodic functions with arbitrary waveforms.

There exists a formal relationship between the educed waveform in the time domain and the power spectrum in the frequency domain:

TIME DOMAIN   FREQUENCY DOMAIN

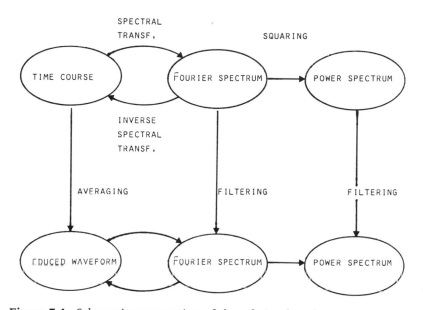

Figure 7.4. Schematic presentation of the relationships between representations in the time domain and in the frequency domain. The fundamental representation in the time domain is the time course. Its counterpart in the frequency domain is the Fourier spectrum. There is a one-to-one mapping between these two forms of representation. The two procedures that yield this mapping are the spectral transformation and the inverse spectral transformation. Power spectra are widely used for graphic representations. They are obtained by computing the sum of the squared Fourier coefficients. The extraction of rhythms can be achieved in both domains by different procedures, namely, an averaging procedure that yields the educed waveform in the time domain and a filtering procedure in the frequency domain.

a given waveform can be transformed into one and only one power spectrum. However, different waveforms may yield the same power spectrum. This is due to the nature of the power spectrum: in contrast to the Fourier spectrum, it does not contain information about the phase of the spectral components (Figure 7.4).

Influence of Phase Shifts in Higher Harmonics. The Fourier spectrum of the educed waveform (Figure 7.5B) was modified by altering the phase angle of the 12.0-hour spectral component by an increment of 6

150

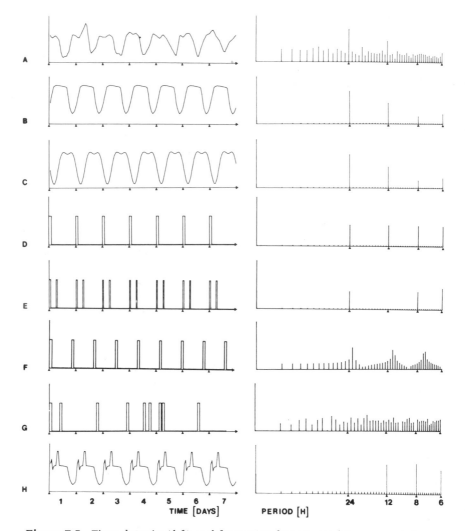

Figure 7.5. Time domain (*left*) and frequency domain (*right*) representations. **A.** Body temperature during 7 days (S 6 in state R, days 2–8). **B.** Educed waveform of body temperature (S 6 in state R, days 1–13). **C.** Waveform obtained by altering the phase angle of the 12.0-hour component of spectrum **B** by an increment of 6 hours. **D, E, F, G.** Variants of a process that is in state "on" for 2 hours per day and "off" for 22 hours per day. The variants **D, E,** and **F** are deterministic: in **D** the process is "on" for the first 2 hours every day; in **E,** the "on" phase is partitioned into two 1-hour "on" intervals with an intermediate "off" interval of 5 hours; and in **F** the duration of the "off" interval is reduced to 20 hours. The variant **G** is a simple stochastic process—the time interval between consecutive 2-hour "on" phases is a random quantity, with a duration

hours. The power spectrum remains unaltered by this modification. However, the periodic time function obtained by an inverse spectral transformation (Figure 7.5C left) obviously has a different shape in comparison to the function shown in Figure 7.5B. This shows that (1) the higher harmonics in the power spectrum (components at 12.0, 8.0, and 6.0 hours) contribute to the waveform of the 24-hour rhythm and (2) the power spectrum does not contain information about the phase of the spectral components.

Masking Effects. It is important to discuss how so-called masking factors can influence spectral representations. In order to demonstrate this, we consider a process that influences body temperature, namely, motor activity. During a fast walk, body temperature increases with a delay of about 20 minutes and the time course shows a transient rise (called masking effect). A fixed amount of motor activity can be carried out in different temporal patterns. For example, a walk from place A to place B and back can either be carried out without interruption, or the walker can rest at place B for some time before resuming the walk back. He can perform the activity during the same period of time every day or he can do it at different times. How do such alterations in the temporal schedule of motor activity affect the spectral representation of the temperature? We attempt to answer this question in two steps.

---

that is equally distributed in (0, 44), i.e., each value between 0 and 44 hours for the duration of the "off" interval has the same probability. **H.** Waveform **B** superimposed by an evoked component (process **E**).

The length of the time series was 13 days, the period of observation for subject S 6 in state R. The data were processed by the standard procedures used for the analysis of the observational data from our study. The power magnitude is represented here and in Figure 7.6 by a nonlinear scale (square root of magnitude) in order to demonstrate also the smaller portions of the power distribution. The frequency resolution of the power spectra is slightly different from the resolution of the spectra in Figure 7.6 because those were computed for periods of 14 days in most cases.

Some information on how to read spectra can be learned from this figure: (1) strictly periodic processes whose period is a factor of the duration of the observation interval have spectra with lines only at 24 hours and its factors, namely, 12, 8, 6, . . . hours (**B, C, D, E,** and **H**); (2) if the period of a strictly periodic process is not a submultiple of the observation interval (the period is 22 hours in **F**), a leakage of power into the entire frequency range can be observed; (3) randomness in the temporal organization of the "on" phases changes the structure of the spectrum fundamentally (**G**)—lines become random quantities that are approximately equally distributed over the entire frequency range; and, (4) a strictly periodic masking component does not affect the basic structure of the spectrum, but it affects the magnitude of the spectral lines.

First, we discuss spectral representations of different patterns in the time domain. The time domain representations (Figures 7.5D,E,F,G left) should be interpreted as indicator functions of motor activity: the state is "on" during a walk and "off" (0) otherwise. We demonstrate four different schedules for the temporal organization of an activity that, over an extended period, is performed for an average of 2 hours per day.

When the activity events occur in stable temporal relationship with the geophysical day, a 24-hour rhythm results (Figures 7.5D,E) and the power spectra exhibit the typical form for rhythms, which has been described above. Different temporal schedules of the activity are represented by different distributions of the power to the four lines.

Periodic temporal patterns whose periods are not integral submultiples of the duration of the analyzed time interval (in our study 336 hours in the majority of cases), in other words, rhythms with periods deviating from 24 hours, have spectra with regular peak-and-trough patterns (Figure 7.5F).

Random patterns in the time domain (Figure 7.5G) yield spectra whose lines have randomly distributed magnitudes. Their distributions are determined by the probability laws that govern the processes in the time domain. The magnitude of the lines in the present example shows random variations across the entire period band.

Let us now try to answer the above question, namely, how spectral representations are influenced by masking effects. We make the simplifying assumption that, temporally, the evoked reaction of body temperature to motor activity is closely related to the occurrence of the activity, that is, the time course of the evoked component in the temperature is highly correlated with the temporal pattern of the activity. Moreover, we assume that the evoked component is additively superimposed on the time course of the body temperature. In this case, the value of the temperature at each time point is the sum of two values, the value of the 24-hour rhythm (Figure 7.5B) plus the evoked component (Figure 7.5E). Thus, the observed course of temperature may be the result of a superposition of a 24-hour rhythm and a periodic masking component (Figure 7.5H).

In the power spectrum, information about the composition of the time course from these two functions—in the following called "elementary functions"—is in most cases not displayed in evident form, because both functions may have power assigned to the 24.0-, 12.0-, 8.0-, and 6.0-hour spectral components. In this case the components may be enhanced, diminished, or even completely averaged out depending on the phase relationships. Obviously, in such cases the magnitude of the components of the power spectrum of the composed function is less than the sum of the respective components in the power spectra of the two elementary functions.

Using Power Spectra as a Tool

The preceding discussion has shown that the influence of masking factors on the spectral representation can be complex. With one special model for the additive decomposition of the observed time function into elementary functions, the relationship between a decomposition in the time domain and its equivalent in the spectral representation is formally simple, namely, with the Fourier model of harmonic sine and cosine functions. In this case each elementary function in the time domain is represented by one and only one spectral component, namely, a spectral line. The examples discussed here demonstrate that such simple decompositions in the frequency domain are not obtained with other classes of elementary time functions.

Given this situation, how should we interpret a prominent line in a power spectrum? A precondition is that it be reliable. If this is the case, the line indicates a periodically operating oscillator. If, in addition, there are no prominent subharmonics, the oscillator generates an approximately sinusoidal rhythm. However, if there are prominent subharmonics two cases are possible: (1) the oscillator generates a nonsinusoidal rhythm and the subharmonics result from the shape of the rhythms; or (2) another oscillator is operating at a subharmonic frequency. Therefore, prominent lines in spectra must be interpreted with great caution, and the question whether separate lines indicate biologically meaningful component processes must be investigated from a substantial psychobiologic perspective rather than from a formal mathematical and data-processing perspective.

Although the interpretation of spectra can be difficult and the method of spectral analysis as such does not solve the problem of detecting biologically meaningful factors, spectral representations and, particularly, power spectra are useful methods in exploratory data analyses. We demonstrate this by some of the results from our study. Figure 7.6 shows the power spectra of urinary potassium.

The power spectra shown here all exhibit a complex structure. The existence of 24-hour rhythms in almost all cases is evident. Moreover, and in contrast to the method of educed waveforms, the power spectrum reveals how the entire power, that is, the variability of the time series, is distributed across the period domain. For instance, it can easily be seen how much power is assigned to the ultradian and infradian period

154

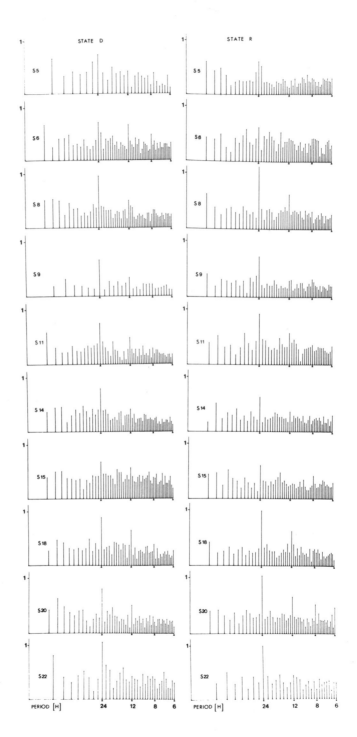

bands. Such a partitioning of the total power with respect to different period bands can yield additional information about the observed processes.

Summary

In the second part of this chapter we have attempted to demonstrate the relationships between (1) our working hypotheses and questions, (2) the structure and content of the data base, and (3) our methods of data analysis, in particular, educed waveforms and power spectra. Even during the planning phase of the study, our major concern was to create data structures and computational procedures that would be mutually compatible and would permit an extensive exploration guided by our working hypotheses and questions. In the preceding sections we have described certain details of our approach to data analysis, which is based on methods that are now classical in chronobiology. We have also demonstrated some important methodologic limitations of this approach. Even with advanced computational procedures of the kind that we have used, data analysis in biologic rhythm research remains a difficult and sensitive task. It requires not only theoretical knowledge about the

---

Figure 7.6. Power spectra of urinary potassium (K) from ten subjects in the state of depression (*left*) and in the state of remission (*right*).

Method. The computation is based on interpolated hourly values: power spectra were computed by the mixed radix Fast Fourier algorithm. The scale units for the power (*y* axis) are identical for all subjects and both states. The unit is mval/hr. The graphical representation of the power is the square root of the power magnitude. The frequency resolution is determined by the length of the observation interval (14 days in most cases): spectral lines 1–12 represent components in the infradian frequency range and lines 13, 14, 15, and 16 represent components with periods of 25.8, 24.0, 22.4, and 21.0 hours, respectively, that is, the circadian frequency range according to the classical chronobiologic definition. As the higher frequencies are approached, the reliability of the spectral representation is limited by the sampling interval: components with periods of not less than 6 hours are reliably measured using a sampling interval of 3 hours. The 24-hour component in the data (compare the educed waveform, Figure 7.3) is decomposed into spectral components with the period 24 hours and its factors, namely, 12.0, 8.0, and 6.0 hours.

Remarks. In the majority of the spectra the 24.0-hour lines are prominent. However, there are spectra in which no significant power is assigned to 24.0 hours (e.g., S 5 in D). Prominent lines at 12.0 hours can be seen in some spectra (e.g., S 6 in D). There are cases where the power is almost equally distributed (e.g., S 6 in R); this indicates the absence of periodic components in the data. The range of variation for the relative magnitude of the most prominent spectral line ranges from 14% (S 5 in R) to 69% (S 8 in R).

156   G. Dirlich et al.

mathematical background, but experience based on domain-specific applications as well. Great caution must be exercised in applying methods that extract and represent information in a form that is still unfamiliar to many researchers in the field. The methods discussed here yield only descriptions of the ongoing processes and they do not necessarily suggest appropriate models and hypotheses. Certainly, they cannot replace the empirical work on which the conception and testing of psychobiologic hypotheses must be based.

We believe that it remains a very important task to explore the free scope for the design of chronobiologic studies within the given constraints of clinical research, while simultaneously exploring the power, the limitations, and the pitfalls of the methods of data analysis. Moreover, we are confronted with the difficult task of posing hypotheses and questions, designing studies and analyzing data, and choosing methods and tools in such a way that all are mutually compatible.

We should like to thank H.-D. Rohde for creative programing and I. Bickert for designing the figures.

REFERENCES

Atkinson M, Kripke DF, Wolf SR (1975): Autorhythmometry in manic-depressives. Chronobiologia 2:325–335.

Dirlich G, Kammerloher A, Schulz H, et al (1981): Temporal coordination of rest–activity cycle, body temperature, urinary free cortisol, and mood in a patient with 48-hour unipolar-depressive cycles in clinical and time-cue-free environments. Biol Psychiatry 16:163–179.

Doerr P, Zerssen D von (1983): Die zirkadiane Ausscheidung an freiem Harncortisol während der depressiven Phase und im freien Intervall bei Patienten mit einer endogenen Depression. In Faust V, Hole G (eds): Depressionen. Stuttgart, Hippokrates, pp 142–150.

Doerr P, Zerssen D von, Fischler M, Schulz H (1979): Relationship between mood changes and adrenal cortical activity in a patient with 48-hour unipolar-depressive cycles. J Affective Disord 1:93–104.

Emrich HM, Aldenhoff JB, Cramon D von (1977): Registration of motor activity in postcomatous states. Excerpta Medica 427:33.

Emrich HM, Lund R, Zerssen D von (1979): Vegetative Funktionen und körperliche Aktivität in der endogenen Depression. Verlaufsuntersuchungen von Speichelsekretion, Temperatur und Motorik bei einem Patienten mit 48-Stunden-Zyklus. Arch Psychiatr und Nervenkrank 227:227–240.

Enright J (1981): Data analysis. In Aschoff J (ed): Handbook of Behavioral Neurobiology, Vol 4: Biological Rhythms. New York, Plenum pp 21–39.

Giedke H, Fratranska H, Doerr P, et al (1974): Tagesperiodik der Rektaltemperatur, sowie Ausscheidung von Elektrolyten, Katecholaminmetaboliten und 17-Hydroxicorticosteroiden mit dem Harn beim Menschen mit und ohne Lichtzeitgeber. Int Arch Arbeitsmedizin 32:43–66.

Halberg F (1968): Physiologic considerations underlying rhythmometry, with special reference to emotional illness. In de Ajuriaguerra J (ed): Cycles Biologiques et Psychiatrie, Symposium Bel Air III, Geneve, Septembre 1967. Geneve, Georg, and Paris, Mason, pp 73–126.

Koopmans LH (1974): The Spectral Analysis of Time Series. New York, Academic.

Kripke DF (1983): Phase-advance theories for affective illness. In Wehr TA, Goodwin FK (eds): Circadian Rhythms in Psychiatry. Pacific Grove, CA, Boxwood, pp 41–69.

Kripke DF, Mullaney DJ, Atkinson M, Wolf S (1978): Circadian rhythm disorders in manic depressives. Biol Psychiatry 13:335–351.

Lund R, Kammerloher A, Dirlich G (1983): Body temperature in endogenously depressed patients during depression and remission. In Wehr TA, Goodwin FK (eds): Circadian Rhythms in Psychiatry. Pacific Grove, CA, Boxwood, pp 77–88.

Lund R, Berger M, Schulz H (1985): Körpertemperatur und REM-Schlaf bei affektiven Störungen. In Ferstl R, Rey E-R, Vaitl D (eds): Klinische Psychologie, Psychophysiologische Merkmale klinischer Symptome, Band II Depression und Schizophrenie. Weinheim, Beltz, pp 48–69.

Papoušek M (1975): Chronobiologische Aspekte der Zyclothymie. Fortschr Neurol Psychiatr Grenzgebiete 43:381.

Pflug B, Erikson R, Johnsson A (1976): Depression and daily temperature: A longterm study. Acta Psychiatr Scand 54:254–266.

Pirke KM, Stamm D (1970): Die Bestimmung von Natrium, Kalium und Calzium im Harn mit dem Filterflammenphotometer. Z Klin Chem Klin Biochem 8, 241–248.

Schulz H, Tetzlaff W (1982): Distribution of REM latencies after sleep interruption in depressive patients and control subjects. Biol Psychiatry 17:1367–1376.

Schulz H, Lund R (1985): On the origin of early REM episodes in the sleep of depressed patients. A comparison of three hypotheses. Psychiatry Res 16:65–77.

Schulz H, Lund R, Cording C, Dirlich G (1979): Bimodal distribution of REM sleep latencies in depression. Biol Psychiatry 14:595–600.

Wever RA (1979): The Circadian System of Man. New York, Springer.

Zerssen D von (1983): Chronobiology of depression. In Angst H (ed): The Origins of Depression: Current Concepts and Approaches. Dahlem Konferenzen. Berlin, Springer, pp 253–271.

Zerssen D von (1986): Clinical Self-Rating Scales (CSRS) of the Munich Psychiatric Information System (PSYCHIS München): In Sartorius N, Ban TA (eds): Assessment of Depression. Berlin, Springer, pp 270–303.

Zerssen D von, with the collaboration of Koeller D-M (1976): Klinische Selbstbeurteilungs-Skalen (KSb-S) aus dem Münchener Psychiatrischen Informations-System (PSYCHIS München): a) Allgemeiner Teil. b) Die Befindli-chkeits-Skala. Weinheim, Beltz.

Zerssen D von, Doerr P (1980): The role of the hypothalamo—pituitary—adrenocortical system in psychiatric disorders. Adv Biol Psychiatry 5:85–106.

Zerssen D von, Lund R, Doerr P, et al (1979): 48-hour-cycles of depression and their biological concomitants with and without "zeitgebers." A case report. In Saletu B, Berner P, Hollister L (eds): Neuropsychopharmacology. New York, Pergamon, pp 233–245.

Zerssen D von, Dirlich G, Fischler M (1983): Influence of an abnormal time routine and therapeutic measures on 48-hour cycles of affective disorders: Chronobiological considerations. In Wehr TA, Goodwin FK (eds): Circadian Rhythms in Psychiatry. Pacific Grove, CA, Boxwood, pp 109–127.

Zerssen D von, Barthelmes H, Dirlich G, et al (1985): Circadian rhythms in endogenous depression. Psychiatry Res 16:51–63.

8

What is Wrong with Circadian Clocks in Depression?

Detlev von Zerssen

CIRCADIAN PHENOMENA IN DEPRESSION

Circadian phenomena in the clinical features of the endogenous (melancholic) subtype of major depressive disorder were first described in the latter part of the nineteenth century (Krafft-Ebing, 1874). The most frequently observed phenomena of this kind are diurnal variations in the severity of depression, with the highest degree of severity usually occurring in the morning, and increasing interruptions of night sleep with early morning awakening (Papoušek, 1975; Wehr and Goodwin, 1981, 1983; von Zerssen, 1983). A more rare phenomenon is the occurrence of 48-hour periods of depression, one "bad" (depressive) day alternating with one "good" (symptom-free) day in unipolar patients, or with one manic/hypomanic day in bipolar patients (von Zerssen et al., 1983). The switch from the normal or the manic/hypomanic state to depression tends to occur during night sleep (Sitaram et al., 1978; von Zerssen et al., 1979). The effect of sleep deprivation on the clinical course of endogenous depression (Gillin, 1983) is to alleviate the depressive state in half to two-thirds of the patients for 1–2 days. Partial sleep deprivation during the second (Schilgen and Tölle, 1980), but not during the first half of the night (Goetze and Tölle, 1981), is similarly effective. A more

159

sustained effectiveness was ascribed to deprivation of REM sleep, rather than deprivation of non-REM sleep, over several weeks (Vogel et al., 1980). This observation is noteworthy in view of the findings regarding EEG sleep parameters in major depression (Gillin et al., 1984; Thase and Kupfer, 1986): In over half of the patients, the first REM sleep period occurs earlier, lasts longer, and exhibits more eye movements than in normals, whereas slow-wave sleep (SWS) is usually reduced; furthermore, REM sleep is suppressed by almost all antidepressant drugs.

CHRONOBIOLOGIC CONCEPTS OF DEPRESSION

During the last two decades, several attempts have been made to explain the circadian phenomena in depression using theoretical models of circadian rhythms (cf. Papoušek, 1975; Rusak, 1984; Wehr and Goodwin, 1981, 1983). The theoretical models were developed by chronobiologists on the basis of experimental research in animals and healthy human volunteers (cf. Aschoff, 1981; Aschoff et al., 1982a; Minors and Waterhouse, 1981; Suda et al., 1979; Wever, 1979). Among these models, the two-oscillator model, which was conceptualized and formalized by Wever (1979) and slightly modified by Kronauer et al. (1982), and the two-process model of sleep regulation, which was conceptualized by Borbély (1982) and formalized by Daan et al. (1984), have received much attention in research on depression.

According to the *two-oscillator model*, a strong circadian oscillator, the "master clock," modulates the time course of most biologic functions (e.g., cortisol secretion, core body temperature, urinary excretion of sodium and potassium). It interacts with a weaker circadian oscillator that modulates the sleep–wake cycle and the time course of certain biologic (e.g., urinary calcium excretion) and most psychologic functions (e.g., reaction time and psychomotor speed). The weaker oscillator is more easily influenced by "zeitgebers," namely, a variety of environmental stimuli, such as bright light and social interactions, but the stronger oscillator then follows the rhythm of its weaker companion within a certain range of entrainment.

Overt circadian rhythms depend not only on the functions of these two oscillators, the so-called internal clocks, but are also influenced by masking effects (Aschoff et al., 1982b; Wever, 1979). Masking effects can be subdivided into external and internal ones. Environmental stimuli (e.g., meals) constitute external masking factors. Interactions among overt circadian rhythms (e.g., fatigue, motor activity, and core body temperature) are the basis of internal masking phenomena. Masking may increase the range of circadian oscillation (positive masking), reduce it (negative masking), or modify the shape of the rhythm.

Within the *two-process model of sleep regulation*, as formulated by Borbély (1982), the function of the stronger circadian oscillator (the "master clock") is represented by process C. Process S is conceptualized as a sleep factor that increases during wakefulness and decreases during sleep. It can be operationalized by means of a frequency analysis of the sleep EEG as the amount of delta sleep. In Daan's extension of the model, not only the threshold for awakening but also that of falling asleep is modulated by process C. The sleep–wake cycle results from an interaction of processes S and C. This model was also used to explain sleep disturbances in depression (Borbély et al., 1984; Borbély and Wirz-Justice, 1982). It was postulated that there was a deficiency of the sleep factor during episodes of the disorder. This assumption would explain the patients' hyposomnia, with early morning awakening and the lack of slow-wave sleep (SWS) and a compensatory increase of REM activity at the beginning of night sleep. Within this theoretical framework, the therapeutic effect of sleep deprivation in depression was ascribed to the accumulation of the sleep factor during the sleep-deprived night. The relapse into depression after 1 or 2 days was referred to as a decrement of the factor during the subsequent sleep period(s).

Most chronobiologic concepts of depression are, however, based on the two-oscillator model conceived by Wever and Kronauer. It is usually assumed that either both these oscillators together or the stronger one and/or the coupling forces that entrain the rhythms of the clocks to external time cues are defective during depressive episodes (Wehr and Goodwin, 1981, 1983). The *desynchronization* hypothesis of rapid cycling even assumes a persistent "free-run" of some circadian rhythms, due to an uncoupling during *and* outside the episodes of the disorder (Halberg, 1968). The periodic (or quasi-periodic) nature of rapidly cycling affective disorders is, in this case, interpreted as a beat phenomenon resulting from the interaction of the free-running rhythm(s) with the other rhythms that remain entrained to the 24-hour routine of the environment (Kripke et al., 1978).

Another chronobiologic concept, which can be partially formulated within the context of the desynchronization hypothesis, is the *phase advance* of biologic rhythms in depression (Kripke, 1983; Wehr and Goodwin, 1981, 1983). This hypothesis is based on a set of empirical findings concerning an early timing of either the maximum or the minimum[1] of overt circadian rhythms in depressed patients. It is pos-

---

[1] See glossary in Wever (1979) for terminology.

Table 8.1. Hypothetical Dysfunctions of the Circadian "Master Clock" and Their Consequences for Overt Biological Rhythms

Questions Regarding the "Master Clock"	Expectations Regarding Overt Rhythms
1. Does the clock run faster (slower) in depressives, even in a 24-hour routine?	Free run with a period below (above) 24 hours
2. Is the clock time advanced (delayed) in relation to the 24-hour routine?	Phase advance (delay)
3. Is the function of the clock quantitatively reduced?	Attenuated range of oscillation with low variability
4. Does the clock work irregularly?	Attenuated range of oscillation with high variability

tulated that during episodes of depression, the stronger oscillator is time advanced in relation to the weaker one, which remains adapted to the external time routine. Consequently, a corresponding time advance in this routine should (via the resulting advance of the sleep–wake cycle) normalize the deviant phase relationships within the circadian system and thereby improve the clinical condition. Indeed, the results of preliminary sleep-advance experiments in depressed patients were, at least partially, in accordance with this expectation (Wehr et al., 1979).

In addition to changes of the period and the phase of circadian rhythms in depression, it could also be assumed that the intensity or regularity of internal clocks was impaired. Such an impairment would result in a diminution of the *range of oscillation* of overt rhythms (Table 8.1), as has indeed been observed by several investigators (Avery et al., 1982a; Beck-Friis et al., 1985; Lobban et al., 1963; Lund et al., 1983; Pflug and Martin, 1980; Sachar et al, 1973).

EVIDENCE FOR A DYSFUNCTION OF INTERNAL CLOCKS IN DEPRESSION

Unfortunately, the empirical basis of all these theoretical assumptions is rather small, and most findings regarding abnormal biologic rhythms, with the exception of those mentioned in the introduction, are inconsistent (von Zerssen, 1983). This is particularly true with respect to the functions of the main circadian pacemaker (the "master clock"). For example, Pflug and coworkers (1976) observed an additional 22.5-hour component in the power spectrum of oral temperature of one female patient during one episode of depression (bipolar II). They were, however, unable to replicate this finding either in the same patient during subsequent episodes or in five other patients studied longitudinally (Pflug et al., 1981). Neither Halberg (1982) nor Kripke (1983) have provided any further evidence of free-running periods of the cortisol or the temperature rhythms in depressives, that would have supported their earlier findings (Halberg, 1968; Kripke et al., 1978).

In two intensively studied cases of a bipolar (Jenner et al., 1967) and a unipolar depressive (Dirlich et al., 1981) displaying regular 48-hour cycles of the disorder, there was no indication of a free-running 16-hour period in any of the autonomic functions studied (including cortisol excretion and body temperature). The presence of such a 16-hour period would have been expected on the basis of Halberg's desynchronization hypothesis (von Zerssen et al., 1983). In one of these cases, the rhythm changed promptly from a cycle length of 48 to 44 hours when the patient was exposed to a 22-hour routine (Jenner et al., 1968). This finding cannot be explained in terms of the desynchronization hypothesis unless the free-running period had changed in proportion to the change in the environmental time schedule, in which case it would not be *free* running. Therefore, this hypothesis lacks predictive validity and should no longer be regarded as a plausible explanation of regular cycles of affective disorders.

Findings in favor of the phase advance hypothesis of depression are greater in number than findings related to the free-running periods. An advance of the circadian maximum was reported for several hormonal rhythms: cortisol (Dietzel et al., 1986), prolactin (Mendlewicz, 1984; Mendlewicz et al., 1980), melatonin (Beck-Friis et al., 1985; Mendlewicz, 1984), and growth hormone (Linkowski et al., 1985a,b). More frequently, an advance of the circadian minimum was reported with respect to the cortisol rhythm (Jarrett et al., 1983; Linkowski et al., 1985b; Rubin and Poland, 1982; Sherman and Pfohl, 1985; Yamaguchi et al., 1978). However, none of these investigators reported a concordant time shift for the maximum *and* the minimum. This casts some doubt on the interpretation of these phenomena to represent a phase advance of the internal clock governing overt circadian rhythms.

Early REM episodes in depression were hypothetically related to the phase advance in the circadian rhythms of body temperature, hormonal secretion, and other body functions (Wehr and Goodwin, 1981, 1983). However, patients exhibiting short REM latency at the beginning of nocturnal sleep also tend to have short REM latencies after artificial interruptions of sleep in the middle of the night (Schulz and Tetzlaff, 1982) as well as during daytime naps (Kupfer et al., 1981; Pugnetti et al., 1982). Therefore, a shortening of REM latency during episodes of depression can be regarded as a sleep-onset phenomenon that does not reflect the phase advance of the circadian REM-propensity cycle that was suggested by Wehr and Goodwin (1981, 1983) and by Kripke (1983).

It should be pointed out in this context that time shifts in the circadian maximum of hormonal rhythms were not found in several well-controlled investigations with respect to cortisol (Halbreich et al., 1985; Rubin and Poland, 1982; Sachar et al., 1973; Sachar, 1975; von Zerssen et al., 1985a), prolactin (Berger et al., 1986), and melatonin (Thompson et al., 1985). The earlier onset of nighttime cortisol secretion in depression reported by several groups (cf. also Halbreich et al., 1985) could be ascribed to sleep disturbances (Rubin and Poland, 1982) because it also occurs in normal subjects during sleep deprivation (Weitzman et al., 1983) and can be induced by the same procedure in depressed patients (Berger et al., 1986). The "phase advance" of the growth hormone (GH) maximum reported by Linkowski et al. (1985a) can be simply described as a lack of the normal SWS-related peak of GH secretion at the beginning of the night sleep (cf. Schilkrut et al., 1975) and a greater number and magnitude of GH peaks during wakefulness in some depressives. Since fluctuations in GH secretion are apparently not under the influence of the main circadian pacemaker (Parker et al., 1980), these findings can hardly be regarded as supportive of the phase advance hypothesis. Rather, they represent the dependence of GH secretion on sleep stages and stress (cf. Brown et al., 1978; Mendelson, 1982).

Avery et al. (1982a) advocated the phase advance hypothesis because of an intraindividual association of REM latency and the time of the nocturnal minimum of body temperature in depressives before and after recovery. However, compared with the average educed waveforms (i.e., averaged 24-hour curves) of the control subjects' body temperature, the depressives presented a delayed minimum (Avery et al., 1982b). This is exactly the opposite of what would be expected on the basis of the phase advance hypothesis (Figure 8.1a). Finally, in four patients with affective disorder who were observed in isolation from time cues, Wehr et al. (1985) obtained no support of Halberg's desynchronization hypothesis of rapid cycling or of their own phase advance hypothesis as a state marker of depression.

A somewhat more consistent finding than the phase advance is

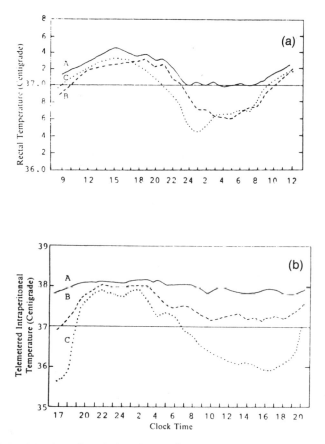

Figure 8.1. (a) Diurnal variation in rectal temperature in 7 subjects with primary depression (A) before recovery, (B) after recovery, and (C) in 12 controls of similar sex and age distribution. Temperature recorded every 3 hours from 9:00 AM to 6:00 PM and every hour from 6:00 PM to 9:00 AM (during continous nocturnal monitoring) (according to Avery et al., 1982b, modified). (b) Effect of taking rectal temperature measurements on intraperitoneal temperature (rat). Temperature curves over a 24-hour period of three groups of rats (*n* = 4 per group). A—rectal measurement every hour; B—rectal measurement every 4 hours; C—unhandled. Telemetered readings plotted every 15 minutes (according to Miles, 1962, simplified). (Reproduced from von Zerssen, 1983, with permission.)

the attenuation of the range of circadian oscillations of several body variables, including plasma cortisol (Sachar et al., 1973) and body temperature (Avery et al., 1982a; Lobban et al., 1963; Lund et al., 1983). However, the findings regarding the cortisol rhythm do not agree with either earlier studies (cf. Aschoff, 1980) or more recent ones (Dietzel et al., 1986; Halbreich et al., 1985; Rubin and Poland, 1982). Moreover, they are contradicted by the results of a large-scale chronobiologic investigation from our group (see Chapter 7), which included the circadian variation in urinary free cortisol (UFC), a variable that grossly parallels the circadian variation in plasma cortisol. In this study, a significant increase in the range of circadian variation could be demonstrated for depressives when compared with their own state after remission and with values obtained from normal controls of similar age and sex distribution (von Zerssen et al., 1985a, 1985b).

Apparently, the circadian variation in the secretion of cortisol during episodes of depression depends on factors such as emotional stress and its circadian variation due to diurnal mood swings (von Zerssen and Doerr, 1980; von Zerssen et al., 1984, 1986). Whereas the cortisol rhythm was enhanced in our depressives, their temperature rhythm was somewhat attenuated. It is, therefore, virtually impossible to draw any firm conclusions about associated dysfunctions of the driving oscillator of cortisol and temperature, i.e., the "master clock." Does it work less intensely or less regularly than in a normal state, thereby resulting in attenuated overt rhythms (as in the case of body temperature), or does it work more intensely or more regularly, thereby accentuating overt rhythms (as in the case of UFC)?

Since findings concerning sleep disturbances in depression are much more consistent (see Thase and Kupfer, 1986) than those referring to sleep-independent circadian rhythms, it appears more plausible to assume that the disorder originates from a dysfunction of the sleep process S. In Borbély's model, this process interacts with the circadian system in initiating, maintaining, and terminating sleep. However, a lack of the sleep factor during depression could hardly explain several empirical findings concerning the sleep disturbances of depressives (cf. van den Hoofdakker and Beersma, 1984). For example, the short latency of the first REM episode occurs in the same patients independently of the amount of SWS, which is assumed to reflect the level of the hypothetical sleep factor (Schulz and Lund, 1985; van den Hoofdakker and Beersma, 1985). Furthermore, the majority of depressive symptoms are clearly not sleep related, and therefore they cannot be understood in the context of this hypothesis.

A NEW VISTA OF CIRCADIAN PHENOMENA IN DEPRESSION

Because of the many incongruities between chronobiologic hypotheses of depression and empirical findings, it seems advisable to seek alternative explanations regarding the circadian features of depressive symptomatology. Such an attempt was undertaken by the present author several years ago in a survey of chronobiologic research on depression (von Zerssen, 1983). The following was concluded:

1. The function of the main circadian pacemaker is fairly well preserved in depression.
2. Findings related to abnormalities in circadian rhythms were either invalid or could be explained by masking effects of the disorder on overt rhythms.
3. The disease process could become entrained to the circadian system. The occurrence of the circadian phenomena mentioned in the introduction was thus explained as a consequence of this entrainment.

Furthermore, it was postulated that the disease process was more closely related to the sleep process than to the main circadian pacemaker. This view was extended in subsequent articles based on findings of our own chronobiologic investigations (von Zerssen et al., 1985a; 1985b). The following is an attempt to integrate the present state of knowledge into a concept of interactions between the disease process, the circadian system, and the sleep-producing system. An effort is made to account for the influence of external time cues on the circadian and the sleep-producing systems.

It is postulated that the disease process underlying depressive symptomatology originates neither in the main circadian pacemaker, assumed to be located in the anterior hypothalamus (Moore, 1979; Rusak and Zucker, 1979), nor in parts of the sleep-producing system, namely, the raphe system (Jouvet, 1974). In fact, it may be related to both of them. This could be due to the presumed localization of the disease between the brain region producing circadian rhythmicity and the region producing the sleep state. The relationship of the disease process underlying depression to sleep-producing processes seems to be stronger than the association with processes responsible for circadian rhythms. The following three reasons support this contention:

(1) Although there are cases of typical endogenous depression

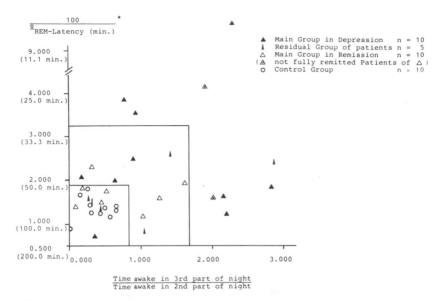

Figure 8.2. Distribution of depressed (black symbols) and nondepressed subjects (white symbols) according to two sleep parameters. Inner borderline indicates sector of normals; outer borderline (double the distance of the inner one) indicates sector of patients remitted from depression. Corresponding values of REM latency are in parentheses.

without obvious sleep disturbances, the majority of endogenous depressives exhibit abnormalities in their sleep pattern. Sleep disturbances, including early morning awakening, tend to increase with the severity of the disorder. In contrast, diurnal variation of depressive symptoms occurs in about 50% of depressives (Hall et al., 1964; von Zerssen et al., 1985a, 1985b; cf. Mellerup and Rafaelsen, 1979) and often disappears at the peak of a depressive episode (Middelhoff, 1967; Waldmann, 1972). It appears that a circadian modulation of the disease process can occur only when this process is of moderate intensity. With increasing severity of depression, the influence of the circadian system on this process decreases whereas the sleep-producing system becomes increasingly involved.

(2) The sleep disturbances of melancholic patients are more persistent than any other abnormality in their circadian rhythms. Figure 8.2 presents sleep data from subjects studied in our investigation (Schulz and Lund, 1983, 1985; Schulz et al., 1978). Each subject has been characterized by two circadian sleep parameters. One is the reciprocal value

of REM latency expressed in minutes and multiplied by 100. (The values of REM latency were inverted in order to obtain increasing scale values with increasing degrees of abnormality.) The second parameter relates to the ratio of time spent awake during the last third and the second third of the night. The subjects had to be awakened during the second third of the night in order to obtain certain measures. The values represent the mean of eight to ten nights of polysomnographic recordings. The area within the inner borderline includes the values of all control subjects. The values of the 15 depressives are located outside this borderline, with the exception of 3 subjects. A similar difference is found with respect to the values of the controls and the ten remitted patients. Four of the remitted patients appear in the same area as the healthy subjects, but all others are distributed outside this area. Values from four patients in remission are located between the inner and the outer borders. Two insufficiently recovered patients and seven of the patients studied during a depressive episode exhibit values beyond the outer border.

It is therefore concluded that the two circadian sleep parameters distinguish depressed from healthy subjects but that remitted patients tend to have values within the lower range of those obtained during the depressive episode. Because other circadian parameters are usually less frequently and less profoundly disturbed during depression, and because they usually normalize completely with clinical recovery (von Zerssen et al., 1985a), the sleep abnormalities can hardly be attributed to a dysfunction of the main circadian clock. Rather, they represent very sensitive indicators of a residual activity of the disease process or a constitutional predisposition to episodes of depression.

(3) Sleep intensifies depression (Gillin et al., 1984). This observation may explain, at least in part, the most typical form of diurnal variation in the severity of the disorder—a morning low and subsequent clinical improvement during wakefulness. This interpretation is in accord with the therapeutic effect of sleep deprivation (Gillin, 1983). In a single case study with a highly variable sleep–wake schedule, improvement occurred after sustained wakefulness. Relapses invariably occurred after sleep, independent of the time of day (Knowles et al., 1979).

Consonant with the above assumption, changes from a normal or manic/hypomanic state into depression within 48-hour cycles tend to occur during night sleep (Sitaram et al., 1978; von Zerssen et al., 1979). We have studied such a case under conditions free of time cues in the isolation unit at Andechs for two consecutive weeks (Dirlich et al., 1981; von Zerssen et al., 1983). The changes occurred during night sleep despite internal desynchronization with a markedly shortened and irregular sleep—wake cycle (Doerr et al., 1979). The mood changes were no longer bound to a particular section of the circadian cycle of the now free-running rhythms of autonomic functions (von Zerssen and Doerr, 1980). Nonetheless, this patient continued to exhibit 48-hour cycles of depression. This implies that the disease process was under the influence of the now free-running circadian system with approximately the same period as under entrained conditions (Dirlich et al., 1981). In spite of internal desynchronization, the correlation between depression scores and the excretion of UFC over time was even higher during the period of isolation from time cues ($r = 0.82$) than under the 24-hour regime of hospital life ($r = 0.73$) (Doerr et al., 1979). Based on these findings, we suspect that a linkage exists between the disease process and the circadian variation in the activity of the hypothalamic—pituitary—adrenocortical system (HPAS).

The above mentioned case provides a further argument in favor of an involvement of the circadian system in the periodicity of the disease process, possibly via the circadian variation in the activity of the HPAS. After the patient was transferred from the isolation unit to our psychiatric ward, total sleep deprivation was instituted after a "good" day, in order to prevent the predicted sleep-bound switch to depression. Between 4:00 and 5:00 AM, the patient suddenly noticed a deterioration in his emotional state and relapsed into depression, as would usually occur during sleep (von Zerssen et al., 1983). At this time, the switch-on process of his depression paralleled the increase in the activity of the HPAS. This observation suggests an entrainment of the disease process to the main circadian pacemaker, possibly mediated via the HPAS. A similar coupling may occur with respect to the diurnal variation in the severity of the disorder during depressive episodes of longer duration. This is indicated by the similarity of the average educed waveforms of UFC and depression scores in patients with significant diurnal variation of mood, and by a significant interindividual correlation between the acrophases[2] of UFC and depression scores (von Zerssen et al., 1985a).

Circabidian and circadian changes in the clinical symptoms of depression can be explained by an entrainment of the disease process to the main circadian pacemaker and by an interaction of the disease process with the sleep-producing system. Changes in overt circadian rhythms of physiologic (e.g., core body temperature) and biochemical (e.g., UFC) rhythms during episodes of depression can be conceived of as masking effects of disease symptoms and their behavioral and phys-

---

[2] See glossary in Wever (1979) for terminology.

iologic consequences on these rhythms. For example, the increased activity of the HPAS is suspected to be principally due to stress because of "psychic pain" (Carroll et al., 1980; von Zerssen et al., 1984, 1986). A flattening of the circadian curve of cortisol secretion/excretion may occur at a high level of stress-induced hypercortisolism in severe depression (von Zerssen and Doerr, 1980).

The flattening of the circadian temperature curve is primarily due to an elevation of the circadian minimum during the night. It can be interpreted as a consequence of stress or the stress-related sleep disturbances of depressives (von Zerssen, 1983; cf. also Beersma et al., 1984). In rats, a flattening of the telemetrically recorded intraperitoneal temperature can be experimentally induced by taking rectal temperatures every 4 hours. If rectal temperatures are taken every hour, the circadian temperature rhythm is almost completely abolished (Miles, 1962; see Figure 8.1b). These phenomena may represent masking effects caused by the experimental procedure and are probably mediated via emotional stress, sleep interruption, and so on (von Zerssen, 1983). Arousal may be the common denominator of the sleep disturbances and the stress experienced by patients during a depressive episode (Zung, 1969; Zung et al., 1964). In the animal experiments, arousal is induced by the experimental situations mentioned above.

OUTLINES OF A MODEL

The components of our concept and their hypothetical interrelationships are presented graphically in Figure 8.3. In this schematic representation, the organismic variables (A–F) are included in a shaded box, the upper part of which symbolizes the area of entrainment and the lower part of which symbolizes that of masking. The relationships between external time cues (G) and organismic variables and the interrelationships among these variables are indicated by arrows whose thickness corresponds to the intensity of the respective relationships. Thus, arrows 1–3 point from the main circadian pacemaker A, the disease process B, and the sleep producing system C to the respective overt organismic phenomena D, E, and F. They represent causal relationships in the strict sense of the word. All other arrows represent entrainment (4–10) of or among the central generators (A, B, C) of the overt phenomena (D, E, F) or masking (11–14) of or among the latter (D, E, F). The numbers of the arrows are used in the following text to indicate the relationships between the components of the model.

It can be easily recognized that external time cues entrain the sleep-

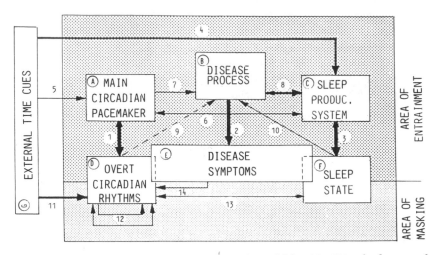

Figure 8.3. Relationships among organismic variables (A–F) and of external time cues (G: "Zeitgebers") to these variables. 1–3: production of overt organismic phenomena (D–F) by central generators (A–C). 4–10: Entrainment of and among central generators (A–C). 11–14: Masking of and among overt rhythms (D).

producing system (4) as well as the main circadian pacemaker (5), both of which entrain the disease process (7 and 8). The main circadian pacemaker and the sleep-producing system also entrain each other (6), and the sleep-producing system is, in addition, also entrained by the disease process (8). It is obvious that the main circadian pacemaker generates overt circadian rhythms (1), the disease process generates the disease symptoms (2), and the sleep-producing system generates the sleep state (3), with feedback (1 and 3) occurring within the physiologic systems. Obviously, the sleep state influences the disease process (10), and overt circadian rhythms presumably exert a similar influence on the disease process as well (9).

Masking is at work in the influence of external time cues on overt circadian rhythms (11), in interactions between overt circadian rhythms, and in a one-sided influence of one overt rhythm upon another (12). Other examples of masking include the influence of the sleep state on overt circadian rhythms and vice versa (13), and that of disease symptoms on overt rhythms (14).

The overlap between disease symptoms, overt circadian rhythms, and the sleep state indicates that rhythmic phenomena, like diurnal variation in the severity of depression and disturbances of the sleep state, are integral parts of the symptomatology of the disorder. The underlying disease process is, however, conceptualized as being separate from the main circadian pacemaker and from the sleep-producing system; it is only coupled to both of them (7 and 8). In this respect, our theoretical concept of circadian phenomena in depression differs fundamentally from other concepts. According to those concepts, the disease process of depression originates either from a dysfunction within the sleep-regulating system (Borbély and Wirz-Justice, 1982) or from a dysfunction of the main circadian pacemaker (the "master clock"), with the disease process causing at least a basic impairment of this clock (Wehr and Goodwin, 1981, 1983). Forthcoming chronobiologic research on depression will have to provide empirical evidence for or against one of these alternative hypotheses.

SUMMARY

Circadian phenomena are typical features of the symptomatology of endogenous depression. They comprise, among others, diurnal variation in the severity of depression, early morning awakening, and the (rare) occurrence of 48-hour cycles of depression. Since Halberg (1968) formulated the desynchronization hypothesis of rapidly cycling manic-depressive disease, several authors have tried to explain the circadian phenomena of depression by postulating dysfunctions of internal clocks assumed to govern circadian rhythms of sleep and wakefulness, autonomic functions, and mental processes. The empirical evidence for such dysfunctions in patients with affective disorders is, however, sparse. Many of the observations regarding disturbed biologic rhythms in depression are contradictory. One of the most consistent findings, the early timing of the first REM episode during night sleep, can be more easily explained as a sleep-onset phenomenon rather than by the assumption of a "phase advance" of the REM propensity cycle because it also occurs after an interruption of night sleep or during daytime naps.

According to this author, circadian phenomena in depression are probably due to a modulation of the disease process underlying depressive symptomatology by the (basically intact!) main circadian pacemaker, the "master clock," rather than due to a dysfunction of this clock or to a primary disturbance within the sleep-producing system. However, the disease process usually involves the sleep-producing system and is, conversely, modulated by it, with sleep tending to trigger or intensify the disease process. Finally, sleep disturbances and other symptoms of depression may exert masking effects on overt circadian rhythms, e.g., attenuating the circadian variation of body temperature, thus imitating a disturbance of the clock (or clocks) governing these rhythms. This view is offered as an alternative to theoretical concepts of a primary or secondary dysfunction of circadian clocks in depression and is intended to stimulate further research on the chronobiology of depression.

REFERENCES

Aschoff J (1980): Wie gestört ist der circadiane Rhythmus bei Depressiven? In Heimann H, Giedke H (eds): Neue Perspektiven in der Depressionsforschung. Bern, Huber, pp 88–99.

Aschoff J (ed) (1981): Handbook of Behavioral Neurobiology, Vol 4: Biological Rhythms. New York, Plenum.

Aschoff J, Daan S, Groos GA (eds) (1982a): Vertebrate Circadian Systems. Structure and Physiology. Berlin, Springer.

Aschoff J, Daan S, Honma K-I (1982b): Zeitgebers, entrainment, and masking: Some unsettled questions. In Aschoff J, Daan S, Groos GA (eds): Vertebrate Circadian Systems, Berlin, Springer, pp 13–24.

Avery DH, Wildschiødtz G, Rafaelsen O (1982a): REM latency and temperature in affective disorder before and after treatment. Biol Psychiatry 17:463–470.

Avery DH, Wildschiødtz G, Rafaelsen OJ (1982b): Nocturnal temperature in affective disorder. J Affective Disord 4:61–71.

Beck-Friis J, Ljunggren J-G, Thorén M, et al (1985): Melatonin, cortisol and ACTH in patients with major depressive disorder and healthy humans with special reference to the outcome of the dexamethasone suppression test. Psychoneuroendocrinology 10:173–186.

Beersma D, Dijk DJ, van den Hoofdakker R, Bloem G (1984): Are differences in the course of body temperature in depression caused by differences in sleep structure? 7th European Sleep Congress, Munich, September 3–7 (Abstract).

Berger M, Zulley J, Höchli D, et al (1986): The activity of different neuroendocrine axes during sleep and sleep deprivation in patients with a major depressive disorder. In Shagass C (ed): Proceedings of the 4th World Congress of Biological Psychiatry, Philadelphia, 1985. New York, Elsevier.

Borbély AA (1982): A two process model of sleep regulation. Hum Neurobiol 1:195–204.

Borbély AA, Wirz-Justice A (1982): Sleep, sleep deprivation and depression. Hum Neurobiol 1:205–210.

Borbély AA, Tobler I, Loepfe M, et al (1984): All-night spectral analysis of the sleep EEG in untreated depressives and normal controls. Psychiatry Res 12:27–33.

Brown GM, Seggie JA, Chambers JW, Prakash GE (1978): Psychoendocrinology and growth hormone: A review. Psychoneuroendocrinology 3:131–153.

Carroll BJ, Greden JF, Feinberg M, et al (1980): Neuroendocrine dysfunction in genetic subtypes of primary unipolar depression. Psychiatry Res 2:251–258.

Daan S, Beersma DGM, Borbély AA (1984): Timing of human sleep: Recovery process gated by a circadian pacemaker. Am J Physiol 246:R161–R178.

Dietzel M, Saletu B, Lesch OM, et al (1986): Light treatment in depressive illness. Polysomnographic, psychometric and neuroendocrinological findings. Eur Neurol.

Dirlich G, Kammerloher A, Schulz H, et al (1981): Temporal coordination of rest–activity cycle, body temperature, urinary free cortisol, and mood in a patient with 48-hour unipolar-depressive cycles in clinical and time-cue-free environments. Biol Psychiatry 16:163–179.

Doerr P, Zerssen D von, Fischler M, Schulz H (1979): Relationship between mood changes and adrenal cortical activity in a patient with 48-hour unipolar-depressive cycles. J Affective Disord 1:93–104.

Gillin JC (1983): The sleep therapies of depression. Prog Neuropsychopharmacol Biol Psychiatry 7:351–364.

Gillin JC, Sitaram N, Wehr T, et al (1984): Sleep and affective illness. In Post RM, Ballenger JC (eds): Neurobiology of Mood Disorders. Baltimore, Williams and Wilkins, pp 157–189.

Goetze U, Tölle R (1981): Antidepressive Wirkung des partiellen Schlafentzuges während der 1. Hälfte der Nacht. Psychiatr Clin 14:129–149.

Halberg F (1968): Physiologic considerations underlying rhythmometry, with special reference to emotional illness. In de Ajuriaguerra J (ed): Cycles Biologiques et Psychiatrie. Symposium Bel-Air III. Genève, Georg; Paris, Masson, pp 73–126.

Halberg F (1982): Quantitative chronobiology and psychoneuroendocrinology. In Collu R, Ducharme JR, Barbeau A, Tolis G (eds): Brain Neurotransmitters and Hormones. New York, Raven, pp 241–256.

Halbreich U, Asnis GM, Shindledecker R, et al (1985): Cortisol secretion in endogenous depression. Arch Gen Psychiatry 42:909–914.

Hall P, Spear FG, Stirland D (1964): Diurnal variation of subjective mood in depressive states. Psychiatr Q 38:529–536.

Jarrett DB, Coble PA, Kupfer DJ (1983): Reduced cortisol latency in depressive illness. Arch Gen Psychiatry 40:506–511.

Jenner FA, Gjessing LR, Cox JR, et al (1967): A manic depressive psychotic with a persistent forty-eight hour cycle. Br J Psychiatry 113:895–910.

Jenner FA, Goodwin JC, Sheridan M, et al (1968): The effect of an altered time regime on biological rhythms in a 48-hour periodic psychosis. Br J Psychiatry 114:215–222.

Jouvet M (1974): The role of monoaminergic neurons in the regulation and function of sleep. In Petre-Quadens O, Schlag JD (eds): Basic Sleep Mechanisms. New York, Academic, pp 207–236.

Knowles JB, Southmayd SE, Delva N, et al (1979): Five variations of sleep deprivation in a depressed woman. Br J Psychiatry 135:403–410.

Krafft-Ebing R von (1874): Die Melancholie. Erlangen, Enke.

Kripke DF (1983): Phase-advance theories for affective illnesses. In Wehr TA, Goodwin FK (eds): Circadian Rhythms in Psychiatry. Pacific Grove, CA, Boxwood, pp 41–69.

Kripke DF, Mullaney DJ, Atkinson M, Wolf S. (1978): Circadian rhythm disorders in manic depressives. Biol Psychiatry 13:335–351.

Kronauer RE, Czeisler CA, Pilato SF, et al (1982): Mathematical model of the human circadian system with two interacting oscillators. Am J Physiol 242 (Regulatory Integrative Compr Physiol 11):R3–R17.

Kupfer DJ, Gillin JC, Coble PA, et al (1981): REM sleep, naps, and depression. Psychiatry Res 5:195–203.

Linkowski P, Mendlewicz J, Kerkhofs M, et al (1985a): Neuroendocrine rhythms in major depressive illness. In Koella WP, Rüther E, Schulz H (eds): Sleep '84. Stuttgart, Gustav Fischer, pp 131–133.

Linkowski P, Mendlewicz J, Leclercq R, et al (1985b): The 24-hour profile of adrenocorticotropin and cortisol in major depressive illness. J Clin Endocrinol 61:1–10.

Lobban M, Tredre B, Elithorn A, Bridges P (1963): Diurnal rhythms of electrolyte excretion in depressive illness. Nature 199:667–669.

Lund R, Kammerloher A, Dirlich G (1983): Body temperature in endogenously depressed patients during depression and remission. In Wehr TA, Goodwin FK (eds): Circadian Rhythms in Psychiatry. Pacific Grove, CA, Boxwood, pp 77–88.

Mellerup ET, Rafaelsen OJ (1979): Circadian rhythms in manic-melancholic disorders. In Essman WB, Valzelli L (eds): Current Developments in Psychopharmacology. New York, Spectrum, Vol 5, pp 51–66.

Mendelson WB (1982): Studies of human growth hormone secretion in sleep and waking. Int Rev Neurobiol 23:367–389.

Mendlewicz J (1984): Alterations in circadian secretion of pituitary and pineal hormones in affective disorders. In Shah NS, Donald AG (eds): Psychoneuroendocrine Dysfunction. New York, Plenum, pp 465–471.

Mendlewicz J, van Cauter E, Linkowski P, et al (1980): The 24-hour profile of prolactin in depression. Life Sci 27:2015–2024.

Middelhoff HD (1967): Tagesrhythmische Schwankungen bei endogen Depressiven im symptomfreien Intervall und während der Phase. Arch Psychiatr Ges Neurol 209:315–339.

Miles GH (1962): Telemetering techniques for periodicity studies. Ann NY Acad Sci 98:858–865.

Minors DS, Waterhouse JM (eds) (1981): Circadian Rhythms and the Human. Boston, Wright PSG.

Moore RY (1979): The anatomy of central neural mechanisms regulating endocrine rhythms. In Krieger DT (ed): Endocrine Rhythms. New York, Raven, pp 63–87.

Papoušek M (1975): Chronobiologische Aspekte der Zyclothymie. Fortschr Neurol Psychiatr 43:381–440.

Parker DC, Rossman LG, Kripke DF, et al (1980): Endocrine rhythms across sleep–wake cycles in normal young men under basal state conditions. In Orem J, Barnes CD (eds): Physiology in Sleep. New York, Academic, pp 145–179.

Pflug B, Martin W (1980): Analyse circadianer Temperaturgänge bei endogener Depression. Arch Psychiatr Nervenkr 229:127–143.

Pflug B, Erikson R, Johnsson A (1976): Depression and daily temperature. A long-term study. Acta Psychiatr Scand 54:254–266.

Pflug B, Johnsson A, Ekse AT (1981): Manic-depressive states and daily temperature. Some circadian studies. Acta Psychiatr Scand 63:277–289.

Pugnetti L, Colombo A, Cazzullo CL, et al (1982): Daytime sleep patterns of primary depressives: A morning nap study. Psychiatry Res 7:287–298.

Rubin RT, Poland RE (1982): The chronoendocrinology of endogenous depression. In Müller EE, MacLeod RM (eds): Neuroendocrine Perspectives. Amsterdam, Elsevier, pp 305–337.

Rusak B (1984): Assessment and significance of rhythm disruptions in affective illness. In Brown GM, Koslow SH, Reichlin S (eds): Neuroendocrinology and Psychiatric Disorder. New York, Raven.

Rusak B, Zucker I (1979): Neural regulation of circadian rhythms. Physiol Rev 59:449–526.

Sachar EJ (1975): Neuroendocrine abnormalities in depressive illness. In Sachar EJ (ed): Topics in Psychoendocrinology. New York, Grune and Stratton, pp 135–156.

Sachar EJ, Hellman L, Roffwarg HP, et al (1973): Disrupted 24-hour patterns of cortisol secretion in psychotic depression. Arch Gen Psychiatry 28:19–24.

Schilgen B, Tölle R (1980): Partial sleep deprivation as therapy for depression. Arch Gen Psychiatry 37:267–271.

Schilkrut R, Chandra O, Osswald M, et al (1975): Growth hormone release during sleep and with thermal stimulation in depressed patients. Neuropsychobiology 1:70–79.

Schulz H, Lund R (1983): Sleep onset REM episodes are associated with circadian parameters of body temperature. A study in depressed patients and normal controls. Biol Psychiatry 18:1411–1426.

Schulz H, Lund R (1985): On the origin of early REM episodes in the sleep of depressed patients. Comparison of three hypotheses. Psychiatry Res 16:65–77.

Schulz H, Tetzlaff W (1982): Distribution of REM latencies after sleep interruption in depressive patients and control subjects. Biol Psychiatry 17:1367–1376.

Schulz H, Lund R, Doerr P (1978): The measurement of change in sleep during depression and remission. Arch Psychiatr Nervenkr 225:233–245.

Sherman BM, Pfohl B (1985): Rhythm-related changes in pituitary–adrenal function in depression. J Affective Disord 9:55–61.

Sitaram N, Gillin JC, Bunney WE Jr (1978): Circadian variation in the time of "switch" of a patient with 48-hour manic-depressive cycles. Biol Psychiatry 13:567–574.

Suda M, Hayaishi O, Nakagawa H (eds) (1979): Biological Rhythms and Their Central Mechanism. Amsterdam, Elsevier.

Thase ME, Kupfer DJ (1986): Current status of EEG sleep in the assessment and treatment of depression. In Burrows GD, Werry JS (eds): Advances in Human Psychopharmacology. Greenwich, CT, JAI Press. vol 4.

Thompson C, Mezey G, Corn T et al (1985): The effect of desipramine upon melatonin and cortisol secretion in depressed and normal subjects. Br J Psychiatry 147:389–393.

van den Hoofdakker RH, Beersma DGM (1984): Sleep deprivation, mood, and sleep physiology. Exp Brain Res (Suppl 8):297–309.

van den Hoofdakker RH, Beersma DGM (1985): On the explanation of short REM latencies in depression. Psychiatry Res 16:155–163.

Vogel GW, Vogel F, McAbee RS, Thurmond AJ (1980): Improvement of depression by REM sleep deprivation. New findings and a theory. Arch Gen Psychiatry 37:247–253.

Waldmann H (1972): Die Tagesschwankung in der Depression als rhythmisches Phänomen. Fortschr Neurol Psychiatr 40:83–104.

Wehr TA, Goodwin FK (1981): Biological rhythms and psychiatry. In Arieti S, Brodie HKH (eds): American Handbook of Psychiatry, 2nd ed, vol 7: Advances and New Directions. New York, Basic Books, pp 46–74.

Wehr TA, Goodwin FK (1983): Biological rhythms in manic-depressive illness. In Wehr TA, Goodwin FK (eds): Circadian Rhythms in Psychiatry. Pacific Grove, CA, Boxwood, pp 129–184.

Wehr TA, Wirz-Justice A, Goodwin FK, et al (1979): Phase advance of the circadian sleep–wake cycle as an antidepressant. Science 206:710–713.

Wehr TA, Sack DA, Duncan WC, et al (1985): Sleep and circadian rhythms in affective patients isolated from external time cues. Psychiatr Res 15:327–339.

Weitzman ED, Zimmerman JC, Czeisler CA,, Ronda J (1983): Cortisol secretion is inhibited during sleep in normal man. J Clin Endocrinol 56:352–358.

Wever RA (1979): The Circadian System of Man. New York, Springer.

Yamaguchi N, Maeda K, Kuromaru S (1978): The effects of sleep deprivation on the circadian rhythm of plasma cortisol levels in depressive patients. Folia Psychiatr Neurol Jpn 32:479–487.

Zerssen D von (1983): Chronobiology of depression. In Angst J (ed): The Origins of Depression: Current Concepts and Approaches. Dahlem Konferenzen. Berlin, Springer, pp 253–271.

Zerssen D von, Doerr P (1980): The role of the hypothalamo–pituitary–adrenocortical system in psychiatric disorders. Adv Biol Psychiatry 5:85–106.

Zerssen D von, Lund R, Doerr P et al (1979): 48-hour-cycles of depression and their biological concomitants with and without "Zeitgebers." A case report. In Saletu B, Berner P, Hollister L (eds): Neuro-Psychopharmacology. Oxford, Pergamon.

Zerssen D von, Dirlich G,, Fischler M (1983): Influence of an abnormal time routine and therapeutic measures on 48-hour cycles of affective disorders: Chronobiological considerations. In Wehr TA, Goodwin FK (eds): Circadian Rhythms in Psychiatry. Pacific Grove, CA, Boxwood, pp 109–127.

Zerssen D von, Berger M, Doerr P (1984): Neuroendocrine dysfunction in subtypes of depression. In Shah NS, Donald AG (eds): Psychoneuroendocrine Dysfunction. New York, Plenum, pp 357–382.

Zerssen D von, Barthelmes H, Dirlich G, et al (1985a): Circadian rhythms in endogenous depression. Psychiatry Res 16:51–63.

Zerssen D von, Dirlich G, Doerr P, et al (1985b): Are biological rhythms disturbed in depression? Acta Psychiatr Belg 624–635.

Zerssen D von, Berger M, Doerr P, et al (1986): The role of the hypothalamo–pituitary–adrenocortical system in depression. In Hippius H, Klerman GL, Matussek N (eds): New Results in Depression Research. Berlin, Springer.

Zung WWK (1969): Effect of antidepressant drugs on sleeping and dreaming. III. On the depressed patient. Biol Psychiatry 1:283–287.

Zung WWK, Wilson WP, Dodson WE (1964): Effect of depressive disorders on sleep EEG responses. Arch Gen Psychiatry 10:439–445.

9

Phase Typing and Bright Light Therapy of Chronobiologic Sleep and Mood Disorders

Alfred J. Lewy and Robert L. Sack

Physiologic effects of light are ubiquitous and well-documented in animals (Aschoff, 1981). The light–dark cycle is an important zeitgeber (time cue) for entraining (synchronizing) circadian rhythms. The length of daylight (the photoperiod) is a major cue for the timing of seasonal rhythms. A third effect of light (that is specific to the pineal gland) is the suppression of nighttime melatonin production.

Although most warm-blooded species tested so far appear to suppress nighttime melatonin production when exposed to relatively dim light (a tonic effect of light), suppression of *human* melatonin production requires bright light. Ordinary room light is rarely greater than 500 lux and is therefore relatively ineffective in suppressing human melatonin production. Exposure to light of 2500 lux suppresses human nighttime melatonin production to near daytime levels; exposure to 1500 lux reduces melatonin production by about 50% (Figures 9.1,9.2) (Lewy et al., 1980b).

Sunlight is also effective in suppressing human melatonin production (Lewy et al., 1980b). Thus, bright artificial light and sunlight suppress melatonin production in humans. Once an intensity threshold is exceeded, the brighter the light, the greater the suppression of melatonin production. More recent studies have delineated this fluence–response relationship and have determined the peak of the action spec-

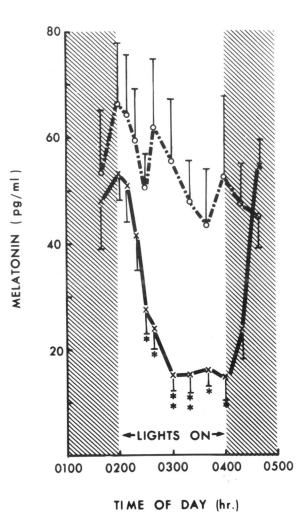

Figure 9.1. Effect of light on melatonin secretion. Each point represents the mean concentration of melatonin (± standard errors) for six subjects. A paired *t* test, comparing exposure to 500 lux (O) with exposure to 2500 lux (×), was performed for each data point. A two-way analysis of variance with repeated measures and the Newman–Keuls statistic for the comparison of means showed significant differences between 2:30 and 4 AM (*, $p < 0.05$; **, $p < 0.01$). From Lewy et al. (1980b), copyright 1980 by the AAAS.

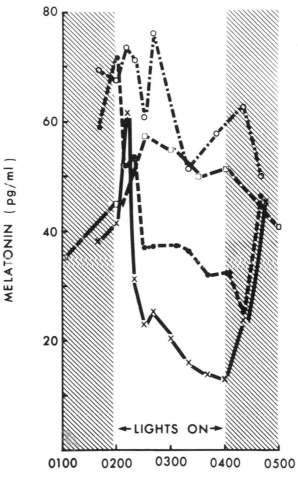

TIME OF DAY (hr.)

Figure 9.2. Effect of different light intensities on melatonin secretion. The averaged values for two subjects are shown. Symbols: (○) 500 lux; (×) 2500 lux; (●) 1500 lux; and (□) asleep in the dark. From Lewy et al. (1980b), copyright 1980 by the AAAS.

trum to be around 509 nm (Brainard et al., 1983, 1985; Lewy et al., 1983a).

The discovery that human melatonin production could be suppressed by bright light (Lewy et al., 1980b) had several important implications: (1) if humans are responsive to bright artificial light (and sunlight), yet are insensitive to ordinary-intensity room light, then humans may have biologic rhythms that are cued by the natural light–dark cycle and the length of natural daylight—unperturbed by the use of ordinary room light; (2) past studies of the effects of light in humans (particularly those in which negative results were obtained) should be repeated using bright light; (3) human biologic rhythms could be experimentally (and perhaps therapeutically) manipulated using bright artificial light; and (4) dim artificial light could be used as a placebo control in such studies—the "bright light–dim light" research paradigm (Lewy, 1981).

Previous studies (reviewed by Lewy et al., 1980b, and by Czeisler et al., 1981) had concluded that light did not affect human pineal function or circadian rhythms. For example, in a study of transmeridian air travel, the finding that subjects who stayed indoors did not reentrain to the new time zone as rapidly as subjects who were allowed to go outside was explained on the basis of increased social cues outdoors (Klein and Wegmann, 1974).

Since the publication of the effect of bright light on human melatonin production (Lewy et al., 1980b), Wever and colleagues (1983) have shown that exposure to 4000-lux artificial light can permit humans to entrain to a 29-hour light–dark cycle. We (Lewy et al., 1984, 1985b, 1985c) have also shown that circadian phase position in humans can be shifted using appropriately timed exposure to bright light (discussed in more detail below).

MELATONIN PRODUCTION—A "MARKER"

In addition to being a useful "biologic marker" for light sensitivity, melatonin production appears to be a highly useful marker for the phase and period of its human endogenous circadian pacemaker. Most markers for biologic rhythms are subject to "masking," examples of which are stress-induced increases in cortisol levels (Czeisler et al., 1979) and changes in core body temperature due to locomotor activity (Weitzman et al., 1979). Melatonin production, however, does not appear to be affected by diet (Arendt, 1979; Herbert and Reiter, 1981), the stages of sleep (Vaughan et al., 1978; Vaughan et al., 1979a; Weinberg et al., 1979, authors' unpublished data), with the exception of one report (Birkeland, 1982), sleep deprivation (Jimerson et al., 1977; Akerstedt et al., 1979), or acute changes in the activity–rest cycle (Jimerson et al., 1977; Lynch et al., 1977). Exercise during the day has been reported by one group to stimulate daytime immunoreactive melatonin (Carr et al., 1981); however, this report is not in agreement with other studies in which stress does not appear to affect melatonin production (Illnerova, 1976; Klein and Parfitt, 1976; Parfitt and Klein, 1977; Vaughan et al., 1979b; Theintz et al., 1984; Sizonenko, personal communication).

The use of melatonin as a biologic marker in humans depends on the capability to measure melatonin levels in the peripheral circulation and on the exclusively pineal origin of circulating levels of melatonin. The gas chromatographic–negative chemical ionization mass spectrometric technique (Lewy and Markey, 1978) is generally recognized to be the most accurate of the melatonin assays (Arendt, 1981; Rollag, 1981; Brown et al., 1983). It is also recognized (Brown et al., 1983; Lynch, 1983) to be among the most sensitive of the melatonin assays (the minimal detectable concentration in plasma is less than 1 pg/ml). Pinealectomy appears to abolish plasma melatonin and urinary 6-hydroxymelatonin levels; therefore, measurement of plasma melatonin and urinary 6-hydroxymelatonin are valid markers for pineal function (Lewy et al., 1980a; Markey and Buell, 1982; Tetsuo et al., 1982; Neuwelt and Lewy, 1983).

Although β-adrenergic and norepinephrine uptake blockers can, respectively, decrease and increase human melatonin production (Vaughan et al., 1976; Hanssen et al., 1977; Moore et al., 1979; Lewy, 1983a; Golden, 1984; Cowen et al., 1985; Sack and Lewy, 1986), light is the only environmental factor known to affect melatonin production (Lewy et al., 1980b). Potential masking effects can therefore be avoided by reducing light intensity below threshold. Because the precise threshold is not yet known, ambient light should be dim during the evening, night, and morning. Under these conditions, melatonin production appears to be a highly useful marker for the phase and period of its endogenous pacemaker. The onset of melatonin production is probably the most useful part of the secretory curve because the increasing development of subsensitivity of the pineal's β-adrenergic receptors throughout the night may influence the timing of the maximal level and the offset of melatonin production (Kebabian et al., 1975; Romero and Axelrod, 1975; Zatz et al., 1976).

THE CLOCK-GATE MODEL AND THE DLMO

Use of the plasma melatonin curve (particularly the onset of nighttime melatonin production) as a marker for circadian phase position requires avoidance of bright light exposure, because we have evidence that bright light exposure in the evening suppresses the onset of melatonin production (Lewy et al., 1984, 1985b). In a study of four normal subjects during the summer of 1983, plasma melatonin curves were obtained before and during 1 week of advanced dusk (dusk was advanced from between 7:30 and 9:00 PM to 4:00 PM). On the first night of advanced dusk the onset of melatonin production advanced from 10:00 to 8:30 PM, suggesting an "unmasking" of the onset of melatonin production (there was no significant change in the offset). By the end of the week, the onset shifted earlier by an additional hour (as did the offset). During the second week of this study, dawn was delayed from between 6:00 and 7:30 AM to 9:00 AM. No immediate change in the onset or offset of melatonin production was noted the first few days. However, by the end of the week the onset and offset had delayed by about 1 hour. These data suggest the existence of a phase-response curve (PRC), in which bright light exposure in the evening delays (shifts to a later time) the underlying circadian pacemaker and bright light exposure in the morning advances (shifts to an earlier time) the underlying circadian pacemaker [see below, under The Phase-Response Curve (PRC)].

These data also suggest that late evening light has an additional tonic or suppressant effect that delays the onset of melatonin production. Therefore, in using the onset of melatonin production as a marker for circadian phase position, subjects should not be exposed to bright light after 5:00 or 6:00 PM on the night of blood sampling. We term this paradigm the dim light melatonin onset (DLMO). The DLMO may be a useful way in which to use plasma melatonin levels as a marker for circadian phase position.

The data of the above study are consistent with the "clock-gate" model that explains how light regulates the onset and offset of nighttime melatonin production (Lewy, 1983a). This model was originally conceived as an alternative to the two-oscillator model that had been proposed to explain the apparent paradoxical (opposite) shifts in phase position in the onset and the offset of melatonin production as the photoperiod changes in duration throughout the year (Illnerova and Vanecek, 1980, 1982a, 1982b; Elliott and Tamarkin, 1982). The clock-gate model can be explained as follows (Figure 9.3): In animals whose intrinsic endogenous periods are greater than 24 hours, circadian phase

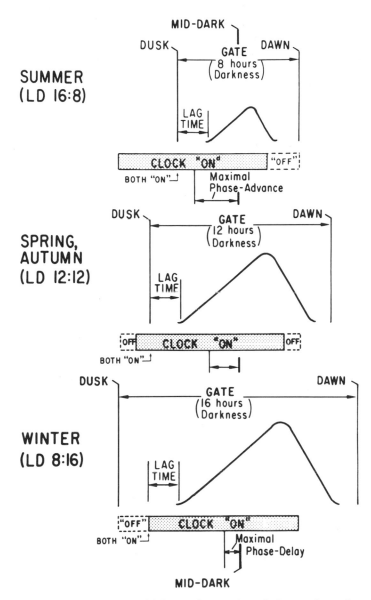

Figure 9.3. "Clock-gate" model for explaining how light regulates the pattern of nighttime melatonin production. From Lewy (1983a), with permission.

position should cue more to dawn than to dusk, as the interval between them changes during the year. Therefore, one might predict that the onset and offset of melatonin production would be earlier in the summer than in the winter. Although this is true for the offset of melatonin production, the opposite occurs with regard to the onset (that is, it is delayed in the summer compared to the winter), which results in the longer duration of nighttime production in the winter compared to the summer (Rollag et al., 1978; Arendt, 1979; Griffiths et al., 1979; Illnerova and Vanecek, 1980; Hoffmann et al., 1980; Tamarkin et al., 1980; Goldman et al., 1981; Petterborg et al., 1981).

The clock-gate model suggests that whereas the *endogenous pacemaker* for melatonin may be relatively advanced in the summer compared to the winter, the seemingly paradoxical late melatonin onset noted in long (summer) photoperiods could be the result of a suppressant effect of evening light on melatonin production. The suppressant effect of light in the evening may not have been considered previously because of the lag time in the onset of melatonin production of at least 1–2 hours following the beginning of sympathetic stimulation of the pineal. [One to two hours is apparently required for transcription and translation of the enzymes necessary for synthesis of melatonin (Romero et al., 1975).] The clock-gate model can explain the opposite changes in phase position in the onset and the offset that occur during the year without the need to assume more than one endogenous circadian oscillator; this model also provides the theoretical basis for avoiding bright light in the evening when using the melatonin onset for marking circadian phase position—the dim light melatonin onset (DLMO).

The clock-gate model predicts (Lewy, 1983) that the phase of the melatonin circadian production rhythm should be advanced in the summer compared to the winter in animals (such as humans) whose intrinsic periods are greater than 24 hours (Wever, 1979). Two recent studies have substantiated this prediction (Illnerova et al., 1985; Arendt et al., personal communication).

ANATOMY OF THE CIRCADIAN SYSTEM

Melatonin production appears to be a highly useful biologic marker in part because of the way in which the nighttime increase is regulated. Sympathetic stimulation results in the release of norepinephrine and the stimulation of β_1-adrenergic receptors on the pinealocytes (Romero et al., 1975). The anatomic pathways (Figure 9.4) mediating the effects of

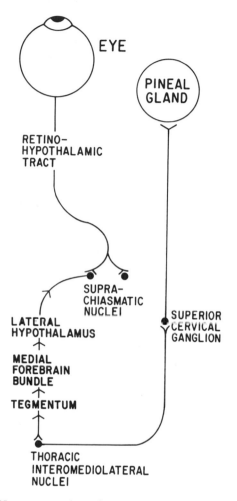

EYE

PINEAL GLAND

RETINO-HYPOTHALAMIC TRACT

SUPRA-CHIASMATIC NUCLEI

LATERAL HYPOTHALAMUS

SUPERIOR CERVICAL GANGLION

MEDIAL FOREBRAIN BUNDLE

TEGMENTUM

THORACIC INTEROMEDIOLATERAL NUCLEI

Figure 9.4. Neuroanatomic pathway between the retina and the pineal gland. From Lewy (1983a), with permission.

light on melatonin production have been described in a number of experimental animals. An endogenous hypothalamic pacemaker, the suprachiasmatic nucleus (SCN), generates a self-sustaining circadian oscillation in sympathetic impulses that results in pineal production of melatonin (Ariens Kappers, 1960; Moore and Eichler, 1972; Stephan and Zucker, 1972). The SCN may be the locus of the endogenous pacemaker for all circadian rhythms, although other pacemakers might exist.

Effects of light on the SCN are mediated by the retinohypothalamic tract (Moore and Lenn, 1972; Moore and Klein, 1974), which extends from the retina to the hypothalamus, innervating both the contralateral (70%) and the ipsilateral (30%) SCN (Hendrickson et al., 1972). The number of synapses between the SCN and the sympathetic outflow is not known. This pathway traverses the tuberal and lateral hypothalamus, the medial forebrain bundle, and the rostral part of the tegmentum, terminating in the interomediolateral nuclei of the upper thoracic segments, where preganglionic sympathetic fibers originate (Ariens Kappers, 1979; Ariens Kappers et al., 1979). [Recent evidence suggests that this pathway passes through the paraventricular nucleus of the hypothalamus (Klein et al., 1983; Pickard and Turek, 1983).] These neurons synapse in the superior cervical ganglia with postganglionic neurons that reenter the brain through the tentorium cerebelli as the nervi conarii (Ariens Kappers, 1960).

After a shift in the light–dark cycle, the circadian melatonin production rhythm gradually resumes its proper phase (Wurtman et al., 1963). In constant dark, the melatonin production rhythm is "free running" (Ralph et al., 1971); no longer entrained by the light–dark cycle, this rhythm displays the period of its endogenous circadian pacemaker.

STUDIES OF BLIND SUBJECTS

In humans, as in lower animals, the light–dark cycle appears to be important in the synchronization of the melatonin production rhythm. In sighted individuals, the onset of melatonin production generally begins 1–4 hours before 11:00 PM and falls at or before dawn (Lewy and Markey, 1978). In a recent investigation (Lewy and Newsome, 1983), two-thirds of ten blind subjects had melatonin patterns with unusual phase positions (some were phase advanced and others were phase delayed).

Two of these subjects were studied longitudinally; they displayed markedly unusual circadian rhythms. One subject's melatonin circadian production rhythm appeared to be 120° out of phase with his (normally entrained) activity–rest cycle on four successive weeks (the same phase position noted 16 months earlier). The onset of production began after 6:00 AM and reached a maximum between 10:00 AM and 12:00 noon on each of four occasions at 1-week intervals (as well as on one occasion 16 months earlier). Because of this unusual phase position, this subject's melatonin circadian production rhythm was probably entrained to some 24-hour time cue other than the environmental light–dark cycle.

The second subject appeared to have a free-running melatonin circadian production rhythm despite the fact that, similar to the first blind subject (and indeed most blind individuals), his activity–rest cycle appeared to be normally entrained. Each week his melatonin rhythm was 4–6 hours delayed compared to the week before. Therefore, this subject had a circadian melatonin production rhythm of approximately 24.7 hours, which was probably the free-running period of his endogenous pacemaker no longer entrained to the light–dark cycle. His melatonin circadian production rhythm was therefore continually going in and out of phase with his activity–rest cycle.

Thus, the light–dark cycle appears to be important for the normal entrainment of the human circadian melatonin production rhythm. Identification of the unknown zeitgeber that permitted the first blind subject to entrain (albeit in an unusual phase position) might be helpful to other blind subjects who are not able to entrain. (It is of course possible, although unlikely, that the first subject was also free running, but with a period very close to 24 hours.) Clearly, in some blind people, the activity–rest cycle is not capable of entraining either the melatonin rhythm or the temperature rhythm. (Our preliminary data suggest that the circadian temperature rhythm is also free running in blind subjects whose melatonin circadian production rhythm is free running.) Studies of blind individuals not only may yield important information about circadian rhythms in blind people but may also aid in the understanding of the human circadian system in general.

Recently, we have studied seven other totally blind individuals longitudinally (Sack et al., 1986). Two had circadian melatonin production rhythms that are normally entrained, one had an ambiguous pattern, and four were clearly free running. Of the four free-running subjects, one had a period of 24.61 hours and the other a period of 25.06 hours. Both of these subjects were studied again 1 year later and the periods were exactly the same (24.57 and 25.07), indicating that this rhythm is stable. Furthermore, it was found that the timing of the rhythm was very precise; employing a regression equation, the onset of melatonin production could be predicted weeks in advance with an accuracy of ±30 minutes.

Free-running circadian rhythms in blind people are probably a source of unappreciated symptomatology. One of the subjects rated his sleep quality every day for almost 3 months on a scale from 1 (best) to 5 (worst) without any knowledge of his circadian melatonin production rhythm. Although his activity–rest cycle appeared to be essentially in phase, the quality of his sleep varied greatly and was highly correlated with the phase of his melatonin rhythm.

During one 3-week period, this subject was given oral melatonin (5 mg) at 10:00 PM in an attempt to entrain his rhythm [as suggested by the rodent experiments of Redman et al. (1983)]. Treatment was begun just before the endogenous melatonin rhythm was coming into normal phase. An 8-hour phase advance in the melatonin rhythm was observed that was clearly related to exogenous melatonin administration. This experiment suggests that circulating melatonin may influence the function of the endogenous circadian pacemaker in humans.

THE PHASE-RESPONSE CURVE (PRC)

If the human response to light is similar to that of other species, then presumably it can be described by a phase-response curve (PRC). The PRC has been demonstrated in animals who are free running in constant dark (DeCoursey, 1960; Pittendrigh and Daan, 1976; Pittendrigh, 1981; Hoban and Sulzman, 1985). Under these conditions, circadian rhythms are governed by an endogenous circadian pacemaker [whose intrinsic period is termed tau (τ)] no longer entrained to the environmental light–dark cycle. Under constant conditions, the activity phase of the activity–rest cycle is termed "subjective night" in nocturnal animals and "subjective day" in diurnal animals (and vice versa for the rest phase). The terms "subjective dusk" and "subjective dawn" indicate the transitions between subjective day and subjective night.

If a free-running animal in constant darkness is exposed to a 15-minute pulse of light, the phase of its activity–rest cycle changes over the next few days. In both diurnal and nocturnal animals, when a pulse of light is presented during subjective day, it has relatively little effect. However, during subjective night the light pulse causes a phase advance if it occurs in the latter half of the night, and causes a phase delay if it occurs during the initial half of the night. The closer the light pulse occurs to the middle of the night, the greater the magnitude of the response in either direction. There is an inflection point in the middle of the night that separates the greatest phase delay from the greatest phase advance.

The study described under The Clock-Gate Model and the DLMO, which demonstrated a suppressant (or tonic) effect of bright evening light, also provides evidence for phasic effects of light and suggests the existence of a PRC in humans. The first week of advanced dusk in that study, the melatonin onset advanced 1.5 hours the first night and remained at that phase position for at least one more night. By the end

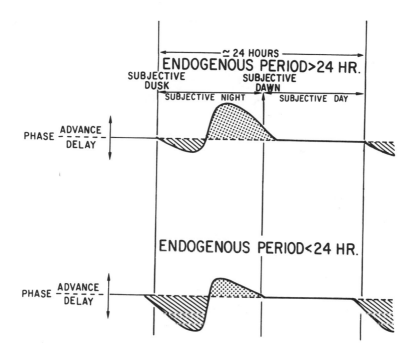

Figure 9.5. Typical phase-response curves for animals with endogenous periods greater than (*top*) and less than (*bottom*) 24 hours.

of the week, however, the melatonin onset had advanced an additional hour and the melatonin offset had also advanced approximately 1 hour compared to its phase position at the beginning of the week. These gradual advances, several days after advancing dusk, suggest an entrainment effect of light consistent with the existence of a PRC in humans with a delay portion in the evening. During the second week of that study, when dawn was delayed to 9:00 AM, the melatonin onset was delayed 1 hour by the end of the week and the melatonin offset was also delayed approximately 1 hour compared to its phase position at the beginning of the week. These gradual delays, several days after delaying dawn, suggest an entrainment effect of light consistent with the existence of a PRC in humans, with an advance portion in the morning.

Under entrained conditions, the margins of the photoperiod acting on the PRC are considered to be important for entrainment. In animals with $\tau > 24$ hours, the area under the illuminated advance portion of the PRC must be greater than the area under the illuminated delay portion, in order to assure stable steady-state entrainment to a 24-hour light–dark cycle (Figure 9.5, middle). [In an animal with $\tau < 24$ hours, the area under the delay portion of the PRC is greater than the area under the advance portion of the curve (Figure 9.5, bottom).] The greater the difference between τ and 24 hours, the more asymmetric the PRC. Humans generally have $\tau > 24$ hours (Wever, 1979). Therefore, every day we must use the advance portion of our PRC more than the delay portion, not only to compensate for the period of the endogenous pacemaker but also to compensate for any phase delay that might occur due to the effect of late afternoon light acting on the delay portion of the PRC. Thus, the area under the illuminated phase advance portion of the PRC in humans is presumably more pronounced than the area under the illuminated phase delay portion.

STUDIES OF MANIC-DEPRESSIVE PATIENTS

In a preliminary study (Lewy et al., 1981), four bipolar patients (two manic and two depressed), who were matched for age but not sex with a group of six normal volunteers, appeared to be supersensitive to light. Exposure to 500 lux suppressed melatonin production in these patients by 50%, whereas normal subjects were not significantly affected at this intensity. [These results were statistically significant at the $p < 0.02$ level (analysis of variance).] Exposure to 1500 lux almost completely suppressed the patients, whereas normal subjects were only suppressed by 50% at this intensity and required 2500 lux for complete suppression. (Patients were not receiving any medications in seven of the eight instances.) Subsequently, 11 additional euthymic (well-state) patients with a history of manic-depressive illness were compared to 24 normal subjects (Lewy et al., 1985a); these patients also appeared to be supersensitive to light, in that exposure to 500 lux suppressed their nighttime melatonin production twice as much as compared to the normal subjects ($p = 0.003$). Supersensitivity to light may therefore be a "trait marker" for manic-depressive illness.

TREATMENT OF WINTER DEPRESSION WITH BRIGHT ARTIFICIAL LIGHT

Bright light is now being used to manipulate biologic rhythms in humans. Although some seasonal rhythms have been identified in humans, this historically has not been a very active area of research. Despite the correlation between amplitude of seasonal rhythms and latitude, lack of direct evidence for photoperiodism in humans may have diminished enthusiasm for doing seasonal studies. Suppression of melatonin production by bright light exposure (Lewy et al., 1980b), however, suggests that humans may be responsive to the change in sunlight duration throughout the year unperturbed by ordinary artificial light.

In a preliminary study during the winter of 1980, a manic-depressive patient with a 13-year history of winter depression was treated with high-intensity light (Lewy et al., 1982). For 10 days, he was exposed to 3 hours of 2000-lux fluorescent light (capable of suppressing melatonin production) between 6:00 and 9:00 AM and between 4:00 and 7:00 PM. After 4 days, he switched out of his depression. Since then, more patients have been studied at Oregon Health Sciences University (Lewy et al., 1984, 1985c) and at the National Institute of Mental Health (Rosenthal et al., 1984, 1985). Using the bright light–dim light research paradigm (Lewy, 1981) in a modified crossover design, it was found that bright light was very effective but dim light had little effect (Rosenthal et al., 1984).

In the treatment of winter depression, bright light exposure in the morning alone is much more effective than evening light alone and may be more effective than the combination of morning plus evening bright light exposure (Lewy et al., 1984, 1985c, 1987). (In our more recent studies, morning bright light was scheduled from 6:00 to 8:00 AM; evening bright light was scheduled from 8:00 to 10:00 PM.) The response is seen within 3–7 days, although if sleep time has to be advanced to accommodate the early morning bright light exposure the optimal response may take a few more days, since it is probably the phase angle abnormality (delayed sleep or sleep-dependent processes with respect to the other circadian rhythms) that causes mood disturbances in phase-delayed disorders (Lewy et al., 1985c). It should also be noted that too much morning bright light can overly phase advance winter depressive patients, causing a return of depressive symptoms after a transient remission.

TREATMENT OF PHASE-ADVANCED AND PHASE-DELAYED CIRCADIAN RHYTHM DISORDERS

Exposure to bright light according to our hypothesized PRC has the predicted effects on shifting circadian phase position. Exposure to bright light in the evening (and avoidance of bright light in the morning) delays the timing of the DLMO and the nighttime temperature minimum and lengthens REM latency. Exposure to bright light in the morning (and avoidance of bright light in the evening) advances the timing of the DLMO and the nighttime temperature minimum and shortens REM latency (Lewy et al., 1984, 1985c, 1987; Sack et al., 1986).

Therefore, affective disorders can be associated with *either* phase-advanced circadian rhythms (as noted by Papoušek, 1975; Kripke et al., 1978; Wehr and Goodwin, 1981) *or* phase-delayed circadian rhythms [as suggested by our winter depressive patients (Lewy et al., 1987)]. "Phase typing" (Lewy et al., 1984, 1985c), that is, assessing circadian phase position in an individual with a sleep or mood disorder, may be necessary to determine if an individual has a chronobiologic disorder. Phase typing patients according to whether they are phase advanced or phase delayed may be a useful way to understand other psychologic and psychobiologic aspects of these patients. Currently, we think that patients should be phase typed on an individual basis, although most winter depressives seem to be phase delayed, as suggested by their preferential response to morning light exposure. We also think that most bipolar depressed patients with morning hypersomnia are phase delayed [and not phase advanced, as suggested by Kripke et al. (1978) and Wehr et al. (1979)] and should therefore preferentially respond to morning light.

After the patient has been phase typed, we recommend that bright light be scheduled on the basis of our hypothesized phase-response curve (Lewy et al., 1983b): patients with phase-advanced circadian rhythms should respond best to bright light in the evening (avoiding bright light in the morning), whereas patients with phase-delayed circadian rhythms should respond best to bright light in morning (avoiding bright light in the evening). We have also described the use of these principles in treating endogenous depressives with phase-advanced circadian rhythms and in treating patients with delayed (and advanced) sleep phase syndromes, as well as in the treatment of winter depression (Lewy et al., 1983b; Lewy, 1984; Lewy et al., 1984, 1985c, 1985d) and in ameliorating "jet lag" (Daan and Lewy, 1984). In the future, it may be possible to phase type individuals using the DLMO. However, at the present time sleep offset time appears to be a useful marker for circadian phase type. It seems likely that appropriately timed exposure to bright light can "correct" circadian phase position.

There is some disagreement among research groups as to the "correct" time for bright light exposure. For example, Kripke (1981) and Kripke et al. (1983) have chosen to concentrate their studies on treating major (presumably phase-advanced) depression with bright light exposure in the morning, and, more recently, morning and evening. On the other hand, we have evidence that exposure to bright light in the evening (and avoidance of bright light in the morning) is most effective for these presumably phase-advanced patients (who have early morning awakening) (Lewy et al., 1984, 1985c, 1985d).

We also disagree with Rosenthal et al. (1985) and James et al. (1985), who recommend bright light in the evening for the treatment of winter depression, stating that morning light does not appear to be critical for the response. On the contrary (as mentioned above), we have found that this group of (probably phase-delayed) patients respond much better to exposure to bright light in the morning (with avoidance of bright light in the evening) than they do to exposure to bright light in the evening or in both the morning and evening (Lewy et al., 1984, 1985c, 1987).

THE CLOSED-LOOP MODEL

Many questions about the effects of light in humans remain unanswered. A model is needed that places greater importance than did previous models on the effects of light on the human circadian system. In this spirit, a "closed-loop" model is proposed (Lewy, 1983a, 1983b) that can accommodate either the one- or two-oscillator models (Eastman, 1982; Kronauer et al., 1982; Wever, 1982; Winfree, 1982; Daan et al., 1984) to clarify how light entrains human circadian rhythms (Figure 9.6).

The essence of the closed-loop model is that light may have two different effects on the human circadian system: a direct zeitgeber effect and a social cue effect. In the case of the circadian melatonin production rhythm, the direct zeitgeber effect is presumably mediated by the retinohypothalamic tract on the SCN. The melatonin–temperature rhythm (we have evidence in some blind subjects that suggests that the circadian temperature rhythm and the circadian melatonin production rhythm are controlled by the same oscillator) may be more responsive than the activity–rest cycle to the direct zeitgeber effect of light, whereas the activity–rest cycle may be more responsive to the social cue effect of light. Core body temperature (or its endogenous pacemaker) influences the times of sleep onset and offset (Zulley, 1979; Czeisler et al., 1980); this is indicated in the model. The closing of the loop is accomplished by the activity–rest cycle superimposing its structure upon the light–dark cycle—in that opening and closing the eyes affects ocularly me-

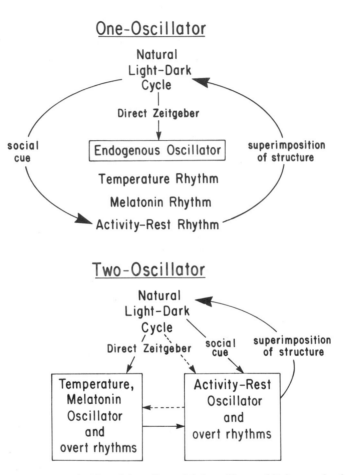

Figure 9.6. Proposed "closed-loop" model for effects of light on the human circadian system. This model assumes that the temperature (melatonin) oscillator is more sensitive to the zeitgeber property of the light–dark cycle and that the activity–rest cycle (or oscillator, depending on whether or not a separate endogenous circadian pacemaker regulates the activity–rest cycle) is more sensitive to the social cue property of the light–dark cycle. The "loop" is completed by the superimposition of structure upon the light–dark cycle by the activity–rest cycle (thorough opening and closing of the eyes).

diated light perception. Such a closed-loop system might provide for stable steady-state entrainment.

The closed-loop model emphasizes the dual effect of light on the circadian system—as a zeitgeber and a social cue. The strength of the social cue depends on whether the light–dark cycle is absolute (total darkness) or relative (reading lamps permitted during the "dark" phase). The strength of the zeitgeber depends on the intensity of the light (and the individual's sensitivity to light) during the "light" phase. The activity–rest cycle may be more responsive to the social cue effect of light; the melatonin–temperature rhythm may be more responsive to the zeitgeber effect of light.

The closed-loop model also suggests how sleep time might affect circadian rhythms in patients with sleep and mood disorders. Particularly, the time of sleep offset might have a critical role in initiating and perpetuating a change in circadian phase position. For example, patients with morning hypersomnia (such as many of our winter depressive patients) could be preventing bright light from illuminating the advance portion of the PRC, thus in turn, delaying circadian phase position, including the phase of the sleep–wake cycle. Such a vicious circle could also be present in patients with phase-advanced circadian rhythms whose early awakening could further advance their circadian rhythms due to earlier exposure to bright light.

Whether or not the primary cause of the phase disturbance is the result of an abnormality in the circadian system (special studies may be needed to determine such causality), the circadian system is certainly involved in the phenomenology of the phase disturbance. Shifting the times of dawn and dusk is one approach to defining the role of the circadian system in sleep and mood disorders. Even if it is eventually shown that shifts in circadian phase position are regularly associated with affective disorders, and even if "correcting" circadian phase position using appropriately timed exposure to bright light proves to be an effective treatment paradigm, many other questions come to mind. For instance, why do only *some* people become manic or depressed in association with a change in circadian phase position, since many people advance or delay their circadian phase positions (after transmeridian flight, for example) and do not have clinically significant mood episodes? The relative strengths of the zeitgebers for entraining rhythms in sighted as well as totally blind individuals also remain to be determined.

SUMMARY

We have determined that there are three critical parameters for light to be chronobiologically active in humans—intensity, wavelength, and timing. We know that light must be sufficiently bright (probably greater than about 2000 lux), although we do not know the precise range of effective intensities. The peak wavelengths for the effect (around 509 nm) are found in most light sources. Patients suspected of having a chronobiologic component to their sleep or mood disorder should be phase typed (phase advanced vs. phase delayed); then the correct timing can be decided based on our hypothesized PRC—bright light exposure in the morning should advance circadian phase position, and bright light exposure in the evening should delay circadian phase position. Delineation of these three critical parameters for light to be chronobiologically active in humans will hopefully help to clarify the basic principles by which light therapy can be tested and administered.

REFERENCES

Akerstedt T, Froberg JE, Friberg Y, Wetterberg L (1979): Melatonin secretion, body temperature and subjective arousal during 64 hours of sleep deprivation. Psychoneuroendocrinology 4:219–225.

Arendt J (1979): Radioimmunoassayable melatonin: Circulating patterns in man and sheep. Prog Brain Res 52:249–258.

Arendt J (1981): Current status of assay methods of melatonin. In Birau N, Schloot W (eds): Melatonin—Current Status and Perspectives. New York, Pergamon, pp 3–7.

Ariens Kappers J (1960): The development, topographical relations and innervation of the epiphysis cerebri in the albino rat. Z Zellforsch Mikrosk Anat 52:163–215.

Ariens Kappers J (1979): Short history of pineal discovery and research. Prog Brain Res 52:3–22.

Ariens Kappers J, Smith AR, DeVries RAC (1979): The mammalian pineal gland and its control of hypothalamic activity. Prog Brain Res 52:149–174.

Aschoff J (ed) (1981): Handbook of Behavioral Neurobiology. New York, Plenum, vol 4.

Birkeland AJ (1982): Plasma melatonin levels and nocturnal transitions between sleep and wakefulness. Neuroendocrinology 34:126–131.

Brainard GC, Lewy AJ, Menaker M, et al (1983): Dose–response relationship between light irradiance and the suppression of plasma melatonin in normal volunteers. Presented at the Endocrine Society 65th Annual Meeting, June 8–10, San Antonio, TX.

Brainard GC, Lewy AJ, Menaker M, et al (1985): Effect of light wavelength on the suppression of nocturnal plasma melatonin in normal volunteers. Ann NY Acad Sci 453:376–378.

Brown GM, Grota LJ, Pulido O, et al (1983): Application of immunologic techniques to the study of pineal indolealkylamines. In Reiter RJ (ed): Pineal Research Reviews. New York, Alan R. Liss, vol 1, pp 207–246.

Carr DB, Reppert SM, Bullen B, et al (1981): Plasma melatonin increases during exercise in women. J Clin Endocrinol Metab 53:224–225.

Cowen PJ, Green AR, Graham-Smith DG, Braddock LE (1985): Plasma melatonin during desmethylimipramine treatment: Evidence for changes in nor-adrenergic transmission. Br J Clin Pharmacol 19:1215–1228.

Czeisler CA, Moore-Ede MC, Regestein QR, et al (1979): Episodic 24-hour cortisol secretory rhythm during cardiac surgery. J Clin Endocrinol Metab 42:273–283.

Czeisler CA, Weitzman ED, Moore-Ede MC, et al (1980): Human sleep: Its duration and organization depend on its circadian phase. Science 210:1264–1266.

Czeisler CA, Richardson GS, Zimmerman JC, et al (1981): Entrainment of human circadian rhythms by light-dark cycles: A reassessment. Photochem Photobiol 34:239–247.

Daan S, Lewy AJ (1984): Scheduled exposure to daylight: A potential strategy to reduce "jet lag" following transmeridian flight. Psychopharmacol Bull 20::566–568.

Daan S, Beersma DGM, Borbely AA (1984): Timing of human sleep: Recovery process gated by a circadian pacemaker. Am J Physiol 246 (Regul Integr Comp Physiol 15):R161–R178.

DeCoursey PJ (1960): Daily light sensitivity rhythm in a rodent. Science 131:33–35.

Eastman C (1982): The phase-shift model of spontaneous internal de-synchronization in humans. In Aschoff J, Daan S, Groos GA (eds): Vertebrate Circadian Systems. Structure and Physiology. Berlin, Springer-Verlag, pp 262–267.

Elliott JA, Tamarkin L (1982): Phase relationship of two circadian oscillators regulates pineal melatonin rhythm in Syrian hamsters. Endocrinology 110:A326.

Golden RN (1984): A new marker for noradenergic function in man? Presented at the American Psychiatric Association Meeting, Los Angeles, CA, May 5–11.

Goldman B, Hall V, Hollister C, et al (1981): Diurnal changes in pineal melatonin content in four rodent species: Relationship to photoperiodism. Biol Reprod 24:778–783.

Griffiths D, Seamark RF, Bryden MM (1979): Summer and winter cycles in plasma melatonin levels in the elephant seal (Mirounga leonina). Aust J Biol Sci 32:581–586.

Hanssen T, Heyden T, Sundberg T, Wetterberg L (1977): Effect of pro-pranolol on serum-melatonin. Lancet 2:309–310.

Hendrickson SE, Wagoner N, Cowan WM (1972): Autoradiographic and electron microscopic study of retino-hypothalamic connections. Z Zellerforsch 125:1–26.

Herbert DC, Reiter RJ (1981): Influence of protein-calorie malnutrition on the circadian rhythm of pineal melatonin in the rat. Soc Exp Biol Med 166:360–363.

Hoban TM, Sulzman SM (1985): Light effects on the circadian timing system of a diurnal primate—The squirrel monkey. Am J Physiol 249:R274–80.

Hoffman K, Illnerova H, Vanecek H (1980): Pineal N-acetyltransferase activity in the Djungarian hamster. Naturwissenschaften 67:408–409.

Illnerova H (1976): The effects of immobilization of the activity of serotonin N-acetyltransferase in the rat epiphysis. In Usdin E, Kvetnansky R, Kopin IJ (eds): Catecholamines and Stress. New York, Pergamon, pp 129–136.

Illnerova H, Vanecek J (1980): Pineal rhythm in N-acetyltransferase activity in rats under different artificial photoperiods and in natural daylight in the course of a year. Neuroendocrinology 31:321–326.

Illnerova H, Vanecek J (1982a): Complex control of the circadian rhythm in N-acetyltransferase activity in the rat pineal gland. In Aschoff J, Daan S, Groos G (eds): Vertebrate Circadian Systems. Structure and Physiology. Berlin, Springer-Verlag, pp 285–296.

Illnerova H, Vanecek J (1982b): Two-oscillator structure of the pacemaker controlling the circadian rhythm of N-acetyltransferase in the rat pineal gland. J Comp Physiol 145:539–548.

Illnerova H, Zvolsky P, Vanecek J (1985): The circadian rhythm in plasma melatonin concentration of the urbanized man: The effect of summer and winter time. Brain Res 328:186–189.

James SP, Wehr TA, Sack DA, et al (1985): Treatment of seasonal affective disorder with light in the evening. Br J Psychiatry 147:424–428.

Jimerson DC, Lynch HJ, Post RM, et al (1977): Urinary melatonin rhythms during sleep deprivation in depressed patients and normals. Life Sci 20:1501–1508.

Kebabian JW, Zatz M, Romero JA, Axelrod J (1975): Rapid changes in rat pineal beta-adrenergic receptor. Alterations in 1-(^{3}H) alprenolol binding and adenylate cyclase. Proc Natl Acad Sci USA 72:3735–3739

Klein DC, Parfitt A (1976): A protective role of nerve endings in stress-stimulated increase in pineal N-acetyltransferase activity. In Usdin E, Kvetnansky R, Kopin IJ (eds): Catecholamines and Stress. New York, Pergamon, pp 119–128.

Klein DC, Smoot R, Weller JL, et al (1983): Lesions of the paraventricular nucleus area of the hypothalamus disrupt the suprachiasmatic–spinal cord circuit in the melatonin rhythm generating system. Brain Res Bull 10:647–652.

Klein KE, Wegmann H-M (1974): The resynchronization of psychomotor performance circadian rhythm after transmeridian flights as a result of flight direction and mode of activity. In Scheving LE, Halberg FF, Pauly JE (eds): Chronobiology. Stuttgart, George Thieme Purl, pp 564–570.

Kripke DF (1981): Photoperiodic mechanisms for depression and its treatment. In Perris C, Struwe G, Jansson B (eds): Biological Psychiatry 1981. Amsterdam, Elsevier, pp 1249–1252.

Kripke DF, Mullaney DJ, Atkinson M, Wolf S (1978): Circadian rhythm disorders in manic-depressives. Biol Psychiatry 13:335–350.

Kripke DF, Risch SC, Janowsky D (1983): Bright white light alleviates depression. Psychiatry Res 10:105–112.

Kronauer RE, Czeisler CA, Pilato SF, et al (1982): Mathematical model of the human circadian system with two interacting oscillators. Am J Physiol 242 (Regul Integr Comp Physiol 11):R3–R17.

Lewy AJ (1981): The effects of light in man: Melatonin secretion, circadian sleep and affective disorders, and the bright light/dim light paradigm. Sleep Res 10:297.

Lewy AJ (1983a): Biochemistry and regulation of mammalian melatonin production. In Relkin RM (ed): The Pineal Gland. New York, Elsevier, pp 77–128.

Lewy AJ (1983b): Effects of light on melatonin secretion and the circadian system of man. In Wehr TA, Goodwin FK (eds): Circadian Rhythms in Psychiatry, Biological Rhythms and Psychiatry. Pacific Grove, CA, Boxwood, pp 203–219.

Lewy AJ (1984): Human melatonin secretion (II): A marker for the circadian system of man and the effects of light. In Post RM, Ballenger JC (eds): Neurobiology of Mood Disorders. Baltimore, Williams and Wilkins, pp 215–226.

Lewy AJ, Markey SP (1978): Analysis of melatonin in human plasma by gas chromatography negative chemical ionization mass spectrometry. Science 201:741–743.

Lewy AJ, Newsome DA (1983): Different types of melatonin rhythms in some blind subjects. J Clin Endocrinol Metab 56:1103–1107.

Lewy AJ, Tetsuo M, Markey SP, et al (1980a): Pinealectomy abolishes plasma melatonin in the rat. J Clin Endocrinol Metab 50:204–205.

Lewy AJ, Wehr TA, Goodwin FK, et al (1980b): Light supppresses melatonin secretion in humans. Science 210:1267–1269.

Lewy AJ, Wehr TA, Goodwin FK, et al (1981): Manic-depressive patients may be supersensitive to light. Lancet 1:383–384.

Lewy AJ, Kern HE, Rosenthal NE, Wehr TA (1982): Bright artificial light treatment of a manic-depressive patient with a seasonal mood cycle. Am J Psychiatry 139:1496–1498.

Lewy A, Brainard G, Menaker M, et al (1983a): Fluence–response relationship between light irradiance, suppression of melatonin production, and treatment of "winter depression." Neuroendocrinology Lett 5:409.

Lewy AJ, Sack RL, Fredrickson RH, et al (1983b): The use of bright light in the treatment of chronobiologic sleep and mood disorders: The phase-response curve. Psychopharmacol Bull 19:523–525.

Lewy AJ, Sack RL, Singer CM (1984): Assessment and treatment of chronobiologic disorders using plasma melatonin levels and bright light exposure: The clock-gate model and the phase response curve. Psychopharmacol Bull 20:561–565.

Lewy AJ, Nurnberger JI, Wehr TA, et al (1985a): Supersensitivity to light: Possible trait marker for manic-depressive illness. Am J Psychiatry 142:725–727.

Lewy AJ, Sack RL, Singer CM (1985b): Immediate and delayed effects of bright light on human melatonin production: Shifting "dawn" and "dusk" shifts the dim light melatonin onset (DLMO). Ann NY Acad Sci 453:253–259.

Lewy AJ, Sack RL, Singer CM (1985c): Treating phase typed chronobiologic sleep and mood disorders using appropriately timed bright artificial light. Psychopharmacol Bull 21:368–372.

Lewy AJ, Sack RL, Singer CM (1985d): Melatonin, light and chronobiological disorders. In Evered D, Clark S (eds): Photoperiodism, Melatonin and the Pineal. London, Pitman, pp 231–252.

Lynch HJ (1983): Assay methodology. In Relkin R (ed): The Pineal Gland, Current Endocrinology: Basic and Clinical Aspects. New York, Elsevier, pp 129–150.

Lynch HJ, Jimerson DC, Osaki Y, et al (1977): Entrainment of rhythmic melatonin secretion in man to a 12-hour phase shift in the light dark cycle. Life Sci 23:1557–1564.

Markey SP, Buell PE (1982): Pinealectomy abolishes 6-hydroxymelatonin excretion by male rats. Endocrinology 111:425–426.

Moore DC, Paunier L, Sizonenko PC (1979): Effect of adrenergic stimulation and blockade on melatonin secretion in the human. Prog Brain Res 52:517–521.

Moore RY, Eichler VB (1972): Loss of circadian adrenal corticosterone rhythm following suprachiasmatic lesions in the rat. Brain Res 42:201–206.

Moore RY, Lenn NJ (1972): A retinohypothalamic projection in the rat. J Comp Neurol 146:1–14.

Moore RY, Klein DC (1974): Visual pathways and the central neural control of a circadian rhythm in pineal serotonin N-acetyltransferase activity. Brain Res 71:17–33.

Neuwelt EA, Lewy AJ (1983): Disappearance of plasma melatonin after removal of a neoplastic pineal gland. N Engl J Med 308:1132–1135.

Papoušek M (1975): Chronobiological aspects of cyclothymia. Fortschr Neurol Psychiatr 43:381–440.

Parfitt A, Klein DC (1977): Increase caused by desmethylimipramine in the production of (^{3}H) melatonin by isolated pineal glands. Biochem Pharmacol 26:904–905.

Petterborg LJ, Richardson BA, Reiter RJ (1981): Effect of long or short photoperiod on pineal melatonin content in the white-footed mouse, *Peromyscus leucopus*. Life Sci 29:1623–1627.

Pickard GE, Turek FW (1983): The hypothalamic paraventricular nucleus mediates the photoperiodic control of reproduction but not the effects of light on the circadian rhythm of activity. Neurosci Lett 43:67–72.

Pittendrigh CS (1981): Circadian systems: Entrainment. In Aschoff J (ed):

Handbook of Behavioral Neurobiology, vol 4: Biological Rhythms. New York, Plenum, pp 95–124.

Pittendrigh CS, Daan S (1976): A functional analysis of circadian pacemakers in nocturnal rodents. IV. Entrainment: Pacemaker as clock. J Comp Physiol 106:291–331.

Ralph CL, Mull D, Lynch HJ, Hedlund L (1971): A melatonin rhythm persists in rat pineals in darkness. Endocrinology 89:1361–1366.

Redman J, Armstrong S, Ng KT (1983): Free-running activity rhythms in the rat: Entrainment by melatonin. Science 219:1089–1091.

Rollag MD (1981): Methods for measuring pineal hormones. In Reiter RJ (ed): The Pineal Gland, Anatomy and Biochemistry. Boca Raton, FL, CRC Press, vol 1, pp 273–302.

Rollag MD, O'Callaghan PL, Niswender GD (1978): Serum melatonin concentrations during different stages of the annual reproductive cycle in ewes. Biol Reprod 18:279–285.

Romero JA, Axelrod J (1975): Regulation of sensitivity to beta-adrenergic stimulation in induction of pineal *N*-acetyltransferase. Proc Natl Acad Sci USA 72:1661–1665.

Romero JA, Zatz M, Axelrod J (1975): Beta-adrenergic stimulation of pineal *N*-acetyltransferase: Adenosine 3',5'-cyclic monophosphate stimulates both RNA and protein synthesis. Proc Natl Acad Sci USA 72:2107–2111.

Rosenthal NE, Sack DA, Gillin JC, et al: (1984): Seasonal affective disorder. Arch Gen Psychiatry 41:72–80.

Rosenthal NE, Sack DA, Carpenter CJ, et al (1985): Antidepressant effects of light in seasonal affective disorder. Am J Psychiatry 142:163–170.

Sack RL, Lewy AJ (1986): Desmethylimipramine treatment increases melatonin production in humans. Biol Psychiatry 21:406–410.

Sack RL, Lewy AJ, Miller LS, Singer CM (1986): Effects of morning versus evening bright light exposure on REM latency. Biol Psychiatry 21:410–413.

Sack RL, Hoben TM, Lewy AJ (1987): Free-running melatonin rhythms in totally blind people. Sleep Research, in press.

Stephan FK, Zucker I (1972): Circadian rhythms in drinking behavior and locomotor activity of rats are eliminated by hypothalamic lesions. Proc Natl Acad Sci USA 69:1583–1586.

Tamarkin L, Reppert SM, Klein DC, et al (1980): Studies on the daily pattern of pineal melatonin in the Syrian hamster. Endocrinology 107:1525–1529.

Tetsuo M, Perlow MJ, Mishkin M, Markey SP (1982): Light exposure reduces and pinealectomy virtually stops urinary excretion of 6-hydroxymelatonin by Rhesus monkeys. Endocrinology 110:997–1003.

Theintz GE, Lang U, Deriaz O, et al (1984): Day-time plasma melatonin response to physical exercise in humans. J Steroid Biochem 20:1470.

Vaughan GM, Pelham RW, Pang SF, et al (1976): Nocturnal elevation of plasma melatonin and urinary 5-hydroxyindole acetic acid in young men: Attempts at modification by brief changes in environmental lighting and sleep and by autonomic drugs. J Clin Endocrinol Metab 42:752–764.

Vaughan GM, Allen JP, Tullis W, et al (1978): Overnight plasma profiles of melatonin and certain adenohypophyseal hormones in men. J Clin Endocrinol Metab 47:566–571.

Vaughan GM, Bell R, De La Pena A (1979a): Nocturnal plasma melatonin in humans: Episodic pattern and influence of light. Neurosci Lett 14:81–84.

Vaughan GM, McDonald SD, Jordan RM, et al (1979b): Melatonin, pituitary function and stress in humans. Psychoneuroendocrinology 4:351–362.

Wehr TA, Goodwin FK (1981): Biological rhythms and psychiatry. In Arieti S, Brodie HKH (eds): American Handbook of Psychiatry, 2nd ed. New York, Basic Books, vol 7, pp 46–74.

Wehr TA, Wirz-Justice A, Goodwin FK, et al (1979): Phase advance of the circadian sleep–wake cycle as an antidepressant. Science 206:710–713.

Weinberg J, D'Eletto RD, Weitzman ED, et al (1979): Circulatory melatonin in man: Episodic secretion throughout the dark–light cycle. J Clin Endocrinol Metab 48:114–118.

Weitzman ED, Czeisler CA, Moore-Ede MC (1979): Sleep–wake, neuroendocrine and body temperature circadian rhythms under entrained and nonentrained (free-running) conditions in man. In Suda M, Hayaishi O, Nakagawa H (eds): Biological Rhythms and Their Central Mechanisms. New York, Elsevier, pp 199–227.

Wever RA (1979): The Circadian System of Man: Results of Experiments Under Temporal Isolation. New York, Springer-Verlag.

Wever RA (1982): Commentary on the mathematical model of the human circadian system. Am J Physiol 242 (Regul Integr Comp Physiol 11):R17–R21.

Wever RA, Polasek J, Wildgruber CM (1983): Bright light affects human circadian rhythms. Pflugers Arch 396:85–87.

Winfree AT (1982): The tides of human consciousness: Descriptions and questions. Am J Physiol 242 (Regul Integr Comp Physiol 11):R163–R166.

Wurtman RJ, Axelrod J, Phillips LS (1963): Melatonin synthesis in the pineal gland: Control by light. Science 142:1071–1073.

Zatz M, Kebabian J, Romero JA, et al (1976): Pineal adrenergic receptor: Correlation of binding of ^{3}H-alprenolol with stimulation of adenylate cyclase. J Pharmacol Exp Ther 196:714–722.

Zulley J (1979): Der Einfluss von Zeitgebern auf den Schlaf des Menschen. Frankfurt, Fischer.

10

Treatment of Major Depressive Disorders by Bright White Light for 5 Days

Daniel F. Kripke, J. Christian Gillin,
Daniel J. Mullaney, S. Craig Risch, and
David S. Janowsky

In two previous studies, we have shown that a single hour of bright white light treatment decreases symptoms of Major Depressive Disorders on the same day of treatment (Kripke, 1981; Kripke et al, 1983a,b). In both studies, the benefit was 1 to 3 points on Hamilton and Beck depression rating scales. In the first study, the effect was small, but statistically significant. In the second study, the effect was slightly smaller and of borderline significance. Thus, the effect of a single hour of bright light treatment seems to be substantially less than has been found with similar patients treated with a single all-night sleep deprivation (Schilgen and Tolle, 1980; Gillin, 1983). On the other hand, it is doubtful one could obtain as much benefit with a single hour of psychotherapy, a single hour of imipramine treatment, or even a single session of electroconvulsive therapy. These customary treatments of serious depression usually require several days or weeks of continuous and repeated treatments before benefits can be appreciated. Thus, the weakness of the effect noted could be due to the brevity of treatment.

We have hypothesized that bright light treatments of patients with major depression are analogous to the photoperiodic effects of light in rodents (Kripke, 1984). Although the effects of light on pineal melatonin secretion are almost immediate, photoperiodic effects on gonadal growth and reproductive behavior in rodents require several weeks before maximal impact is achieved (Reiter, 1980; Elliott and Goldman,

207

Table 10.1. Comparison of Depression and Photoperiodic Responses

Animal	*Human*
Seasonal infertility	Human depression
Altered noradrenergic induction/ conversion of serotonin to melatonin, possibly suppressed through a cholinergically mediated pathway	Hypothesized decreased noradrenergic and serotonergic synaptic transmission Excessive cholinergic neurotransmission
Decreased production of thyroid hormones, cortisol, prolactin, LH, FSH, and gonadal steroids	Decreased production of thyroid stimulating hormone, prolactin, LH, and possibly testosterone and estrogen. Excess production of cortisol.
Decreased breeding behaviors, decreased aggressive behaviors, sometimes behavioral inactivity	Decreased libido, decreased concentration, motivation, and assertiveness. At times, retardation.
Weight changes	Weight changes

1981). Thus, one might expect similar delays in obtaining the neuroendocrine effects of light treatment among depressed subjects. There are numerous resemblances between the photoperiodic depression of reproduction found in lower mammals and depression in humans (Table 10.1).

In somewhat analogous experiments, Rosenthal and colleagues (1984, 1985a,b) have tested effects of extending the photoperiod with bright light upon patients with winter depression. In these studies, quite dramatic decreases in depressive symptoms were obtained, beginning after 3–4 days of treatment. These results also suggested that a longer treatment duration was needed.

With these considerations, we decided to study the effects of 5 days of bright white light treatment as contrasted with 5 days of control dim red light treatment on patients with Major Depressive Disorders.

METHODS

Subjects

All subjects were veteran inpatients at the Mental Health Clinical Research Center, located in the San Diego Veterans Administration Medical

Center. Fourteen of the fifteen subjects were males. Their mean age was 46 years (range 34–57). Between January 1983 and March 1984, patients were selected if they had Beck and Hamilton depression ratings of at least 15 upon entry in the study, were depressed, and were free of major psychotropic drugs. One patient had to be placed on doxepin 150–200 mg during both the white light and red light treatments, which were given in that order. As it happened, this patient's depression ratings did not vary from baseline to the end of the study. Of the 15 patients initially entering the study, 1 dropped out and 14 completed the entire protocol.

Schedule of Affective Disorders interviews were given and consensus research diagnoses established (Research Diagnostic Criteria), in some cases after the study began. Of the 14 subjects who completed the study, 11 were diagnosed as having Major Depressive Disorders, of whom 1 was bipolar and 6 endogenous. Two subjects were schizoaffective and one had a minor depressive disorder. Five of the fourteen had mean REM latencies of less than 60 minutes. Of eight subjects who were tested with 1.0 mg dexamethasone at 11:00 PM, three had plasma cortisols exceeding 5.0 μg/dl the next day at 4:00 or 11:00 PM.

Protocol

Patients signed written informed consent. After 1–4 days of baseline ratings (mean 2.5 days), subjects were randomly assigned to either bright light or dim light treatments for 5 days.

In the bright light treatment, subjects were placed in a bedroom equipped with fluorescent lights capable of illuminating the room at intensities varying from 300 to 4500 lux in different directions at eye level, measuring through a cosine diffuser and photometric filter with a UDT40X photometer. The first seven patients used Vitalite fluorescent supplied by a portable eye-level fixture. The next seven patients used cool-white fluorescent mounted in overhead fixtures. Subjects were permitted to retire in a single-patient room at their normal ward bedtime, usually 10:00 to 11:00 PM. At 5:00 AM, they were awakened by staff and immediately exposed to the bright white light illumination, which reached full intensity over a period of 1.5 minutes. Subjects were asked to remain in the room in the bright light exposure, apart from quick trips to the bathroom, until 6:00 AM, when the lights were extinguished. Subjects were encouraged to return to sleep until their normal time of awakening (around 7:00 AM). After six subjects had been studied, it was noted that the effects of the bright light treatment were weak, and it was decided to add an additional hour of bright white light treatment for the final eight patients (from 9:00 to 10:00 PM) to the 5:00 to 6:00 AM treatment described above.

The control dim-light treatments were similarly given from 5:00 to 6:00 AM ($N = 14$) and from 9:00 to 10:00 PM ($N = 8$), except that the room was then illuminated by only two dim fluorescent bulbs covered by a red Plexiglas filter. The red filter was selected on the basis of evidence that red light is ineffective in suppressing melatonin (Brainard et al., 1984, 1985). The red light provided illumination of approximately 3–30 lux. The dim red light provided comfortable vision in the room but was somewhat dim for reading. Thus, subjects were allowed to watch a black and white television during both the bright and dim light treatments, the screen of which gave illumination of approximately 10 lux. When subjects were up and about the ward outside of light treatments, they were exposed to the usual ward fluorescent lighting, which after sunset ranged from about 20–100 lux.

After the 5 days of treatment with either bright white or dim red light and a 2-day "washout," each subject was crossed over to the opposite bright light or dim light treatment for an additional 5 days. Finally, a posttreatment rating was obtained 3–5 days after the last light treatment. Not all patients remained drug free during this follow-up.

Since no significant differences were found between methods of bright light treatment, the subjects receiving 5:00 to 6:00 AM Vitalite light treatments only and those receiving 9:00 to 10:00 PM plus 5:00 to 6:00 AM cool-white fluorescent treatments were combined for purposes of analysis.

Mood Ratings

Patients were rated twice daily on the Hamilton Depression Scale by a rater blind to their type of light exposure. A 24-item Hamilton scale was used to determine if the 15-point entry criterion for the study was met, but in subsequent analyses, the three sleep-related items were removed to obtain a 21-item scale undistorted by experimental awakenings. Subjects also completed Beck self-ratings twice daily. After removing the question about sleep, 20 Beck items were totaled. In addition, subjects completed a circadian mood rating form with an abscissa of 24 hours and an ordinate consisting of a 125-mm glad–sad visual analogue scale. Thus, subjects were encouraged in this self-rating form to indicate both the phase and amplitude of their daily mood fluctuation as well as the day-to-day changes in depressive feelings. The mood scores were analyzed by least-squares determination of the best-fitting 24-hour cosine.

EEG

All-night EEG sleep recordings were obtained as often as possible, generally one or two nights during baseline and two to three nights in each condition (bright light and dim light). EEG recordings were also used to assure that the patients remained awake during the treatment from 5:00 to 6:00 AM and to assess how much patients slept after the morning light treatments.

RESULTS

On the first day after treatment, there was no improvement as compared to baseline with either the bright white light or dim red light treatment (Figures 10.1, 10.2). Nevertheless, a progressive improvement occurred over the 5 days while the patients were treated with bright white light. Although after 5 days of bright white light treatment, depression scores fell significantly from baseline, there was a minimal reduction in depres-

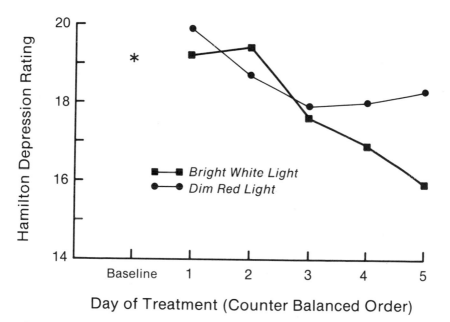

Figure 10.1. Hamilton Depression Scale ratings of the subjects while exposed to 5 days of dim red light treatment (*thin line*) and 5 days of bright white light treatment (*thick line*).

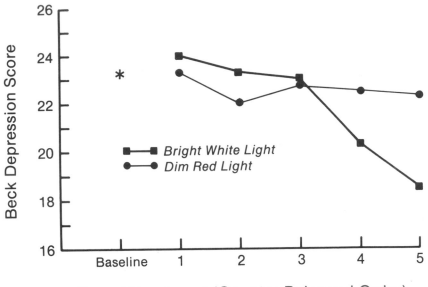

Figure 10.2. Beck Depression Scale self-ratings of subjects exposed to 5 days of dim red light treatment (*thin line*) and 5 days of bright white light treatment (*thick line*).

sion ratings when the patients were treated with control dim red light for 5 days. A more definite progressive improvement occurred when the patients were treated with bright white light (Figures 10.1, 10.2). In the 21-item Hamilton ratings, the depression scores decreased nonsignificantly, from a mean baseline of 19.1 to 18.2, after 5 days of control dim red light treatment ($p = 0.59$). At the end of 5 days of bright white light treatments, the Hamilton ratings decreased significantly, from the 19.1 baseline to 15.9 ($p = 0.05$). Similarly, in the 20-item Beck self-ratings, depression scores decreased nonsignificantly, from a mean baseline of 23.2 to 22.3, at the end of the dim red light treatment ($p = 0.63$), and decreased significantly, from the 23.2 baseline to 18.5, at the end of bright white light treatment ($p = 0.02$). Nevertheless, at no point during the treatments was the contrast of ratings *between* bright white light and dim red light treatments significant, nor was the contrast significant between the regression slopes of the depression scores during the two treatments. An increase in depression scores was noted following termination of bright white light treatment, whether it was given

Table 10.2. Treatment Effects on Sleep

	Mean +/− SD of EEG Sleep Scoring Results		
	Baseline	*Dim Red Light*	*Bright White Light*
Total sleep time	310 min ± 94	367 min ± 62	371 min ± 59
Sleep after 5:00–6:00 AM awakening	Not applicable	51 ± 30	47 ± 36
REM latency	65 ± 47	72 ± 33	72 ± 47
REM sleep	76 ± 43	78 ± 30	85 ± 29
Stage 3–4 sleep	54 ± 41	54 ± 32	54 ± 29
REM percent	24% ± 9%	25% ± 9%	26% ± 8%
Stage 3–4 percent	16% ± 11%	17% ± 10%	17% ± 9%

first or second. The posttreatment Hamilton ratings averaged 16.8 and the Beck ratings 21.8. Thus, in a two-way analysis of variance (ANOVA) with repeated measures, using the order of treatment as the second factor, there were no order effects or order–treatment interactions.

There was no significant change in the mean circadian mood self-ratings from baseline to light treatment. Nevertheless, the *amplitude* of the daily changes in mood decreased from baseline (5.3 mm out of 125 mm) to either dim light (3.3 mm) or bright light (2.9 mm) treatment ($p = 0.008$), there being no significant difference between dim and bright. No significant change in the circadian phase of self-reported mood was noted.

Perhaps due to "first-night" effects, subjects slept more during both light treatments than during the baseline (Table 10.2). Thus, the 5:00 AM awakening did not result in sleep deprivation. Nevertheless, comparing the bright light and dim light treatments, there were no significant differences in total sleep time, REM latency, minutes or percentage of REM sleep, or minutes or percentage of slow-wave sleep (stages 3 and 4). Furthermore, the amounts of sleep obtained in the morning after the bright light and dim light treatments did not differ significantly.

DISCUSSION

These results extend our previous findings that treatments with bright white light decrease the symptoms of patients with Major Depressive Disorders. A progressive improvement was noted during 5 days of bright light treatment, so that although the effects on the first day were less than those previously noted, the effects by the fifth day were greater. Unfortunately, these results must be considered equivocal, for although the depression scores were significantly lower than baseline by the end of 5 days of bright white light treatment, the improvement was not statistically significantly superior to that obtained with the counterbalanced control treatment. In view of our previous results, it is unlikely that there is no true difference between the antidepressant effects of bright white light and dim red light treatments. On the other hand, the magnitude of the effects we obtained here are not of great clinical significance, whatever their statistical reliability.

The data suggest that even greater progressive effects might be obtained with still longer durations of treatment (Figures 10.1, 10.2) and we are presently experimenting with longer treatment durations. We hope that colleagues in other centers will join in this task, to increase the numbers of subjects being studied.

We have been concerned whether our patients were receiving light that was sufficient in quality and quantity to obtain the desired effects. Although our lighting fixtures clearly provided sufficient illumination to suppress melatonin when the patients were looking toward the lights, it is of course difficult to ensure the direction of a person's gaze from moment to moment. By installing overhead fixtures, we have attempted to provide enough light to result in the suppression of melatonin, regardless of the subject's position in his bedroom: however, we have not completed enough melatonin assays to validate the effectiveness of our lighting. An impression has been created without any direct evidence that Vitalite fluorescent light might be more effective in treating depression than other forms of bright artificial lighting. We have found no evidence that this is so. Indeed, in the green wavelengths from 500–520 nm, which are most likely to suppress melatonin (Brainard et al., 1984, 1985), our measurements show that 40-W Vitalite fluorescents actually give less light than ordinary cool-white bulbs of identical size and rated power consumption.

It is possible that we have failed to utilize an optimal duration of light exposure. The stronger results of Rosenthal and colleagues (1984, 1985a,b) were obtained with 6 hours of bright light exposure a day. Furthermore, a preliminary report of Dietzel et al. (1984) suggested that 6 hours of light exposure a day may be rapidly effective in patients with Major Depressive Disorders. Nevertheless, we found no difference between the groups receiving 1 versus 2 hours of light treatment per day. Rosenthal and colleagues have not found their 6-hour pattern of light treatment to be as effective in pilot subjects with nonseasonal Major

Depressive Disorders as in their seasonal patients (Rosenthal, personal communication).

It would appear most likely that our patient group is less sensitive to the benefits of bright light treatment than the winter depressives described by Rosenthal and colleagues. Our patients differed from the winter depressives in sex ratio, by their inpatient status (though their depression ratings were not greater), and, most strikingly, by their clinical syndromes. The winter depressives are probably a group uniquely sensitive to light. None of our patients showed a distinct history of winter predominance of symptoms. We have extensively reviewed this group of patients, together with the patients of our previous studies, to determine whether the time of year of treatment, age, sex, RDC diagnosis, or markers such as REM latency, early awakening, or dexamethasone resistance predict the favorable responders. We have not yet found any clinical descriptor that predicts which of our patients will respond most favorably.

A remaining possibility is that a different form of photoperiod treatment would be better for the patient with Major Depressive Disorder. Since we began our studies in these patients, evidence has appeared that patients with Major Depressive Disorder actually secrete less melatonin at night than age-matched controls (Mendlewicz et al., 1980; Beck-Friis et al., 1984; Claustrat et al., 1984; Checkley and Arendt, 1984; Kocsis et al., 1984; Steiner and Brown, 1984). Furthermore, manic-depressive patients seem more sensitive to suppression of melatonin by light than do control subjects (Lewy et al., 1981).

In view of these findings, efforts to suppress major depressives' nocturnal melatonin with bright light might seem somewhat illogical, since this would tend to exacerbate a melatonin deficiency. Simple melatonin suppression is unlikely to be the mechanism of the beneficial effects we have previously described.

Two possible alternative beneficial effects of light treatment for patients with Major Depressive Disorders should be considered. First, bright light could reset the phase of abnormal circadian rhythms in depressed patients. If a rhythm is abnormally advanced, and light exposures reset the phase of this rhythm, one might expect evening light rather than morning light to produce beneficial phase resetting (Lewy, 1984; Lewy et al., 1984). If this were true, however, we might have expected the addition of our 9:00 to 10:00 PM treatment to show increased benefit, which was not the case. If light primarily advances the phase of some rhythm systems that are distinct from those abnormally advanced among patients with Major Depressive Disorders, the morning light would tend to correct the abnormal internal phase relationships among body circadian rhythms. We need much more data about the actual effects of light treatments on circadian rhythms.

Second, Beck-Friis and colleagues (1985) have suggested that an evening bright light exposure, although producing a momentary melatonin suppression, actually facilitates rebound increases in plasma melatonin later in the night, when melatonin approaches its peak. Thus, daytime or evening bright light exposure might actually increase melatonin secretion overnight and correct the low secretion described among patients with Major Depressive Disorders. Light treatments might also produce more tolerance to bright light and correct hypersensitivity to light suppression of melatonin (Lynch et al., 1981). The most effective time for such exposures has not yet been determined; however, it is quite unlikely that the 5:00 to 6:00 AM morning exposure or the 9:00 to 10:00 PM evening exposure would be optimal.

Thus, the present results can be viewed as promising steps toward a treatment approach that needs further development. Either the duration of the treatment needs to be extended beyond 5 days, or the timing of the treatment needs to be optimized. Our current methods are unready for clinical application.

The possibility that optimal timing of light treatments could produce increased benefit in patients with Major Depressive Disorders is an exciting possibility for future study. In an ongoing study, we are exposing patients to bright light from 8:00 to 11:00 PM for seven evenings. Preliminary results suggest that a more robust response may be obtained, but further subjects must be studied.

This work was supported by NIMH MH38822, by NIMH RSDA MH00117 (to DFK), by NIMH CRC MH30914, and by the Veterans Administration.

REFERENCES

Beck-Friis J, von Rosen D, Kjellman BF, et al (1984): Melatonin in relation to body measures, sex, age, season and the use of drugs in patients with major affective disorders and healthy subjects. Psychoneuroendocrinology 9:261–277.

Beck-Friis J, Borg G, Wetterberg L (1985): Rebound increase of nocturnal serum melatonin levels following evening suppression by bright light exposure in healthy men: Relation to cortisol levels and morning exposure. Ann NY Acad Sci 453:371–375.

Brainard GC, Richardson BA, King TS, et al (1984): The influence of different light spectra on the suppression of pineal melatonin content in the Syrian hamster. Brain Res 294:333–339.

Brainard GC, Lewy AJ, Menaker M, et al (1985): Effect of light wavelength on the suppression of nocturnal plasma melatonin in normal volunteers. Ann NY Acad Sci 453:376–378.

Checkley S, Arendt J (1984): Pharmacoendocrine studies of GH, PRL, and melatonin in patients with affective illness. In Brown GM, Koslau SH, Reichlin S (eds): Neuroendocrinology and Psychiatric Disorders. New York, Raven, pp 165–190.

Claustrat B, Chazot G, Brun J, et al (1984): A chronobiological study of melatonin and cortisol secretion in depressed subjects: Plasma melatonin, a biochemical marker in major depression. Biol Psychiatry 19:1215–1228.

Dietzel M, Saletu B, Waldhauser F, et al (1984): Effects of bright light and practical sleep deprivation: Polysomnographic and neuroendocrine variables. Munich, Germany, 7th European Sleep Congress Abstracts, p 335.

Elliott JZ, Goldman BD (1981): Seasonal reproduction: Photoperiodism and biological clocks. In Adler NT (ed): Neuroendocrinology of Reproduction. New York, Plenum, pp 377–423.

Gillin JC (1983): The sleep therapies of depression. Prog Neuropsychopharmacol Biol Psychiatry 7:351–364.

Kocsis JH, Brown RP, Frazer A, et al (1984): Serum melatonin in melancholia. Los Angeles, APA Annual Meeting, New Research Abstracts, p NR54.

Kripke DF (1981): Photoperiodic mechanisms for depression and its treatment. In Perris C, Struwe G, Jansson B (eds): Biological Psychiatry 1981. Amsterdam, Elsevier, pp 1249–1252.

Kripke DF (1984): Critical interval hypothesis for depression. Chronobiol Int 1:73–80.

Kripke DF, Risch SC, Janowsky D (1983a): Bright white light alleviates depression. Psychiatry Res 10:105–112.

Kripke DF, Risch SC, Janowsky DS (1983b): Lighting up depression. Psychopharmacol Bull 19:526–530.

Lewy AJ (1984): Human melatonin secretion (II): A marker for the circadian system and the effects of light. In Post RM, Ballenger JC (eds): Neurobiology of Mood Disorders. Baltimore, Williams and Wilkins, pp 215–226.

Lewy AJ, Wehr TA, Goodwin FK, et al (1981): Manic-depressive patients may be supersensitive to light. Lancet 1:383–384.

Lewy AJ, Sack RA, Singer CL (1984): Chronobiology and neuropsychiatric disorders. Psychopharmacol Bull 20:561–565.

Lynch HL, Rivest RW, Ronsheim PM, et al (1981): Light intensity and the control of melatonin secretion in rats. Neuroendocrinology 33:181–185.

Mendlewicz J, Branchey L, Weinberg U, et al (1980): The 24 hour pattern of plasma melatonin in depressed patients before and after treatment. Comm Psychopharmacol 4:49–55.

Reiter RJ (1980): The pineal and its hormones in the control of reproduction in mammals. Endocrine Rev 1:109–131.

Rosenthal NE, Sack DA, Gillin JC, et al (1984): Seasonal affective disorder: A description of the syndrome and preliminary findings with light therapy. Arch Gen Psychiatry 41:72–80.

Rosenthal NE, Sack DA, Carpenter CJ, et al (1985a): Antidepressant effects of light in seasonal affective disorder. Am J Psychiatry 142:163–170.

Rosenthal NE, Sack DA, James SP, et al (1985b): Seasonal affective disorder and phototherapy. Ann NY Acad Sci 453:260–269.

Schilgen B, Tolle R (1980): Partial sleep deprivation as therapy for depression. Arch Gen Psychiatry 37:267–271.

Steiner M, Brown GM (1984): Melatonin/cortisol ratio: A biological marker? Los Angeles, APA Annual Meeting, New Research Abstracts, p NR53.

11

Infradian Rhythms and Affective Disorders

M. R. Eastwood and J. L. Whitton

Biologic processes are rhythmic and oscillate between two limits under the control of adaptive or homeostatic mechanisms. These cyclic patterns may be very simple or extremely complex; they may last from a fraction of a second to many years. Infradian rhythms are defined as "pertaining to a period of more than 24 hours; applied to the rhythmic repetition of certain phenomena in living organisms occurring in cycles of more than a day." (Dorland's Illustrated Medical Dictionary, 1981). Infradian rhythms (greater than 24 hours) are found in both normal and ill individuals (Hersey, 1931; Gjessing and Gjessing, 1961; Richter, 1965; Sollberger, 1965; Jenner et al., 1967; Richter, 1968; Luce, 1970; Nelson, 1971; Dorland and Brinker, 1973; Sothern, 1974; Broughton, 1975; Slarney et al., 1977; Whitton, 1978; Parlee, 1978; Reynolds et al., 1978; Eastwood and Stiasny, 1978; Wehr and Goodwin, 1979; Wehr et al., 1979; Jenner and Damas-Mora, 1979). They may be associated with endocrine and neurochemical processes (Takahashi and Gjessing, 1974; Watotani, 1974; Descovitch et al., 1974; Doering et al., 1975; Smals et al., 1977; Arendt et al., 1978; Carlsson et al., 1980; Wirz-Justice and Richter, 1979; Swade and Coppen, 1980) or be entrained by zeitgebers in the environment (Malin and Srivastava, 1979; Lewy et al., 1981; Whitton et al., 1982). These rhythms may be fundamental in our conceptualization of human behavior.

The long-cycle periodicity of human mood states has only recently become the focus of systematic study. Although subtle psychologic changes comprising long mood undulations have been found to occur in normal individuals, most mood swings are so gradual that they are not obvious and often are masked by daily random fluctuations. This is in dramatic contrast to the striking mood alterations that occur in individuals with major affective disorders, which may vary in severity from mild, but nevertheless distressing, alterations in mood to the most disabling psychotic states. The causes of these shifts are still debated, and their relationship to normal variations in hedonic levels are still unclear. It may be that all individuals experience subclinical rhythms of mood of a regular periodic nature and that in the affective disorders the severity or amplitude is larger, leading to a clinically defined affective disorder. In this sense, it has been suggested that some cases of recurrent affective disorder are pathologic expressions of normal rhythms (Wehr and Goodwin, 1978).

SEASONALITY

Annual rhythms have been reported for temperature (Kleitman, 1949), patterns of sleep (Kleitman, 1963), urinary 17-keto-steroids (Hamburger, 1954), blood cholesterol (Jellinek and Looney, 1936), and timing of menses (Valsik, 1965). Seasonal variation also has been implicated in myocardial infarction (Freeman et al., 1976), diabetes (Gamble and Taylor, 1969), and peptic ulcers (Bodhe and Mokashi, 1975). A relationship between mood and season has also long been assumed, with both Hippocrates and Socrates connecting melancholia to season. Goshen (1967) considered insanity to be more common in temperate climates and during the summer months. Huntington (1938) reported a series of European studies that tended to support these observations. In a cross-national study of three German-speaking countries, Angst et al. (1968) found evidence of spring and fall peaks only for endogenous depression; in Germany itself, Faust and Sarreither (1975) observed that patients suffering from schizophrenia and endogenous depression tended to be admitted to the hospital in "warm" weather, whereas patients with neurotic depressions did not exhibit such seasonal variation. An examination by Symonds and Williams (1976) of patients admitted with a diagnosis of mania in England and Wales revealed a significant seasonal trend for women but not men, the peak occurring in August and September. In the United States, Zung and Green (1974) and Kraines (1957) found that hospital admissions for depression had a nonsignificant tendency to peak in March/April; Kraines's study also showed a significant peak in September. Unfortunately, the major epidemiologic studies have not been analyzed for seasonality, although Kellner (1966) found no seasonal variation in the frequency of neuroses seen by general practitioners. However, in his survey of sickness in England and Wales, Stocks (1949) found that the highest prevalence of "nervous complaints" was in October and November, and McCartney (1962) found a higher referral for depressive reactions in the autumn.

The seed work for one of the authors (M.R.E.) was an interest in electroconvulsive therapy (ECT). An investigation, undertaken to rebuff the notion that ECT was given randomly, showed that its application was seasonal, with peaks in the spring and the fall. Since there was evidence extant that suicide and affective disorders also had such patterning, it was decided to correlate the three phenomena.

It was found that the seasonal variations for depression, suicide, and ECT coincided with peaks occurring in the Ontario spring and fall (Eastwood and Peacocke, 1976). Thus, the seasonal variations for suicide and psychotic depression are similar in Ontario. This is in agreement with the findings of Lester (1971) for suicide in the United States. It is noteworthy that the variation for suicide corresponds more to the seasonal variation for major or psychotic depression than for neurotic depression. Higher incidence of depressive illness (particularly major) at certain times of the year would thereby increase the risk of suicide. This contrasts with Durkheim's contention, supported by Lester (1971), that the most important factor influencing suicide rates at these times is altered social activity (Durkheim, 1897).

In order to expand on the preliminary results, a more extensive study was undertaken (Eastwood and Stiasny, 1978). The admission date and discharge diagnoses for all psychiatric admissions to provincial inpatient facilities were obtained from the Ontario Ministry of Health for the period 1969–1974 inclusive. All adult psychiatric diagnoses (ICDA-8) were examined, with the exception of mental retardation, physical disorders of psychogenic origin, special symptoms not elsewhere classified, and mental disorders not specified as psychotic associated with physical conditions. During the 6-year period the average number of annual admissions to Ontario psychiatric facilities was 43,000.

The admission frequencies for these diagnoses were grouped by season (as defined by the solstices and equinoxes) for the 6-year period and standardized so as to yield equal seasons of 91.3 days. Naturally defined seasons were employed, in preference to those defined by calendar months. Because Ontario's latitude extends from 42° to 55° north, the onset and duration of the seasons vary throughout the province. Admissions were further broken down by sex and age.

On inspection, it became apparent that the number of admissions for selected diagnoses was growing (total admissions at an 8.5% compounded rate); therefore, regression coefficients were computed and subtracted from those groupings that showed a statistically significant linear trend. Overall, these regression analyses accounted for 85% of the variability in admissions. Had adjustments to account for growth in admissions not been made, conclusions about a given season being higher than a preceding season could have been artifactual. That is, it would have been difficult to determine whether a seasonal increase was a true effect or a result of the expected growth in the sample.

The mode of analysis carried out on the resulting seasonal frequencies was the chi-square goodness of fit. A diagnosis was not considered noteworthy unless it showed overall seasonal variability and at least one season that showed significant deviation from the expected. A 0.001 alpha cutoff was adopted for both the overall tests of seasonality (the sum of a diagnosis' deviation from expected) and the tests of specific seasons within each diagnosis. This was done in order to hold the statistical power constant throughout the very large number of tests to be performed and also because the chi-square test may be oversensitive to deviations in extremely large samples.

The results showed that of all the psychiatric diagnoses, only endogenous depressions (ICD 296, 298), neurotic depressions (300.4), and alcoholism (303) showed significant seasonal variation ($p < 0.001$). It was noted that the number of endogenous depressions was higher in the spring and lower in the winter than expected, whereas neurotic depressions were higher in the fall and lower in the summer than expected. Alcoholism, also, was higher than expected in the spring but lower than expected in the fall. Schizoaffective disorder and mania did not show seasonal variation.

The consistency of the seasonal variation by year was then examined. For endogenous depression it was found that 22 of the 24 seasons followed the expected trend, for neurotic depression 17 out of 24 seasons, and for alcoholism 19 out of 24 seasons (Figure 11.1).

The pathway between onset of illness and admission to the hospital depends upon such factors as threshold of complaint, availability of services, and hospital policies. In Ontario there are ample psychiatric facilities, and the assumption was made that those with the more severe illnesses stand an equal and considerable chance of being admitted throughout the year. Although hospital data represent only a small pro-

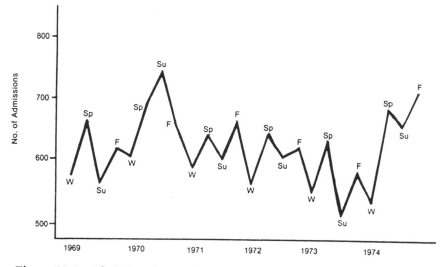

Figure 11.1. Admissions by season for endogenous depressions between the years 1969 and 1974. The four seasons are indicated as follows: W = winter; Sp = spring; Su = summer; F = fall. Reproduced with permission from Arch Gen Psychiatry 35(June 1978):769–771. Copyright 1978, American Medical Association.

portion of mental illness, they probably reflect the seasonal pattern for the severe forms and, to some extent, the milder forms. The findings showed a high level of consistency for the three psychiatric disorders and should be reliable given the number of years examined, the large sample size, and the use of naturally occurring intervals. It seems un-likely that "anniversary" depressions and the possibility of people "learning" to expect to be readmitted at certain times of the year are obfuscating factors. It seemed that there was a causal nexus between season and mood, and it was not clear whether social, biologic, or cli-mactic factors were involved.

PERIODICITIES IN NORMAL PERSONS

The existence of infradian periodicities in the mood of normal subjects has been studied for more than half a century. Hersey (1931) was the first to report human mood fluctuations. Since then further reports (Nel-son, 1971; Dorland and Brinker, 1973) have appeared. Individuals with precisely timed episodes of manic-depressive psychosis have been recognized (Jenner et al., 1967; Gjessing and Gjessing, 1961) and anecdotal case reports have suggested that mood rhythms do occur, at least over a short interval of time. Initially, therefore, Whitton (1978) addressed the question of whether normal individuals exhibit sustained periodicities in mood variables over a long period of time.

In a yearlong study, 85 normal individuals agreed to make daily assessments of their physical health, number of hours of sleep the preceding night, general level of anxiety, creativity, and mood. The ratings

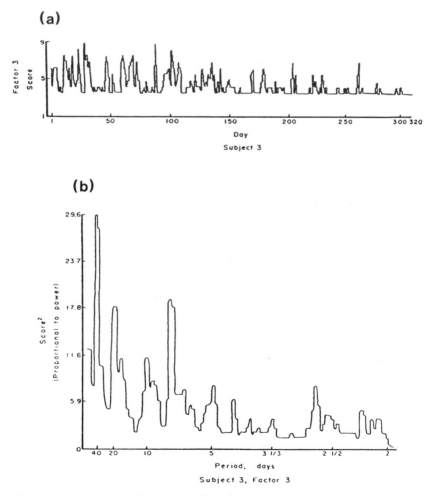

Figure 11.2. (a) Periodicities in self-reports of health, sleep, and mood variables. (b) Spectral transformations of data in (a). Reproduced with permission from Journal of Psychosomatic Research 22(1978):111.

were completed on a self-report scale at the same time each day. Eighteen subjects successfully complied for at least 320 days. Subject dropouts occurred primarily between 26 and 126 days and were due to either an inability to rate at the same time each day or a lack of continuing interest.

Visual inspection of the data, as a time series, revealed several periodicities in a background of noise. This suggested the application of spectral analysis (Jenkins and Watts, 1968), which is a statistical technique for decomposing the variance of a time series in two constituent periodicities and is explained more fully in a later section. Care was taken to exclude cycles that were not significantly present throughout the study. An example of the data from a subject is presented in Figure 11.2(a) and its spectral transformation is given in Figure 11.2(b). Figure 11.2(b) illustrates that the variance of the data in Figure 11.2(a) can be explained by underlying periodicities at 43, 17, and 7 days, with minor nonsignificant peaks accounting for the residue. The spectral analysis suggests that the fluctuations that are seen in Figure 11.2(a) are best explained in terms of these three independent cycles. This does not imply, as can be seen by visual inspection of Figure 11.2(a), that there is a smooth waxing and waning in these periodicities and is only a statistical accounting of the variance.

Of all of the time series, 54.6% contained significant cycles. No significant difference occurred with respect to sex or age. The distribution was skewed towards longer periods, with 56.1% of the periods being 3–8 weeks long, 32.3% between 1 and 3 weeks, and the remainder 1 week or less.

This study was later replicated in 15 normal subjects who rated 11 subjective measures twice daily for 90 days. It was found that 48% of the time series had significant and stable periodicities. Again the distribution of the periods was skewed towards longer cycles, with 46% being in the 3–8-week interval. These preliminary findings led to the major study presented later.

INSTRUMENT

It was soon realized that a new instrument was needed to measure mood daily, as previous instruments had been either too brief or too cumbersome. The purpose was not to fabricate a diagnostic tool but rather to design a brief rating instrument capable of assessing the inner subjective state of an individual over time. Self-report, which is readily obtained, was thought to be the most reasonable means by which to collect quantitative psychopathology data, as the descriptions it provides of a subject's moods are difficult to obtain otherwise (Epstein, 1979). It should also be noted that it has been found that external observation is no more accurate than self-report (Irwin et al., 1979). There was a need then to have affective symptoms measured daily in order to have a high degree of spectral resolution in time series analysis and high rating compliance.

A practical instrument for daily measurement of affective symptoms is the graphic self-rating scale. The most commonly used has been the 100-mm Visual Analogue Scale (VAS) (Guilford, 1954; Aitken, 1969, 1970), which has been reported to be reliable, valid, and clinically useful for measuring mood over time within individual patients (Zealley and Aitken, 1969). Because the standard scale is measured using a ruler, this type of measurement is not practical in lengthy studies involving frequent measurement and many subjects. The alternative was the Segmented Graphic Rating Scale (Kellner and Sheffield, 1968).

A 90-day study was undertaken to (1) investigate problems in compliance, (2) compare the VAS in the 100-m format with the VAS in a 9-point segmented format (SVAS), (3) compare morning and evening ratings, and (4) determine which subjective states to measure. A total of 36 subjects, 18 outpatients with recurrent affective disorders and 18 controls, participated in the study. Initially, each subject completed the General Health Questionnaire (GHQ) (Goldberg, 1972), the Eysenck Personality Inventory (EPI) (Eysenck and Eysenck, 1969), and the Recent Life Events Scale (Paykel et al., 1971). The rating scale consisted of 11 items: hours slept the previous night, a 100-mm VAS, a 9-point SVAS, and 8 other subjective variables in a 9-point segmented format. The eight subjective variables were psychic anxiety, somatic anxiety, irritability, tiredness, concentration, intellectual efficiency, physical well-being, and a unique item that the subject believed to be periodic in himself. Six of these variables had been used in previous research, in which 94% of subjects showed significant infradian cycles on one or more of the variables (Whitton, 1978). A team of psychiatrists involved in treating affective disorders selected the remaining factors. Care was taken to include a wide range of variables relevant to affective state, which, in the psychiatrists' clinical experience, would best indicate potential for infradian cycles. Subjects were instructed to complete the 11-item questionnaire upon arising and again 12 hours later. Subjects were told that their ratings were to reflect their immediate feelings and that questionnaires were not to be completed retrospectively if they had not been completed at the indicated times.

An examination of subject compliance revealed that 67% of the subjects completed the project after 90 days. Noncompliant subjects were more likely to be patients and to be older; they also tended to drop out within the first 3 weeks of the study. The GHQ, EPI, and Recent Life Events Scale did not vary significantly with subject compliance. The majority of subjects preferred the 9-point segmented format to the 100-mm format because it was easier for them to assign a number to mood than use the finer discrimination required by the VAS. There was a significant correlation between the VAS and SVAS scores, and there were no significant differences in the mean number of cycles per subject or in the mean cycle length of the most significant cycle. Importantly, there was no significant difference between format type and the variance of the two halves of each series. The morning SVAS format was the most consistent, with 69% of the cases having no tendency to decline over time. Although compliance was the same for morning and evening, subjects preferred the morning rating time because it suited their daily routines.

The subjects reported that the 11-item questionnaire was tedious, that some items were redundant, and that compliance would be better with a shorter instrument. The segmented format was selected for the final instrument because it was preferred by the subjects and produced the same results as the VAS.

The 11 items were intercorrelated. From the matrix of correlations there were two groupings of items: (1) the psychic anxiety, somatic anxiety, and irritability items; and (2) the fatigue, concentration, and intellectual efficiency items. The former group was collapsed into an anxiety scale and the latter into an energy scale. Mood was significantly correlated with all items except sleep. Sleep, retained out of interest, was in fact not correlated with any of the above items. The unique item was dropped on the basis of being overly idiosyncratic.

The three items, mood, anxiety, and energy, are given bipolar ratings. At the ends are the extremes conceptualized by the subject with their average in the middle. These points are not therefore theoretical concepts or representative of populations but peculiar to the rater. Changes measured by the scale are particular to the subject. A single morning rating was chosen because of subject preference and the absence of systematic differences between morning and evening ratings within subjects or between groups.

Although the project was primarily concerned with the development of a practical rating scale, time-series analyses were performed on the data. It was found that 48% of the time series had significant and stable periodicities as compared with the 54% reported by Whitton earlier. The cycle length was skewed towards longer cycles. The scale (Eastwood et al., 1984) is shown in Figure 11.3.

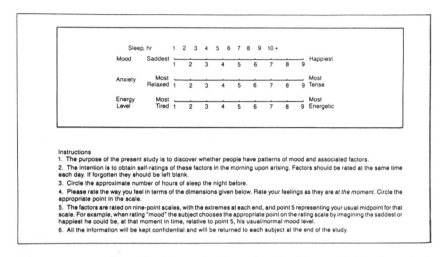

Figure 11.3. Daily self-rating scale. Reproduced with permission from Arch Gen Psychiatry 42(March 1978):295–299. Copyright 1985, American Medical Association.

STATISTICAL METHODS

The measurement of infradian rhythms of mood has two aspects; (1) the development of an effective instrument to rate mood consistently over a long period of time; and (2) the analytic methods that will search for slow cycles and their correlation with external factors.

There are two approaches that are used to describe and analyze a time series—the time domain and the frequency domain. Time-domain methods include autocorrelation and cross-correlation measures. Frequency-domain methods are based on the spectral density function, which describes how the variance in a time series may be accounted for by cyclic components at different frequencies. Traditional spectral analysis decomposes the variance (second moment of a time series) into constituent frequencies. For bivariate series, the cross spectrum, and its derivative the coherence, measures covariances between two series at each frequency.

To detect periodicities in the data, spectral analysis was employed, and, to establish correlations with external factors, coherence analysis was used. Spectral analysis was used because the data, considered as a time series, indicated from visual inspection that it contained periodicities in a background of noise. Each raw time series was completed with zeros at each end (as necessary) to construct a 512-point series. The mean of the data was removed and the data were then transformed to the frequency domain using a Fast Fourier Transform. The spectral estimators were smoothed with weights ($\frac{1}{4}$, $\frac{1}{2}$, $\frac{1}{4}$), resulting in a bandwidth of approximately 0.00586 cycles/day (cpd) and a nyquist frequency of 0.5 cpd. The period of a frequency was expressed as the central period (median) for its appropriate bandwidth interval. Thus, periods from 26.74 days to 31.059 days were all expressed as 28 days. (The central frequency for this bandwidth is 0.03515625 cpd, which, to the nearest day, is 28 days.)

Care was taken to exclude cycles that were not significantly present throughout the entire recording time. Power spectra were performed on each completed time series, and on the first half and second half of each series. A peak in the power spectrum was considered statistically significant if its 95% confidence limit did not include the expected value for Gaussian noise, and if the same peak was significant in power spectra on both the first and second halves of the time series and in the spectrum of the complete time series. Small but significant peaks near the expected noise value were rejected if the spectrum had evidence of broadband noise.

The spectra were expressed as plots of amplitude at each periodicity from 256 days to 2 days. For purposes of analysis, periods from 128 days to 3 days were used, thus eliminating a possible long-term linear drift or recording bias and small, rapid, 1-day variations. An engineering rule of thumb suggests that one needs to record for 2.34 times the longest cycle that is desired to be accurately detected (Otnes and Enochson, 1972; Jenkins and Watts, 1968). If a seasonal cycle is defined as 180 days, a recording time of 14 months is approximately 5 times the length of seasonal cycles and assures more than adequate detection of seasonal cycles. (The term seasonal is not a periodicity that precisely recurs seasonally but a rhythm that is approximately or nearly seasonal in its recurrence.)

To assess the degree of correlation between the subjects' data and external factors (e.g., weather variables), the coherence statistic was used. Coherence, which is the frequency analogue of the correlation coefficient, is well known in both time series and EEG analysis. It was established that mood is composed of several fluctuating rhythms; weather variables such as temperature and solar flux also appeared to be subtended by periodicities (Whitton et al., 1982).

Coherence measures the correlation at each frequency. Ordinary correlation tends to average relationships across all frequencies. Two variables may share a significant association at a certain frequency, and yet the Pearson product moment coefficient may not be significant. A novel method of using the coherence statistic to detect relationships between mood and weather was developed. An extension of the lagged cross correlation is the lagged coherence. Analogously with the lagged cross correlation, the weather data was shifted back with respect to each subject's data from 0 to 50 days and the coherence function calculated for each lag (Whitton et al., 1984).

Lagged coherence results in a three-dimensional surface (the axes are coherence correlation, frequency, and lag). Because the coherence is not significant unless periodicities are in-phase throughout most of the record, the act of lagging one of the series allows underlying periodicities to become in-phase. The lag is then an index of the time delay in the relationship between weather and the other variables. The lag coherence was employed in this novel manner because it was evident from the pilot studies that there was a delay in the effect of weather on subjective variables such as mood.

Correction of bias for coherence and calculation of 90% of confidence intervals were performed using the method of Benignus (1969). Because waves of even very small amplitude, if they are in phase, will have large coherence values, the following measures to determine a significant coherence estimate were employed: its p value was less than 0.1; its 90% confidence interval did not overlap that of a value whose interval overlapped zero; the cross-spectrum amplitude was not in the 90% interval of that expected for noise; and the spectrum of the subject's data had a significant peak at that frequency.

The use of the coherence statistic was demonstrated in data from a 42-year-old male who completed the instrumentation rating scale for 369 consecutive days (Whitton et al., 1984). Each day upon arising he rated hours slept, mood, anxiety, and energy for that moment in time. Weather data for Toronto, where the subject lived, were obtained from Environment Canada, the Canadian Weather Service. Data were obtained for the rating period, including the 50 days prior to his starting date of June 10, 1979. The relationship between the psychologic variables and solar flux, temperature, humidity, and barometric pressure was examined.

No significant Pearson product moment correlations between the weather and the subject's data were found in this study. However, we found several instances of significant coherence relationships between weather and the subject's psychologic variables. Currently, these results are being investigated in a study of 66 subjects who are self-rating for 14 months. The frequency-domain coherence method is more sensitive to linear interactions between variables than is the time-domain correlation approach and may be helpful in increasing our understanding of the relationship between weather or other environmental variables and mood.

INFRADIAN RHYTHMS: A COMPARISON OF PATIENTS WITH AFFECTIVE DISORDERS AND NORMALS

Our group had arrived at the stage where convergence of the investigative approaches was possible. We understood that there was a need to examine daily recordings of mood over long periods of time for both psychiatric cases and normal individuals. The instrument had been designed and the mathematics had been resolved. It was thought to be of fundamental epidemiologic and biologic importance to establish the relationship of mood alterations in affective illness to normal subclinical rhythms.

The culmination of previous work led to an investigation (Eastwood et al., 1985) that further examined the existence and nature of cycles of affective symptoms in patients being treated for a major affective disorder and a normal population. There were two hypotheses: (1) affective symptoms, principally mood, are continuously distributed variables with a periodic component, that is, both affectively disordered individuals and healthy controls have cycles; and (2) the significant difference between disorder and normality in the analysis of these periodicities is in amplitude.

The subjects were studied for 14 months. Thirty patients with a major affective disorder, determined by the Research Diagnostic Criteria (RDC) (Spitzer et al., 1978) and by the Schedule for Affective Disorder and Schizophrenia (SADS) (Endicott and Spitzer, 1978) participated. Twenty-five had bipolar and five had unipolar affective disorders. These subjects were independently treated with medication by their attending psychiatrists. Each patient was matched for age and sex with a healthy control. Four extra control subjects were included. Thus, this group comprised 34 individuals. The controls were free of any history of treated psychiatric illness as measured by the RDC and SADS. In addition to the interview, all subjects were given the General Health Questionnaire (Goldberg, 1972), the Eysenck Personality Inventory (Eysenck and Eysenck, 1969) and the Paykel Recent Life Events Scale (Paykel et al., 1971). Each subject was asked to enter, every morning upon arising, on a 9-point segmented graphic scale, the number of hours slept plus three bipolar ratings of mood, anxiety, and energy levels. The scales were bound in a compact checkbook format sufficient for 1 month. These were collected through regular contact with the subjects to increase compliance.

One-third of the subjects were male and two-thirds were female; the mean age was 43 years (standard deviation 13.8 years). Two-thirds were married and most had completed high school, with one-fifth having completed graduate school. Patients and controls did not differ, except that the patient group scored significantly higher on the General Health Questionnaire.

The data, as time series, demonstrated periodicities in a background of noise and thus spectral analysis was required. Eighty-one percent of the total sample had significant periodicities. Of all the significant cycles, 35% were seasonal (greater than 85 days), 15% were monthly, and 14% were weekly or less. Of the mood cycles, 32% were seasonal, 20% were monthly, and 5% were weekly or less. There was no effect of sex. The number of cycles in each of the four self-report measures was approximate, with a skew towards longer cycles. The only significant difference between the patient and control groups was that the patient group had significantly more mood cycles than did the controls. The control group had more sleep cycles of exactly 7 days, which is likely to be an artifact of having a more orderly life-style with weekend patterning. Significant and sustained mood cycles were found in 60% of the patients and 41% of the controls, with a skew towards longer cycles. In summary, the periodicity and distribution of cycle length was not different between patients and controls, although the patients had more cycles of total mood.

The average amplitude of the most significant cycle for each variable for the two groups was plotted against cycle length. The patients had a greater amplitude for a seasonal sleep and energy rhythm and at several mood rhythms in the region of 3–7 weeks. When the average amplitude of the most significant cycle for all variables was plotted against cycle length, there were significant differences in the average amplitude of rhythms of 85, 51, 43, and 26 days' duration (Figure 11.4).

The principal difference between the two groups was amplitude of cycles, and hence affective symptoms may be considered a variant of normal hedonic states. No difference was found between bipolar and unipolar patients. The patients were on different medications, but there was no pharmacologic effect on cycle length or amplitude. In summary, affective symptoms appear to be universal, with a periodic component that differs in degree rather than kind; the pattern of cycles for the ill is defined by amplitude. This makes affective disorder akin to hyper-

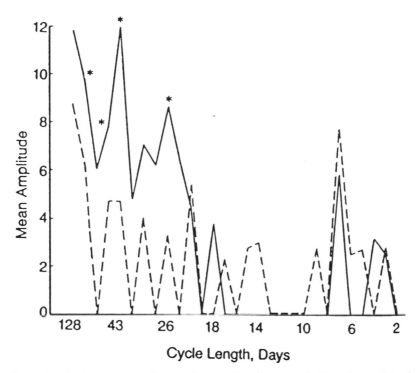

Figure 11.4. Average amplitude of most significant cycle for all variables for affective disorder (*solid line*) and healthy control (*broken line*) groups plotted against cycle length. Reproduced with permission from Arch Gen Psychiatry 42(March 1985):295–299. Coyright 1985, American Medical Association.

tension and diabetes wherein a physiologic variable shades into a pathologic variant.

The finding that half of the rhythms were seasonal is in accord with earlier findings that the affective disorders exhibit seasonal variation. This leads to the hypothesis that some infradian mood cycles may be driven or timed by meteorology. The results also suggest that affective changes are more common than was earlier realized. Rennie (1942) found that only half of his cases of mood disorder had three or more episodes, whereas Bratfos and Haug (1968) quoted Kraepelin to the effect that 60% or 70% of his cases had only one episode and few had more than four. Shobe and Brion (1971) reported that 45% of his cases had only one episode. Angst et al. (1973) reported that the mean number of episodes for bipolar cases was eight to nine and for unipolar cases was five to six. In our study, 60% of the patients and 41% of the controls had significant mood cycles. Clearly, any prevalence study would have to bear this in mind and the definition of "caseness" would depend upon the time of year, the population sampled, and the phase of the individual's mood periodicity at the time of sampling (Eastwood and Kramer, 1981).

SUBSIDIARY STUDIES

The origin or cause of infradian rhythms has not been established. Although weather is suspected to affect emotion, social behavior, and various cyclical physiologic measures, specific environmental variables have not been adequately assessed. The data collected in the first study (Whitton et al., 1982) were examined in relation to various weather features. Daily reports of the number of sunspots, solar flux, maximum and minimum temperatures, humidity, three measures of wind and three measures of precipitation, and four 6-hour barometric recordings were obtained from the Canadian Weather Service. Correlations between subject's data and weather time series were analyzed. The two sets of data were properly aligned, and then, as in the pilot study, weather data were shifted back 1 day in time with respect to the subject's ratings. A maximum correlation and a time lag (in the range 0–50 days) was thus obtained. Pearson product moment correlations greater than or equal to 0.6, with a probability of 10%, were reported.

Of the weather variables only four had significant correlations with subjects' time series (Whitton et al., 1982). The correlations varied from 0.6 to 0.97, with an average of 0.75. Solar flux had the greatest number of correlations (44.4%) with the subjective variables. This was followed by barometric pressure (41.7%), maximum daily temperatures (39.8%), and 8:00 AM relative humidity (38.9%). This weather effect was probably related to the rate of environmental temperature change. The rate of environmental cooling or warming depends on changes in solar flux, barometric pressure, temperature, and humidity—the four variables found in this study to correlate with psychologic variables.

It was also found that the time lag (weather preceding subject's cycle) fell into four approximate groups: 7, 6, 5, and 2 weeks. Solar flux had, across all subjects, an average time lag of 36.4 days (standard deviation 12.6), with similar values for the other three important weather variables.

Work is currently in progress to assess the effects of lithium upon mood change. Subjects are 26 remitted outpatients with major affective disorders (11 taking only lithium) and a control group of 22 healthy individuals who are participating with informed consent in the yearlong study. This study provides an opportunity to examine whether patients taking lithium only have mood stability over a 1-year period in comparison to patients taking other medications and healthy controls. Initial results are that bipolar patients taking lithium only have less mood variability than the control group or the other two patient groups. The findings are consistent with those of Folstein et al. (1982), who reported an unusual mood stability in patients taking lithium.

It would appear then that infradian rhythms occur both in individuals with mood disorders and in the mentally healthy. It is not known whether these are governed by internal clocks and zeitgebers, such as the effect of photoperiodism on melatonin (Lewy, 1983).

This work is exacting and requires a strict methodology, high compliance, and considerable patience. The results require duplication in such groups as those persons with affective disorders, both bipolar and unipolar, of both sexes at different ages, those taking prophylactic medications such as lithium carbonate, carbamazepine, and antidepressants, kinships of all kinds, including twins, and employment situations such as shift work. Cycles that are revealed should be related to other behaviors such as accidents, alcohol ingestion, and suicidal ideation, and to environmental variables. It may prove possible to indict those factors antecedent and subsequent to affective cycles.

SUMMARY

Over a decade ago, this team of investigators was drawn together by a common interest in infradian rhythms and affective disorders. The team designed a self-report instrument to measure mood and allied symptoms; developed statistical methods to measure such data in terms of rhythms; examined, in a long-term study, the existence of infradian rhythms in subjects with and without affective disorders; and, finally, considered how these rhythms correlated with weather variables.

Epidemiologic data from disparate centers suggest that affective disorders (and suicide) are seasonal in that they peak in the spring and fall. This finding excites interest because it implies that this type of illness may be predictable to some extent and possibly preventable. Furthermore, the finding may be linked with current interest in changes of light, mood, and the neurohormone melatonin. It is conceivable, but as yet not demonstrated, that certain affective disorders are triggered at certain times of the year by weather effects. This biogenic theory is at least as plausible as any psychogenic or sociogenic hypotheses.

236 M. R. Eastwood, J. L. Whitton

The lengthy study of infradian rhythms showed that 90-day cycles were the most common; intriguingly, these cycles occurred both in individuals with an affective disorder and in controls, with cycles differing only in amplitude. This suggests that mood disorder, like many medical illnesses, is a pathologic variant of a physiologic variable.

What remains to be done is to show how infradian rhythms actually fit into the calendar year, any relationship they may have with weather, and if and how such rhythms have a significant impact on health and behavior.

The authors would like to thank Pat Kramer and Alice Peter for their very able assistance in this work.

REFERENCES

Aitken RCB (1969): Measurement of feelings using visual analogue scales. Proc R Soc Med 62:989.

Aitken RCB (1970): Communication of symptoms. Psychother Psychosom 18:74.

Angst J, Grof P, Hippius H, et al (1968): La psychose manico-depressive, est-elle periodique ou intermittente? In Cycles Biologiques et Psychiatrie. Geneve, George and Cie, SA.

Angst J, Baastrup B, Grof P, et al (1973): The course of monopolar depression and bipolar psychosis. Psychiatr Neurol Neurochir 76:489.

Arendt J, Wirz-Justice A, Viven B, Symons A (1978): Seasonal variations of melatonin in different species. Neurosci Lett (Suppl 1):198.

Benignus VA (1969): Estimation of the coherence spectrum and its confidence interval using the Fast Fourier Transformation. IEEE Trans Audio Electroacoust 17:145.

Bodhe YG, Mokashi RY (1975): Seasonal variations in the incidence of peptic ulcers perforations. Int J Biometeorol 19:85.

Bratfos O, Haug JO (1968): The course of manic-depressive psychosis. Acta Psychiatr Scand 44:89.

Broughton R (1975): Biorhythmic variations in consciousness and psychological functions. Can Psychol Rev 16:217.

Carlsson A, Svennerhold L, Winblad B (1980): Seasonal and circadian monoamine variations in human brains examined postmortem. Acta Psychiatr Scand Suppl 280:75.

Descovitch GC, Montalbetti N, Kuhl JH, et al (1974). Age and catecholamine rhythms. Chronobiologia 1:163.

Doering CH, Kraimer HC, Brodie HKH, et al (1975): A cycle of plasma testosterone in the human male. J Clin Endocrinol Metabol 40:492.

Dorland J, Brinker N (1973): Fluctuations in human mood. J Interdiscipl Cycle Res 4:25.

Dorland's Illustrated Medical Dictionary, 26th ed. (1985): Philadephia, Saunders.

Durkheim E (1897): Le Suicide. Paris. Translation (1952): Suicide: A Study in Sociology, Spaulding JA, Simpson C. London, Routledge and Kegan Paul.

Eastwood MR, Peacocke J (1976): Seasonal patterns of suicide, depression and electroconvulsive therapy. Br J Psychiatry 129:472.

Eastwood MR, Stiasny S (1978): Psychiatric disorder, hospital admission, and season. Arch Gen Psychiatry 35:769.

Eastwood MR, Kramer PM (1981): Epidemiology and depression. Psychol Med 11:229.

Eastwood MR, Whitton JL, Kramer PM (1984): A brief instrument for longitudinal monitoring of mood states. Psychiatry Res 11:119.

Eastwood MR, Whitton JL, Kramer PM (1985): Infradian rhythms: A comparison of affective disorders and normal persons. Arch Gen Psychiatry 42:295.

Endicott J, Spitzer RL (1978): A diagnostic interview: The schedule for affective disorders and schizophrenia. Arch Gen Psychiatry 35:837.

Epstein S (1979): The ecological study of emotions in humans. In Pliner P, Blankstein K, Spegel I (eds): Advances in the Study of Communication and Affect: Perception of Emotion in Self and Others. New York, Plenum.

Eysenck HJ, Eysenck SB (1969): Eysenck Personality Inventory. San Diego, Education and Industrial Testing Service.

Faust V, Sarreither P (1975): Jahreszeit und psychische Krankheit. Med Klin 70:467.

Folstein MF, DePaulo JR, Trepp K (1982): Unusual mood stability in patients taking lithium. Br J Psychiatry 140:188.

Freeman JW, McGlashan ND, Loughhead MG (1976): Temperature and the incidence of acute myocardial infarction in a temperate climate. Am Heart J 92:405.

Gamble DR, Taylor KW (1969): Seasonal incidence of diabetes mellitus. Br Med J 3:631.

Gjessing R, Gjessing LR (1961): Some main trends in the clinical aspects of periodic catatonia. Acta Psychiatr Scand 37:1.

Goldberg DP (1972): The Detection of Psychiatric Illness by Questionnaire. London, Oxford University Press.

Goshen CE (1967): Documentary History of Psychiatry. London, Vision Press.

Guilford JP (1954): Psychometric Methods. New York, McGraw Hill.

Hamburger C (1954): Six years daily 17-ketosteroid determinations on one subject: Seasonal variations and independence of volume and urine. Acta Endocrinol 17:116.

Hersey RB (1931): Emotional cycles in man. J Ment Sci 77:151.

Huntington E (1938): Season of Birth; Its Relation to Human Ability. New York, Wiley.

Irwin R, Kammann R, Dixon G (1979): If you want to know how happy I am, you'll have to ask me. NZ Psychol 8:10.

Jellinek EM, Looney JM (1936): Studies in seasonal variations of physiologic functions: The seasonal variation of blood cholesterol. Biometric Bull 1:83.

Jenkins GM, Watts DG (1968): Spectral Analysis and Its Applications. San Francisco, Holden-Day.

Jenner FA, Damas-Mora J (1979): Cyclic processes and abnormal behavior. In Van Praag HM, Lade MH, Rafaelsen OJ, Sacher EJ (eds): Handbook of Biological Psychiatry. New York, Marcel Dekker.

Jenner FA, Gjessing LR, Cox JR, et al (1967): A manic-depressive psychotic with a persistent 48-hour cycle. Br J Psychiatry 113:895.

Kellner R (1966): The seasonal prevalence of neurosis. Br J Psychiatry 112:69.

Kellner R, Sheffield BF (1968): The use of self-rating scales in a single-patient multiple cross-over trial. Br J Psychiatry 114:193.

Kleitman N (1949): Biological rhythms. Physiol Rev 29:1.

Kleitman N (1963): Sleep and Wakefulness, 2nd ed. Chicago, University of Chicago Press.

Kraines S (1957): Mental Depressions and Their Treatment. New York, Macmillan.

Lester D (1971): Seasonal variation in suicidal deaths. Br J Psychiatry 118:627.

Lewy AJ (1983): Effects of light on melatonin secretion and the circadian system of man. In Wehr TA, Goodwin FK (eds): Circadian Rhythms in Psychiatry. Pacific Grove, CA, Boxwood.

Lewy AJ, Wehr TA, Goodwin FK, et al (1981): Manic-depressive patients may be supersensitive to light. Lancet 1:383.

Luce GG (1970): Biological Rhythms in Psychiatry and Medicine. Education and Welfare Publication No. 2088, U.S. Department of Health.

Malin SRC, Srivastava BJ (1979): Correlation between heart attacks and magnetic activity. Nature 277:646.

McCartney JL (1962): Seasonal variation in psychiatric illness. Psychosomatics 3:312.

Nelson TM (1971): Student mood during a full academic year. J Psychosom Res 15:113.

Otnes RK, Enochson L (1972): Digital Time-Series Analysis. New York, Wiley.

Parlee MB (1978): The rhythms in men's lives. Psychol Today 4:82.

Paykel ES, Prusoff BA, Uhlenhuth EH (1971): Scaling of life events. Arch Gen Psychiatry 25:340.

Rennie TAC (1942): Prognosis in manic-depressive psychoses. Am J Psychiatry 98:801.

Reynolds TD, White WA, London WP, Yorke JA (1978): Behavioral rhythms in schizophrenia. J Nerv Ment Dis 166:489.

Richter CP (1965): Biological Clocks in Medicine and Psychiatry. Springfield, IL, Thomas.

Richter CP (1968): Periodic phenomena in man and animals. In Michael RP (ed): Endocrinology and Human Behavior. Oxford, Oxford University Press.

Shobe FO, Brion P (1971): Long-term prognosis in manic-depressive illness. Arch Gen Psychiatry 24:334.

Slarney PR, Breitner JCS, Rabins PV (1977): Variability of mood and hysterical traits in normal women. J Psychiatr Res 13:155.

Smals AGH, Ross HA, Kloppenborg PW (1977): Seasonal variation in serum T3 and T4 levels in man. J Clin Endocrinol Metabol 44:998.

Sollberger A (1965): Biological Rhythm Research. New York, Elsevier.

Sothern RB (1974): Low-frequency rhythms in the beard growth of a man. In Scheving LE, Halberg F, Pauly JE (eds): Chronobiology. Tokyo, Igaku, Shoin.

Spitzer RL, Endicott J, Robins E (1978): Research diagnostic criteria: Rationale and reliability. Arch Gen Psychiatry 35:773.

Stocks P (1949): Sickness in the Population of England and Wales in 1944–1947. London, HMSO (Studies on Medical and Population Subjects, No. 2).

Swade C, Coppen A. Seasonal variations in biochemical factors related to depressive illness. J Affective Disord 2:249.

Symonds RL, Williams P (1976): Seasonal variation in the incidence of mania. Br J Psychiatry 129:45.

Takahashi S, Gjessing LR (1974): Longitudinal study of catecholamine metabolism in periodic catatonia. In Lissak K, (ed): Hormones and Brain Function. New York, Plenum.

Valsik JA (1965): The seasonal rhythm of menarche: A review. Hum Biol 37:75.

Watotani N (1974): Endocrinological studies on periodic psychoses. In Lissak K (ed): Hormones and Brain Function. New York, Plenum.

Wehr TA, Goodwin FK (1978): Biological rhythms and affective illness. Weekly Psychiatry Update Series 28:1.

Wehr TA, Goodwin FK (1979): Rapid cycling in manic-depressives induced by tricyclic antidepressants. Arch Gen Psychiatry 36:555.

Wehr TA, Wirz-Justice A, Goodwin FK, et al (1979): Phase advance of the circadian sleep-wake cycle as an antidepressant. Science 206:710.

Whitton JL (1978): Periodicities in self-reports of health, sleep and mood variables. J Psychosom Res 22:111.

Whitton JL, Kramer PM, Eastwood MR (1982): Weather and infradian rhythms in self-reports of health, sleep and mood measures. J Psychosom Res 26:231.

Whitton JL, Kramer PM, Peter AM, et al (1984): Infradian mood rhythms: Measurement and relationship to weather. J Interdiscipl Cycle Res 15:81.

Wirz-Justice A, Richter R (1979): Seasonality in biochemical determinations: A source of variance and a clue to the temporal incidence of affective illness. Psychiatry Res 1:53.

Zealley AK, Aitken RCB (1969): Measurement of mood. Proc R Soc Med 62:993.

Zung WWK, Green RL (1974): Seasonal variation of suicide and depression. Arch Gen Psychiatry 30:89.

12

Circadian Rhythms in Human Performance and Subjective Activation

Timothy H. Monk

This chapter is concerned with changes in human performance efficiency and subjective feelings of alertness over the 24-hour day. It begins by tracing the development of the conceptual framework in which circadian performance rhythms have been considered. This framework developed from notions of simple mental fatigue, at the turn of the century. It evolved, through explanations based on the temperature rhythm, which dominated from the 1930s to the early 1970s, to current explanations that emphasize the multifaceted nature of circadian performance rhythms, and consider the mechanisms and oscillatory systems that underlie them. Circadian rhythmicity is also considered in subjective feelings of alertness or activation, and its relationship to the temperature oscillator and the sleep–wake cycle is discussed.

PERFORMANCE EFFICIENCY

Early Studies

As Lavie points out in his 1980 review, the study of circadian rhythms in human performance can be traced to Lombard's studies at the end of the nineteenth century. Thus, the study of human circadian performance rhythms predates that of physiologic rhythms, and the coinage of the term "circadian," by over half a century. Much of this early work was carried out in what was then the new discipline of educational psychology, and was concerned with the applied problem of determining the optimal time of day for the teaching of academic subjects (e.g., Gates, 1916; Laird, 1925). However, even "mainstream" psychologists were aware of time-of-day effects, and Ebbinghaus, for example, controlled for them in his pioneering memory experiments at the end of the nineteenth century.

Because of the educational background of the researchers, the tasks studied were usually the more cognitive ones such as mental arithmetic and memory for prose. Although the results were far from uniform, the general trend was towards a morning superiority. Gates (1916) concluded "in general, the forenoon is the best time for strictly mental work . . . while the afternoon may best be taken up with school subjects in which motor factors are predominant." Later, in a rather jaundiced review of the area, Freeman and Hovland (1934) concluded that there was an afternoon superiority for motor and sensory performance, but rather mixed effects for more cognitive tasks. Various explanations were put forward for the effects, but many were based upon the notion of a buildup in "mental fatigue" over the day. In modern terms, we would categorize these explanations as being based primarily on the sleep–wake cycle and/or the circadian processes underlying it. As we shall see later on, other investigators have used a rather different approach, basing their explanations on the other major circadian cycle of study, namely, the circadian *temperature* rhythm.

The Work of Kleitman and Colquhoun

Following Freeman and Hovland's rather negative review of the area in 1934, the study of time-of-day effects in human performance tended to be rather neglected. It was not until the 1950s and 1960s that any major new research was published. This work was primarily concerned with relatively simple perceptual–motor and vigilance detection tasks with a comparatively low cognitive load. Kleitman (1963), an early pioneer of sleep research, performed several time-of-day experiments on himself and his colleagues, using mainly reaction time and card dealing tasks. Kleitman was particularly struck by the parallelism that occurred between the time-of-day curves of temperature and performance efficiency. He developed this theme in shiftwork and watchkeeping studies (Kleitman and Jackson, 1950), showing that the parallelism was preserved, even when the subject was phase adjusting to an acute change in routine. Kleitman believed that there was a *causal* relationship between the two, and asserted that there was little need for performance tests, since performance efficiency could be inferred from the (much more easily measured) body temperature rhythm. Unfortunately, this notion of a single performance rhythm, always parallel to the body temperature rhythm, has become widely accepted in the field of chronobiology, and has proved to be remarkably resilient, despite much evidence contrary to it (see below).

In the 1960s, Colquhoun and his coworkers at Cambridge addressed the question of which naval watchkeeping schedules were optimal with regard to sonar detection performance. Many different tasks were used, although most were either of a "vigilance" nature (i.e., the detection of very infrequently occurring targets), or were fairly routine tasks such as card sorting that required a simple "throughput" of information and little cognitive involvement (Hockey and Colquhoun, 1972). Like Kleitman, Colquhoun was very struck by the parallelism that appeared between body temperature and performance, even when subjects were on watchkeeping rotas that involved nightwork (Colquhoun, 1971). Unlike Kleitman, however, Colquhoun was careful to avoid ascribing any causal relationship between the two. Instead, a mechanism involving a rhythm in basal arousal was invoked as a mediating factor (Colquhoun, 1971).

Colquhoun regarded arousal to be the inverse of sleepiness, and he hypothesized that there was a circadian rhythm in arousal that was essentially parallel to that in body temperature (apart from the "postlunch dip") (Hockey and Colquhoun, 1972). The arousal rhythm was considered to mediate changes in performance level through an "inverted U" relationship, whereby rises in arousal level were associated with improvements in performance up to a certain arousal level, after which performance started to decline. In the general area of arousal and performance, the Yerkes–Dodson law postulates such a relationship, with the optimal arousal level of a task dependent upon its complexity, the more complex tasks having a lower optimal arousal level (Kahneman, 1973).

The mechanism of the inverted U was useful because of a finding that Colquhoun's group regarded as slightly anomalous, namely the *decline* in performance over much of the waking day that they had observed in the memory task of digit span (Blake, 1967). By invoking the arousal model, this apparent anomaly could be explained by postulating that digit span had a low optimal arousal, with the time-of-day variation thus occurring on the *falling* arm of the inverted U. A further advantage was that time of day could then be regarded as just another arousing agent like white noise, or knowledge of results. A series of experiments

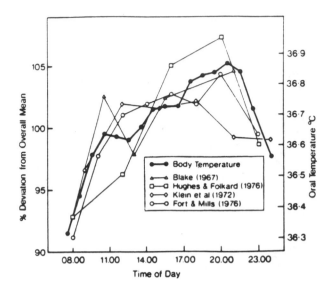

Figure 12.1. The time-of-day effect in serial visual search speed from four different studies (after Monk, 1979). Reproduced by permission.

involving the combination of these agents could then be carried out, and the various interactions explored in detail (see Blake, 1971, for a partial summary). These produced results that were in agreement with the model. However, one of the problems of the inverted U concept is that of tautology, with very few patterns of results being in conflict with the theory, so that the positive findings are perhaps not entirely surprising. Colquhoun did not specify the arousal rhythm any further, and the "arousal model" remained a rather nebulous (but useful) hypothetical construct that had descriptive, rather than quantitatively predictive, validity. Attempts to correlate it with more conventional measures of psychophysiologic arousal largely failed (Gale et al., 1972), and a later attempt to quantify it had only limited predictive success (Monk, 1982).

Thus, through the 1960s and early 1970s, the notion was of a single performance rhythm usually parallel to the temperature rhythm, with the exception of memory tasks such as digit span, whose rhythms were explained in terms of superoptimal arousal. As can be seen in Figure 12.1, for some tasks at least, the parallelism with temperature is quite striking. This notion persisted until the mid-1970s when Folkard (1975), who was a member of Colquhoun's group, studied the time-

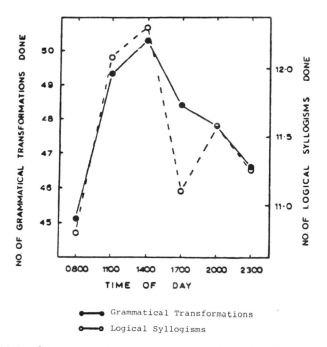

Figure 12.2. The average time-of-day function ($n = 36$) for performance at two cognitively loaded tasks (after Folkard, 1975). Reprinted by permission.

of-day effect in two complex cognitive tasks, namely, logical syllogisms and the Baddeley reasoning test (Baddeley, 1968). These tasks represented a dramatic departure in that they involved the subject in fairly involved thought processes and could not simply be worked through in a routine fashion. The results are shown in Figure 12.2, which reveals time-of-day curves having a midday peak, unlike either the digit span or simple repetitive task time-of-day functions. This result heralded a new approach to the study of circadian performance rhythms, with more emphasis on the differences between circadian performance rhythms than on their similarities, and greater theoretical richness in considering the *mechanisms* by which circadian performance rhythms might occur.

The following sections cover the research performed between the mid-1970s and the present, which can be divided into research concerned with "pure" memory tasks, "working" memory tasks, simple repetitive tasks, subjective activation, and the underlying oscillatory mechanisms.

Pure Memory Tasks

Even from the early studies, it was clear that the time-of-day function for memory was very different from that for other tasks. Later research, by Baddeley and colleagues (1970) and Hockey and colleagues (1972), confirmed that for relatively "pure" tasks of immediate memory (i.e., memory tested within a few minutes of presentation) performance was better in the morning than in the afternoon or evening. This result was explained by the arousal model, by postulating that high arousal interfered with immediate memory, and that the time-of-day range in arousal coincided with the *falling* arm of the inverted U. This agreed with evidence from outside the time-of-day area that arousing manipulations such as anxiety could produce decrements in immediate memory performance (see review by Craik and Blankstein, 1975). In contrast, a more robust finding from these arousal manipulation studies was that high arousal was actually beneficial to *long-term* memory for the material. Thus, if one waited a few days rather than a few minutes before testing the memory, the high arousal presentation condition resulted in *superior* performance.

These findings suggest that the time-of-day function for long-term memory might be very different (in terms of time-of-presentation effects) from that of immediate memory. Thus, the time of day giving an arousal level that was optimal for immediate memory might be associated with a suboptimal arousal level for long-term memory. That prediction was tested by Folkard and coworkers (1977), who presented a story to groups of schoolchildren at either morning (9:00 AM) or afternoon (3:00 PM) sessions. Memory for the material was tested either immediately after presentation, or after a delay of 1 week. The predictions of the model were perfectly validated. The morning presentation group performed better than the afternoon group on the immediate test, but worse than them on the delayed test (time of *testing* for the memory appeared to have no effect). Interestingly, the magnitude of the time-of-day effects for immediate and delayed tests were 64% and 44%, respectively, of the difference in performance due to the 1-week delay. Clearly, even when one is only considering differences between 9:00 AM and 3:00 PM, time-of-day effects are important and striking. In practical terms, of course, the study has ramifications for the scheduling of school time-tables, which had been the focus of the early studies. Thus, for good long-term retention, afternoon teaching might be more efficient.

The schoolchildren study was later validated at more extreme times of day using night nurses, comparing memory for a training film presented at either 4:00 AM or 8:30 PM. Again, the conclusions of the arousal

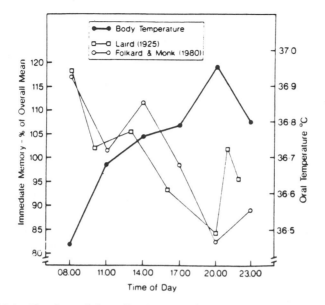

Figure 12.3. The time-of-day effect in immediate memory for information presented in prose (from Folkard and Monk, 1980). Reprinted by permission.

model were validated, with a crossover between immediate and delayed memory occurring (Monk and Folkard, 1978) and time of *recall* again proving to be irrelevant. This has ramifications for those who "burn the midnight oil" in study. In the early hours of the morning (when arousal is low), one's good immediate memory might mislead one into thinking that the material has been successfully committed to memory, whereas long-term retention of the material might actually be rather poor.

A time-of-day function for immediate memory was determined by Folkard and Monk (1980). As can be seen in Figure 12.3 (taken from that paper), the observed decline over the waking day coincided very well with that found by Laird (1925) over half a century earlier, and was markedly different from the rise over the day observed in body temperature. Again, the reader's attention is drawn to the *magnitude* of the effect.

Further detail regarding the mechanisms by which memory performance changed over the day was investigated by Folkard and collaborators in a series of experiments. The work is summarized in Folkard (1982). Essentially, it revealed that subvocal rehearsal is an important mediating factor and is more in evidence in the morning than in the evening, where more semantically based rehearsal strategies tend to predominate. Thus, manipulations such as articulatory suppression, semantic and syntactic confusability, and presentation modality and rate all serve to dramatically affect the observed time-of-day function. These results are important in demonstrating that time-of-day differences need not merely be quantitative in the capacity of the information processing system but may reflect qualitative changes in the way in which information is processed.

Working Memory Tasks

As described above, it was the investigation of time-of-day effects in working memory tasks such as verbal reasoning that brought about an "opening up" of research in the area of circadian performance rhythm (Folkard, 1975). The dramatic changes in the relationship between temperature and performance rhythms that can be wrought by simply increasing the memory load of the task are illustrated in Figure 12.4. The good parallelism between temperature and performance rhythms (top panel) is seen to break down (middle panel) and eventually become inverted (bottom panel) as the memory load of the task is increased. Thus, even within the same basic task (in this case a serial search task), increasing the memory load can totally alter the associated time-of-day function (Folkard and Monk, 1979).

In a later study (Monk et al., 1978), it was shown that the memory load of a task affects not only the phase of the circadian performance rhythm, but also its rate of phase adjustment to a change in routine (e.g., to nightwork). This difference in phase adjustment rate is difficult to account for in terms of the standard arousal model and will be reconsidered when the multioscillatory nature of circadian performance rhythms is discussed.

Simple Repetitive Tasks

Until the late 1970s, the study of circadian performance rhythms in simple repetitive tasks, which had little or no cognitive or memory component, tended to be rather neglected because of the pervading belief in a consistent parallelism with temperature. However, when a collection of time-of-day functions for simple repetitive tasks was made (Monk and Leng, 1982), the expected uniformity (and parallelism with temperature) was far from evident. This heterogeneity, together with further experiments by Monk and Leng, suggested that, similar to memory tasks, simple repetitive tasks have time-of-day functions that are me-

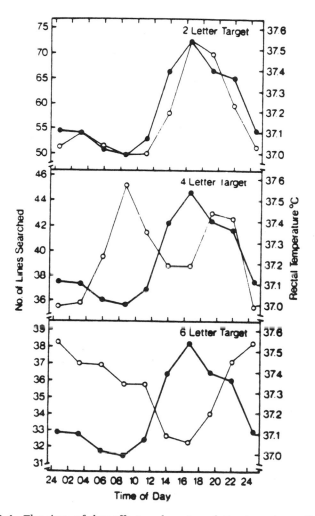

Figure 12.4. The time-of-day effect on low (two-letter target), medium (four-letter target), and high (six-letter target) working memory load versions of a visual search task together with that in body temperature (●——●). From Folkard S, and Monk TH. Shiftwork and performance. Human Factors 21/4 (1979): 486. Copyright 1979, by the Human Factors Society, Inc. and reproduced by permission.

diated by changes in *strategy*, rather than by simple changes in the information processing *capacity* of the brain. Essentially, the pattern of results suggested that the gains in performance *speed* over the waking day (Figure 12.1) were won at the expense of a worsening in accuracy by the adoption of a "fast but inaccurate" strategy late in the waking day. Using a computer analogy, the changes in performance observed over the day appear to result from a decrease in the *number* of program steps used to complete the task, rather than from an increase in the *rate* at which program steps can be executed. Thus, although there is undoubtedly some diurnal variation in information processing capacity, it is the variation in strategy that appears to be the more important determinant of time-of-day effects in performance.

Underlying Oscillatory Mechanisms

The nature of the underlying oscillator mechanisms is to some extent independent of the findings regarding strategy changes that have been discussed above. Thus, a change in strategy can either spring from a change in underlying arousal (Monk, 1982; Monk and Leng, 1982), or from a change in some other oscillatory mechanism. Moreover, as Monk and Leng (1982) discuss, there is suggestive evidence that a relaxation in performance criterion (i.e., a trend towards inaccuracy) can occur as a natural consequence of a mild increase in arousal. The finding that cannot be explained by a simple model is the difference in phase adjustment rates that has been observed between cognitive and simple repetitive tasks, with the former showing faster adjustment rates than the latter (Folkard and Monk, 1979, 1983). This has led to the hypothesis that different performance rhythms can be under multiple oscillatory control, much as the physiologic rhythms are.

Experiments to test this hypothesis have involved subjects living in temporal isolation. Three types of experiments have been performed, and all three have produced evidence that intertask differences are also reflected in differences in oscillatory control, although the exact form that such differences take is not always uniform. First, there are standard "free-running" experiments in which subjects in temporal isolation are free to select their own timings of sleep, wakefulness, and meals. A battery of performance tests is given several times throughout each waking day, the experiment lasting several weeks (Monk et al., 1984). By determining the dominant periodicities in the different performance measures, one can plot the equivalent of a power spectrum for each performance measure. Intertask differences in these plots then suggest possible differences in underlying oscillatory control. An example is il-

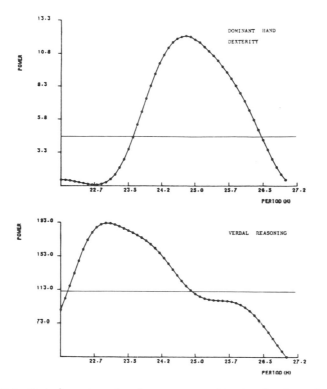

Figure 12.5. Period spectra of performance speed in the dominant hand dexterity and verbal reasoning tasks. The "power" is expressed in squared seconds of amplitude. Points above the line are significant at the 5% level or better (after Monk et al., 1984). Reprinted by permission.

lustrated in Figure 12.5, which shows results of a free-running subject whose circadian rhythm in a cognitive (verbal reasoning) task had a shorter period than it did in a manual dexterity task. Although not all subjects show such dramatic differences, it would appear that there is a tendency for the free-running rhythms of cognitive tasks to have shorter periods than those of simple repetitive tasks (Monk et al., 1984).

In the second and third types of temporal isolation experiments, artificially long or short days are imposed upon the subject. In "fractional desynchronization" experiments, day lengths are progressively shortened or lengthened, with each day length different from the one before it. Differences in underlying oscillatory control then become apparent as different circadian rhythms reach the limit of their particular range of entrainment and break away from the progressively shortening or

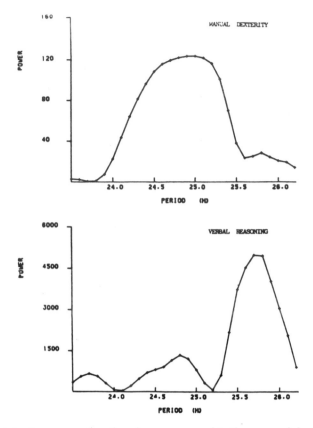

Figure 12.6. Power spectra of performance speed in the manual dexterity (peg-board) task and in the verbal reasoning task. Each power spectrum was produced by a bandpass filtering technique applied to the 155 latencies. The power is expressed in squared units of 0.1 seconds. Reprinted by permission from Nature, Vol. 304, No. 5926, p. 545. Copyright © 1983 Macmillan Journals Limited.

lengthening sleep–wake cycle at different periods (Wever, 1979). When a battery of performance tests is given using this technique, cognitive tasks are found to break off at shorter periods than are associated with simple repetitive tasks (Folkard et al., 1983).

In "forced desynchronization" experiments, one artificially long or short day length, outside the range of entrainment of the temperature oscillator, is enforced for many weeks. This oscillator then runs at its "natural" period (typically close to 25 hours), while the sleep–wake cycle remains driven at the imposed day length. As in the free-running studies, the equivalent of power spectra can be plotted for different performance measures, and intertask differences in these plots used to suggest differences in underlying oscillatory control. An example is shown in Figure 12.6, where the imposed sleep–wake cycle was of a 25.8-hour period, and the temperature oscillator ran at a period of 24.8-hours. When simple manual dexterity was compared with a cognitive (verbal reasoning) task, it was found that the rhythmic behavior of the former tended to be dominated by the temperature oscillator, while that of the latter tended to be dominated more by the cycle of sleep and wakefulness (and/or the oscillator underlying it) (Monk et al., 1983b). Thus, this experiment again showed intertask differences related to cognitive complexity, although these were not directly equivalent to those observed in the free-running and fractional desynchronization experiments.

Conclusions

There is not one single performance rhythm, but many. Different tasks are associated with different time-of-day functions, adjusting at different rates to a change in schedule, and under different oscillatory control. The cognitive complexity or working memory load of a task appears to be an important index of its circadian behavior, although even within the area of memory, there are dramatic differences between short- and long-term retention. The mechanisms underlying these differences in both memory and nonmemory tasks appear to be based primarily upon changes in *strategy* rather than solely upon changes in *capacity*. The oscillatory control underlying these changes appears to depend upon both the temperature oscillator and sleep–wake cycle, with the particular pattern again dependent upon various aspects of the task.

SUBJECTIVE ACTIVATION

In addition to the more objective measurement of performance efficiency, one can ask subjects for their own subjective rating of alertness at different times of day. There are various techniques for doing this, the three most popular being mood adjective checklists, in which subjects ascribe ratings of agreement to long lists of adjectives (e.g., Thayer, 1978), simple numerical ratings scales (e.g., Wever, 1979), and Visual Analogue Scales (VASs) in which subjects place a mark on a 10-cm line labeled "very sleepy" at one end, and "very alert" at the other (e.g., Folkard et al., 1978). In this discussion we focus on alertness as the variable in question; one could as well use the same techniques to measure "subjective sleepiness," in which case the time-of-day function would be a "mirror image" of the function given by alertness.

In a review of a number of studies, Folkard (1982) found that (regardless of the method used) there was usually a midday (or early afternoon) peak in alertness for normal subjects on a diurnal ("day-oriented") routine. This result is rather surprising in view of the conventional wisdom (and premise of the arousal theory) that alertness should be parallel to body temperature, showing a peak in the late afternoon or evening (Colquhoun, 1971). The following section discusses in detail the relationship between the circadian rhythms of subjective alertness and temperature, with the aim of bringing about a preliminary understanding of the circadian mechanisms that underlie subjective feelings of alertness. In this discussion, it should be remembered that the psychologic variable is *subjective* alertness, which may or may not have any relationship at all to "true" psychophysiologic activation (Gale et al., 1972) or to the ability of the subject to fall asleep on request (Richardson et al., 1982).

Alertness and Temperature

By its very definition, a rating of subjective alertness is effectively barred from the sleep time of the individual. This means that alertness ratings are usually restricted to the "normal" (7:00 AM to 12:00 midnight) hours of wakefulness. However, either by keeping subjects awake continuously, or by studying nightworkers, one can obtain sensible readings through the night hours. Using the former technique, Froberg (1977) showed a clear circadian rhythm in alertness (during a 72-hour sleep deprivation experiment) that was essentially parallel to the temperature rhythm (Figure 12.7), although it was, of course, superimposed on an overall decreasing trend. Despite that trend, there was a significant positive correlation between the two variables ($r = 0.683, p < 0.01$). Since the routine of the subjects was constant, and they were unaware of clock time, this result clearly implicates the endogenous circadian oscillator responsible for the body temperature rhythm (referred to henceforth as "the temperature oscillator") as one determinant of subjective alertness.

Monk and Embrey (1981) studied a group of rapidly rotating nightworkers. Every 2 hours, while on shift, the subjects gave ratings of alertness and measured their oral temperature. By averaging over a whole month, it was possible to obtain 24-hour cycles for each measure (Figure 12.8). Because the shift system was a rapidly rotating one, there were no significant phase adjustment effects [indeed the phase of the

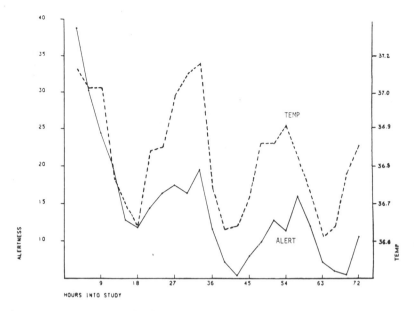

Figure 12.7. Circadian rhythms in body temperature and self rated alertness in 15 subjects experiencing 72 hours of sleep deprivation (after Froberg, 1977).

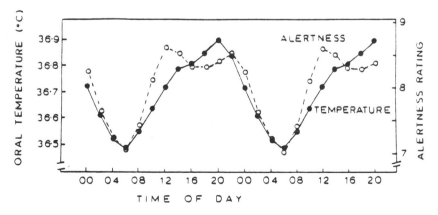

Figure 12.8. The circadian rhythms of oral temperature (●——●) and self-rated alertness (○ − − − ○). Two cycles of the 12 points defining each rhythm have been plotted. Reprinted with permission from Monk TH and Embrey DE, A field study of circadian rhythms in actual and interpolated task performance. In Reinberg A, et al (eds), Night and Shift Work: Biological and Shift Aspects, Copyright 1981, Pergamon Books Ltd.

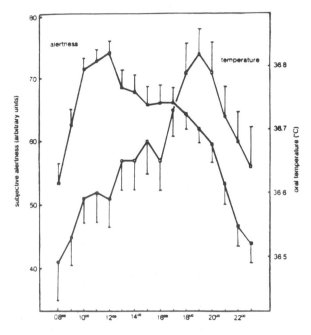

Figure 12.9. Experiment 2 ($n = 38$). Time-of-day effects in subjective alertness and oral temperature, plotted together with plus or minus one standard error (after Monk et al., 1983a). Reprinted by permission.

temperature rhythm was strikingly close to that found by Colquhoun (1971) in normal diurnal subjects]. Although the troughs of temperature and alertness coincided, the same was not true for the *peaks*. The temperature rhythm showed the usual peak at about 8:00 PM, while the alertness rhythm had two peaks, one nearly coinciding with the temperature peak, the other occurring considerably earlier (at about midday). The coincidence of the two troughs again confirms the importance of the temperature oscillator as a determinant of alertness, but the midday peak in alertness suggests that in this situation, namely, subjects who were not time isolated and were sleeping normally (at night) while on daywork, some other factor was involved.

This phase difference in the time of peak of the two measures was confirmed in two studies on normal diurnal subjects (36 students, 38 members of the general public) reported by Monk et al (1983a). Figure 12.9 shows the results of the second of those studies.

Clearly, the most parsimonious explanation for the difference is that the sleep–wake cycle (and/or the circadian process underlying it) is also having an effect. This is not implausible, in view of the obvious link between sleepiness and going to bed! It is thus of interest to separate out the two components, for example, by using a forced desynchronization technique in which the temperature oscillator is made to run at a different period from the sleep–wake cycle. That was done in several forced desynchronization experiments similar to the one illustrated in Figure 12.6 in the discussion of performance rhythms. Subjective ratings were obtained about six times per day using a VAS technique comprising a question, followed by a 10-cm line with the words "very little" at one end and "very much" at the other. The subject was required to place a mark to indicate where his answer lay, at that time, in terms of his normal range of feelings. At each testing session, a total of nine mood assessments were made (Monk et al., 1985). We consider here the two questions: "How sleepy do you feel?" and "How alert do you feel?" The response was scored in terms of the distance of the mark from the left hand ("very little") end, measured in arbitrary units.

Four studies were performed (PB01, PB02, PB03, PB04) on healthy young men aged between 19 and 27.[1] In each study the subject lived in temporal isolation for several weeks on a strict routine of bedtime, waketime, and meals. That routine corresponded to a "day" length that was either longer (PB01, 25.8 hours; PB02, 25.8 hours; PB03, 26.0 hours) or shorter (PB04, 23.0 hours) in period than the temperature oscillator could (under these circumstances) be entrained to. As a consequence, a desynchronization was induced, with the temperature oscillator "free-running" at its "natural" period (typically close to 25 hours), in contrast to the imposed period of the sleep–wake cycle.

Figure 12.10 illustrates the "power spectra" in temperature, alertness, and sleepiness for study PB01. The major peak of the temperature power spectrum at 24.8 hours corresponds to the "natural" period of the temperature oscillator for this subject; the secondary peak at 25.8 hours corresponds to the periodic changes in temperature evoked by the rhythm of sleeping and waking. Measures of alertness and sleepiness also showed significant spectral peaks at these two periodicities, but for them the sleep–wake cycle period was more powerfully in evidence.

The bimodal power spectra plotted in Figure 12.10 were typical of those found in all four studies. Only the "alertness" measures of study PB04 failed to show statistically significant peaks at both the natural temperature oscillator period and the period of the imposed sleep–wake

[1] These studies were carried out at the Institute of Chronobiology, Cornell University Medical College, by J.E. Fookson, M.L. Moline, C.P. Pollak, and the late E.D. Weitzman in collaboration with the present author.

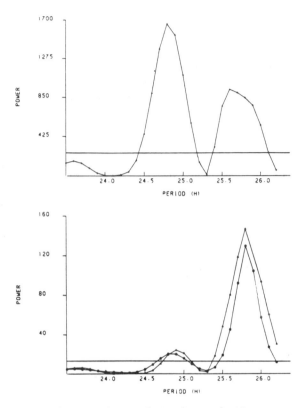

Figure 12.10. Experiment 1 (imposed 25.8-hour "day"): Power spectra of rectal temperature (upper panel) and of subjective alertness (O———O) and subjective sleepiness (▲———▲) (lower panel). The power of the temperature is expressed in squared units of 0.01°F, that of the subjective measures in arbitrary units. Points above the line are significant at the 5% level or better.

cycle. For each subject, separate analyses could thus be made by fitting sinusoids to the time series (Monk and Fort, 1983, after Halberg et al., 1967) at both "temperature oscillator" and "sleep–wake cycle" periods, and obtaining phase (time of peak) estimates for each. The results are summarized in Table 12.1. In terms of "temperature oscillator days," there was a close parallelism between temperature and subjective activation, with a mean difference between the two peaks of less than 70 minutes. In terms of the imposed "sleep–wake cycle days," the peak alertness occurred an average of 8.2 hours after wake time, and the trough in sleepiness 6.4 hours after wake time, thus coinciding reasonably well (but not perfectly) with the midday peak in subjective acti-

Table 12.1. Times of Greatest Subjective Activation

Subject	Period (hr)	Time of Greatness Alertness (hr)	Time of Least Sleepiness (hr)
"Temperature Oscillator Days" (at length of temperature oscillator period) *Measure: Difference in Hours from Temperature Peak*			
PB01	24.8	+ 1.59	− 2.09
PB02	24.3	+ 0.70	+ 0.56
PB03	24.5	+ 0.92	+ 0.79
PB04	24.3	n.s.	+ 0.25
Mean		+ 1.07	− 0.12
"Sleep–Wake Cycle Days" (at length of imposed sleep/wake cycle) *Measure: Difference in Hours from Wake Time*			
PB01	25.8	+ 7.64	+ 5.74
PB02	25.8	+ 7.68	+ 5.46
PB03	26.0	+ 9.38	+ 8.08
PB04	23.0	n.s.	+ 6.48
Mean		+ 8.23	+ 6.44

vation found in most normal day-oriented individuals (Folkard, 1983; Monk et al., 1983a).

The notion of "dual input" from temperature oscillator and sleep–wake cycle is attractive from both theoretical and practical points of view. In terms of theory, we see that there is indeed a rhythm in alertness that is parallel to the temperature rhythm, thus confirming a major tenet of the arousal theory of circadian performance rhythms. In Froberg's 72-hour sleep deprivation experiments (Figure 12.7) this is the only factor present, and there is thus a good parallelism between alertness and temperature. When sleep is allowed (Figures 12.8 and 12.9), a sleep–wake component appears, producing the observed difference in the timing of the two peaks. In practical terms, we have an explanation for the disrupted sleep experienced by the shift worker and air traveler, whose temperature oscillators may take several days to completely adjust to a change in routine and may thus be producing an inappropriately phased circadian alertness component.

Conclusions

Like performance rhythms, circadian rhythms in subjective alertness are not solely under the control of the temperature rhythm oscillator, al-

260 T. H. Monk

though that is indeed an important determinant. Rather, there would appear to be inputs both from the oscillator and from the cycle of sleep and wakefulness. Further experimentation is needed before we can conclude whether the latter effect stems from simply a learned anticipation of sleep, or from a second endogenous circadian process. That process may correspond to either an oscillator (Wever, 1975; Kronauer et al., 1982) or a capacitor (Borbély, 1982) in its action.

The author is extremely grateful to Dr. Simon Folkard and Professor W. Peter Colquhoun, who played a major role in shaping his ideas about circadian performance rhythms, and to his former colleagues at Cornell, Dr. Jeffrey E. Fookson, Dr. Margaret L. Moline, and Dr. Charles P. Pollak, who collaborated with him in the temporal isolation studies that were started under the guidance of the late Elliot D. Weitzman, M.D. The financial support of grants MH37814-02 and AG04135-01 from the National Institute of Mental Health and National Institute on Aging, and cooperative agreement NCC 2-253 with NASA-Ames, is also acknowledged.

REFERENCES

Baddeley AD (1968): A three-minute reasoning test based on grammatical transformation. Psychon Sci 10:341–342.

Baddeley AD, Hatter JE, Scott D, Snashall A (1970): Memory and time of day. Q J Exp Psychol 22:605–609.

Blake MJF (1967): Time of day effects on performance in a range of tasks. Psychon Sci 9:349–350.

Blake MJF (1971): Temperament and time of day. In Colquhoun WP (ed): Biological Rhythms and Human Performance. London, Academic, pp 109–148.

Borbély AA (1982): A two-process model of sleep regulation. Hum Neurobiol 1:195–204.

Colquhoun WP (1971): Circadian variations in mental efficiency. In Colquhoun WP (ed): Biological Rhythms and Human Performance. London, Academic, pp 39–107.

Craik FIM, Blankstein KR (1975): Psychophysiology and human memory. In Venables PH, Christie MJ (eds): Research in Psychophysiology. London, Wiley, pp 388–417.

Folkard S (1975): Diurnal variation in logical reasoning. Br J Psychol 66:1–8.

Folkard S (1982): Circadian rhythms and human memory. In Brown FM,

Graeber RC (eds): Rhythmic Aspects of Behavior. Hillsdale, NJ, Lawrence Erlbaum, pp 241–272.

Folkard S (1983): Diurnal variation in human performance. In Hockey GRJ (ed): Stress and Fatigue in Human Performance. Chichester, Wiley, pp 245–272.

Folkard S, Monk TH (1979): Shiftwork and performance. Hum Factors 21:483–492.

Folkard S, Monk TH (1980): Circadian rhythms in human memory. Br J Psychol 71:295–307.

Folkard S, Monk TH (1983): Chronopsychology: Circadian rhythms and human performance. In Gale A, Edwards J (eds): Physiological Correlates of Human Behavior. London, Academic, pp 57–78.

Folkard S, Monk TH, Bradbury R, Rosenthall J (1977): Time of day effects in school children's immediate and delayed recall of meaningful material. Br J Psychol 68:45–50.

Folkard S, Monk TH, Lobban MC (1978): Short- and long-term adjustment of circadian rhythms in "permanent" night nurses. Ergonomics 21:785–799.

Folkard S, Wever RA, Wildgruber CM (1983): Multioscillatory control of circadian rhythms in human performance. Nature 305:223–226.

Freeman GL, Hovland CI (1934): Diurnal variations in performance and related physiological processes. Psychol Bull 31:777–799.

Froberg JE (1977): Twenty-four-hour patterns in human performance, subjective and physiological variables and differences between morning and evening active subjects. Biol Psychiatry 5:119–134.

Gale A, Harpman B, Lucas B (1972): Time of day and the EEG: Some negative results. Psychon Sci 28:269–271.

Gates AI (1916): Variations in efficiency during the day, together with practice effects, sex differences, and correlations. Univ Calif Publ Psychol 2:1–156.

Halberg F, Tong YL, Johnson EA (1967): Circadian system phase—An aspect of temporal morphology procedures and illustrative examples. In von Mayerback H (ed): The Cellular Aspects of Biorhythms. Berlin, Springer, pp 20–48.

Hockey GRJ, Colquhoun WP (1972): Diurnal variation in human performance: A review. In Colquhoun WP (ed): Aspects of Human Efficiency—Diurnal Rhythm and Loss of Sleep. London, English Universities Press, pp 39–107.

Hockey GRJ, Davies S, Gray MM (1972): Forgetting as a function of sleep at different times of day. Q J Exp Psychol 24:389–393.

Kahneman D (1973): Attention and Effort. New York, Prentice-Hall.

Kleitman N (1963): Sleep and Wakefulness. Chicago, University of Chicago Press.

Kleitman N, Jackson DP (1950): Body temperature and performance under different routines. J Appl Psychol 3:309–328.

Kronauer RE, Czeisler CA, Pilato SF, et al (1982): Mathematical model of the human circadian system with two interacting oscillators. Am J Physiol 242 (Regul Integr Comp Physiol 11):R3–R17.

Laird DA (1925): Relative performance of college students as conditioned by time of day and day of week. J Exp Psychol 8:50–63.

Lavie P (1980): The search for cycles in mental performance: From Lombard to Kleitman. Chronobiologia 7:247–256.

Monk TH (1979): Temporal effects in visual search. In Clare JN, Sinclair MA (eds): Search and the Human Observer. London, Taylor & Francis, pp 30–39.

Monk TH (1982): The arousal model of time of day effects in human performance efficiency. Chronobiologia 9:49–54.

Monk TH, Embrey DE (1981): A field study of circadian rhythms in actual and interpolated task performance. In Reinberg A, Vieux N, and Andlauer P (eds): Night and Shift Work: Biological and Social Aspects. Oxford, Pergamon, pp 473–480.

Monk TH, Folkard S (1978): Concealed inefficiency of late-night study. Nature 273:296–297.

Monk TH, Leng VC (1982): Time of day effects in simple repetitive tasks: Some possible mechanisms. Acta Psychol 51:207–221.

Monk TH, Fort A (1983): COSINA—A cosine curve fitting program suitable for small computers. Int J Chronobiol 8:193–222.

Monk TH, Knauth P, Folkard S, Rutenfranz J (1978): Memory based performance measures in studies of shiftwork. Ergonomics 21:819–826.

Monk TH, Leng VC, Folkard S, Weitzman ED (1983a): Circadian rhythms in subjective alertness and core body temperature. Chronobiologia 10:49–55.

Monk TH, Weitzman ED, Fookson JE, et al (1983b): Task variables determine which biological clock controls circadian rhythms in human performance. Nature 304:543–545.

Monk TH, Weitzman ED, Fookson JE, Moline ML (1984): Circadian rhythms in human performance efficiency under free-running conditions. Chronobiologia 11:343–354.

Monk TH, Fookson JE, Kream J, et al (1985): Circadian factors during sustained performance: Background and methodology. Behav Res Meth Instrum Comput 17:19–26.

Richardson GS, Carskadon MA, Orav EJ, Dement WC (1982): Circadian variation of sleep tendency in elderly and young adult subjects. Sleep 5:582–594.

Thayer RE (1978): Toward a psychological theory of multidimensional activation (arousal). Motiv Emot 2:1–35.

Wever R (1975): The circadian multi-oscillator system of man. Int J Chronobiol 3:19–55.

Wever R (1979): The Circadian System of Man: Results of Experiments Under Temporal Isolation. New York, Springer-Verlag.

13

Effects of Lithium Salts on Circadian Rhythms

Wolfgang Engelmann

The circadian system of individuals suffering from major depression appears to differ from that of normals (Wehr et al., 1979). A central question relates to a possible causal relationship between depressive illness and the abnormality of the circadian system. Are depressive symptoms caused by the disturbance(s) in the circadian system (Figure 13.1a) or is the circadian system affected by this mental disorder (Figure 13.1b)? Alternatively, the disturbance of the circadian system and the affective disorder could both be due to a third factor (Figure 13.1c). The problem is further complicated by the fact that major depression is not well defined and might comprise a number of subgroups. Only few of these subgroups, such as the endogenous type, might pertain to the above considerations (Figure 13.1d) (Schuyler, 1974).

One argument in support of a causal relationship between endogenous depression and abnormalities in the circadian system is the fact that lithium salts (Li^+) interfere profoundly with circadian rhythms (Emrich, 1982; Wirz-Justice, 1982; Goodwin et al., 1982; Johnson, 1975). It is well established that Li^+ has definite therapeutic effects in bipolar and possibly in unipolar manic-depressive illness (Schou, 1973, 1976).

At the time when Li^+ was discovered to affect circadian rhythms,

This chapter is dedicated to Prof. E. Bünning on the occasion of his 80th birthday.

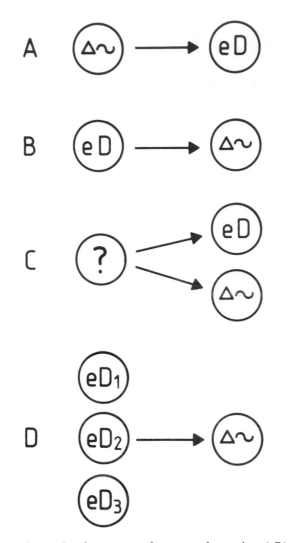

Figure 13.1. Relationship between endogenous depression (eD) and altered circadian system (△∼). **A.** An altered circadian system is the cause of depression. **B.** Depression leads to alterations in the circadian system. **C.** Both the disturbance of the circadian system and the affective disorder are caused by an unknown common factor. **D.** Only one subgroup of depression is associated with disturbances in the circadian system.

only a few substances were known to exert such an influence. The circadian system's general insensitivity to chemical substances had been assumed and its homeostatic behavior had been claimed (Richter, 1965; Pittendrigh and Caldarola, 1973). However, since then, a significant number of substances have been shown to affect circadian rhythms, and more are constantly being added (Woolum and Strumwasser, 1983; Mayer et al., 1985). Work along these lines has shown that protein synthesis and membrane properties are essential parts to the proper functioning of the circadian system. Unfortunately, the general picture is still unclear, and even the basic question of whether different circadian rhythms in different organisms utilize the same mechanisms remains unanswered.

In this chapter, I review the effects of Li$^+$ on circadian rhythms in different organisms (from unicellulars to man), discuss some of the mechanisms involved, and review recent attempts to simulate the effects of Li$^+$ using a feedback model for circadian rhythms.

EFFECTS OF LI$^+$ ON CIRCADIAN RHYTHMS IN UNICELLULARS, PLANTS, FUNGI, ANIMALS, AND MAN

Unicellulars

In unicellulars such as *Skeletonema*, Li$^+$, up to 1.5 mM, increases the period of the cell division rhythm from 26.7 to 29.3 hours in a concentration-dependent manner (Ostgaard et al., 1982). Concentrations above 1.5 mM are toxic. The Li$^+$ effect in this unicellular is temperature independent (between 5° and 22°C), contrary to the findings in *Kalanchoe*. In the green alga *Euglena gracilis*, Li$^+$ induces period lengthening of the circadian rhythm of mobility (Kreuels, personal communication). In contrast, Li$^+$ has been reported to have no effect on the phototactic response rhythm in *Chlamydomonas* (Goodenough et al., 1981) but the concentrations used (0.64 mM) may have been too low.

Fungi

Li$^+$, at a 10-mM concentration, increases by 1.5 hours the period length of the rhythmic formation of conidia in the mutant bd of *Neurospora crassa*. The wild type of *Neurospora crassa* can be induced to show a circadian conidiation rhythm by applying Rb$^+$ ions. Under normal conditions, this rhythm is shown only by the mutant bd. Rb^+ seems to slow the turnover of plasmalemma adenosine triphosphatases (ATPases) (Gall and Lysek, 1981). Zonated growth is induced by H^+ and all alkali ions (Lysek and Schrüfer, 1981).

Higher Plants

Kandeler (1970) reported that Li^+ diminishes the action of phyto-chrome on the photoperiodic flower induction in the long-day plant, *Lemna gibba* G1, and the short-day plant, *Lemna perpusilla* 6746. Since photoperiodic time measurement uses the circadian clock (Bünning, 1936), this effect of Li^+ could also result from an effect on the period of the circadian system. We tried to ascertain whether Li^+ would affect a directly observable rhythm, namely, the petal movement rhythm of *Kalanchoe blossfeldiana*. Li^+ lengthened the period in a dose-dependent manner under conditions of continuous physiologic darkness (Engel-mann, 1973).

The effect was more pronounced at lower temperatures (17°C) and disappeared at higher temperatures (27°C) (Engelmann et al., 1976). This observation indicates a possible involvement of ATPases, since Swann and Albers (1979) have reported that (Na^+-K^+)-ATPase has a similar temperature dependence. Furthermore, the lengthening effect relates to the increased interval for the opening of the petals (Engelmann et al., 1976), which is an active process likely to involve ATPases. Plasma-membrane ATPases are probably not directly involved in the function of the circadian clock: vanadate, which inhibits the ATPase, does not change the period of the clock, but affects only the phase (Eckhardt and Engelmann, 1984). This might indicate an indirect effect of vanadate on clock-driven processes, which in turn feed back to the basic oscillator, thereby changing its phase (Engelmann et al., 1984).

The period lengthening effect of Li^+ in *Kalanchoe* under conditions of continuous darkness (DD) is due to a slowing of the underlying os-cillator (Engelmann et al., 1974b). This lengthening effect of Li^+ is not found under continuous light (LL) conditions. The rhythm under DD is different from the rhythm under LL. I have termed these rhythms "light-on," "light-off" rhythms (Engelmann, 1967). We have used them to describe differences in the amplitude of oscillations in *Kalanchoe* under different light–dark (LD) cycles (Engelmann and Honegger, 1967), the time course of eclosion of *Drosophila* flies out of the puparium (Engel-mann, 1966), and various photoperiodic phenomena.

The idea of two rhythms interacting with each other has been termed "internal coincidence" (Pittendrigh, 1972) and "morning–evening oscillator" (Pittendrigh, 1981). The point is that at least in the case of the *Kalanchoe* petal rhythm, Li$^+$ appears to affect only the "light-off" rhythm. This might be an interesting model for lithium's effect in correcting the postulated disturbed phase relationship of one of the two oscillators in endogenous depression. Such a relationship has been subsumed under the "phase-advance hypothesis" (Wehr and Goodwin, 1981; Wehr et al., 1982).

The underlying physiology of the "light-on" and "light-off" rhythm in plants similar to *Kalanchoe* was studied recently by Wilkins (1983, 1984). The dark oscillator is connected with processes pumping malate into the vacuole of the plant cell, until malate production is inhibited via a feedback mechanism. The oscillator in LL is connected with processes of malate metabolism and the photosynthetic pathway.

Whether coupling of oscillators plays any role in the case of *Kalanchoe* for the determination of period length is not known. It is more likely that the oscillators in the individual cells are independent of each other and synchronized via external time cues such as the LD cycle (Schrempf, 1975).

Li$^+$ increases the period of circadian rhythms not only in *Kalanchoe* but also in other higher plants. In *Oxalis regnellii*, the period of the leaflet movement rhythm is increased in a dose-dependent manner (Johnsson et al., 1981). Li$^+$ pulses have to be 24 hours long in order to lead to a permanent phase shift, and only delays are found. The antidepressant imipramine shifts the phase of the rhythm of *Oxalis* leaflets; only phase advances are seen. When imipramine is administered chronically, Rinnan and coworkers (1985) have found that the period is not changed. These authors suggested that the effect of antidepressants such as Li$^+$ and imipramine might be understood on a basic cellular level and would not have to be restricted to the nervous system.

The effect of Li$^+$ on the photoperiodic reaction of Lemna has been mentioned earlier. Kondo (1984) studied the K$^+$ uptake rhythm of *Lemna* and found Li$^+$, at 0.5 mM, to lengthen the period from 25.5 to 27 hours. This appears to be an effect specific to Li$^+$, since Rb$^+$ and other cations are ineffective. The effect of Li$^+$ is reversed by very small concentrations of Na$^+$ (0.2 μM). Li$^+$ seems to compete with Na$^+$ for active sites. Na$^+$ and Li$^+$ show similar physical properties and physiologic effects; however, the affinity of the sites is much higher for Na$^+$ than it is for Li$^+$. Membrane processes and/or activity of membrane-bound enzymes inside the cells appear to be involved. The leaf movement rhythm of *Trifolium repens* is slowed by Li$^+$ from 27.5 hours in controls to 28.8 hours at 2 mM of Li$^+$ given chronically (Engelmann, unpublished). A similar effect is found in *Phaseolus*, from 26.2 hours in controls to 27.4 hours at 3 mM of Li^+, and to 28.1 hours at 3.5 mM of Li^+ (Mayer, unpublished).

Photoperiodic flower induction is also affected by Li^+. The critical daylengths of the short-day plants *Pharbitis nil* and *Chenopodium rubrum* are lengthened, as would be expected if Li^+ indeed slowed the underlying oscillator responsible for the photoperiodic time measurement (Engelmann et al., 1976).

Lower Animals

The eye and optic nerve preparation from the marine snail *Aplysia* is well known for the circadian rhythm of its compound action potential (Jacklet, 1981). If Li^+ is present in the medium, it produces a dose-dependent lengthening of the period of up to 9 hours at 40 mM concentration (Strumwasser and Viele, 1980; Woolum and Strumwasser, 1983). As in *Neurospora*, protein synthesis and membrane processes, such as Ca^{++} uptake and release by mitochondria, seem to be intricately involved in the mechanism of this rhythm (Feldman and Dunlap, 1983).

The period of locomotor activity rhythm in *Drosophila* is lengthened by 0.4 hours if Li^+ is present in the drinking water at 1 mM concentration (Mack, 1980). This effect may be due to Li^+ competing with K^+, since a K^+-free diet also leads to a period lengthening (of 0.25 hours) and addition of K^+ to the K^+-free diet shortens the period again. K^+ pulses given at different phases advance the rhythm, with a maximum effect of 5 hours. Chronic Rb^+ lengthens the period by 0.6 hours.

The eclosion rhythm of adult *Drosphila pseudoobscura* is not affected by the addition of Li^+ (up to 10 mM) to the medium in which the larvae grow (Reinhard, unpublished).

In the cockroach *Leucophaea maderae*, Li^+ concentrations of 10–50 mM lengthen the period of the locomotor activity rhythm by 0.10 hours and by 0.18 hours at 100 mM (Hofmann et al., 1978). In most cases, the lengthening of the period is observed immediately after Li^+ has been added to the drinking water. In a few cases it takes several days for the lengthening effect to become detectable, and some of the animals do not change period at all. Rb^+ shortens the period by 0.16 hours (50 mM) (Engelmann and Casper, 1984). Rb^+ often shows opposite effects to Li^+.

The range of entrainment is broadened by Li^+. This was shown by driving the locomotor activity rhythm in LD cycles both longer and shorter than 24 hours (Reinhard, 1983). If Li^+ only lengthened the period, a shift of the range of entrainment to longer periods would be expected. The broadening of the range could be due to

1. an increase in the sensitivity of the photoreceptors or of the oscillator to the zeitgeber;
2. a weakening of the oscillator strength; or
3. a change in the mutual coupling strength of oscillators by Li^+.

Increase of sensitivity of the photoreceptors to the zeitgeber, has, however, been ruled out by testing the threshold sensitivity to synchronizing light−dark cycles in cockroaches receiving Li^+ (Rauch et al., 1986). Contrary to expectation, sensitivity decreases slightly under Li^+.

Vertebrates

In isolated goldfish Li^+ increases the period of the circadian swimming activity from 24 to 24.5 hours. Interestingly, groups of fish already show an increase in period length to 24.5 hours in the absence of Li^+. Addition of Li^+ to the water does not lead to a further increase in the period (Kavaliers, 1981). Li^+ impairs the responsiveness to environmental stimuli, but this effect is overcome when stimulus intensity increases due to the grouping of the fish. These findings, as they relate to stimulation from the environment, sleep disturbances, and defense mechanisms against these symptoms, have been discussed by Johnson (1979). Thus, Li^+ reduces the significance attributed to environmental stimuli.

A single oral dose of Li^+ shortens the roosting activity cycle of canaries, when administered early, but not late, in the activity period. The birds studied were able to select their own LD cycles (Wahlström, 1968).

In the bat *Taphozous melanopogon,* Li^+ shortens the period length of the locomotor activity rhythm under weak continuous light (of about 5 lux). The longer the free-running period is before Li^+ administration, the greater the shortening of the period by Li^+ (Subbaraj, 1981).

The behavior of Syrian hamsters is not greatly changed by Li^+. For example, running wheel activity remains the same. Sleep duration per daily cycle increases from 48% to 64% but is accompanied by more frequent interruptions by movements. Frequency of attentive postures is reduced. In ultradian rhythms of various behaviors no differences were found between controls and Li^+-treated animals. Fluid intake was reduced to 82% after the addition of Li^+ to the water. The appearance of hamsters receiving Li^+ is characterized by a more shaggy fur, and their body weight is slightly reduced (Delius et al., 1984).

The diurnal pattern of neurotic behavior, emotional reactivity, and central nervous activation in mice is phase displaced under Li^+ treatment (Poirel et al., 1981). Li^+ and tryptophan inhibit the killing responses of muricidal rats (Broderick and Lynch, 1982).

Diurnal rhythms of food and water intake and urine flow in rats are shifted by Li^+ in such a way that minima occur at the time when controls show maxima (Christensen and Agner, 1982). The food intake rhythm of blinded male Wistar rats is slowed by Li^+ (Wirz-Justice et al., 1982).

In rats (Kripke et al., 1979), Syrian hamsters (Engelmann, 1973), and the desert rodent *Meriones* (Hofmann et al., 1978), Li^+ increases the period of the running wheel activity rhythm. In a follow-up study with hamsters, Li^+ lengthened the period in 50% and shortened it in 25% of the animals. The remainder of animals showed no change. No correlation was found between change of period and Li^+ concentration (Delius et al., 1984). Recent experiments from the same laboratory show only period lengthening by Li^+ (Han, 1984). The reasons for these discrepancies are not clear. There is a correlation between period change and period length before Li^+ administration: long periods tend to become shortened and short periods tend to become lengthened (unpublished data). Similar results have been reported for the effect of estradiol on the activity rhythm in rats (Albers, 1981) and valproate in squirrel monkeys (Borsook et al., 1984).

These findings can be explained by a model of coupled oscillators (Delius et al., 1984). The working of coupled oscillators is indicated by the splitting of locomotor activity rhythms into two components in rats and hamsters. Splitting usually occurs under LL, and the frequency of this splitting in hamsters is not changed by Li^+ (Reinhard, unpublished). However, splitting has been reported in blinded rats by Kripke et al. (1979c), who found that Li^+ increased the rate of its occurrence. In contrast, no splitting occurred in sighted hamsters under physiologic darkness (Engelmann, unpublished; Groos, unpublished).

In addition to Li^+, other antidepressants, such as clorgyline and imipramine, increase the period length of the locomotor activity rhythm or they dissociate the morning and evening components of the activity pattern in Syrian hamsters (Wirz-Justice and Campbell, 1982).

Under an LD cycle of a 24-hour day, Li^+ and other antidepressants delay the phase of the rhythm of locomotor activity (Wirz-Justice, 1982), plasma prolactin, corticosterone, parathyroid hormone, Ca^{++} and Mg^{++} (McEachron et al., 1980). In contrast, the rhythms of 5-hydroxytryptamine (5HT) and melatonin are not affected. These findings have been related to an effect of these drugs on the X oscillator only, whereas rhythms driven by the Y oscillator are unaltered (McEachron et al., 1983). The phase-advance hypothesis and therapeutic measures for endogenous depression are both based on these considerations. The upper range of entrainment is shifted by Li⁺ to longer periods in rats (McEachron et al., 1981) and hamsters (Delius et al., 1984). The lower range of entrainment is also shifted by Li⁺ to longer periods in hamsters (Reinhard, 1985). In the hamster experiments, only 1-hour pulses were used per entraining cycle to avoid masking by long light periods. The occurrence of relative coordination served as a measure of synchronization strength. These results can be explained by an increase in the period of the X or Y oscillator, or both, by a change in sensitivity to the entraining light pulses, or by a change in the coupling of oscillators.

The sensitivity to entraining light pulses is indeed changed, as has been shown by Han (1984), who compared phase-response curves to light pulses in controls and hamsters after chronic Li⁺ treatment. Whereas the effect of light pulses during the delaying part is hardly changed in Li⁺, phase advances are reduced (Figure 13.3). The phase-response curve of 1 hour light of 75 lux under Li⁺ is the same as the phase-response curve of 7.5 lux without Li⁺. The implications of these findings are discussed below.

Some pilot experiments by Reinhard (1983) have shown a period lengthening of the body temperature paralleling that of the locomotor activity rhythm in Li⁺-treated hamsters. Maxima of the body temperature rhythm and the locomotor activity rhythm were delayed by Li⁺ under a LD 12:12 cycle. At the upper limit of entrainment (26 hour), internal desynchronization occurs between the temperature rhythm (which free runs) and the locomotor activity rhythm (which shows relative coordination).

Man

Li⁺ delays the sleep cycle by 14.2 minutes in healthy subjects under entrained conditions (normal 24-hour day). Sleep latency is increased by 36 minutes and REM latency by 49 minutes (Sitaram, Gillin, and Bunney, cited as personal communication in Judd and Janowsky, 1981). REM sleep shows a reduction of 22%, an effect common to almost all psychotropic drugs (Lanoir, 1978). Quality and quantity of sleeping and napping are not affected (Kripke et al., 1979a; Lanoir, 1978). The nocturnal temperature minimum is delayed by 15 minutes (Pflug et al., unpublished) and the daily temperature maximum by 2 hours. Finally, the pattern of the temperature curve is flattened (Sasaki et al., 1982).

Under free-running conditions, such as under temporal isolation in a bunker, therapeutic doses of Li⁺ slightly prolong the period of the circadian rhythm of temperature, urinary electrolytes, and urine volume (Wever, 1979). Experiments conducted with subjects under temporal isolation in Spitsbergen (79° N) during the arctic summer showed an increase in period length of core temperature, activity, and sleep–wake cycle by 1.2 hours in four out of eight healthy students receiving therapeutic doses of Li^+, as compared to placebo. On crossing over from placebo to Li^+, it took about 1 week for these effects to become manifest. The mean value of amplitude and signal energy of the sleep–wake cycle were changed in both the Li^+ responders and nonresponders (Johnsson et al., 1979, 1980, 1983). The phase relationship of the free-running temperature rhythm and the sleep–wake rhythm is changed by Li^+ in that temperature peaks earlier. Using the model of coupled oscillators proposed by Wever (1964) and modified by Kronauer and coworkers (1982), these effects of Li^+ on the phase relationship can be explained as an increase in the coupling strength of the Y oscillator with the X oscillator, or as a decrease in the coupling strength of the X oscillator with the Y oscillator (Engelmann et al., 1982; Engelmann and Pflug, 1978). Similar effects would be seen, if Li^+ reduced the strength of the X oscillator. Because in man the Y oscillator has the longer period, a weakening of the X oscillator would increase the period of the Y-driven processes, thereby explaining the changes seen in the period. It appears that Li^+ affects the X oscillator and not the Y oscillator. This conclusion was reached also by McEachron and coworkers (1983), who found the phase of steroids and proteins in adrenal rhythms to be delayed, whereas liver glycogen and pineal serotonin rhythms, both of which are driven by the Y oscillator, were not affected.

LITHIUM, MAMMALIAN CIRCADIAN SYSTEM DISORDERS, SLEEP DISTURBANCES, AND AFFECTIVE ILLNESS

The current understanding of the circadian pacemakers in the central nervous system of mammals focuses on two oscillators. A Y oscillator in the suprachiasmatic nucleus (SCN) of the hypothalamus drives the activity and the sleep–wake cycle and a variety of behavioral, psychologic, physiologic, and biochemical processes. An X oscillator, the precise localization of which in the central nervous system is not yet established, drives core temperature, REM sleep, and other processes. Although this postulate is still being debated (Eastman et al., 1984), it might serve as a working hypothesis to explain some of the observed results. Furthermore, the pineal plays a central role as a converter of the rhythmic inputs of the Y oscillator into hormonal signals of melatonin (see Chapter 9).

A number of chronobiologic alterations have been reported to occur in endogenous depression:

1. altered phase relationships, e.g., phase-advanced REM (Wehr and Wirz-Justice, 1981; Mendlewicz et al., 1983), phase-advanced core temperature rhythm (Atkinson et al., 1975; Mellerup et al., 1978), phase-advanced sleep (Weitzman, 1983), or phase-delayed sleep (Czeisler et al., 1981);

2. aberrant frequencies, e.g., the rhythm of 3-methoxy-4-hydroxyphenylglycol (MHPG) as the major metabolite of brain norepinephrine (Wehr et al., 1980; Pflug et al., 1982), core temperature rhythm (Kripke et al., 1978; Wehr and Wirz-Justice, 1981; Wehr et al., 1982; Tupin, 1970; Pflug et al., 1981; Chapter 2 of this volume);

3. lower amplitudes (Nikitopoulou and Crammer, 1976; Tupin et al., 1968; Tupin, 1973); and

4. larger variabilities of the circadian system (Pflug and Martin, 1980; Pflug, 1984; see, however, Kripke et al., 1979b), which can be traced to the X oscillator. Li$^+$ appears to slow down this oscillator, thus correcting abnormal phase relationships or frequencies. With respect to this correction, it is noteworthy that there is a greater occurrence of internal desynchronization in a zeitgeber-free environment in elderly people, who also show affective symptoms more frequently than do younger individuals.

Li$^+$ is most effective in a subpopulation of manic-depressives with abnormally shortened circadian rhythms, whereas patients with prolonged periods are Li$^+$ nonresponders (Kripke et al., 1979a).

Because the time course of melatonin production is controlled by the Y oscillator in the SCN, we would expect its phase to be normal in patients suffering from endogenous depression even during their depressed state. Indeed, this was reported to be true (Jimerson, 1977). The effect of Li$^+$ on the melatonin rhythm was studied in rats and hamsters. According to one report, the maximum of N-acetyl-transferase (NAT) activity was delayed by 1–3 hours, but N-acetylserotonin and melatonin rhythms were not shifted (Friedman and Yocca, 1981). A similar absence of effect of Li$^+$ on the melatonin rhythm was found by McEachron and coworkers (1983). Based on their data, Seggie and coworkers (1983) claimed that melatonin activity peaked 4 hours earlier under Li$^+$, but their sodium-treated controls in fact appear not to show a phase-shifting effect. Li$^+$ reduces NAT activity and β-adrenergic receptor density in the pineal but has no effect on serotonin, 5-hydroxytryptophane (5HTP), or 5-hydroxyindole acetic acid (5HIAA) concentrations. The effects of light on melatonin are discussed by Lewy and Sack in Chapter 9 of this book. Li$^+$ selectively affects suppression of melatonin by light, but has no influence on the entraining effect of light on the melatonin rhythm (Nair and Hariharasubramanian, 1984). As mentioned earlier, Li$^+$ changes the phase-response curve of hamsters to light pulses. Li$^+$ also prevents the rapid cycling induced by tricyclic antidepressants in female manic-depressives (Wehr and Goodwin, 1979). Period shortening has been observed by administration of estradiol in rodents (Fitzgerald and Zucker, 1976).

SIMULATION OF EFFECTS OF LI$^+$ AND LIGHT ON CIRCADIAN RHYTHMS

Several oscillator models have been applied to the analysis of rhythmic phenomena. A particularly successful model is the feedback model proposed by Johnsson and Karlsson (1972). This model simulates many responses of the petal movement rhythm in *Kalanchoe* to light and temperature perturbations (Karlsson and Johnsson, 1972; Engelmann et al., 1973, 1974a; Engelmann and Johnsson, 1978). It has also been modified to simulate responses of the locomotor activity rhythm of an insect to light and temperature perturbations (Gander and Lewis, 1979; Lewis, 1976). In the design of this model, several components were used that respond in a way comparable to known components of physiologic systems. Furthermore, the unit oscillators were coupled to each other in order to simulate experiments that cannot be explained with single feedback oscillators (Christensen and Lewis, 1982, 1983). The concept of the unit oscillator presupposes that a substance is synthesized within a membrane-bound system and leaves the system supposedly via passive diffusion. Oscillations occur, when the actual concentration of this substance is compared with a reference concentration in a time-delayed feedback. Light destroys this substance (Figure 13.2). For details see the cited references. Simulations with other models (e.g., Wever, 1964) give less satisfactory results (Gander, 1976).

Using this model, we (Engelmann and Lewis, unpublished) have attempted to simulate the experimentally derived phase-response curve of the locomotor activity rhythm of Syrian hamsters to 1 hour of light

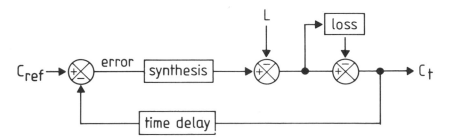

Figure 13.2. Feedback model for simulations of circadian rhythms according to Gander and Lewis (1979). C_{ref}, reference value. C_t, oscillating variable. L is entrance point of light.

pulses (Han, 1984). To account for the asymmetry in the phase response (Figure 13.3), the waveforms of the oscillating entity had to be skewed (Figure 13.4) so that the advancing part of the phase-response curve can be more pronounced than the delaying part. Animals under chronic Li⁺ treatment (in drinking water) show smaller advances when light pulses of identical intensities are administered (Figure 13.3), whereas delays are hardly affected. Under chronic administration of Li⁺ the

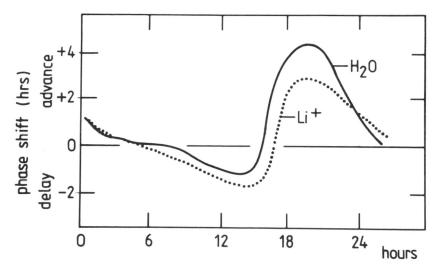

Figure 13.3. Phase-response curve of 1-hour light pulse in Syrian hamster running wheel activity rhythm under water (H_2O) and 47 mM lithium chloride solution (Li⁺).

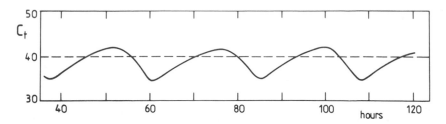

Figure 13.4. Waveform of Syrian hamster oscillator controlling wheel running activity under conditions of continuous darkness. Parameters chosen are synthesis rate = 5, loss rate = 11, upper bound = 40, time delay = 27, C_{ref} = 43. Feedback model of Gander and Lewis (Figure 13.2) and simulation of experimental data in Figure 13.3 are the basis of the simulation.

phase-response curve to light pulses is shifted to the right by 0.5 hour (Figure 13.3). These effects of Li^+ on the phase-response curve to light pulses can be simulated if it is assumed that Li^+ (1) increases the time delay in the model and (2) decreases the sensitivity of the oscillator to light pulses. Time delay is the parameter that is principally responsible for the period length of the oscillation, and an increase leads to longer periods, this being a known property of Li^+. A decrease in the sensitivity of the oscillator to light pulses has not been reported as yet. We do not know whether this decrease takes place at the retinal level, at the SCN

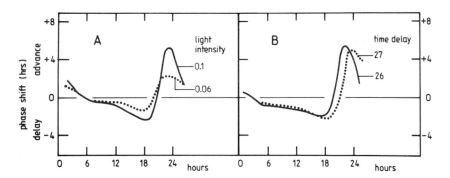

Figure 13.5. The experimentally derived phase response curve of 1-hour light pulse in Figure 13.3 can be simulated using the model in Figure 13.2 and the parameters in Figure 13.4. The effect of Li^+ (reduction of the phase advances, slight shift of the curve to the right) is simulated (a) by reducing the light intensity from 0.1 to 0.06 relative units and (b) by increasing time delay from 26 to 27 relative units (corresponding to 6.5 and 6.75 hours).

level, or in the pathway between the retina and the SCN. Failure to demonstrate experimentally any one of these possibilities would cast serious doubt on the validity of the model used in the simulations. Finally, the results of the simulations might be interpreted on a cellular level as pointing to changes in membrane properties or transport, because time delay is most likely mediated via membrane processes. Li$^+$ is known to interfere with other ions and membrane transport.

LI$^+$ EFFECTS ON BIOCHEMICAL RHYTHMS, NEUROTRANSMITTERS, NEUROTRANSMITTER RECEPTORS, AND HORMONES

Under entrainment conditions Li$^+$ delays a number of biochemical circadian rhythms in rats (McEachron et al., 1982). Other measured rhythms are affected to a lesser extent or not at all. The list of such rhythms includes neurotransmitters and hormones. It is concluded that Li$^+$ shifts the X oscillator and thus selectively affects those rhythms driven by the X and not the Y oscillator (McEachron et al., 1982).

The pineal melatonin rhythm, which is driven by the Y oscillator, is not shifted by Li$^+$ (McEachron et al., 1983). The effect of Li$^+$ on the melatonin rhythm is, however, far from clear, as discussed earlier. The prolactin rhythm in rats is not affected by Li$^+$, according to Seggie and coworkers (1983), whereas McEachron and coworkers (1982) find a delay in plasma prolactin. Parathyroid hormone and corticosterone rhythms are delayed by Li$^+$ (McEachron et al., 1982).

The peak of the daily rhythm of melanocyte-stimulating hormone (αMSH) concentration in rat brain occurs 5 hours earlier under chronic Li$^+$ treatment than in controls, whereas clorgyline and imipramine delay it by 9 hours (O'Donohue et al., 1982). αMSH is a hormone involved in attention and arousal in rats and man (Kafka et al., 1982) and it may also be involved in learning and memory (O'Donohue et al., 1982). Li$^+$ attenuates the increase of growth hormone in rats and man during darkness and delays its acrophase (Seggie et al., 1983; Brown et al., 1981). In contrast, the rhythm of the neurotransmitter serotonin is not shifted by Li$^+$ (McEachron et al., 1982).

The rhythms of the electrolytes Ca^{++} and Mg^{++} are phase delayed by Li$^+$ in rats (McEachron et al., 1980), but the human rhythm of plasma Ca^{++} and Mg^{++} is not affected (Mellerup et al., 1976, 1979).

In rat brain a number of specific binding sites in various neurotransmitter systems undergo circadian changes (Wirz-Justice, 1983).

Chronic treatment with antidepressant drugs, including Li^+, profoundly modify the temporal pattern of these rhythms (Wehr and Wirz-Justice, 1981; Kafka et al., 1983). Li^+ decreases the amplitude of many of these rhythms and those that persist show a delay in phase position by 4 to 12 hours (Kafka et al., 1982) under 24-hour entrainment. The rhythm is abolished by Li^+ in rat forebrain α- and β-adrenergic and benzodiazepine receptors. The prophylactic effect of Li^+ against cycling between mania and depression may include the abolishment of circadian rhythms in α- and β-adrenergic receptors and benzodiazepine rhythms as observed in forebrains of rats. Phase delays of 12 hours are induced by chronic Li^+ administration in rat striatum benzodiazepine receptors, whereas 4-hour phase delays occur in muscarinic receptors and forebrain opiate receptors. Under chronic Li^+ administration, striatal dopamine receptors show two peaks as compared to one in controls. The chronic effect of Li^+ on the rhythmic pattern of neurotransmitters could result from direct influences on the circadian oscillator itself or on the expression of that rhythm. Direct injections into the rat SCN of antidepressants, such as clorgyline and imipramine, which have similar effects on the rhythm to those of Li^+, cause phase delay. Injections in areas adjacent to the SCN are without effect. These findings indicate a direct effect of these agents on the oscillator (Groos and Mason, 1982).

Li^+ activates GABAergic mechanisms in specific brain regions, most notably in the hypothalamus. Other substances, such as sodium valproate, dipropylacetamide, and carbamazepine, all of which affect gamma amino butyric acid (GABA) transmission, are used in acute mania and for the long-term prophylaxis of recurrent manic-depressive episodes in Li^+ nonresponders. These agents increase or decrease the period length of activity and temperature rhythms in squirrel monkeys, probably at the level of the SCN. GABA might therefore play a fundamental role in the regulation of circadian rhythms (Borsook et al., 1984).

BASIC BIOCHEMICAL AND CELLULAR EFFECTS OF LI$^+$

Cellular actions of Li^+ involve metabolic, neuronal, and hormonal systems, the very systems that show aberrations during the course of affective illness. Effects of Li^+ on cellular processes seem to depend partly on ionic substitution. Li^+ can replace Na^+, K^+, Ca^{++}, and Mg^{++} ions and ammonia groups (Ehrlich and Diamond, 1980), including those of biogenic amines in the cells. Thus, it can alter the properties of excitable cells, change neurosecretion and membrane transport processes, and affect the activity of enzymes such as the adenylate cyclase (Pandey and Davis, 1979; Waller et al., 1984). Li$^+$ also inhibits the synthesis of prostaglandin El (Horobin and Manku, 1980).

In snail neurons, Li$^+$ slows the Ca^{++} regulation, thereby increasing intracellular steady-state Ca^{++} concentrations (Aldenhoff and Lux, 1982, 1985). An increase in intracellular Ca^{++} concentration elevates the conductance of the hyperpolarizing ion, K$^+$, under physiologic conditions (Gorman et al., 1982), a mechanism that could slow discharge frequency. Such a mechanism could be of particular importance for biologic rhythms because the activity of pacemaker cells as well as neuroendocrine cells is regulated by Ca^{++} (Petersen and Maruyama, 1984). Li$^+$ facilitates neurotransmitter release from presynaptic terminals and alters the postsynaptic cyclic adenosine monophosphate (cAMP) concentration (Wirz-Justice et al., 1982). Transport ATPases are also affected by Li$^+$ (Duhm, 1982).

Li$^+$ interacts with catecholaminergic, indoleaminergic, and cholinergic systems (Sheard, 1980; Gerbino et al., 1978; Sugrue, 1981). The therapeutic effect of Li$^+$ has been suggested to be the result of changes in postsynaptic receptor sensitivity (Post et al., 1979). In endocrine systems, Li$^+$ blocks the release of thyroid hormone and the synthesis of testosterone (Sheard, 1978; Whybrow and Prange, 1981).

For more detailed information regarding the biochemical and cellular effects of Li$^+$, the reader is referred to some excellent reviews (Emrich et al., 1982; Johnson, 1975; Beumont and Burrows, 1982; Knapp, 1983; Rosenthal and Goodwin, 1982).

The mechanism of circadian oscillation is still unknown. Experimental evidence in various test systems points to the involvement of cytoplasmic protein synthesis in the functioning of circadian clocks (Feldman and Dunlap, 1983; Jacklet, 1981). Membranes have also been discussed as being essential parts of the oscillator mechanism (Engelmann and Schrempf, 1980), but the arguments here are more circumstantial. Some recent studies bring evidence against the involvement of membrane functions in oscillator mechanisms (Scholübbers et al., 1984; Goodenough et al., 1981).

Circadian rhythms appear to control the activity of enzymes that are both rate limiting and rapidly degraded (Johnson et al., 1984). Mitochondria and their Ca^{++} concentration are necessary for normal clock functioning, at least in *Neurospora*, but are not gears of this clock (Nakashima, 1984). Ca^{++} uptake or release seems to play a role in the determination of period length in the circadian oscillator of isolated *Aplysia* eyes (Jacklet, 1973).

CONCLUDING REMARKS

In this chapter, I have reviewed a field in which knowledge is still fragmented and does not permit the consolidation of facts and concepts. There is no doubt that Li^+ affects circadian rhythms in a variety of organisms. However, the way in which the period is changed (mostly lengthened) is unknown. It is unclear whether a single oscillator, one of several oscillators, or the coupling of several oscillators is affected by Li^+. Our knowledge of the control mechanisms of circadian rhythms is insufficient to allow for an accurate assessment of the effects of Li^+ on these mechanisms, which is also true for the action of Li^+ on cellular physiology. I have also tried to demonstrate possible connections between neuropsychiatric disorders, such as manic-depressive illness, and disturbances in the circadian system of man. Again, the hard facts are sparse. In this regard, it would be important to know more about the physiology of circadian rhythms in mammals. For example, is there more than one pacemaker? If so, what is the nature and localization of the X oscillator, and how is it related to the Y oscillator? With regard to the particular topic under review, it would be extremely important to gather data on the behavior of the circadian system of depressed individuals under free-running conditions, with and without Li^+. This would enable us to know whether the disturbance in the circadian system is the cause of the depression or the result of it. There are many other unanswered questions: Do other antidepressants have an effect on circadian rhythms? If manic-depressive illness is indeed the result of a disturbed circadian system, then antidepressants other than Li^+ should, without exception, be expected to influence the circadian system in the same way. Other psychoactive drugs should not exert such an effect on the circadian system, unless they exhibit an antidepressant component. Agents such as light, known to affect the circadian system, could be used therapeutically in correcting these disturbances.

SUMMARY

Li^+ affects circadian systems in a number of organisms ranging from unicellulars to man. In most cases the period is lengthened by Li^+. This lengthening leads to a phase delay of rhythms under a 24-hour synchronization and might be responsible for the therapeutic effect of Li^+ in depression where one of the oscillators is perhaps advanced with respect to the other. Cellular effects of Li^+ include metabolic, neuronal, and hormonal systems. The same systems are altered in affective illness.

Literature search was facilitated by a search from the lithium index of the lithium information center and a literature search by Dr. Schou. I would like to thank Dr. Silyn Roberts, Dr. Halaris, Dr. Johnsson, and Dr. Pflug for reviewing the manuscript.

REFERENCES

Albers HE (1981): Gonadal hormones organize and modulate the circadian system of the rat. Am J Physiol 241:R62–R66.

Aldenhoff JB, Lux HD (1982): Effects of lithium on calcium-dependent membrane properties and on intracellular calcium-concentration in *Helix* neurons. In Emrich HM, Aldenhoff JB, Lux HD (eds): Basic Mechanisms in the Action of Lithium. Amsterdam, Excerpta Medica, pp 50–63.

Aldenhoff JB, Lux HD (1985): Lithium slows neuronal calcium-regulation in the snail *Helix pomatia*. Neurosci Lett 54:103–108.

Atkinson M, Kripke DF, Wolf SR (1975): Autorhythmometry in manic-depressives. Chronobiologia 2:325–335.

Beaumont PJV, Burrows GD (1982): Handbook of Psychiatry and Endocrinology. Amsterdam, Elsevier.

Borsook D, Moore-Ede MC, Hedberg T, et al (1984): Gamma-aminobutyric acid and the neural basis of circadian timekeeping: Implications for pathophysiology and psychopharmacotherapy of circadian based disorders. Annu Rev Chronopharmacol 1:53–56.

Broderick P, Lynch V (1982): Behavioral and biochemical changes induced by lithium and L-tryptophan in muricidal rats. Neuropharmacology 21:671–679.

Brown GM, Grof E, Grof P (1981): Neuroendocrinology of depression: A discussion. Psychopharmacology 17:10–12.

Bünning E (1936): Die endogene Tagesrhythmik als Grundlage der photoperiodischen Reaktion. Ber Deutsch Bot Ges 54:590–607.

Christensen S, Agner T (1982): Effects of lithium on circadian cycles in food and water intake, urinary concentration and body weight in rats. Physiol Behav 28:635–640.

Christensen ND, Lewis RD (1982): The circadian locomotor rhythm of *Hemideina thoracica* (*Orthoptera, Stenopelmatidae*): The circadian clock as a population of interacting oscillators. Physiol Entomol 7:1–13.

Christensen ND, Lewis RD (1983): The circadian locomotor rhythm of *Hemideina thoracica* (*Orthoptera, Stenopelmatidae*): A population of weakly coupled feedback oscillators as a model of the underlying pacemaker. Biol Cybern 47:165–172.

Czeisler CA, Richardson GS, Coleman RM, et al (1981): Chronotherapy:

Resetting the circadian clocks of patients with delayed sleep phase insomnia. Sleep 4:1–21.

Delius K, Günderoth-Palmowski M, Krause I, Engelmann W (1984): Effects of lithium salts on the behavior and the circadian system of *Mesocricetus auratus* W. J. Interdiscipl Cycle Res 15:289–299.

Duhm J (1982): Note on the interaction of lithium ions with the transport function of Na^+-K^+ pump. In Emrich HM, Aldenhoff JB, Lux HD (eds): Basic Mechanisms in the Action of Lithium. Amsterdam, Excerpta Medica, pp 21–27.

Eastman CI, Mistlberger RE, Rechtschaffen A (1984): Suprachiasmatic nuclei lesions eliminate temperature and sleep rhythms in the rat. Physiol Behav 32:357–368.

Eckhardt D, Engelmann W (1984): Involvement of plasmalemma ATPases in circadian rhythm of the succulent herb *Kalanchoe blossfeldiana* (*Crassulaceae*). Ind J Exp Biol 22:189–194.

Ehrlich BE, Diamond JM (1980): Lithium, membranes, and manic-depressive illness. J Membr Biol 52:187–200.

Emrich HM (1982): Prophylactic therapies in affective disorders: Mode of action from a clinical point of view. In Emrich HM, Aldenhoff JB, Lux HD (eds): Basic Mechanisms in the Action of Lithium. Amsterdam, Excerpta Medica, pp 202–214.

Emrich HM, Aldenhoff JB, Lux HD (1982): Basic Mechanisms in the Action of Lithium. Amsterdam, Excerpta Medica.

Engelmann W (1966): Effect of light and dark pulses on the emergence rhythm of *Drosophila pseudoobscura*. Experientia 22:606–608.

Engelmann W (1967): Tagesrhythmisches Schlüpfen von *Drosophila pseudoobscura* und Tagesrhythmische Blütenblattbewegung von *Kalanchoe blossfeldiana* als Überlagerung von An- und Aus-Rhythmen. Nachr Ak Wiss Göttingen II, Math phys Kl 10:141.

Engelmann W (1973): A slowing down of circadian rhythms by lithium ions. Z Naturforsch 28c:733–736.

Engelmann W, Honegger HW (1967): Versuche zur Phasenverschiebung endogener Rhythmen: Blütenblattbewegung von *Kalanchoe blossfeldiana*. Z Naturforsch 22b:200–204.

Engelmann W, Johnsson A (1978): Attenuation of the petal movement rhythm in *Kalanchoe* with light pulses. Physiol Plant 43:68–76.

Engelmann W, Pflug B (1978): Rhythmische Aspékte der Lithiumwirkung. In Heimann H, Pflug B (eds): Rhythmusprobleme in der Psychiatrie, Stuttgart, Gustav Fischer, pp 65–67.

Engelmann W, Schrempf M (1980): Membrane models for circadian rhythms. In Smith KC (ed): Photochemical and Photobiological Reviews 5. New York, Plenum, pp 49–86.

Engelmann W, Casper H (1984): Effect of RbCl on the circadian rhythm of locomotor activity in the cockroach *Leucophaea maderae*. J Interdiscipl Cycle Res 15:17–22.

Engelmann W, Karlsson HG, Johnsson A (1973): Phase shifts in the *Kalanchoe* petal rhythm, caused by light pulses of different duration. A theoretical and experimental study. Internat J. Chronobiol 1:147–156.

Engelmann W, Eger I, Johnsson A, Karlsson HG (1974a): Effect of temperature pulses on the petal rhythm of Kalanchoe: An experimental and theoretical study. Internat J Chronobiol 2:347–358.

Engelmann W, Maurer A, Mühlbach M, Johnsson A (1974b): Action of lithium ions and heavy water in slowing circadian rhythms of petal movement in *Kalanchoe.* J Interdisc Cycle Res 5:199–205.

Engelmann W, Bollig I, Hartmann R (1976): Wirkung von Lithium-Ionen auf zirkadiane Rhythmen. Arzneimittelforsch 26:1085–1086.

Engelmann W, Pflug B, Klemke W, Johnsson A (1982): Lithium-induced change of internal phase relationship of circadian rhythms in humans, and other observations. In Goodwin FK, Wehr TA (eds): Circadian Rhythms in Psychiatry. Pacific Groves, CA, Boxwood, pp 89–107.

Engelmann W, Lang G, Casper H, Hellrung W (1984): Is the oscillator of the *Kalanchoe* petal rhythm directly affected by vanadate? Abst Int Conf Biometheorol Tokyo.

Feldman JF, Dunlap JC (1983): *Neurospora crassa:* A unique system for studying circadian rhythms. Photochem Photobiol Rev 7:319–368.

Fitzgerald KM, Zucker I (1976): Circadian organization of the estrous cycle of the golden hamster. Proc Natl Acad Sci USA 73:2923–2927.

Friedman E, Yocca FD (1981): The effect of chronic lithium treatment on rat pineal *N*-acetyl-transferase rhythm. J Pharmacol Exp Ther 219:121–124.

Gall A, Lysek G (1981): Induction of circadian conidiation by rubidium chloride. Neurospora Newslett 28:13.

Gander PH (1976): A model for the circadian pacemaker of *Hemideina thoracica* derived from the effects of temperature on its activity rhythm. Doctoral thesis, Auckland, New Zealand.

Gander PH, Lewis RD (1979): The circadian locomotor activity rhythm of *Hemideina thoracica* (*Orthoptera*): A feedback model for the underlying clock oscillation. Int J Chronobiol 6:263–280.

Gerbino L, Oleshansky M, Gershon S (1978): Clinical use and mode of action of lithium. In Lipton MA, DiMascio MA, Killam KF (eds): Psychopharmacology: A Generation of Progress. New York, Raven, pp 1261–1275

Goodenough JE, Bruce VG, Carter A (1981): The effects of inhibitors affecting protein synthesis and membrane activity on the *Chlamydomonas reinhardii* phototactic rhythm. Biol Bull 161:371–381.

Goodwin FK, Wirz-Justice A, Wehr TA (1982): Evidence that the pathophysiology of depression and the mechanism of action of antidepressant drugs both involve alterations in circadian rhythms. In Costa E, Racagni G (eds): Typical and Atypical Antidepressants: Clinical Practice. New York, Raven, pp 1–11.

Gorman ALF, Hermann A, Thomas MV (1982): Ionic requirements for membrane oscillations and their dependence on the calcium concentration in a molluscan pacemaker neuron. J Physiol Lond 327:185–217

Groos GA, Mason R (1982): An electrophysiological study of the rat's suprachiasmatic nucleus: A locus for the action of antidepressants. J Physiol Lond 330:40P.

Han SZ (1984): Lithium chloride changes sensitivity of hamster rhythm to light pulses. J Interdisc Cycle Res 15:139–145.

Hofmann K, Günderoth-Palmowski M, Wiedenmann G, Engelmann W (1978): Further evidence for period lengthening effect of Li on circadian rhythms. Z Naturforschung 33c:231–234.

Horobin DF, Manku MS (1980): Possible role of prostaglandin El in the affective disorders and in alcoholism. Br Med J 280:1363–1366.

Jacklet JW (1973): The circadian rhythm in the eye of *Aplysia*. Effects of low calcium and high magnesium. J Comp Physiol 87:329–338.

Jacklet JW (1981): Circadian timing by endogenous oscillators in the nervous system: Toward cellular mechanisms. Biol Bull 160:199–227.

Jimerson JC (1977): Urinary melatonin rhythms during sleep deprivation in depressed patients and normals. Life Sci 20:1501–1508.

Johnson CH, Roeber JF, Hastings JW (1984): Circadian changes in enzyme concentration account for rhythm of enzyme activity in *Gonyaulax*. Science 223:1428–1430.

Johnson FN (1975): Lithium Research and Therapy. London, Academic.

Johnson FN (1979): The psychopharmacology of lithium. Neurosci Biobehav Rev 3:15–30.

Johnsson A, Karlsson HG (1972): A feedback model for biological rhythms. I. Mathematical description and basic properties of the model. J Theor Biol 36:153–174.

Johnsson A, Pflug B, Engelmann W, Klemke W (1979): Effect of lithium carbonate on circadian periodicity in humans. Pharmacopsychiatry 12:423–425.

Johnsson A, Engelmann W, Pflug B, Klemke W (1980): Influence of lithium ions on human circadian rhythms. Z Naturforsch 35c:503–507.

Johnsson A, Johnsen PI, Rinnan T, Skrove D (1981): Basic properties of the circadian leaf movements of *Oxalis regnellii,* and period change due to lithium ions. Physiol Plant 53:361–367.

Johnsson A, Engelmann W, Pflug B, Klemke W (1983): Period lengthening of human circadian rhythm by lithium carbonate, a prophylactic for depressive disorders. Int J Chronobiol 8:129–147.

Judd L, Janowsky D (1981): Lithium: Effects on normal psychological and cognitive behavior. In Perris C, Struwe G, Janssen B (eds): Biological Psychiatry. Amsterdam, Elsevier, pp 657–660.

Kafka MS, Wirz-Justice A, Naber D, et al (1982): Effect of lithium on circadian neurotransmitter receptor rhythms. Neuropsychobiology 8:41–50.

Kafka MS, Wirz-Justice A, Naber D, et al (1983): Circadian rhythms in rat brain neurotransmitter receptors. Fed Proc 42:2796–2801.

Kandeler R (1970): Die Wirkung von Lithium und ADP auf die Phytochromsteuerung der Blütenbildung. Planta (Berlin) 90:203–207.

Karlsson HG, Johnsson A (1972): A feedback model for biological rhythms. II. Comparisons with experimental results, especially on the petal rhythm of *Kalanchoe*. J Theor Biol 36:175–194.

Kavaliers M (1981): Period lengthening and disruption of socially facilitated circadian activity rhythms of goldfish by lithium. Physiol Behav 27:625–628.

Knapp S (1983): Lithium. In Graham-Smith DG, Cohen PJ (eds): Psychopharmacology. 1, Part 1: Preclinical Psychopharmacology. Amsterdam, Excerpta Medica, pp 71–106.

Kondo T (1984): Removal by a trace of sodium of the period lengthening of the potassium uptake rhythm due to lithium in Lemna gibba G3. Plant Physiol 75:1071–1074.

Kripke DF, Mullaney DJ, Atkinson M, Wolf S (1978): Circadian rhythm disorders in manic-depressives. Biol Psychiatry 13:335–350.

Kripke DF, Judd LL, Hubbard B, et al (1979a): The effect of lithium carbonate on the circadian rhythm of sleep in normal human subjects. Biol Psychiatry 14:545–548.

Kripke DF, Mullaney DJ, Atkinson ML, et al (1979b): Circadian rhythm phases in affective illnesses. Chronobiologia 6:365–375.

Kripke DF, Wyborney VG, McEachron D (1979c): Lithium slows rat circadian activity rhythms. Chronobiologia 6:122.

Kronauer RE, Czeisler CA, Pilato SF, et al (1982): Mathematical model of the human circadian system with two interacting oscillators. Am J Physiol 242:R3–R17.

Lanoir J (1978): Lithium and states of alertness. Adv Biosci 21:157–167.

Lewis RD (1976): The circadian rhythm of the weta *Hemideina thoracica* (*Orthoptera*), free-running rhythms, circadian rule and light entrainment. Int J Chronobiol 3:241–254.

Lysek G, Schrüfer K (1981): Wuchsrhythmen (banding) bei *Podospora anserina* (*Ascomycetes*): Wirkung von Alkali-Ionen. Ber Deutsch Bot Ges 94:105–112.

Mack J (1980): Das Multioscillatorsystem von *Drosophila*. Doctoral thesis, University of Tübingen, FRG.

Mayer W-E, Maier M, Flach D (1985): Osmotica, DMSO, PHMB and CN change the period of the circadian clock in the pulvini of *Phaseolus coccineus L.* Chronobiol Internat 2:11–17.

McEachron DL, Kripke DF, Eaves M, et al (1980): The interaction of Li and time-of-day on calcium, magnesium, parathyroid hormone, and calcitonin in rats. Psychiatry Res 7:121–131.

McEachron DL, Kripke DF, Wyborney VG (1981): Lithium promotes entrainment of rats to long circadian light-dark-cycles. Psychiatry Res 5:1–9.

McEachron DL, Kripke DF, Hawkins R, et al (1982): Lithium delays biochemical circadian rhythms in rats. Neuropsychobiology B:12–29.

McEachron DL, Kripke DF, Sharp FR, et al (1983): Lithium delays the phase of running wheel rhythms but not those of pineal melatonin or SCN glucose metabolism in rats. Abstracts of the Society for Neuroscience, 13th Annual Meeting, Boston, November 6–11.

Mellerup ET, Lauritsen B, Dam H, Rafaelsen OJ (1976): Lithium effects on diurnal rhythm of calcium, magnesium, and phosphate metabolism in manic-melancholic disorder. Acta Psychiatr Scand 53:360–370.

Mellerup ET, Widding A, Wildschiøtz ZG, Rafaelsen OJ (1978): Lithium effect on temperature rhythm in psychiatric patients. Acta Pharmacol Toxicol 42:125–129.

Mellerup ET, Widding A, Wildschiøtz ZG, Rafaelsen OJ (1979): Circadian rhythm in manic-melancholic disorders. In Essman WB, Valzelli L (eds): Current Developments in Psychopharmacology New York, SP Medical and Scientific Books, vol 5, pp 51–56.

Mendlewicz J, Hoffmann G, Linkowski P, et al (1983): Chronobiology and manic depression. Neuroendocrine and sleep EEG parameters. In Mendlewicz J, Van Praag HM (eds): Advances in Psychiatry. Basel, Karger, vol 11, pp 128–153.

Nair NVP, Hariharasubramanian N (1984): Circadian rhythms and psychiatry. Br J Psychiatry 145:557–558.

Nakashima H (1984): Calcium inhibits phase shifting of the circadian conidiation rhythm of *Neurospora crassa* by the calcium ionophore A23187. Plant Physiol 74:268–271.

Nikitopoulou G, Crammer JL (1976): Change in diurnal temperature rhythm in manic-depressive illness. Br Med J 1:1311–1314.

O'Donohue TL, Wirz-Justice A, Kafka MS, et al (1982): Effects of chronic lithium, clorgyline, imipramine, fluphenazine and constant darkness on the alpha-melanotropin content and circadian rhythm in rat brain. Eur J Pharmacol 85:1–7.

Ostgaard K, Jensen A, Johnsson A (1982): Lithium ions lengthen the circadian period of growing cultures of the diatom *Skeletonema costatum*. Physiol Plant 55:285–288.

Pandey GN, Davis JM (1979): Cyclic AMP and adenylate cyclase in psychiatric illness. In Palmer GC (ed): Neuropharmacology of Cyclic Nucleotides. New York, Urban, pp 112–51.

Petersen OH, Maruyama (1984): Calcium-activated potassium channels and their role in secretion. Nature 307:693–696.

Pflug B (1984): Circadian rhythms in affective disorders, with special reference to sleep deprivation. In Degen R, Niedermeyer E (eds): Epilepsy, Sleep, and Sleep Deprivation. Amsterdam, Elsevier, pp 59–64.

Pflug B, Martin M (1980): Analyse circadianer Temperaturgänge bei endogener Depression. Arch Psychiatr Nervenkr 229:127–143.

Pflug B, Johnsson A, Tveito-Ekse A (1981): Manic-depressive states and daily temperature. Acta Psychiatr Scand 63:277–289.

Pflug B, Engelmann W, Gaertner HJ (1982): Circadian course of body temperature and the excretion of MHPG and VMA in a patient with bipolar depression. J Neur Transm 53:213–215.

Pittendrigh CS (1972): Circadian surfaces and the diversity of possible roles of circadian organization in photoperiodic induction. Proc Nat Acad Sci 69:2734–2737.

Pittendrigh CS (1981): Circadian systems: Entrainment. In Aschoff J (ed): Handbook of Behavioral Neurobiology. New York, Plenum, vol 4, pp 95–124.

Pittendrigh CS, Caldarola PC (1973): General homeostasis of the frequency of circadian oscillations. Proc Nat Acad Sci USA 70:2697–2701.

Poirel C, Briand M, Hengartner O (1981): On some diurnal variations of emotional reactivity levels in mice treated by lithium, chronopharmacological perspectives in affective illness. In Walker CA (eds): Chronopharmacology and Chronotherapeutics, pp 103–108.

Post RM, Jimerson DC, Bunney WE (1979): Perspectives in the treatment of the psychoneurological disorders: Affective disorders. Progr Neuropsychopharmacol 3:65–74.

Rauch J, Reinhard P, Engelmann W (1986): Effects of lithium chloride on range of entrainment and synchronization in the cockroach Leucophaea maderae. J Interdisc Cycle Res 17:51–68.

Reinhard P (1983): Die Wirkung von Lithium auf das circadiane Verhalten von Schaben und Hamstern in Lichtprogrammen verschiedener Periodenlänge. Doctoral thesis, University of Tübingen, FRG.

Reinhard P (1985): Effect of lithium chloride on the lower range of entrainment in syrian hamsters. J Interdisc Cycle Res 16:227–237.

Richter CP (1965): Biological clocks in medicine and psychiatry. Springfield, IL, Charles C. Thomas.

Rinnan T, Johnsson A, Götestam KG (1985): Imipramine affects circadian leaf movements in *Oxalis regnellii*. Physiol Plant 62:153–156.

Rosenthal NE, Goodwin FK (1982): The role of the lithium ion in medicine. Ann Rev Med 33:555–568.

Sasaki M, Suzuki M, Onda M, et al, (1982): Lithium influence on the circadian rhythm of normal adults. Adv Biosci 40:303–308.

Scholübbers HG, Taylor W, Rensing L (1984): Are membrane properties essential for the circadian rhythm of *Gonyaulax?* Am J Physiol 247:R250–R256.

Schou M (1973): Prophylactic lithium maintenance treatment in recurrent endogenous affective disorders. In: Gershon S, Shopsin B (eds): Lithium, Its Role in Psychiatric Research and Treatment. New York, Plenum, pp 269–294.

Schou M (1976): Clinical prophylactic effects and clinical pharmacology of lithium. Neurosci Res Prog Bull 14:117–124.

Schrempf M (1975): Eigenschaften und Lokalisation des Photorezeptors für phasenver schiebendes Störlicht bei der Blütenblattbewegung von *Kalanchoe blossfeldiana* (v. Poelln.). Doctoral thesis, University of Tübingen, FRG.

Schuyler D (1974): The Depressive Spectrum. New York, Jason Aronson, p 174.

Seggie J, Werstiuk E, Grota L, Brown GM (1983): Chronic lithium treatment and twenty-four-hour rhythm of serum prolactin, growth hormone and melatonin in rats. Prog Neuropsychopharmacol Biol Psychiatry 7:827–830.

Sheard MH (1978): The effect of lithium and other ions on aggressive behavior. Mod Probl Pharmacopsychiatry 13:53–68.

Sheard MH (1980): The biological effects of lithium. Trends Neurosci 3:85–86.

Strumwasser F, Viele DP (1980): Lithium increases the period of neuronal circadian oscillator. Abstract 241.5, Society for Neuroscience, 10th Annual Meeting.

Subbaraj R (1981): Effect of lithium chloride on the circadian rhythm in the flight activity of the microchiropteran bat, *Taphozous melanopogon*. Z Naturforsch 36c:1068–1071.

Sugrue MF (1981): Current concepts of the mechanisms of antidepressant drugs. Pharmacol Ther 13:219–247.

Swann AC, Albers RW (1979): (Na^+-K^+)–adenosine triphosphatase of mammalian brain. J Biol Chem 254:4540–4544.

Tupin JP (1970): Certain circadian rhythms in manic depressives and their response to lithium. Int Pharmacopsychiatry 5:227–232.

Tupin JP (1973): Diurnal temperature and manic-depression. Lancet 2:843.

Tupin JP, Schlagenhauf GK, Creson DL (1968): Lithium effects on electrolyte excretion. Am J Psychiatry 125:536–543.

Wahlström G (1968): Drugs which interfere with the metabolism of monoamines and biological cycles. Bell Air Symposium No 3. Geneve, G. George; Paris, Masson.

Waller DG, Albano JDM, Millar JGB, Polak A (1984): Cyclic AMP responses to parathyroid hormone and glucagon during lithium treatment. Clin Sci 66:557–559.

Wehr TA, Goodwin FK (1979): Rapid cycling in manic-depressives induced by tricyclic antidepressants. Arch Gen Psychiatry 36:555–559.

Wehr TA, Goodwin FK (1981): Biological rhythms and psychiatry. In Arieti S, Brodie HKH (eds): American Handbook of Psychiatry. Advances and New Directions. New York, Basic Books, pp 46–74.

Wehr TA, Wirz-Justice A (1981): Internal coincidence model for sleep deprivation and depression. In Koella WP (ed): Sleep 1980. Circadian Rhythms, Dreams, Noise, and Sleep, Neurophysiology, Therapy, 5th European Congress on Sleep Research, Amsterdam 1980. Basel, Karger, pp 26–33.

Wehr TA, Wirz-Justice A, Lewy AJ, Goodwin FK (1979): Biological rhythm disturbances in affective illness. In Obiols J, Ballus C, Gonzalez Monclus E, Pujol J (eds): Biological Psychiatry Today. Amsterdam, Elsevier, vol A, pp 303–306.

Wehr TA, Muscettola G, Goodwin FK (1980): Urinary 3-methoxy-4-hydroxyphenylglycol circadian rhythm: Early timing (phase advance) in manic-depressives compared with normal subjects. Arch Gen Psychiatry 37:257–263.

Wehr TA, Lewy A, Wirz-Justice A, et al (1982): Antidepressants and a circadian rhythm phase-advance hypothesis of depression. In Collu R, et al (eds): Brain Peptides and Hormones. New York, Raven, pp 263–276.

Weitzman ED (1983): Biological rhythms in man under non-entrained conditions and chronotherapy for delayed sleep phase insomnia. In Mendlewicz J, Van Praag HM (eds): Biological Rhythms and Behavior. Adv. Biological Psychiatry. Basel, Karger, vol 11, pp 136–149.

Wever RA (1964): Ein mathematisches Modell für biologische Schwingungen. Z Tierpsych 21:359–372.

Wever R (1979): The Circadian System of Man. New York, Springer.

Whybrow PC, Prange AJ (1981): A hypothesis of thyroid-catecholamine-receptor interaction: Its relevance to affective illness. Arch Gen Psychiatry 38:106–113.

Wilkins MB (1983): The circadian rhythm of carbon-dioxide metabolism in *Bryophyllum:* The mechanism of phase-shift induction by thermal stimuli. Planta 157:471–480.

Wilkins MB (1984): A rapid circadian rhythm of carbon-dioxide metabolism in *Bryophyllum fedtschenkoi.* Planta 161:381–384.

Wirz-Justice A (1982): The effects of lithium on the circadian system. In Emrich HM, Aldenhoff JB, Lux HD (eds): Basic Mechanisms in the Action of Lithium. Amsterdam, Excerpta Medica, pp 249–258.

Wirz-Justice A (1983): Antidepressant drugs: Effects on the circadian system. In Wehr TA, Goodwin FK (eds): Circadian Rhythms in Psychiatry. Pacific Groves, CA, Boxwood, pp 235–265.

Wirz-Justice A, Campbell IC (1982): Antidepressant drugs can slow or dissociate circadian rhythms. Experientia 38:1301–1309.

Wirz-Justice A, Groos GA, Wehr TA (1982): The neuropharmacology of circadian timekeeping in mammals. In Aschoff J, Daan S, Groos G (eds): Vertebrate circadian systems: Structure and physiology. Berlin, Springer, pp 183–193.

Woolum JC, Strumwasser F (1983): Is the period of the circadian oscillator in the eye of *Aplysia* directly homeostatically regulated? J Comp Physiol A 151:253–269.

14

Circadian Rhythm of Brain Serotonin: Physiologic Control and Pharmacologic Manipulation

P. H. Redfern and K. F. Martin

CONTROL OF CIRCADIAN RHYTHM OF 5-HT CONCENTRATION

The association between psychiatric disorders and disturbed circadian rhythms has generated considerable interest in recent years, as the contents of other chapters in this book demonstrate. In particular, there is increasing evidence associating the affective disorders with a breakdown in circadian synchrony (e.g., see Thompson 1985; Halaris, Chapter 2 of this volume). In 1983, Kripke proposed that during depression there was a phase advance in a subset of circadian rhythms exemplified by body temperature and cortisol secretion. In addition, altered sleep patterns and abnormalities in rapid eye movement (REM) sleep have been reported (Wehr et al., 1983). The observation by Riederer and colleagues (1974) that the excretion of the 5-hydroxytryptamine (5-HT) metabolite 5-hydroxyindoleacetic acid (5-HIAA) is phase advanced in depression is especially interesting, because changes in 5-HT neurotransmission have long been held to be causally implicated in affective disorders (Green and Costain, 1982; Tyrer and Marsden, 1985) and many clinically effective antidepressants interact with 5-HT systems. These considerations, coupled with the fact that 5-HT may be important in the control of circadian rhythms (Rusak and Zucker, 1979), although itself exhibiting a circadian variation in release (Martin and Marsden, 1985) and metabolism (Faradji et al., 1983), make it clear that 5-HT neurotransmission must be an important element in any consideration of the involvement of circadian rhythms and their control mechanisms in the etiology of affective disorders. In this chapter, we discuss the possible mechanisms controlling the 24-hour variation in 5-HT release and metabolism, and the pharmacology of these mechanisms.

NEURAL CONTROL OF CIRCADIAN RHYTHMS

The question of which neuronal pathways and structures are involved in the control of circadian rhythms has been the subject of numerous reviews, of which this section provides a brief summary, in order to place the rest of the chapter in perspective.

It now appears that there are at least two major components of the central neural control of circadian rhythms. First, because the light–dark cycle is the major environmental zeitgeber for synchronization, it is reasonable to assume that elements of the visual pathway provide one major component. Second, the fact that circadian rhythms are free running under constant conditions indicates the presence of an endogenous rhythm-generating mechanism.

The site of the endogenous pacemaker is generally recognized to be the suprachiasmatic nucleus (SCN), which lies in the anterior ventral hypothalamus, either side of the third ventricle (Moore, 1983). This region receives a direct input from the retina via the retinohypothalamic tract (Moore, 1973). In addition, it receives numerous inputs from other parts of the brain (Guldner, 1985). Of these projections, the most pertinent to the present argument are those from the midbrain raphe complex (Azmitia and Segal, 1978). Recent evidence has demonstrated that the 5-HT nerve terminals are principally located in the rostroventral area of the SCN (Van den Pol and Tsujimoto, 1985). Lesions of the midbrain raphe are associated with a loss of circadian rhythmicity in plasma corticosterone levels (Dunn et al., 1983). Loss of a distinct circadian rhythm in plasma ACTH also followed depletion of whole brain 5-HT with pCPA; in these experiments, the recognizable 24-hour rhythmicity in plasma ACTH returned when 5-HTP was administered at 11:00 AM but not when the same dose was given at 11:00 PM (Szafarczyk et al., 1979), further demonstrating the potentially important role of the 5-HT input to the SCN in the control of circadian rhythms.

CIRCADIAN RHYTHMS OF BRAIN 5-HT CONCENTRATION

It is 30 years since Albrecht and coworkers (1956) first reported circadian changes in 5-HT concentrations in mouse brain. This finding has been confirmed and extended to other rodents in numerous other studies (Matussek and Patshke, 1963; Dixit and Buckley, 1967; Scheving et al., 1968; Davies et al., 1972). Although the phase of the rhythm is not identical in all brain regions, the overall pattern is for tissue concentrations of 5-HT to be greatest during the light phase (Quay, 1968; Kan

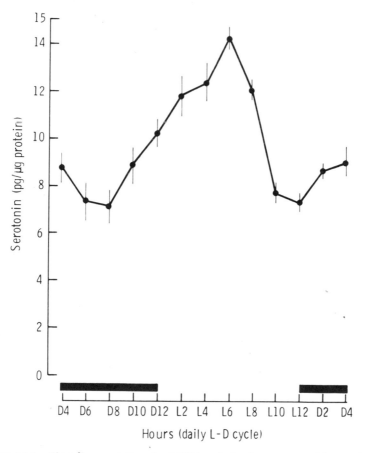

Figure 14.1. Circadian variation in 5-HT levels in the rat suprachiasmatic nucleus (Lighton, unpublished data). Each point represents the mean ± SEM of six animals. The horizontal black bar represents the hours of darkness.

et al., 1977). That this pattern is also found in the SCN can clearly be seen in Figure 14.1 (Lighton, unpublished data).

In 1972, Hery and coworkers published a comprehensive analysis of the factors controlling the diurnal synthesis and metabolism of rat brain 5-HT. They came to the then surprising conclusion that there was a disparity between catabolic and metabolic processes. Synthesis of 5-HT, as measured, for instance, by the rate of tritiated 5-HT accumulation after intracisternal injection of tritiated tryptophan (TRY), was consistently higher during the light phase. In contrast, utilization of 5-HT, as measured by the ratio of tritiated 5-HT to tritiated 5-HIAA following preloading with tritiated TRY, was more rapid during the dark phase, which is, of course, the active phase in nocturnal animals. These conclusions have largely stood the test of time as more sophisticated techniques have permitted a more precise examination of the earlier findings. In the following sections, we consider the possible mechanisms responsible for these circadian changes.

TRYPTOPHAN HYDROXYLASE

Tryptophan hydroxylase (EC 1.14.16.4, L-tryptophan tetrahydropteridine oxygen oxydoreductase) is recognized as the rate-limiting step in the intraneuronal conversion of TRY to 5-HT (Ashcroft et al., 1965; Friedman et al., 1972). It is therefore sensible to look first at the possibility that changes in activity of this enzyme may be involved in the appearance of the 24-hour rhythm in 5-HT synthesis. In vitro investigations in this area have produced conflicting results. A significant 24-hour variation in enzyme activity was reported first by Kan and coworkers (1977) in the rat and by Natali and coworkers (1980) in the mouse. Cahill and Ehret (1981) and Sinei and Redfern (1985) confirmed the presence of a rhythm in the rat, whereas Brown and coworkers (1982) and McLennen and Lees (1978) failed to demonstrate any significant rhythm. Two equally plausible explanations have been put forward to account for these differences First, positive results have been obtained from regional studies, whereas use of whole brain preparations has yielded negative results. Therefore, regional variation in the time of occurrence of peak enzymatic activity (Natali et al., 1980) may lessen the chances of detecting a significant variation in whole brain. Secondly, it seems that the process of homogenization may alter the level of enzyme activity. McLennen and Lees (1978) suggested that disruptive homogenization released an unidentified inhibitor and that the rate of release of this inhibitor could vary with time of day. Retention of the enzyme within synaptosomes, they argued, protected it from the influence of the inhibitor. Against this argument, it has been pointed out by Elks and colleagues (1979) that enzyme activity in homogenates of brain tissue is considerably higher than can be observed in vivo (Kizer et al., 1975; Lin et al., 1969). The process of homogenization, they suggest, maximally activates tryptophan hydroxylase. Elkes and co-workers (1979) further suggested that in this respect homogenization may mimic physiologic depolarization of the serotonergic nerve ending. Using parasagittal sections of rat brain in vitro they were able to show that electrically-evoked depolarization increased both rate of synthesis and rate of release of 5-HT, an effect they attributed to allosteric activation of tryptophan hydroxylase. There is abundant evidence that the stimulation-evoked release of 5-HT from nerves may be inhibited by 5-HT itself, an effect antagonized by the 5-HT receptor antagonist metitepin (Cerrito and Raiteri, 1979; Gothert and Schickter, 1983). In the light of emerging evidence for circadian changes in receptor activity (vide infra), it is tempting to speculate that feedback mechanisms may play a part in regulating, or generating, intraneuronal rhythms of neurotransmitter synthesis. It can be demonstrated, for instance, that antidepressant drugs, chronically administered to rats, can significantly increase intraneuronal tryptophan hydroxylase activity (Redfern and Sinei, 1986) although in this preliminary study no differential effect was seen mid-light compared to mid-dark. However, measurement of the rate of accumulation of 5-HTP, after inhibition of 5-HTP-decarboxylase, showed that the increase in 5-HT levels occurring towards the middle of the light phase was preceded by an increased rate of accumulation of 5-HTP (Sinei and Redfern, unpublished observations).

TRYPTOPHAN-SUBSTRATE CONTROL OF SYNTHESIS

The general finding that brain tryptophan hydroxylase is normally unsaturated with its substrate (Friedman et al., 1972) has led to much speculation on the subject of substrate control of synthesis. There are many instances of altered plasma levels of TRY, or alteration in one of the many variables affecting the relationship between plasma and brain TRY, leading to changed brain levels of TRY, and subsequent changes in brain 5-HT (Fernstrom and Wurtman, 1971; for review, see Curzon, 1979). However, most of this literature describes experiments inducing gross changes that can have little relevance to the physiologic changes under consideration here. Plasma TRY concentration, both free and total, display a circadian rhythm (Niskanen et al, 1976; Hillier and Red-fern, 1977; Hussein and Goedke, 1979; Martin and Redfern, 1985). However, there is evidence to suggest that under physiologic conditions plasma TRY has little influence on brain 5-HT concentrations (Morgan and Yndo, 1973). Further, although there is no doubt that changes in brain TRY concentration can alter brain 5-HT levels, there is no evidence that spontaneous neuronal firing, and consequently the rate of 5-HT release, is in any way altered (Trulson, 1985; Elks et al., 1979). It follows that the behavioral changes associated with, for instance, TRY administration to rats (Graham-Smith, 1971) or to man (Winokur et al., 1986) may be related to changes independent of 5-HT release.

TRYPTOPHAN UPTAKE

In 1972, Hery and coworkers stressed the importance of mechanisms responsible for the uptake of TRY into 5-HT-containing neurons in the control of 5-HT synthesis over 24 hours. Knapp and Mandel (1972) demonstrated the presence of two uptake systems in synaptosomal

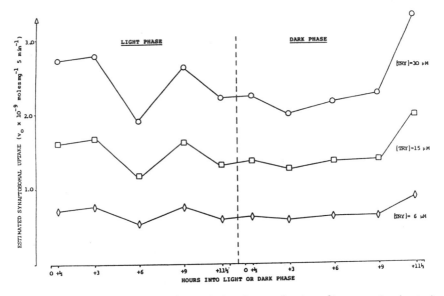

Figure 14.2. Theoretical 24-hr variation in uptake (nmol/mg per 5 minutes) of L-TRY into cortical synaptosomes prepared from rat cortex. Extracellular L-TRY concentration has been assumed to lie in the range 6–30 μM.

preparations from 5-HT rich areas of the brain, both of which displayed Michaelis–Menten kinetics. Recent experiments (Loizou and Redfern, 1986) on the high-affinity (K_m 5.0 × 10^{-5} M) uptake system into cortical synaptosomes, which is energy dependent, temperature sensitive, and susceptible to drug action, have confirmed that the rate of TRY uptake may vary over 24 hours. This study also indicated that extracellular TRY concentrations influenced the rate of TRY uptake only at relatively high extracellular concentrations. (Figure 14.2). Within what we assume to be the physiologic range, variation in both V_{max} and K_m presumably ensure that the ratio of V_{max} to K_m remains constant. If these results are confirmed—and at present we have no explanation of how K_m might be altered—they would indicate that, far from making a significant contribution to the circadian rhythm in rat brain 5-HT concentration, the kinetic properties of the TRY uptake process buffer the system against temporary changes in extracellular TRY concentration. We are, therefore, drawn back to consider that, thus buffered, the internal economy of the 5-HT neuron is likely to be controlled by feedback control of synthesis, as alluded to above, and by control of 5-HT release.

CIRCADIAN RHYTHM IN 5-HT RELEASE AND METABOLISM

The data of Hery and colleagues (1972) demonstrating greater utilization of newly synthesized 5-HT during the dark phase suggested that release of 5-HT was greater during the dark period. However, since Hery and colleagues were not able to distinguish definitively between 5-HIAA arising from released 5-HT and that derived directly from intraneuronal metabolism of 5-HT, their data were inevitably difficult to interpret. The use of newer techniques such as in vivo voltammetry and in vivo intracerebral dialysis have provided new approaches with which to address the question of which factors control 5-HT release. The principles and practicalities of voltammetry and dialysis in vivo have been well reviewed by Marsden and colleagues (1984), and Ungerstedt (1984) respectively, and the interested reader is directed to both of these reviews for detailed information. Briefly, in the case of voltammetry three microelectrodes are implanted intracerebrally. Application of suitable voltages results in oxidation of certain compounds at the surface of one of these electrodes—the working electrode, which is carbon based. Upon oxidation, electrons are released, and these can, with suitable equipment, be measured in the form of an electrical current. In the experiments described here, the working electrode was composed of three pyrolytic

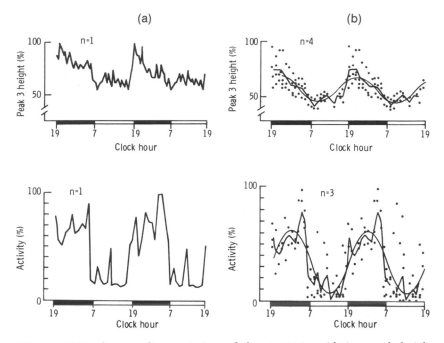

Figure 14.3. The circadian variation of the 5-HIAA oxidation peak height recorded in the SCN of freely moving rats on a 12:12 L–D cycle. (a) illustrates data from a single animal and (b) from four animals. The lower panels illustrate the rest-activity patterns of the animals used for the voltammetry (modified from Faradji et al., 1983, with permission).

carbon fibers (each of 8 μm diameter) held in a pulled glass capillary from which they protruded approximately 300 μm; their fabrication is described fully elsewhere (Marsden and Martin, 1986). Following electrical pretreatment it is possible to differentiate oxidation of ascorbate and DOPAC (peaks 1 + 2) from 5-HIAA (peak 3) using differential pulse voltammetry (Cespuglio et al., 1984).

Intracerebral dialysis involves the implantation of a small-diameter (250 μm) semipermeable dialysis tube folded into a loop and supported by two stainless-steel cannulae into the brain region of interest. This is then perfused with artificial cerebrospinal fluid (CSF) (1 μl/min) and fractions collected for assay by high-performance liquid chromatography (HPLC) with ECD for amines and their metabolites.

Using in vivo voltammetry, Cespuglio and colleagues have demonstrated circadian changes in the extracellular concentration of 5-HIAA in the frontal cortex (Cespuglio et al., 1982) and the SCN (Figure 14.3; Faradji et al., 1983) of freely moving rats. Their data demonstrated two things: first, the extracellular levels of 5-HIAA were highest during the dark period, and second, the greatest changes occurred at the time of transition from light to dark (increase) and dark to light (decrease). Since it is well established that changes in the 5-HIAA oxidation peak reflect changes in 5-HT release (Sharp et al., 1984), these data suggest that 5-HT release increases during the dark period. Recently, further evidence in support of this hypothesis has been obtained. Using a dialysis probe implanted into the ventromedial hypothalamus (VMH), Martin and Marsden (1985) reported that extracellular levels of 5-HT increased during the hour prior to the light–dark transition; this was accompanied by an increase in extracellular 5-HIAA. Similarly, decreases in 5-HT and 5-HIAA concentrations were observed at the transition from dark to light.

CIRCADIAN RHYTHMS IN 5-HT RECEPTOR ACTIVITY

We have already touched on the possibility that feedback inhibition of synthesis and release may be important in controlling the circadian oscillation in presynaptic events. This control could result solely from variation in concentrations of 5-HT within the synaptic cleft, but the possibility that the activity of presynaptic receptors might also vary over 24 hours must be considered. Wesemann et al. (1983) found evidence of circadian variation of 5-HT to binding sites in rat cerebral hemispheres. Circadian rhythms in many other receptor populations have been reported (Kafka et al., 1985). Based on the classification of 5-HT receptors (Peroutka, 1984; Leysen et al., 1984) into 5-HT_1, selectively labeled by tritiated 5-IIT, and 5-HT_2, selectively labeled by tritiated spiperone or tritiated ketanserin, a variety of 5-HT-mediated behaviors have been used to assess the consequences of receptor activation at different points of the light–dark cycle. For example, in mice, the head-twitch induced by 5-methoxy-NN-dimethyl-tryptamine (5MeODMT), generally regarded as a 5-HT_2-mediated response, exhibited a significant circadian rhythm with a peak mid-light. Conversely, the 5-HT syndrome, significant components of which are 5-HT_1 receptor mediated, displayed no variation over 24 hours (Moser and Redfern, 1985a) (Figure 14.4). This lack of periodicity in 5-HT_1-mediated behaviors in the mouse has been confirmed using two 5-HT_1-receptor agonists— RU24969   (1,2,3,6,-tetrahydro-4-pyridinyl)-H-indole   (5-HT_{1B}-selec-

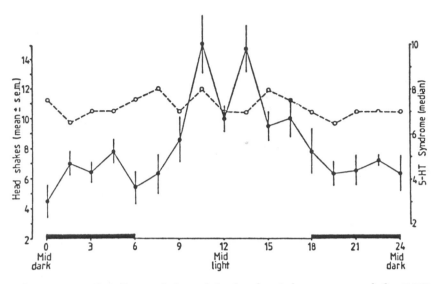

Figure 14.4. Circadian variation of the head twitch response and the 5-HT syndrome in response to 5MeODMT in mice. Filled symbols represent the mean number of head shakes ($\pm$ SEM; $n = 8$) observed in 3 minutes. Open symbols represent the median values for the 5-HT syndrome scored 4 minutes postinjection. Anovar of head shakes: $F = 6.4$ for 16/118 df, $p < 0.01$. (Reprinted with permission from Chronobiology International, Volume 2, Moser PC, Redfern PH, Lack of variation over 24 hours in response to stimulation of 5-HT receptor stimulation in the rat. Copyright 1985, Pergamon Journals Ltd.)

tive) and 8OHDPAT (8-hydroxy-2-(di-*N*-propylamino)tetralin)(5-HT$_{1A}$-selective). Hyperlocomotion induced by RU24969 did not show a circadian rhythm (Moser and Redfern, 1985a), although the ability of metergoline to antagonize the response to RU24969 varied at the two time points tested by Marsden and colleagues (1985). The hypothermia induced by 8OHDPAT also failed to show any circadian variation (Moser and Redfern, 1985b). A similar differentiation between 5-HT$_1$- and 5-HT$_2$-evoked behaviors exists in the rat. Head-twitch responses evoked by 5MeODMT show significant variation, but the time taken to establish the 5-HT$_1$-dependent discriminative cue properties of 5-HTP was independent of circadian influence (Moser and Redfern, 1986). Given that the release of 5-HT has a circadian component, it follows that the degree of physiologic stimulation of postsynaptic receptors will also be circadian in nature. In our behavioral experiments, outlined above, we stimulated the postsynaptic receptors with directly acting exogenous agonists, presumably making the responses independent of endogenous transmitter levels. If our inferences about circadian variation in receptor sensitivity are correct, 5-HT_1 receptors, apparently devoid of circadian changes in sensitivity, would therefore be susceptible to, and would pass on, the circadian variation in 5-HT release. Conversely, since the varying sensitivity of the 5-HT_2-receptor population is approximately $180°$ out of phase with that of transmitter release, i.e., when 5-HT release is highest, receptor activity (whether it is receptor number or affinity that changes we cannot yet say) is lowest, and vice versa. The end result would therefore be to dampen out the consequences of presynaptic oscillations. A similar argument could be applied to presynaptic control of intraneuronal synthesis and turnover of 5-HT.

RECEPTOR-MEDIATED CONTROL OF 5-HT RELEASE IN VIVO

There is now considerable evidence that 5-HT release is under the control of an autoreceptor (for review, see Moret, 1985). Recent evidence has suggested that release and metabolism of 5-HT in the SCN is modulated by the activity of a presynaptic 5-HT_{1B} receptor (Marsden and Martin, 1985a; Martin and Marsden, 1986a). When RU24969 was administered intraperitoneally (10 mg/kg), the height of the 5-HIAA oxidation peak recorded in the SCN decreased. This effect was attenuated by methiothepin, a 5-HT_1- and 5-HT_2-receptor antagonist, but not by the selective 5-HT_2-receptor antagonist ketanserin (Martin and Marsden, 1986a). The response to RU24969 was clearly mediated via a receptor located in the nerve terminal region because 10 μg RU24969 directly injected into the SCN resulted in an 80%–90% decrease in extracellular 5-HIAA concentrations but had no effect when injected into the 5-HT cell body region of the dorsal raphe (Marsden and Martin, 1985a).

The release of 5-HT in the SCN also appears to be under the influence of 5-HT_{1A} receptors. Intravenous administration of 8-OH-DPAT (0.1 mg/kg) is associated with a 30% decrease in peak 3 height (Marsden and Martin, 1986). Ipsapirone, a purported 5-HT_{1A}-receptor antagonist (Goodwin et al., 1986; Martin et al., 1986) was the only 5-HT-receptor antagonist that blocked this effect (Marsden and Martin, 1986). However, the actual site at which 8-OH-DPAT acts remains unclear because it has no effect on extracellular 5-HIAA levels when injected directly into either the SCN or dorsal raphe (Marsden and Martin, 1985b).

In addition, there appears to be tonic control of 5-HT release in the SCN via α_2-adrenoceptors. Administration of idazoxan (500 μg/kg, IV), a selective α_2-adrenoceptor antagonist (Doxey et al., 1983), is associated with a 150% increase in the size of the 5-HIAA oxidation peak in the SCN (Marsden and Martin, 1986). This compound, at the lower dose of 200 µg/kg, also completely blocked the effects of 8-OH-DPAT (Marsden and Martin, 1986). From these data, it is interesting to speculate that, contrary to opinions based on in vitro methodology (Galzin et al., 1984), 5-HT release in the hypothalamus is under tonic control via α_2 adrenoceptors in vivo. Further, the effects of 8-OH-DPAT may involve a catecholaminergic link or be mediated via direct effects on α_2-adrenoceptors whose exact location is presently unknown. As to the possibility of a circadian rhythm in autoreceptor activity, preliminary data from Marsden's laboratory suggests that in mice the biochemical responses to RU24969 exhibit a circadian variation (Martin et al., 1986). Administration of RU24969 decreased tissue levels of 5-HIAA in hypothalamus and brainstem when given 8 hours after the beginning of the light phase but not when given 5 hours into the dark phase, suggesting that the 5-HT_{1B} receptor responsible for the autoregulation of 5-HT release and metabolism exhibits a circadian variation in sensitivity. Obviously, further experiments are required to confirm that these receptors control circadian rhythms in 5-HT release in vivo and to determine the factors that in turn control their sensitivity.

The theory that 5-HT_{1B}-receptor-mediated changes in 5-HT release in the SCN may be important in the control of circadian rhythms has been strengthened by some behavioral data recently presented to the New York Academy of Sciences. When RU24969 was infused directly into the SCN from osmotic mini-pumps over a 14-day period at a rate of 2.5 µg/hr, the entrained circadian rhythm in locomotor activity was completely abolished (Martin and Marsden, 1986b, Figure 14.5). Similar infusions of 0.9% sodium chloride had no effect. It appears, therefore, that the changes in 5-HT release during the light–dark cycle may be important for entrainment since in the above experiments one would assume that the normal 24-hour fluctuations in 5-HT release have been abolished.

PHARMACOLOGIC MANIPULATION OF CIRCADIAN RHYTHMS IN 5-HT FUNCTION

Having considered the mechanisms responsible for the circadian rhythm in 5-HT release and metabolism in rodent brain tissue, we shall finally speculate on the possible physiologic and clinical significance of this rhythm. We believe that the regulatory role of the serotonergic innervation of the SCN may provide a link between two apparently disparate

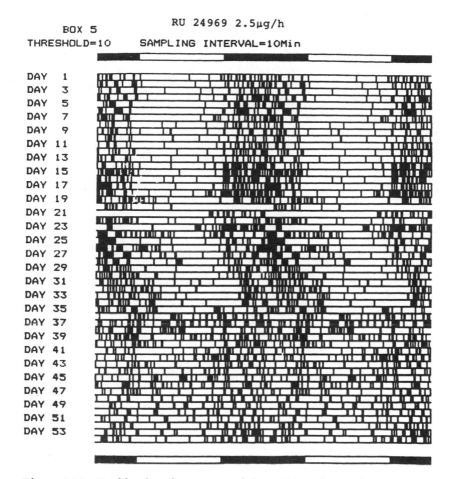

Figure 14.5. Double-plotted actogram of the activity of a single male Wistar rat on a 12:12 L–D cycle. A guide cannula was implanted under pentobarbitone anaesthesia on day 21 and an osmotic minipump connected to an injection cannula implanted on day 35 under halothane anaesthesia. From days 35–49 RU 24969 2.5 μg/hr was infused into the SCN. The hours of darkness are represented by the solid bars at the top and bottom of the figure.

observations. On the one hand, growing evidence supports the hypothesis that depressive illness is related to an abnormality of endogenous circadian rhythms (see review by Wirz-Justice and Wehr, 1983). The common occurrence of early morning awakening and pronounced diurnal mood swings as symptoms of endogenous depression, together with a shortened REM latency (Gillin et al., 1981) lead to the formulation of the hypothesis that "a phase advance in the strong oscillator with reference to the weak oscillator might be a specific cause of some depressions" (Kripke, 1983). On the other hand, one of the few pharmacologic properties common to all clinically effective antidepressants is their ability to affect monoamine transmission and in particular 5-HT mechanisms. In view of the foregoing arguments favoring an essential role for serotonergic neurons in the physiologic control of circadian rhythms, it is tempting to suggest that antidepressants may specifically affect the circadian rhythm(s) of 5-HT function. There is certainly evidence that the monoamine oxidase inhibitor clorgyline causes a phase delay of free-running rhythms in the rat (Wirz-Justice et al., 1982), although this may result from an action on the retina rather than the SCN (Reme et al., 1984). However, evidence that antidepressant drugs specifically affect circadian rhythms of central 5-HT mechanisms is sparse. We have shown that chronic administration to rats of clomipramine, imipramine, and zimelidine significantly alters the proportion of plasma TRY present in the free form at different points of the light–dark cycle (Martin and Redfern, 1985). These results are summarized in Figure 14.6. We have also demonstrated that the altered pattern of plasma TRY resulted in significant alteration of the pattern of change in brain 5-HT and 5-HIAA over 24 hours after chronic, but not acute, dosing with the same three drugs (Martin and Redfern, 1982a,b,c). The effect of chronic administration of clomipramine on brain levels of 5-HT is shown in Figure 14.7. It is evident that the normal peak in 5-HT concentration has become displaced. A preliminary report (Hill et al., 1986) also suggests that chronic imipramine and iprindole, but not fluoxetine or zimelidine, caused phase delays in the wheel-running activity in the mouse.

SUMMARY

In this chapter we have discussed the evidence that 5-HT function varies over 24 hours and the possible mechanisms that exert control over these changes. There is good reason to believe that 5-HT is an important neurotransmitter in the control of circadian rhythms, and therefore further research into its actions is warranted.

Interest in the hypothesis that antidepressant drugs are clinically effective because they facilitate a phase delay of the strong oscillator remains strong. There is at present little evidence that antidepressant drugs directly affect circadian oscillators within the SCN, and it seems to us equally plausible that they may act indirectly, perhaps by making oscillator control mechanisms more susceptible to external zeitgebers.

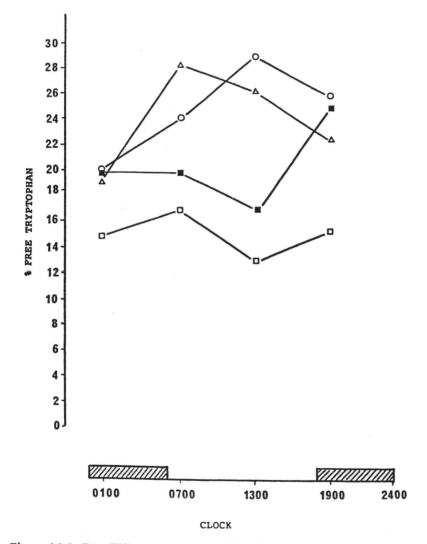

Figure 14.6. Free TRY as a percentage of total TRY concentration in plasma. Effect of 14 days oral administration of imipramine (□), clomipramine (○), and zimelidine (△) 200 μg/ml compared to control (■). $n = 4$. (From Martin and Redfern, 1985, with permission.)

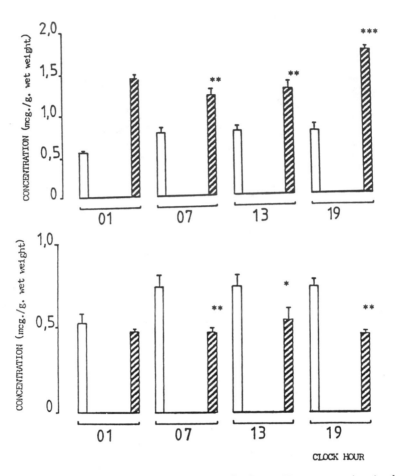

Figure 14.7. Effect of oral clomipramine on brain 5-HT concentration in the rat. Clomipramine was administered in the drinking water at a concentration of 200 μg/ml for 2 days (top diagram) or 14 days (bottom diagram). Open columns—control; hatched columns—drug treated. Mean ± SEM are shown, n = 5 or 6. Difference from control *—$p < 0.05$; **—$p < 0.01$; ***—$p < 0.001$.

We believe these hypotheses are worth testing, but for the time being they must remain largely speculative.

K. F. Martin is a Wellcome Trust Research Fellow in Mental Health.

REFERENCES

Albrecht P, Visscher MB, Bittner JJ, Halberg F (1956): Daily changes in 5-hydroxytryptamine concentration in mouse brain. Proc Soc Exp Biol Med 92:703–706.

Ashcroft GW, Eccleston D, Crawford TBB (1965): 5-Hydroxyindole metabolism in rat brain: A study of intermediate metabolism using the techniques of tryptophan loading. J Neurochem 12:483–492.

Azmitia EC, Segal M (1978): An autoradiographic analysis of the differential projections of the dorsal and median raphe nuclei in the rat. J Comp Neurol 179:641–668.

Brown F, Nicholass J, Redfern PH (1982): Synaptosomal tryptophan hydroxylase activity in rat brain measured over 24 hours. Neurochem Int 4:181–183.

Cahill AL, Ehret CF (1981): Circadian variations in the activity of tyrosine hydroxylase, tyrosine amino transferase and tryptophan hydroxylase: Relationship to catecholamine metabolism. J Neurochem 37:1109–1115.

Cerrito R, Raiteri M (1979): Serotonin release is modulated by presynaptic autoreceptors. Eur J Pharmacol 57:427–430.

Cespuglio R, Faradji H, Crespi F, Jouvet M (1982): Detection by differential pulse voltammetry of 5-hydroxyindolacetic acid in rostral brain areas: Fluctuations occurring during the sleep–waking cycle. 6th European Congress on Sleep Research, Zurich, pp 282–284.

Cespuglio R, Faradji H, Hahn Z, Jouvet M (1984): Voltammetric detection of brain 5-hydroxyindoleamines by means of electrochemically treated carbon fibre electrodes. Chronic recordings for up to one month with movable cerebral electrodes in the sleeping or waking rat. In Marsden CA (ed): Measurement of Neurotransmitter Release in vivo. Chichester, Wiley, pp 173–191.

Curzon G (1979): Relationships between plasma, CSF and brain tryptophan. J Neural Transm Suppl 15:81.

Davies JA, Ancill RJ, Redfern PH (1972): Hallucinogenic drugs and circadian rhythms. Prog Brain Res 36:79–95.

Dixit BN, Buckley JP (1967): Circadian changes in brain 5-HT and plasma corticosterone in the rat. Life Sci 6:755–758.

Doxey JC, Roach AG, Smith CFC (1983): Studies on RX781094: A selective potent and specific antagonist of α_2 adrenoceptors. Br J Pharmacol 78:489–505.

Dunn JD, Johnson DC, Castro AJ (1983): The effect of raphe transection on circadian patterns of corticosterone. Neuroendocrinol Lett 5:233–238.

Elks ML, Youngblood WW, Kizer JS (1979): Serotonin synthesis and release in brain slices: Independence of tryptophan. Brain Res 172:471–486.

Faradji H, Cespuglio R, Jouvet M (1983): Voltammetric measurements of 5-hydroxyindole compounds in the suprachiasmatic nuclei circadian fluctuations. Brain Res 279:111–119.

Fernstrom JD, Wurtman RJ (1971): Brain serotonin content: Physiological dependence on plasma tryptophan levels. Science 173:149–151.

Friedman PA, Kappelman AH, Kaufman S (1972): Partial purification and characterization of tryptophan hydroxylase from rabbit hindbrain. J Biol Chem 247:4165–4173.

Galzin AM, Moret C, Langer SZ (1984): Evidence that exogenous but not endogenous norepinephrine activates the presynaptic alpha-2 adrenoceptors on serotonergic nerve endings in the rat hypothalamus. J Pharmacol Exp Ther 228:725–732.

Gillin JC, Duncan WC, Murphy DL, et al (1981): Age related changes in sleep in depressed and normal subjects. Psychiatry Res 4:73–78.

Goodwin GM, DeSouza RJ, Green AR (1986): The effects of a novel putative 5-HT$_1$ receptor antagonist (TVX Q7821) on 5-HT synthesis and the behavioural effects of 5-HT agonists in mice and rats. Psychopharmacology, in press.

Gothert M, Schickter E (1983): Autoreceptor-mediated inhibition of ^{3}H-5-HT release from rat brain cortex slices by analogues of 5-HT. Life Sci 32:1183–1191.

Graham-Smith DC (1971): Studies in vivo on the relationship between brain tryptophan, brain 5-HT synthesis, and hyperactivity in rats treated with an MAOI and L-tryptophan. J Neurochem 18:1053–1066.

Green AR, Costain DW (1982): Pharmacology and Biochemistry of Psychiatric Disorders. Chichester, Wiley.

Guldner FH (1985): Structure and neural connections of the suprachiasmatic nucleus. In Redfern PH, et al (eds): Circadian Rhythms in the Central Nervous System. London, Macmillan, pp 29–44.

Hery F, Rouer E, Glowinski J (1972): Daily variations of serotonin metabolism in the rat brain. Brain Res 43:445–465.

Hill SJ, Mason R, Reffin D (1986): Differential effect of chronic antidepressant administration on enhanced circadian wheel-running behaviour in the mouse. Br J Pharmacol 85:357P.

Hillier JG, Redfern PH (1977): 24-hour rhythm in serum and brain indoleamines: Tryptophan hydroxylase and MAO activity in the rat. Int J Chronobiol 4:197–210.

Hussein L, Goedke HW (1979): Diurnal rhythm in the plasma level of total and free tryptophan and cortisol in rabbits. Res Exp Med Berlin 176:123–130.

Kafka MS, Marangos PJ, Moore RY (1985): Suprachiasmatic nucleus ablation abolishes circadian rhythms in rat brain neurotransmitter receptors. Brain Res 327:344–347.

Kan JP, Chouvet G, Hery F, et al (1977): Daily variations of various parameters of serotonin metabolism in the rat brain. I. Circadian variations of tryptophan-5-hydroxylase in the raphe nuclei and the striatum. Brain Res 123:125–136.

Kizer JS, Palkovits M, Kopin IJ, et al (1975): Lack of effect of various endocrine manipulations on tryptophan hydroxylase activity of individual nuclei of the hypothalamus, limbic system and midbrain of the rat. Endocrinology 98:743–750.

Knapp S, Mandel AJ (1972): Narcotic drugs: Effects on the serotonin biosynthetic system of the brain. Science 177:1209–1211.

Kripke DF (1983): Phase advance theories for affective illness. In Goodwin E, Wehr T (eds): Circadian Rhythms in Psychiatry: Basic and Clinical Studies. Pacific Grove, CA, Boxwood, pp 41–69.

Leysen JE, de Chattoy de Courcelles D, De Clerk F, et al (1984): Serotonin S_2 receptor binding sites and functional correlates. Neuropharmacology 23:1493–1502.

Lin RC, Costa E, Nett NH, et al (1969): In vivo measurement of 5-HT turnover rates in the rat brain from the conversion of ^{14}C-tryptophan to ^{14}C-5-HT. J Pharmacol Exp Ther 170:232–238.

Loizou G, Redfern PH (1986): Circadian variation in uptake of tryptophan by synaptosomes from the rat cortex. J Pharm Pharmacol 38:89P.

McLennan IS, Lees GJ (1978): Diurnal changes in the kinetic properties of tryptophan hydroxylase from rat brain. J Neurochem 31:557–559.

Marsden CA, Martin KF (1985a): RU24969 decreases 5-HT release in the SCN by acting on 5-HT receptors in the SCN but not the dorsal raphe. Br J Pharmacol 86:219P.

Marsden CA, Martin KF (1985b): In vivo voltammetric evidence that the 5-HT autoreceptor is not of the $5-HT_{1A}$ sub-type. Br J Pharmacol 86:445P.

Marsden CA, Martin KF (1986): Involvement of $5-HT_{1A}$ and α_2-receptors in the decreased 5-hydroxytryptamine release and metabolism in rat suprachiasmatic nucleus after intravenous 8-hydroxy-2-(n-dipropyl amino) retralin. Br J Pharmacol 89:277–287.

Marsden CA, Maidment NT, Brazell MP (1984): An introduction to *in vivo* electrochemistry. In Marsden CA (ed): Measurement of Neurotransmitter Release *in vivo*. Chichester, Wiley, pp 127–151.

Marsden CA, Martin KF, Webb AJ (1985): Diurnal variation in $5-HT_1$ receptor function. Br J Pharmacol 86:398P.

Martin KF, Marsden CA (1985): In vivo diurnal variations of 5-HT release in hypothalamic nuclei. In Redfern PH et al (eds): Circadian Rhythms in the Central Nervous System. London, MacMillan, pp 81–94.

Martin KF, Marsden CA (1986a): *In vivo* voltammetry in the suprachiasmatic nucleus of the rat: Effects of RU24969, methiothepin and ketanserin. Eur J Pharmacol 121:135–140.

Martin KF, Marsden CA (1986b). Pharmacological manipulation of the serotoninergic input to the suprachiasmatic nucleus—An insight into the control of circadian rhythms. Ann NY Acad Sci 473:542–545.

Martin KF, Redfern PH (1982a): The effects of clomipramine on the 24-h variation of 5-HT and tryptophan concentrations in the rat brain. Br J Pharmacol 76:288P.

Martin KF, Redfern PH (1982b): The effect of zimelidine on the 24-h variation of 5-HT and tryptophan concentrations in the rat brain. Br J Pharmacol 77:357P.

Martin KF, Redfern PH (1982c): Modification of 24-h variations in brain tryptophan and 5-HT concentrations by imipramine. Br J Pharmacol 77:511P.

Martin KF, Redfern PH (1985): The effect of antidepressant drugs on 24-hour rhythms of tryptophan metabolism in the rat. Chronobiol Int 2:109–113.

Martin KF, Mason R, McDougal H (1986): Electrophysiological evidence that ipsapirone (TVXQ7821) is a partial agonist at 5-HT_{1A} receptors in the rat hippocampus. Br J Pharmacol 89:729P.

Martin KF, Webb AR, Marsden CA (1986): Behavioural responses to the 5-hydroxytryptamine 1B (5-HT_{1B}) receptor agonist RU24969 may exhibit a circadian variation in the mouse. Chronobiol Int (in press).

Matussek N, Patshke V (1963): Beziehungen des Schlaf und Wachrhythmus zum noradrenalin und serotonin gehalt im zentral nervensystem von Hamstern. Med Exp 11:81–87.

Moore RY (1973): Retinohypothalamic projection in mammals. A comparative study. Brain Res 49:403–409.

Moore RY (1983): Organization and function of a central nervous system circadian oscillator: The suprachiasmatic hypothalamic nuclei. Fed Proc 42:2783–2789.

Moret C (1985). Pharmacology of the serotonin autoreceptor. In Green AR (ed): Neuropharmacology of Serotonin. New York, Oxford University Press, pp 21–49.

Morgan WW, Yndo CA (1973): Daily rhythms in tryptophan and serotonin content in mouse brain: The apparent independence of these parameters from daily changes in food intake and from plasma tryptophan content. Life Sci 12:395–408.

Moser PC, Redfern PH (1985a): Circadian variation in behavioural responses to central 5-HT receptor stimulation in the mouse. Psychopharmacology 86:223–237.

Moser PC, Redfern PH (1985b): Lack of variation over 24 hours in response to stimulation of 5-HT receptor stimulation in the rat. Chronobiol Int 2:235–238.

Moser PC, Redfern PH (1986): Circadian rhythms in behaviours mediated by 5-HT receptor stimulation in the rat. Annu Rev Chronopharmacol 3:13–16.

Natali JP, McRae-Degueurce A, Chouvet G, Pujol JP (1980): Genetic studies of daily variation of first-step enzymes of monoamines metabolism in the brain of inbred strains of mice and hybrids—I. daily variations of tryptophan hydroxylase activity in the nuclei raphe dorsalis, raphe centralis and in the striatum. Brain Res 123:125–136.

Niskanen F, Huttunen M, Tamminen T, Jaaskelainen J (1976): The daily rhythm of plasma tryptophan and tyrosine in depression. Br J Psychiatry 128:67–73.

Peroutka SJ (1984): 5-HT_1 receptor sites and functional correlates. Neuropharmacology. 23:1487–1492.

Quay WB (1968): Differences in circadian rhythms in 5-hydroxytryptamine according to brain region. Am J Physiol 215:1448–1453.

Redfern PH, Sinei K (1986): Effect of chronic administration of mianserin and clomipramine on tryptophan-5-hydroxylase activity in rat brain. Br J Pharmacol 88:342P.

Reme C, Wirz-Justice A, Aeberhard B, Rhyner A (1984): Chronic clorgyline dampens rat retinal rhythms. Brain Res 298:99–106.

Riederer T, Birksmayer W, Neumeyer E, et al (1974): The daily rhythm of HVA, VMA (VA) and 5-HIAA in depression-syndrome. J Neural Transm 35:23.

Rusak B, Zucker I (1979): Neural regulation of circadian rhythms. Physiol Rev 59:449–526.

Scheving LE, Harrison WH, Gordon P, Pauly JE (1968): Daily fluctuations (circadian and ultradian) in biogenic amines of the rat brain. Am J Physiol 214:166–173.

Sharp T, Maidment NT, Brazell MP, ct al (1984): Changes in monoamine metabolites measured by simultaneous *in vivo* differential pulse voltammetry and intracerebral dialysis. Neuroscience 4:1213–1221.

Sinei K, Redfern PH (1985): 24-hour variation in synaptosomal tryptophan-5-hydroxylase activity in rat brain. In Redfern PH, et al (eds): Circadian Rhythms in the Central Nervous System. London, Macmillan, pp 193–198.

Szafarczyk A, Ixart G, Malaval J, et al (1979): Effects of lesions of the suprachiasmatic nuclei and *p*-chlorophenylalamine on the circadian rhythms of adrenocorticotrophic hormone and corticosterone in the plasma and on locomotor activity of rats. J Endocrinol 83:1–16.

Thompson C (1985): Circadian rhythms in clinical perspective. In Redfern PH, et al (eds): Circadian rhythms in the central nervous system. London, Macmillan, pp 163–176.

Trulson ME (1985): Dietary tryptophan does not alter the function of brain serotonin neurons. Life Sci 37:1072.

Tyrer P, Marsden CA (1985): New antidepressants: Is there anything new they tell us about depression? Trends Neurosci 8:427–431.

Ungerstedt U (1984): Measurement of neurotransmitter release by intracranial dialysis. In Marsden CA (ed): Measurement of Neurotransmitter Release *in vivo*. Chichester, Wiley, pp 81–106.

Van Den Pol AN, Tsujimoto KL (1985): Neurotransmitters of the hypothalamic suprachiasmatic nucleus: Immunocytochemical analysis of 25 neuronal antigens. Neuroscience 15:1049–1086.

Wehr TA, Sack D, Rosenthal N, et al (1983): Circadian rhythm disturbances in manic-depressive illness. Fed Proc 42:2809–2814.

Wesemann W, Weiner N, Rotsch M, Schulz E (1983): Serotonin binding in rat brain: Circadian rhythm and effect of sleep deprivation. Neural Transm Suppl 18:287–294.

Winokur A, Lindberg ND, Lucki I, et al (1986): Hormonal and behavioural effects associated with intravenous L-tryptophan administration. Psychopharmacology 88:213–219.

Wirz-Justice A, Wehr TA (1983): Neuropharmacology and biological rhythms. Adv Biol Psychiatry 11:20–34.

Wirz-Justice A, Groos GA, Wehr TA (1982): The neuropharmacology of circadian timekeeping in mammals. In Aschoff J, Daan S, Groos GA. (eds): Vertebrate Circadian Systems, Structure and Physiology. Berlin, Springer-Verlag.

15

Circadian Rhythms in Discrete Brain Regions

Marian S. Kafka

This chapter discusses some studies of circadian rhythms in the rat (Kafka et al., 1986a,b,c). As there is good reason to believe that similar processes occur in mammals in general, the relationships that are discussed may exist in the human and may be related not only to behaviors, but to the affective and cognitive mental processes that lead to behaviors. Changes in the rhythms, in their relationships to one another, in their amplitudes, and, in fact, in their existence, might alter feelings, thoughts, and behaviors, and, for these reasons, play a role in affective disorders and schizophrenia.

Receptor binding in the rat brain varies over the 24-hour day (Kafka et al, 1983). Circadian and ultradian (Kafka et al., 1983, 1985) rhythms in α_1- and β-adrenergic, acetylcholine muscarinic (ACh), opiate, and benzodiazepine (BDZ) receptors have been demonstrated in "forebrain," namely, all the brain rostral to cerebellum, except striatum. Benzodiazepine and dopamine (DA) receptor rhythms were also present in striatum. To begin to relate circadian rhythms in functional processes with those in receptors and neurotransmitter secretion, studies were designed to investigate whether receptor rhythms were present in discrete brain regions and if those rhythms correlated with rhythmic changes in secretion and putative second messenger generation in the same regions, and with physiologic, and behavioral rhythms in the animals.

CIRCADIAN RHYTHMS IN RECEPTORS

Male Sprague–Dawley rats were maintained for about 3 weeks in a controlled light–dark environment, after which they were enucleated to eliminate time cues, then maintained for 2–3 days, and killed at six 4-hour intervals over a 24-hour period. Their brains were quickly removed and frozen, and then dissected and stored for the measurement of binding.

Circadian rhythms in adrenergic receptors were found in a number of discrete brain regions (Figure 15.1). Unimodal rhythms in specific binding to the α_1-adrenergic receptor were found in the following cerebral cortical regions: frontal, cingulate, piriform, parietal, temporal, and occipital cortices, and in olfactory bulb. In all of these regions the peak-specific binding occurred in middle to late subjective night, i.e., the dark phase of the light–dark cycle, when the animals were sighted, except for piriform cortex in which the peak was in the middle of subjective day, i.e., the light phase of the light–dark cycle (Figure 15.1a). Unimodal circadian rhythms were also found in α_1-receptor binding in noncortical regions—hypothalamus, hippocampus, pons-medulla, caudate-putamen and thalamus-septum. No rhythm was found in cerebellum. All regions in which circadian rhythms in binding to the α_1-receptor were found, except olfactory bulb, and frontal and piriform cortex, had prolonged peaks in binding.

Unimodal circadian rhythms in specific binding to the α_2-receptor were found in frontal, parietal, and temporal cortex and pons-medulla, with no rhythms in cingulate, piriform, or occipital cortex, or hypothalamus (Figure 15.1b). Peak binding in frontal, temporal, and parietal cortex and pons-medulla occurred during subjective night.

Unimodal circadian rhythms in specific binding to the β-receptor were found in a number of cortical regions—olfactory bulb, piriform, insular, parietal, and temporal cortices (Figure 15.1c). Unimodal circadian rhythms were also found in hypothalamus and cerebellum (Figure 15.1c). No rhythm was found in frontal, entorhinal, cingulate, or occipital cortex, or in hippocampus, pons-medulla or caudate-putamen (Figure 15.1c). Binding in all rhythmic regions, except olfactory bulb and piriform cortex, was maximal in subjective night and minimal at 10 AM, i.e., the beginning of subjective day.

The regional 24-hour mean adrenergic receptor binding varied threefold to fourfold, with cortical regions higher; hypothalamus just lower than the cortex in α_1- and β-receptors; and piriform cortex strikingly high in α_2-receptors (Table 15.1).

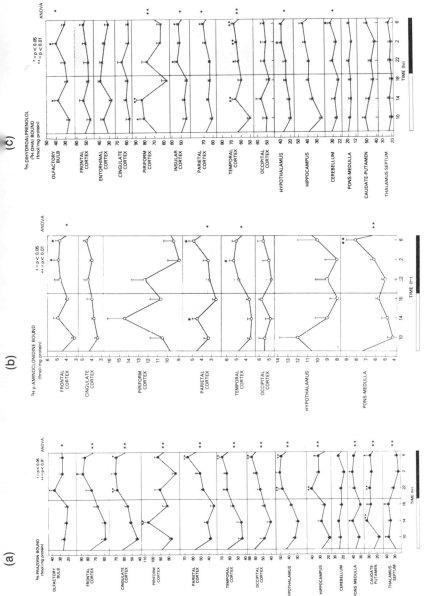

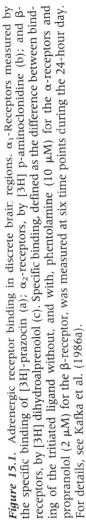

Figure 15.1. Adrenergic receptor binding in discrete brain regions. α_1-Receptors measured by the specific binding of [3H]-prazosin (a); α_2-receptors, by [3H] p-aminoclonidine (b); and β-receptors, by [3H] dihydroalprenolol (c). Specific binding, defined as the difference between binding of the tritiated ligand without, and with, phentolamine (10 μM) for the α-receptors and propranolol (2 μM) for the β-receptor, was measured at six time points during the 24-hour day. For details, see Kafka et al. (1986a).

Table 15.1. Regional 24-Hour Mean Receptor Binding^a

Brain region	α_1	α_2	β	ACh	BDZ
Olfactory bulb	27 ± 2 (35)	—	32 ± 1 (44)	170 ± 10 (35)	432 ± 13 (40)
Frontal cortex	71 ± 3 (42)	4 ± 0.2 (44)	48 ± 2 (44)	431 ± 11 (42)	443 ± 28 (47)
Insular cortex	—	—	48 ± 1 (45)	—	—
Entorhinal cortex	—	—	34 ± 1 (45)	—	—
Cingulate cortex	59 ± 2 (48)	4 ± 0.2 (46)	60 ± 1 (48)	—	—
Piriform cortex	88 ± 3 (42)	11 ± 0.6 (48)	72 ± 2 (42)	—	—
Parietal cortex	44 ± 2 (43)	4 ± 0.2 (43)	66 ± 1 (43)	495 ± 11 (45)	790 ± 20 (45)
Temporal cortex	56 ± 2 (42)	4 ± 0.2 (45)	63 ± 11 (42)	—	—
Occipital cortex	52 ± 2 (44)	5 ± 0.3 (44)	51 ± 2 (48)	483 ± 11 (46)	743 ± 21 (43)
Hypothalamus	41 ± 2 (48)	9 ± 0.5 (44)	34 ± 1 (47)	—	—
Hippocampus	29 ± 2 (41)	—	30 ± 1 (43)	313 ± 11 (44)	213 ± 10 (40)
Amygdala	—	—	—	—	454 ± 10 (45)
Nucleus accumbens	—	—	—	533 ± 11 (44)	303 ± 13 (48)
Thalamus-septum	32 ± 1 (41)	—	21 ± 1 (45)	195 ± 6 (47)	199 ± 6 (44)
Caudate-putamen	27 ± 1 (41)	—	47 ± 1 (43)	401 ± 11 (41)	179 ± 7 (48)
Pons-medulla	36 ± 1 (41)	6 ± 0.3 (47)	18 ± 1 (47)	149 ± 3 (48)	166 ± 5 (44)
Olfactory tubercle	—	—	—	—	317 ± 12 (48)
Cerebellum	22 ± 1 (41)	—	28 ± 1 (44)	53 ± 1 (42)	142 ± 5 (42)

^{a} Mean ± SEM. The number of measurements appears in parentheses.

In muscarinic acetylcholinergic (ACh) receptors and benzodiaze-pine (BDZ) receptors, circadian rhythms were also found in many dis-crete regions. Unimodal circadian rhythms in specific binding to ACh receptors were found in olfactory bulb, parietal cortex, and caudate-putamen. No rhythms were found in frontal or occipital cortex, nucleus accumbens, hippocampus, thalamus-septum, pons-medulla, or cere-bellum (Figure 15.2a). In the regions in which rhythms were present, maximal binding occurred in subjective night.

Unimodal circadian rhythms in specific binding to BDZ receptors were found in olfactory bulb and frontal cortex, olfactory tubercle, nu-cleus accumbens, amygdala, caudate-putamen, hippocampus, and cer-ebellum. No rhythms were found in parietal or occipital cortex, pons-medulla, or thalamus-septum (Figure 15.2b). Peak binding occurred in the middle of subjective day in frontal cortex, olfactory tubercle, nucleus accumbens, amygdala, caudate-putamen, and hippocampus; in con-trast, peak binding occurred in the middle of subjective night in olfactory bulb and cerebellum.

The variation among regions was, for both ACh and BDZ receptors, threefold to fourfold.

Because there was not enough tissue to measure saturation iso-therms, it is not certain whether the rhythms in specific binding to re-ceptors reflect rhythms in receptor number, affinity, or both. In previous experiments, however, the affinities of these receptors did not change during the course of the day (Kafka et al., 1983 and 1986b; Wirz-Justice et al., 1983), suggesting that the rhythms in specific binding measure the number of receptors. In spite of a certain variability, all the rhythms measured in receptor binding were unimodal, that is, circadian rhythms without ultradian (endogenous rhythms with periods of less than 24 hours) features.

There is a circadian rhythm in binding to the α_1-adrenergic re-ceptor in most brain regions investigated. The cerebellum, the only re-gion in which no circadian rhythm in α_1-receptor binding was found, is also the region with the least amount of binding, and a region in which it has been reported that there is no stimulation of cyclic aden-osine monophosphate (cAMP) production (Daly et al., 1981). Perhaps the α_1-receptor is not very important in cerebellar functions, including those functions that vary across the day.

Failure to observe significant circadian rhythms in the α_2-receptor in half the regions measured, including hypothalamus, may indicate that the regions are arrhythmic, that they are not rhythmic at the time of year they were measured (Kafka et al., 1983), or that rhythms in even smaller regions, for example, hypothalamic nuclei, may be present

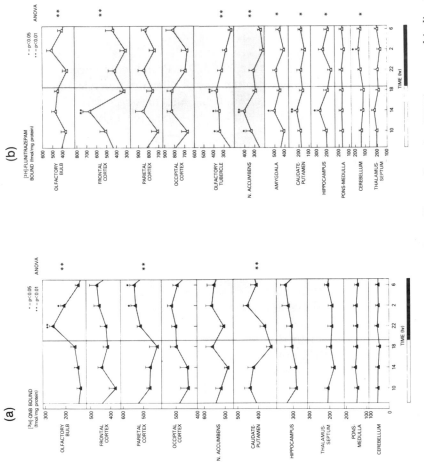
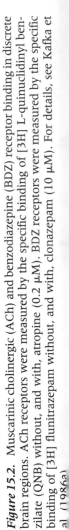

Figure 15.2. Muscarinic cholinergic (ACh) and benzodiazepine (BDZ) receptor binding in discrete brain regions. ACh receptors were measured by the specific binding of [3H] L-quinuclidinyl benzilate (QNB) without, and with, atropine (0.2 μM). BDZ receptors were measured by the specific binding of [3H] flunitrazepam without, and with, clonazepam (10 μM). For details, see Kafka et al. (1986a).

but cancel each other or be of insufficient amplitude to be discerned when the region as a whole is studied. Evidence in support of one of the latter possibilities comes from the reported occurrence of an α_2-receptor circadian rhythm in the medial hypothalamus (Krauchi et al., 1984) and in some hypothalamic nuclei (Leibowitz et al., 1984).

Because the density of β-receptors is markedly different in different cell layers of a single region (Palacios and Kuhar, 1980) and the parts of the brain measured in our study are not small enough to have homogeneous cell populations, the rhythms measured, even in discrete anatomic regions, may be a composite of the β-receptor rhythms of many cell types. At subjective dawn, the concurrent minima in all regions exhibiting β-receptor circadian rhythms, except piriform cortex, might indicate a diminution in β-receptor-mediated events. On the other hand, if the overall activity of β-receptors in the brain is inhibitory, perhaps the fall in receptors at subjective dawn disinhibits, permitting the rest cycle to begin (Hilakivi, 1983).

Binding to the ACh receptor was maximal in all three rhythmic regions in subjective night. Perhaps ACh receptors mediate behaviors during the rats' active period. As no rhythms were found in the majority of regions studied, perhaps the ACh receptor is arrhythmic in these regions. Although it is not possible, for the reasons mentioned above, to rule out the occurrence of rhythms in smaller parts of any of these regions, the relatively small nucleus accumbens was without rhythm.

Peak binding to the BDZ receptor occurred in the middle of subjective day in frontal cortex, olfactory tubercle, nucleus accumbens, amygdala, hippocampus, and caudate-putamen, suggesting that BDZ receptors may mediate events in the rats' rest phase. In contrast, in olfactory bulb and cerebellum, the peak occurrence of the BDZ receptor binding in the middle of subjective night suggests a role of BDZ receptors in mediating events in the rats' active phase.

In summary, peak binding to adrenergic and ACh receptors occurred during subjective night in most regions in which rhythms were found. In contrast, peak binding to BDZ receptors occurred during subjective day. The adrenergic receptors and the ACh receptor may mediate activity, and the processes and behaviors that accompany it, during the active phase of the rat, a nocturnal animal. The BDZ receptors, on the other hand, may mediate rest, and the processes accompanying it.

CIRCADIAN RHYTHMS IN METABOLITES

Not only have circadian rhythms in receptors been measured, but daily rhythms in the concentrations of rat brain biogenic amines have been

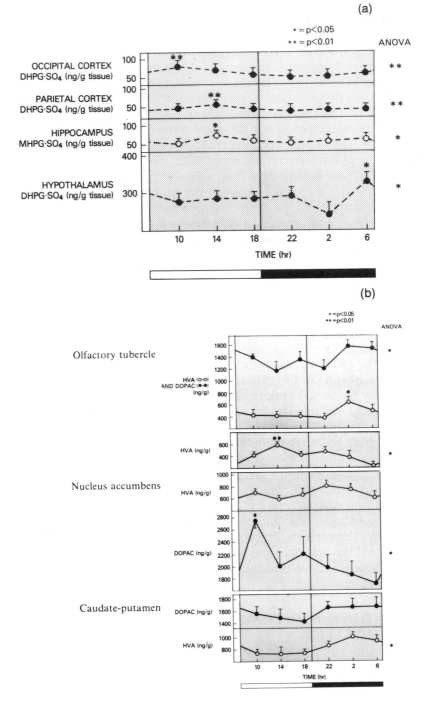

reported (Scheving et al., 1986; Simon and George, 1975, Hillier et al., 1975; Turner et al., 1981), and changes in neurotransmitter secretion and turnover have been shown to alter the levels of neurotransmitter receptors (Creese and Snyder, 1979; Reisine, 1981; Bylund and U'Prichard, 1983). Circadian (unimodal) rhythms in norepinephrine (NE) and DA metabolites occur in discrete brain regions.

Four frozen, pooled regional samples were prepared and analyzed simultaneously for norepinephrine (NE) metabolites, 3-methoxy-4-hydroxyphenylglycol (MHPG), and 3,4-dihydroxyphenylglycol (DHPG) by a gas chromatographic mass spectometric assay (Ellsworth et al., 1983). Conjugated MHPG and DHPG (as sulfates) represent the majority of reduced NE metabolites present in rat brain (Ellsworth et al., 1982). The dopamine metabolites homovanillic acid (HVA) and 3,4-dihydroxyphenylacetic acid (DOPAC) were analyzed by a gas chromatographic mass spectrometric method measuring the free, unconjugated, acidic DA metabolites (Bacopoulos et al., 1979). A significant portion of rodent DA acidic metabolites are in the free form.

A circadian rhythm in MHPG concentration, found in the hippocampus, peaked in the middle of subjective day; and no rhythms were found in frontal, cingulate, parietal, piriform, insular, or temporal cortex, pons-medulla, cerebellum, thalamus-septum, or hypothalamus (Figure 15.3a). A circadian rhythm with a peak at 10:00 AM may exist in occipital cortex. The magnitude of the MHPG concentration at that time point is not reliable, however, because of an insufficient number of samples. Circadian rhythms in DHPG concentration were found in occipital and parietal cortex, and in hypothalamus. Peak DHPG concentrations in cortex were in early to middle subjective day; and in hypothalamus, at subjective dawn (Figure 15.3a). The rhythms in NE metabolites were unimodal, and the regional variation in the NE metabolites was fourfold to sixfold.

Norepinephrine, secreted at presynaptic terminals in rat brain, is metabolized to DHPG and MHPG, the former, probably intraneuronally, and the latter, extraneuronally. In rat brain both MHPG and DHPG provide a measure of central NE metabolism and noradrenergic activity. Circadian rhythms in NE metabolites were found in very few of the brain regions examined; in MHPG, only in hippocampus, the peaks occurring early in subjective day in occipital and parietal cortex and

---

Figure 15.3. The concentrations of (a) norepinephrine (NE) and (b) dopamine (DA) metabolites in discrete brain regions. (a) MHPG·SO$_4$ and DHPG·SO$_4$ (b) HVA and DOPAC were measured by gas chromatography mass spectrometry. For details, see Kafka et al. (1986b).

hippocampus, and at dawn in hypothalamus. Though rhythms existing in very small regions may have been missed in measuring the regions selected in this study, the data suggest that presynaptic NE metabolism, including NE secretion, is not rhythmic in most brain regions. For this reason, rhythms in NE secretion are, in general, not likely to confer the rhythms measured in adrenergic receptors.

Circadian rhythms were also present in DA metabolites. Circadian rhythms in HVA concentration were observed in olfactory tubercle and amygdala. The peak concentration in olfactory tubercle was in the middle of subjective night and, in amygdala, in the middle of subjective day (Figure 15.3b). No rhythm was found in nucleus accumbens or caudate-putamen. A circadian rhythm in DOPAC concentration was found in nucleus accumbens, the peak concentration occurring early in subjective day. No rhythm was found in olfactory tubercle or caudate-putamen (Figure 15.3b). The rhythms in DA metabolites were unimodal, and the 24-hour concentration of DA metabolites varied onefold to twofold.

Rat brain DA metabolites provide a measure of dopaminergic cell activity, because their concentrations depend on the rates of DA turnover and release (Bacopoulos et al., 1979). Circadian rhythms in HVA concentration were found in olfactory tubercle and amygdala; circadian rhythms in DOPAC concentration were found only in nucleus accumbens. For the reasons mentioned above, rhythms may have been missed. The data suggest, however, that DA release often is not rhythmic.

CIRCADIAN RHYTHMS IN SECOND MESSENGERS

In rat brain, agonist occupancy of the α_1- and β-adrenergic receptors stimulated the production of cAMP (Daly et al., 1981). In addition, daily rhythms in brain cAMP concentration have been reported (Choma et al., 1979; Valases et al., 1980). In our studies, rats were killed at 4-hour intervals over a 24-hour period, by focused microwave irradiation to the head. The brains were removed, sliced, and frozen, and discrete regions dissected for measurement of cyclic guanosine monophosphate (cGMP) and cAMP by radioimmunoassay.

Circadian rhythms in cGMP concentration were found in frontal poles, frontal, cingulate, insular, piriform, temporal, and occipital cortex, olfactory tubercle, nucleus accumbens, caudate-putamen, amygdala, hypothalamus, and hippocampus. No rhythm was observed in parietal cortex (Figure 15.3).

The peak concentration of cGMP occurred in subjective night in frontal poles, frontal, cingulate, insular, and occipital cortex, nucleus accumbens, hypothalamus, and hippocampus (Figure 15.4a). In contrast to regions with peaks in subjective night, regions with peak cGMP concentrations in subjective day included insular, piriform, and temporal cortex, olfactory tubercle, caudate-putamen, and amygdala. The 24-hour mean cGMP concentration varied 123-fold, being highest in the nucleus accumbens and lowest in cingulate cortex. This variation was an order of magnitude larger than that of any other variable measured in the studies. The rhythms in cGMP were circadian (unimodal).

The role of cGMP in neural tissue is not clear. Changes in the concentration of cGMP could be a cause, or a result, of changes in neuronal activity. Another possibility is that cGMP acts, not as an activator of ion fluxes and neurotransmitter release, but as modulator of processes that restore neurons after periods of activity (Symposium, Fed Proc 42, 1983; Goldberg and Haddox, 1977). In contrast to the release of NE and DA, the concentration of cGMP displays rhythms of considerable amplitude in all regions measured except parietal cortex.

Muscarinic cholinergic M1 receptors and α_1-adrenergic receptors may stimulate polyphosphoinositide hydrolysis, and, with it, generate cGMP (Berridge et al., 1982; Berridge and Irvine, 1984). The only region measured in our study in which both cholinergic receptors and cGMP were rhythmic is caudate-putamen. Cyclic GMP is high at subjective dusk and during early subjective night, a rhythmic pattern contrasting with that observed in cholinergic receptor binding, which has its trough at that time (Kafka et al., 1986a). The data suggest that the rhythm in cholinergic receptors (although M1 and M2 receptors were not measured separately) does not confer the caudate-putamen cGMP rhythm. In contrast, cortical α_1-receptor rhythms and cGMP rhythms peak in subjective night, with the exception of piriform, in which both are rhythmic, and temporal cortex, in which α_1-receptors are not rhythmic but cGMP is. In caudate-putamen, hippocampus, and hypothalamus, the increase in α_1-receptor binding slightly precedes increasing cGMP concentrations. It is possible, then, that α_1-receptor rhythms in frontal, cingulate, piriform, and occipital cortex, caudate-putamen, hypothalamus, and hippocampus trigger an intraneuronal cascade, conferring a rhythm in cGMP concentration. Though not measured in this study, α_1-receptor-mediated polyphosphoinositide hydrolysis itself could have circadian rhythmicity, and because it regulates many cell functions, may be a very important brain modulator of functions that vary across the day.

In contrast to cGMP, cAMP was rhythmic in relatively few discrete

324

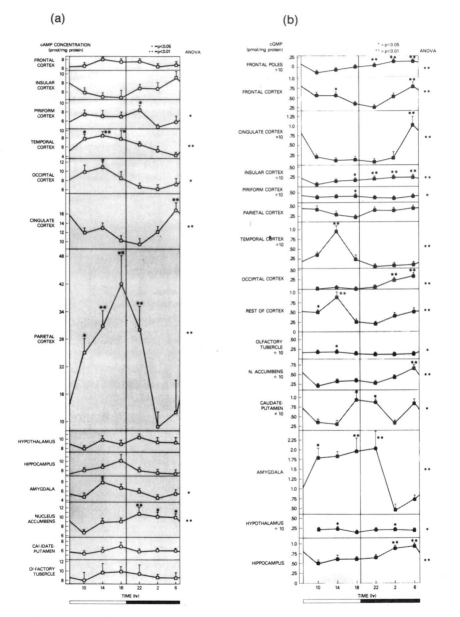

Figure 15.4. The concentrations of (a) cAMP and (b) cGMP in discrete brain regions. Both were measured by radioimmunoassay. For details, see Kafka et al. (1986b).

regions. Rhythms in cAMP concentration were observed in piriform, temporal, occipital, cingulate, and parietal cortex, and in amygdala and nucleus accumbens. No rhythms were found in frontal or insular cortex, hypothalamus, hippocampus, caudate-putamen, or olfactory tubercle (Figure 15.4b). When the cAMP concentration was rhythmic in cortex, the rhythmic patterns differed with the cortical region. The temporal, occipital, and parietal rhythms peaked during subjective day, the peak in parietal cortex extending into subjective night. The cAMP concentration in piriform and cingulate cortex peaked in subjective night, the cingulate peak occurring at subjective dawn. The patterns in cAMP concentration also differed from one another in the nine limbic regions measured. Like the rhythms in cGMP concentration, the rhythms in cingulate cortex and nucleus accumbens peaked in subjective night, and, in amygdala, in subjective day. Unlike the cGMP concentration, the cAMP concentration was without circadian rhythm in frontal and insular cortex, hypothalamus, hippocampus, caudate-putamen, and olfactory tubercle.

The 24-hour mean concentration of cAMP varied fourfold, a range similar to those in receptors and metabolites.

Circadian rhythmicity in cAMP concentration occurred more often in cortical than in noncortical brain regions. The most rostral cortical regions, including the frontal poles (not shown), did not undergo circadian rhythms. As these regions are high in DA innervation, DA-stimulated cAMP production may not be rhythmic. Two other areas innervated by dopaminergic tracts were measured: the nucleus accumbens had a prolonged peak in cAMP concentration in subjective night, and no rhythm was measured in the caudate-putamen cAMP concentration.

The relationships between circadian rhythms in cAMP and cGMP and the circadian rhythms in adrenergic receptors are not simple. In regions in which both are rhythmic, the patterns in cAMP and cGMP concentration are similar, except for parietal and occipital cortex, in which they are opposite in phase. In all regions in which a rhythm in cAMP concentration is found, there is a rhythm in α_1-receptors, and, in some regions, in β-receptors as well (Figures 15.1 and 15.4b). Adrenergic-receptor binding was not measured in nucleus accumbens or amygdala, but, like the cyclic nucleotide concentrations, binding to the α_1-receptor in the cingulate cortex peaked in subjective night.

In diurnal man, plasma cAMP, and, in monkeys, CSF cAMP, are high in the light and low in the dark (Markianos and Lykouras, 1981; Perlow et al., 1977). In the nocturnal rat, cAMP concentrations in discrete brain regions are higher during waking than during sleep, except in the cerebellum (Ogasahara et al., 1977). The increased cAMP level early in subjective night might play a role in wakefulness in these nocturnal animals.

Cyclic AMP concentration seems to be coupled with the rhythm in α_1-receptor binding in cingulate cortex. In other regions in which the cAMP concentration is rhythmic, its peak is in subjective day, when adrenergic peaks are in subjective night, and vice versa. Though the circadian rhythm in NE-stimulated cAMP production in cortical slices follows the rhythms in α_1- and β-receptor number (Kafka et al., 1986b), cAMP production in vivo does not appear to be as closely coupled to adrenergic receptor rhythms in most regions. In four of five regions in which cAMP is rhythmic, adrenergic receptor rhythms are not similar, whereas in one, the cingulate, they are. In five regions in which cAMP concentration is not rhythmic, adrenergic-receptor binding is rhythmic.

Regulation of cAMP concentration and the circadian rhythms in cAMP concentration seem to be complex. If adrenergic transmission alone is considered, the magnitude of the cAMP concentration, its rhythmicity and the timing of its peaks (phase) in some regions, and its arrhythmicity in other regions, could be affected by a number of parts of the system, in addition to receptors. The level of NE or epinephrine (E) in the synapse could change both the magnitude and the rhythm of the cAMP concentration. Some enzymes, important in the synthesis and breakdown of adrenergic transmitters, and in the breakdown of cAMP, vary over the course of the day, and variations in these enzymes could modulate the concentration of cAMP present. Transmitter systems, other than the NE system, stimulate or inhibit adenylate cyclase, and probably affect the concentration of cAMP at different times of day. Among transmitter systems altering cAMP production are the muscarinic ACh, DA, and opiate systems, whose receptors (Kafka et al., 1983) and transmitters have been shown to undergo circadian rhythms. Many additional putative transmitters or modulators, in which circadian rhythms have not yet been investigated, for example, adenosine and histamine, alter adenylate cyclase activity. A large number of peptides stimulate or inhibit adenylate cyclase, and daily or circadian rhythms in the concentrations of two of them, α-MSH (O'Donohue et al., 1982) and arginine vasopressin (Kafka et al., 1986c), have been reported.

Just as brain regions differ in their functions, they also differ in their neurochemical parameters that show circadian rhythmicity. The concentration of cAMP in cells has been shown to regulate protein phosphorylation and activation (Greengard, 1979). Understanding the significance of the presence or absence of a regional circadian rhythm in cAMP concentration depends upon a more profound understanding than is currently available of the functional interactions between transmitter systems innervating that region.

Both the presence and the absence of regional rhythms in cAMP and cGMP concentration may be the result of rhythmic changes in the adrenergic system, or complex, even rhythmic, interactions between a multiplicity of transmitter systems. The presence of regional circadian rhythms in cAMP and cGMP concentrations may be important in regulating the biochemical reactions, physiologic processes, and behaviors that permit animals to adapt to daily events in the environment. The absence of regional circadian rhythms in these cyclic nucleotide concentrations may, on the other hand, help to maintain a constant internal milieu, despite changes in the external environment throughout the day.

RELATIONSHIP BETWEEN BEHAVIORAL RHYTHMS, PLASMA CORTICOSTERONE, AND HYPOTHALAMIC CIRCADIAN RHYTHMS

The hypothalamus, and, in particular, the suprachiasmatic nuclei (SCN), play a central role in the generation of circadian rhythms, including regulation of feeding, drinking, locomotor activity, and corticosterone secretion (Aschoff, 1981). The well-established circadian rhythms in these physiologic processes and behaviors were compared with circadian rhythms in the hypothalamic noradrenergic system, cAMP, cGMP, and SCN arginine vasopressin (AVP). Food and water consumption and locomotor activity were measured during six 4-hour intervals over the 24-hour day. Plasma corticosterone and adrenocorticotropin (ACTH), and AVP in the SCN were measured by radioimmunoassay.

Under the conditions of constant darkness in which these rats lived, eating, drinking, and locomotor activity followed the well-known circadian patterns of nocturnal behavior (Figure 15.5), and indicated that the animals were at similar phases even after some days of free run. Plasma corticosterone followed the characteristic pattern in rats of a rise at dusk and a minimum at dawn, somewhat elevated values in the dark phase, due probably to a slight stress response. No rhythm was found in ACTH concentration. Specific binding to both β- and to α_1-adrenergic receptors in the hypothalamus peaked in subjective night, with troughs at the beginning of subjective day. No rhythm was found in specific binding to α_2-adrenergic receptors (Figure 15.5). The concentration of

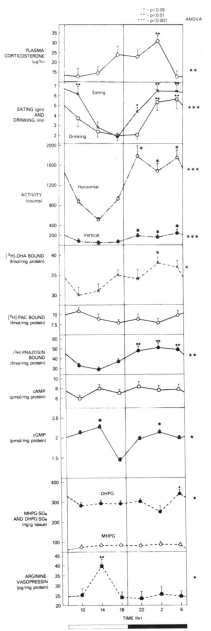

Figure 15.5. Circadian rhythms in plasma corticosterone, eating, drinking, locomotion, SCN AVP, and some variables in the whole hypothalamus. For details, see Kafka et al. (1986c).

hypothalamic cGMP was the same at all times, with the exception of a fall at dusk, whereas no rhythm was found in hypothalamic cAMP concentration (Figure 15.5). The concentration of DHPG was similar throughout the day, with the exception of a peak at dawn, while no significant changes occurred in hypothalamic MHPG concentration (Figure 15.5). The concentration of AVP in the SCN peaked sharply at 2:00 PM and remained low at all other time points (Figure 15.5).

The hypothalamus is a region of great importance in the control of circadian rhythms (Aschoff, 1981; Symposium, Fed Proc 42, 1983). The SCN of the anterior hypothalamus are thought to be the rat circadian pacemaker (Moore, 1983) that, via efferents to other hypothalamic nuclei, drives rhythms in pituitary hormones, and through them, hormones of pituitary target endocrine glands, such as the adrenal cortex. The noradrenergic system in the hypothalamic paraventricular nuclei regulates feeding and corticosterone rhythms; and medial and lateral hypothalamic control of ingestive behaviors is correlated with α_2-and β-adrenergic receptor rhythms, respectively (Krauchi et al., 1984).

Feeding, drinking, locomotor activity, and corticosterone levels all were high in subjective night, and, in general, low in subjective day, following established patterns. The rhythms were not disturbed by enucleation, and remained of large amplitude.

Specific binding to hypothalamic α_1- and β-adrenergic receptors, indicative probably of the number of receptors, is also greater in subjective night, suggesting that α_1- and β-receptors may mediate adrenergic transmission during the rat's active phase. No rhythm was found in α_1-receptor binding. In smaller hypothalamic regions, however, in α_2-receptors, circadian rhythms have been found, for example, in the paraventricular, suprachiasmatic, and supraoptic nuclei, but not in other hypothalamic areas (Leibowitz et al, 1984). Binding to α_2-receptors in the paraventricular nucleus of the medial hypothalamus increased when feeding increased. As it is likely that a receptor rhythm measured in whole hypothalamus represents a composite of rhythms present or lacking in discrete nuclei (or even smaller units), the parallel patterns in increased nocturnal behaviors and α_1- and β-receptor binding can be acknowledged, but not interpreted. A detailed understanding of the role of receptors in consumption and satiation will require additional studies in which receptor rhythms in nuclei or parts of nuclei are related to the eating and drinking behaviors of the whole animal.

By phosphorylating neuronal proteins, cAMP seems to act as second messenger for a number of neurotransmitters and hormones, including α_1- and β-receptors in the hypothalamus (Daly et al., 1981). The role of cGMP is less clear, though neurotransmitters and hormones, through the hydrolysis of polyphosphoinositides, initiate a cascade of cellular metabolic events, among which is an increase in cGMP concentration (Kafka et al., 1986b). Of the receptors measured in the current study, the α_1-adrenergic receptor stimulates both of these systems; the M2-muscarinic receptor, adenylate cyclase, and the M1-muscarinic receptor, polyphosphoinositide, break down. The β-adrenergic receptor stimulates, and the α_2-adrenergic receptor inhibits, cAMP production.

Cyclic GMP concentration in hypothalamus was level throughout the 24-hour day, with the exception of a low point at dusk. If cGMP is acting as a second messenger, perhaps it mediates inhibition of the onset of locomotor and ingestive behaviors, and a fall in its concentration permits them to begin. Cyclic AMP concentration, which showed no rhythm in the hypothalamus, is probably controlled by a large number of factors in addition to the number of α_1- and β-receptors, which themselves were rhythmic.

In hypothalamus, the peak in DHPG concentration as well as α_1- and β-receptor binding, at subjective dawn, suggests that at that time of day hypothalamic noradrenergic transmission is increased. As the rest phase of the activity cycle begins then, such increased transmission might inhibit activity.

Arginine vasopressin, a putative peptide neurotransmitter, is intrinsic to the SCN (Moore, 1983). The AVP concentration has a discrete peak at 2:00 AM in the SCN, and at all other times is low. The peak AVP concentration occurs just after the midpoint of the increases in SCN circadian rhythms in deoxyglucose uptake (Schwartz et al., 1980) and neuronal firing (Inouye and Kawamura, 1982; Green and Gillette, 1982; Groos and Hendriks, 1982), processes of energy utilization and electrical activity related to the pacemaker activities of the SCN (Inouye and Kawamura, 1982). The function of AVP, which does not seem to play an essential role in the SCN's rhythm-generating function, however, is not known.

The comparison of variables in the hypothalamus has underlined the need to compare circadian rhythms in behaviors with circadian rhythms in even smaller brain regions than those examined in these studies (e.g., hypothalamic nuclei). By this means, biochemical and physiologic processes involved in the rhythmic features of a behavior may be discriminated from processes necessary only to the manifestation of the behavior. It is clear, however, that in studying a number of relatively discrete brain areas, different rhythms are manifested, and the complexity of receptor rhythms is shown. In addition, the parallel measurement of receptor rhythms and rhythms in second messengers suggests that there are regional differences in feedback mechanisms, as can be inferred from the positive correlations in some regions, negative ones in others, and none at all in still others. Only by linking functional measures, biochemical and behavioral, to changes in receptor number and transmitter secretion, can we understand the significance of the changes that occur over the course of the 24-hour day.

CONCLUSION

An important point that emerges from these studies is that the circadian rhythm measured in each variable is reproducible. The studies were run in two identical parts, 4 days apart, because logistics made it impossible to accomplish all the measurements in a statistically adequate number of rats in a single study. The data from the two parts of the study were not significantly different statistically, and comparable data from the two parts were combined. From these data it becomes clear that receptor rhythms, which can vary with brain region and rat strain, replicate when conditions are maintained constant. For this reason, modifications of circadian rhythms with psychoactive drugs (Kafka et al., 1983; Kafka, 1985) are probably significant and not due to experimental variability. Previous studies have shown that a number of drugs, including the antidepressants, imipramine and clorgyline, the antimanic-antidepressant, lithium, and the neuroleptic, fluphenazine, alter the circadian rhythms of brain receptors. Sleep deprivation, which is immediately but very briefly, antidepressant, did not change the rhythms.

Changes in rhythms of receptors, neurotransmitters and their metabolites, and second messenger intracellular effector systems in brain could profoundly affect transmission in the CNS. Changes in transmission, in turn, may underlie the disorders in some patients with affective illness (Wehr et al., 1983) and schizophrenia (Kafka and Kafka, 1983). Measurement of receptors, transmitters, and second messengers across the 24-hour day in humans may help to elucidate the etiologies of psychiatric disorders. Cerebrospinal fluid or plasma measurements and measurements in available blood cells (Kafka and Paul, 1986) might indicate when neurotransmitter systems are changing; and correlating daily rhythmic changes in transmitter systems with symptoms of a psychiatric disorder might suggest whether the rhythmic changes contribute to the etiology of that disorder.

REFERENCES

Aschoff J (1981): In Aschoff J (ed): Handbook of Behavioral Neurobiology. Vol 4: Biological Rhythms, New York, Plenum, pp 81–93.

Bacopoulos NG, Hattox SE, Roth RH (1979): 3,4-dihydroxyphenylacetic acid and homovanillic acid in rat plasma: Possible indicators of central dopaminergic activity. Eur J Pharmacol 56:225–236.

Berridge MJ, Irvine RF (1984): Inositol trisphosphate, a novel second messenger in cellular signal transduction. Nature 312:315–321.

Berridge MJ, Downes CP, Hanley MR (1982): Lithium amplifies agonist-dependent phosphatidylinositol responses in brain and salivary glands, Biochem J 206:587–595.

Bylund DB, U'Prichard DC (1983): Characterization of alpha-1- and alpha-2-adrenergic receptors. Int Rev Neurobiol 24:343–431.

Choma PP, Puri AK, Volicer L (1979): Circadian rhythm of cyclic nucleotide and GABA levels in the rat brain. Pharmacology 19:307–314.

Creese I, and Snyder SH (1979): Nigrostriatal lesions enhance striatal [3H]-apomorphine and [3H]-spiroperiodol binding. Eur J Pharmacol 56:277–281.

Daly JW, Padgett W, Creveling CR, et al (1981): Cyclic AMP-generating systems: Regional differences in activation by adrenergic receptors in rat brain. J Neurosci 1:45–59.

Ellsworth JD, Redmond DE Jr, Roth RH (1982): Plasma and cerebrospinal fluid 3-methoxy-4-hydroxyphenylethylene glycol (MHPG) as indices of brain norepinephrine metabolism in primates. Brain Res 235:115–124.

Ellsworth JD, Roth RH, Redmond DE Jr (1983): Relative importance of 3-methoxy-4-hydroxyphenylglycol and 3,4-dihydroxyphenylglycol as norepinephrine metabolites in rat, monkey and humans. J Neurochem 41:786–793.

Goldberg ND, Haddox MK (1977): Cyclic GMP metabolism and involvement in biological regulation. Annu Rev Biochem 46:823–896.

Green DJ, Gillette R (1982): Circadian rhythm of firing rate recorded from single cells in the rat suprachiasmatic brain slice. Brain Res 245:198–200.

Greengard P (1979): Phosphorylated proteins as physiological effectors. Science 199:146–152.

Groos G, Hendriks J (1982): Circadian rhythms in electrical discharge of rat suprachiasmatic neurones recorded in vitro. Neurosci Lett 34:283–288.

Hilakivi I (1983): The role of beta- and alpha-adrenoceptors in the regulation of the states of the sleep-waking cycle in the cat. Brain Res 277:109–118.

Hillier JG, Martin PR, Redfern PH (1975): A possible interaction between 24h rhythms in catecholamine and 5-hydroxytryptamine concentration in the rat brain. J Pharm Pharmacol (Suppl) 27:1–40.

Inouye ST, Kawamura H (1982): Characteristics of a circadian pacemaker in the suprachiasmatic nucleus. J Comp Physiol 146:153–160.

Kafka JS, Kafka MS (1983): Timing processes and mental illness. Seventh World Congress of Psychiatry, Vienna.

Kafka MS (1985): The effects of antidepressants on circadian rhythms in brain neurotransmitter receptors. Acta Pharmacol Toxicol 56 (Suppl 1):162–169.

Kafka MS, Paul SM (1986): Platelet alpha-2-adrenergic receptors in depression. Arch Gen Psychiat 31:92–95.

Kafka MS, Wirz-Justice A, Naber D, et al (1983): Circadian rhythms in rat brain neurotransmitter receptors. Fed Proc 42:2796–2801.

Kafka MS, Marrangos PJ, Moore RY (1985): Suprachrasmatic nucleus ablation abolishes circadian rhythms in rat brain neurotransmitter receptors. Brain Res 327:344–347.

Kafka MS, Benedito MA, Blendy JA, Tokola NA (1986a): Circadian rhythms in neurotransmitter receptors in discrete rat brain regions. Chronobiol Int 3:91–100.

Kafka MS, Benedito MA, Roth RH (1986b): Circadian rhythms in catecholamine metabolites and cyclic nucleotide production. Chronobiol Int 3:101–115.

Kafka MS, Benedito MA, Steele LK, et al (1986c): Relationships between behavioral rhythms, plasma corticosterone and hypothalamic circadian rhythms. Chronobiol Int 3:117–122.

Krauchi K, Wirz-Justice A, Morimasa T, et al (1984): Hypothalamic alpha-2- and beta-adrenoceptor rhythms are correlated with circadian feeding: Evidence from chronic methamphetamine treatment and withdrawal. Brain Res 321:83–90.

Leibowitz SF, Jhanwar-Uniyal M, Roland CR (1984): Circadian rhythms of circulating corticosterone and extrahypothalamic areas of rat brain. Soc Neurosci Abstr 10:294.

Markianos M, Lykouras L (1981): Circadian rhythms of dopamine-beta-hydroxylase and cAMP in plasma of controls and patients with affective disorders. J Neural Transm 50:149–155.

Moore RY (1983): Organization and function of a central nervous system circadian oscillator: The suprachiasmatic hypothalamic nucleus. Fed Proc 42:2783–2789.

O'Donohue TL, Wirz-Justice A, Kafka MS, et al (1982): Effects of chronic lithium, clorgyline, imipramine, fluphenazine and constant darkness on the alpha-melanotropin content and circadian rhythm in rat brain. Eur J Pharmacol 85:1–7.

Ogasahara S, Taguchi Y, Wada H (1977): Changes in the levels of cyclic nucleotides in rat brain during the sleep–wakefulness cycle. Brain Res 213:163–170.

Palacious JM, Kuhar MJ (1980): β-adrenergic receptor localization by light microscopic autoradiography. Science 208:1378–1380.

Perlow MJ, Festoff B, Gordon EK, et al (1977): Daily fluctuation in the concentration of cAMP in the concious primate brain. Brain Res 126:391–396.

Reisine T (1981): Adaptive changes in catecholamine receptors in the central nervous system. Neuroscience 6:1471–1502.

Scheving LE, Harrison WH, Gordon P, Pauly JE (1968): Daily fluctuations in biogenic amines of the rat brain. Am J Physiol 214:166–173.

Schwartz WJ, Davidsen LC, Smith CB (1980): In-vivo metabolic activity of a putative circadian oscillator, the rat suprachiasmatic nucleus. J Comp Neurol 189:157–167.

Simon ML, George R (1975): Diurnal variations in plasma corticosterone and growth hormone as correlated with regional variations in norepinephrine, dopamine, and serotonin content of rat brain. Neuroendocrinolology 17:125–138.

Symposium (1983): Central nervous system control of mammalian circadian rhythms. Fed Proc 42:2782–2814.

Symposium (1983): Cyclic GMP in the nervous system. Fed Proc 42:3098–3113.

Turner BB, Wilens TE, Schroeder KA, et al (1981): Comparison of brainstem and adrenal circadian patterns of epinephrine synthesis. Neuroendocrinology 32:257–261.

Valases C, Wright SR Jr, Catravas GN (1980): Diurnal changes in cyclic neucleotide levels in the hypothalamus of the rat. Exp Brain Res 40:261–264.

Wehr TA, Sack D, Rosenthal N, et al (1983): Circadian rhythm disturbances in manic-depressive illness. Fed Proc 42:2809–2814.

Wirz-Justice A, Krauchi K, Campbell IC, Feer H (1983): Adrenoceptor changes in spontaneous hypertensive rats: A circadian approach. Brain Res 262:233–242.

Young WS III, Kuhar MJ (1980): Noradrenergic alpha-1 and beta-2 receptors: Light microscopic autoradiographic localization. Proc Natl Acad Sci USA 77:1696–1700.

Index